DREAMS FROM OUR FOUNDING FATHERS

DREAMS FROM OUR FOUNDING FATHERS

FIRST PRINCIPLES IN THE AGE OF OBAMA

RON DESANTIS

ISBN 978-1-934666-80-7

Cover Design by Mary Fisher Design

Published and distributed by:
High-Pitched Hum Publishing
321 15th Street North
Jacksonville Beach, Florida 32250

Contact High-Pitched Hum Publishing at www.highpitchedhum.net

To Casey

Contents

PART FIVE: "FEW AND DEFINED"

PART SIX: JUDICIAL AUTHORITY AND THE POLITICS OF EMPATHY

PART SEVEN: LEADERSHIP

PART EIGHT: THE NATIONAL CHARACTER

PREFACE

"I...do solemnly swear that I will support and defend the Constitution of the United States against all enemies, foreign and domestic; that I will bear true faith and allegiance to the same; that I take this obligation freely, without any mental reservation or purpose of evasion; and that I will well and faithfully discharge the duties of the office on which I am about to enter. So help me God."

This is the oath of office taken by commissioned officers in the United States Armed Forces, an oath I had taken for the first time in 2004 when I received and accepted commission for active duty service in the United States Navy, and that I again took in early 2010 as I prepared to leave active duty service and assume duties as an officer in the Navy Reserve. When I took the oath in 2004, I was less concerned with the meaning of the oath itself than with the reality that I was leaving behind civilian life, that our nation was more heavily engaged in shooting wars overseas that at any point since Vietnam, and that I wanted to do what I could to support the effort.

By the time I took the oath for my reserve commission in 2010, I became intrigued with the primacy that the oath places on the Constitution. The oath does not pledge its taker to the defense of the land owned and governed by the United States or to the population of American citizens, but, instead, to a particular form of government. Part of this fascination, no doubt, was due to the fact that I was taking the oath against the backdrop of a political environment in which the power of the federal government was being expanded beyond traditional limits. From assuming control of automobile companies to transmogrifying the nation's health care system, President Barack Obama and his congressional allies seemed to be effectuating a self-described transformation of the American republic, even in the face of what was, at times, overwhelming public disapproval.

That these changes were being brought about by a political class that exhibited what I saw as an almost casual disregard for the Constitution further highlighted, in my mind, the centrality of the

Constitution to the oath of office, especially since the Constitution has the same primacy in the oath taken by members of Congress. When the debate over the health care overhaul reached a feverish pitch, then-House Speaker Nancy Pelosi was asked by a reporter to identify the constitutional basis that authorized Congress to force citizens to purchase private health insurance, which is something without parallel in American history. Pelosi bristled with contempt at the mere notion that the Constitution might constrain her political ambitions. "Are you serious? Are you serious?" she asked before shaking her head in disgust. She did not answer the question.

Pelosi's incredulity about a question regarding basic constitutional power appears to be symptomatic of a larger malady of ignorance afflicting a sizable chunk of elected officials. In late 2008, the results of a civics test administered by the Intercollegiate Studies Institute (ISI) to members of the American public made minor headlines because the results suggested that a significant number of Americans lack a working knowledge of the Constitution, American history, and economics. The kicker, though, was that elected officials comprised the one identifiable group that scored substantially lower than the public as a whole. "It is disturbing enough that the general public failed ISI's civic literacy test, but when you consider the even more dismal scores of elected officials, you have to be concerned," said Josiah Bunting, chairman of the National Civic Literacy Board at ISI. "How can political leaders make informed decisions if they don't understand the American experience?" Indeed.

I soon started to question whether the nation's political leaders even take seriously their duty to support and defend the Constitution. An inclination to spend other people's money, a lust to control the lives of their fellow citizens and a desire to perpetuate oneself in office are all characteristic of some of the most powerful political figures in the country, and it is easy to see how such figures could let these ignoble desires supplant a rigorous constitutional fidelity. With trillions of dollars of taxpayer money at the disposal of the political class, it seems like they consider the Constitution to be a quaint afterthought, a sometimes annoying impediment to their desire to redistribute the money of their fellow citizens and to engage in social engineering.

What is more, President Obama came to office after having pledged to enact far-reaching changes in the foundations of American society. He styled himself a "progressive," which summoned the ghosts of those early-20th century "reformers" who criticized the Founding Fathers and expressed contempt for the Constitution. Just as those progressives sought to reorient American's bedrock principles away from individual liberty and limited government and towards progressive central planning and a large administrative state, Obama seemed to be trying to reformulate our core operating principles in a way that furthered this progressive vision. Moving America towards a European-style bureaucratic Leviathan undercuts the ethos of constitutionalism that the Founding Fathers bequeathed to us. By my lights, it will be sad indeed if the nation departs from the foundational principles that the Founders pledged their lives, their fortunes and their sacred honor to establish.

Ron DeSantis
July 2011

Part One

Obama and the Return to First Principles

1

FUNDAMENTAL TRANSFORMATION

When viewers tuned into CNBC on February 19, 2009, little did they know they were about to witness the beginning of one of the largest grassroots political movements in American history. The station's morning business show, *Squawk Box*, featured a discussion of a new home foreclosure policy proposed by the new presidential administration of Barack Obama, who, buttressed by a fawning press, was enjoying a smooth honeymoon period and high public approval ratings. Reporting from the floor of the Chicago Mercantile Exchange, Rick Santelli was not buying the hype about Obama. Though few had publicly rebuked the popular new president, Santelli ripped Obama and his bailout policies for "promoting bad behavior." According to Santelli, the federal government was rewarding financial irresponsibility with generous assistance—a perversion of incentives and a punishment, in effect, of those who did not need a bailout due to making sound decisions. Receiving encouragement from a crowd of people on the trading floor, Santelli bellowed, "President Obama, are you listening?"

Santelli argued that Obama's big spending policies, such as the $814,000,000,000 economic stimulus bill[1] enacted earlier that month, were doomed to failure because "you can't buy your way into prosperity." Referencing the Keynesian economic theory that each dollar spent by the government expands the economy by *more* than a dollar, he said that "if the multiplier that all of these Washington economists are selling us is over one...then we never have to worry about the economy again. The government should spend a trillion dollars an hour because we'll get $1.5 trillion back!" Things seemed to be getting so out of hand that Santelli was "thinking of having a

Chicago Tea Party in July. All you capitalists that want to show up to Lake Michigan, I'm gonna start organizing." Santelli cited the need to foster a return to first principles, because "if you read our founding fathers, people like Benjamin Franklin and Jefferson….What we're doing in this country now is making them roll over in their graves."[2]

Santelli's on-air protest became an instant sensation: within a week, the Santelli "tea party" video had been viewed several million times on the internet. At the time of the Santelli "rant," there had not been much forceful public opposition to the Obama agenda, so his forthright statement became a rallying cry for those disenchanted with the implementation of "change." At the same time, had Santelli's statement been nothing more than a knee-jerk, anti-Obama diatribe, it is unlikely that it would have caught on in the manner that it did. Instead, by invoking the Founding Fathers against the unprecedented expansion of the federal government, Santelli raised concerns about the very nature of the "change" that Obama was advocating; namely, whether such "change" reaffirmed the nation's bedrock values or whether it represented a departure from them.

The tea party movement that soon spread throughout the country represented a powerful political force, but the fact that such a movement even developed was, at least at the time, surprising. For one thing, Barack Obama was not billed as a typical politician. As the first African-American candidate to be elected president, he was already considered to be an historic figure. He seemed to epitomize the type of leader that could transcend old divisions and serve as a unifying force in government. Indeed, Obama implicitly marketed his presidential candidacy as one dedicated to a post-racial America, to the idea that, as he proclaimed to the 2004 Democratic National Convention in the speech that catapulted him to national prominence, "there's not a black America and white America and Latino America and Asian America; there's the United States of America."[3] This was peculiarly a candidate-centered appeal: only Obama, as the son of a mother from Kansas and a father from Kenya, so the theory went, could deliver America to its post-racial nirvana.

Obama's electoral victory represented a triumph of the American notion that one's potential for achievement is limited only by one's talent, initiative and determination. The specter of President-elect Obama striding onto the stage in Chicago's Grant Park on election night to give his victory speech stood as a powerful symbol of the possibilities of the American experiment. He told the crowd his election was "the answer" to "anyone out there who still doubts that America is a place where all things are possible, who still wonders if the dream of our founders is alive in our time."[4] Obama's political rise was historically meteoric: in the span of little more than four years, he moved seamlessly from the obscurity of the Illinois legislature to the keynote speech at the 2004 Democratic National Convention, and then from a short, undistinguished tenure in the U.S. Senate to the president-elect of the United States.

On the surface, Obama did not seem to be a polarizing figure like his most recent predecessors, Bill Clinton and George W. Bush. Beginning with his 2004 DNC address, Obama consistently pitched himself as an oracle of post-partisan bliss, an enlightened statesman that eschewed what he considered to be tired debates and worn-out dogmas. In this respect, Obama was less like Ronald Reagan, whose appeal rested on unwavering convictions—to limit government at home and defeat communism abroad—and, ironically, given Obama's educational and professional background, more like the great military leaders, such as Dwight Eisenhower, who won the presidency based on their personal attributes. Just as most voters in 1952 could agree that they liked Ike, even if they couldn't agree why they did, so too in 2008 could most voters agree that they wanted "change they could believe in," even if most couldn't agree what that meant. Irrespective of any political program, as the first African-American nominee of a major political party, Obama *was* change, a vessel for the hopes and dreams of Americans from all walks of life.

The media attention that greeted his election and inauguration was, predictably, euphoric. Part of this, no doubt, stemmed from the newsworthiness of Obama breaking the presidential color barrier. The fact that he attained the presidency against the longest of odds—he was the lowly, freshman senator who defeated the heavily favored former First Lady and Senator Hillary Clinton in a spirited primary—also added to the Obama aura. Another important factor was the undeniable fact that Obama's political orientation represented the type of elite brand of progressive politics that magnetically attracted political journalists inside the Washington-New York axis. This was made clear in comic fashion when MSNBC's liberal talk show host Chris Matthews noted that he "felt this thrill going up my leg" when he heard Barack Obama give a primary night victory speech.

Bringing large Democratic majorities in both houses of Congress with him to Washington, Obama, some suggested, was leading a structural political realignment that, while organized around Obama the individual, portended an era of left-of-center federal government activism. James Carville, a well-known Democratic political strategist, was so sure that Obama's election signaled a sea change in American politics that he wrote a book titled *40 More Years: How the Democrats Will Rule the Next Generation.* As the leader of a new political order, journalists began drawing comparisons between Obama and other noteworthy political leaders, including liberal luminaries like Franklin D. Roosevelt and John F. Kennedy, and even Obama's fellow Illinoisan and the preeminent Republican president, Abraham Lincoln.

But for all the high expectations and adulatory media coverage, there remained an absence of scrutiny about the type of political program that Obama would pursue. The theme of his presidential campaign had been "change," an inherently and perhaps intentionally vague concept that allowed Obama to avoid taking more detailed positions and to become the default candidate for those unhappy with the nation's direction. To be sure, Obama made it clear that, at the very least, "change" meant that he was *not* George W. Bush, who by the end of his term was, according to public polling, spectacularly unpopular.

But there was also reason to suspect that Obama saw himself as a change agent of historic proportions, as someone who could, as he said during the primary against Hillary Clinton, "put us on a fundamentally different path."[5] He did not want to be president "just to hold office," but instead said he wanted to "transform a nation."[6] As the campaign drew to a close, and with the political winds blowing strongly at his back, Obama told a crowd in Missouri that "we are five days from fundamentally transforming the United States of America."[7]

It would be a mistake to dismiss Obama's embrace of "transformational change" as some sort of overheated campaign rhetoric. Obama's expressed desire to transform America was not merely a way to differentiate himself from an unpopular incumbent; instead, the theme of transformational change was one to which he had dedicated his entire adult life. In an interview with the Associated Press following his election as the first black president of the *Harvard Law Review* in April of 1990, Obama proclaimed his intention to "reshape America in a way that is less mean-spirited and more generous." He wanted, he said, "to be part of a transformation of this country."[8] It is striking that, nearly twenty years before his presidential campaign and while still a relatively young man, Obama used language virtually identical to his campaign rhetoric to express a desire to transform a country that he deemed too mean-spirited, and it is doubtful that he would have trumpeted "transformational change" if he wanted to reorient America towards its traditional principles rather than take America into hitherto unchartered waters. For her part, Michelle Obama was more explicit about her husband's transformational project, telling voters that "Barack knows that we are going to have to make sacrifices, we are going to have to change our conversation, we're going to have to change our traditions, our history."[9]

Many great leaders throughout American history have been "change" agents, but most sought conservative change that rested on the nation's fundamental principles—often explicitly invoking the Founding Fathers. Abraham Lincoln, who, as the Great Emancipator, was responsible for some of the most far-reaching change in the nation's history, drew a sharp line against any extension of slavery into the territories, but did so in a way that reaffirmed the country's founding principles against the recent sweep of events that he correctly saw as veering from those principles. In fact, in his famous address to New York City's Cooper Union in anticipation of the presidential campaign of 1860, Lincoln attacked the views of Stephen A. Douglas, who claimed that the Constitution's creators supported his pro-slavery position, by scrutinizing the public positions of all of the delegates to the Constitutional Convention regarding the authority of Congress to ban slavery in the territories.

After demonstrating that most of the delegates thought the Constitution allowed the federal government to prohibit slavery in the territories, Lincoln urged that "as those fathers marked it, so let it be again marked, as an evil not to be extended."[10] During his most famous speech, delivered in the midst of the Civil War in commemoration of the dedication of the cemetery at Gettysburg, Lincoln famously placed the entire struggle in the context of reaffirming the nation's founding principles: the task, he said, was to make sure that the dead did not die in vain, and that "this nation, under God, shall have a new birth of freedom—and that government of the people, by the people, and for the people, shall not perish from the earth."

A century later, a young Baptist preacher from Atlanta picked up the torch of reaffirmation-based change from Lincoln. Seeking to rally the American people against the pernicious practices of racial segregation and racial discrimination, Dr. Martin Luther King Jr. stood in front of the Lincoln Memorial to declare that "when the architects of our republic wrote the magnificent words of the Constitution and the Declaration of Independence, they were signing a promissory note to which every American was to fall heir."[11] More than 100 years after the outbreak of the Civil War, Dr. King implored America to "cash this check, a check that will give us upon demand the riches of freedom and the security of justice." Dr. King did not dream of a transformation of America in which the foundational principles of the nation were tossed aside; he simply asked that African-Americans be recognized as full participants in the American constitutional drama. Even in his final speech in Memphis, Tennessee in 1968, King made clear that he embraced the basic tenets of American life: "All we say to America," he said, "is, 'be true to what you said on paper.'"[12] Had King sought to transform society in a way that diverged from the basic principles articulated by the Founding Fathers and championed by Abraham Lincoln, it is unlikely that he would have attained his status as a towering figure in American history.

That Obama spoke of "transforming" America in a way that, at the very least, eschewed the strong reaffirmation element of a Lincoln or a King is not something that drew much attention in the early days of his presidency. Media reports instead drew parallels between the faltering American economy of 2009 and the Great Depression of the 1930s, and cast Obama as a would-be FDR tasked with saving America from falling further into the economic abyss. *The New York Times* trumpeted Obama's Inaugural Address as having "swept away eight years of President George Bush's false choices and failed policies and promised to recommit to America's most cherished ideals." *The Times* was comforted "that with Mr. Obama's help, this battered nation will be able to draw together and mend itself."[13]

The following month, when Obama signed the $814,000,000,000 American Recovery and Reinvestment Act, also known as the "stimulus" bill, many saw it as the most ambitious federal spending initiative since Roosevelt's New Deal. "No one's going to have 100 days like Franklin Roosevelt again," said Allan Lichtman, a liberal political history professor at American University in Washington. "But leaving aside that impossible comparison, Obama's accomplishments stack up very well."[14] With a gargantuan stimulus package under his belt and with commanding legislative majorities in Congress, Obama was riding a wave of public approval and continued exaltation by the major media outlets.

The adulation proved to be short-lived. Taking office on the heels of an unprecedented spending initiative—the Troubled Asset Relief Program (TARP) that provided taxpayer-financed capital injections to financial institutions—designed to prevent the collapse of the financial system (which was signed into law by his predecessor, but which Obama continued and expanded into unanticipated areas), Obama nevertheless proceeded to push a number of boldly left-of-center initiatives that heralded the type of fundamental change to which he had alluded in the campaign: in addition to the $814,000,000,000 "stimulus" bill that dramatically exacerbated an already exploding budget deficit, he pushed for a federal overhaul of the nation's health care system that created a new federal entitlement and put America on a course to a government-run, single-payer system, and championed proposals in the fields of energy and education that required an unprecedented expansion of the federal government. But that was not all. To help deal with some of the aftershocks of the financial meltdown from the previous autumn, Obama proposed more bailouts—for union-heavy General Motors and for those facing a home mortgage foreclosure. Within a very short time after taking office, his efforts at transformational change started to stir discontent among the public and created the impetus for a revitalized conservative opposition to his policies.

When Santelli invoked the need for a tea party dedicated to the nation's founding principles, he was giving voice to a widespread, if latent, feeling among a substantial number of Americans that Obama's political project was transforming the United States into a country they no longer recognized. It was this nagging feeling that caused many Americans to trumpet the need to return to first principles. Soon after Santelli made his case against Obama's policies, Americans throughout the country began organizing individual tea parties in which individual participants seemed to share a belief in limited government, a desire to reduce federal spending, and an opposition to federal bailouts of private industry, as well to the tax increases that will eventually, but inevitably, follow the spike in spending.

Most significantly, the expansion of government in Washington seemed to many to represent a direct challenge to the Founding Fathers' vision of America as a land of individual liberty and as a nation with a Constitution that limited government's power to few, enumerated functions. Accordingly, a renewed interest developed, among a sizable number of citizens not limited to self-described supporters of the tea party movement, in the views and values of the Founders and in foundational documents such as the Declaration of Independence and the Constitution. This nostalgia for the Founding Fathers even fueled sales of powdered wigs, as Americans sought unorthodox ways to reconnect with the nation's original leading lights. One could not attend a major tea party event without running into a number of activists dressed up as one of the Founders.[15]

Some disagreed with those who invoked the Founders for support for their opposition to Obama's policies. These critics contended that the tea party activists were selectively reading history; according to this view, the Founding Fathers "seldom agreed about anything," so any attempt to invoke the Founders against the Obama governing ethos was futile.[16] Former President Bill Clinton saw clear differences between then and now, arguing that the contemporary political debate was about "taxation by duly, honestly elected representatives that you don't happen to agree with that you can vote out at the next election and two years after that and two years after that."[17] According to this view, Obama was not transforming America in a way that diverged from the nation's first principles—many of the people who were protesting against the Obama administration were simply upset that their side lost the election. They were, essentially, throwing a Founding Fathers-inspired temper tantrum.

Some even suggested that the entire tea party enterprise was nothing more than an elaborate cover for racial bias against Barack Obama. According to these critics, those who asserted that Obama was straying from foundational American values were right to note that America was changing. The change, though, did not stem from any failure to keep faith with the Founding Fathers, but was a function of the nation's increasing cultural diversity, signified by Obama, the self-described "mutt." This view presupposes, without evidence, that an underlying racial animus motivates vast swaths of the American electorate. It is also affirmatively belied by the fact that, since the 1950s, Obama's initial 68% presidential approval rating has been surpassed only by President John F. Kennedy's first public rating in 1961. Since a mere 12% of voters disapproved of the newly inaugurated President Obama, one would have to assume that a cancerous racial prejudice suddenly infected a large number of Americans after January 20, 2009, but before public opposition to Obama's policies began to flourish.[18] That there existed little reason to think that those opposing the Obama agenda were doing so for reasons other than a legitimate philosophical disagreement with his policies was underscored by Obama's concession that there was a broad group of people "who are legitimately concerned about the deficit, who are legitimately concerned that the federal government may be taking on too much."[19]

Later, as opposition to Obama's "change" agenda hardened and as the 2010 political season matured, it became even more difficult to castigate Santelli-inspired tea party activists as motivated by racial animosity rather than by philosophical principle. For example, in South Carolina, the birthplace of secession and the former home to Dixiecrat candidates like Strom Thurmond who, as a Southern Democrat, supported racial segregation in the 1948 presidential campaign, the candidates who earned tea party support tended to be anti-establishment candidates with diverse backgrounds. State Representative Nikki Haley, an Indian-American supported by tea party activists, won the GOP gubernatorial primary by defeating the Lieutenant Governor, the Attorney General, and a sitting U.S. Congressman—all white, male establishment Republicans. Tim Scott, an African-American also backed by the tea party movement, earned a resounding victory in the Republican primary in the congressional district encompassing Charleston and Ft. Sumter. He defeated the son of Strom Thurmond in the primary. Both were elected to office in November 2010. If, in fact, voters were identifying with the tea party due to racial prejudice, then they had an awfully strange way of showing it.

Beyond the diversion of racial prejudice, much of the discussion in the press focused on if and how the political opposition to Obama's policies affected the ongoing political debate in the United States. Not surprisingly, this focus tended to revolve around the partisan concern of whether tea party activists would benefit the Republican Party or hurt its electoral prospects. This is an interesting discussion point, but is ultimately far less important than the critique advanced by Rick Santelli, among others, that the Obama agenda represented a divergence from the principles championed by the American Founders.

As we will see, Santelli and other critics were right to invoke the Founding Fathers in opposition to the Obama agenda: the "transformational change" pursued by President Barack Obama and by his allies in Congress is, on a number of fronts, irreconcilable with the political principles espoused by the Constitution's creators. This is because Obama does not seek to reaffirm the nation's political foundations, but instead wants to reformulate them. And it is not even that the "change" he seeks is not merely unfaithful to the Founders' political ethos, though it surely is; in many important respects, Obama's quest to "fundamentally transform the United States of America" represents the type of political program that the Constitution was designed to prevent.

2

"FIRST PRINCIPLES AND MAIN PILLARS OF THE FABRIC"

"IN DISQUISITIONS of every kind," Alexander Hamilton wrote in *The Federalist* No. 31, "there are certain primary truths, or first principles, upon which all subsequent reasoning must depend. These contain internal evidence which, antecedent to all reflection or combination, commands the assent of the mind. Where it produces not this effect, it must proceed either from some disorder in the organs of perception, or from the influence of some strong interest, or passion, or prejudice."[1]

For "disquisitions" about American politics, the principles underlying the United States Constitution represent precisely the type of principles that Hamilton referenced in his essay in *The Federalist.* These principles are exemplified in the protections for individual liberty contained in the Bill of Rights, as well as later amendments such as the Thirteenth, Fourteenth, and Fifteenth Amendments, but also include—and, indeed, are primarily rooted in—the structural foundations of constitutional government, from the separation of powers and checks and balances to the limited, enumerated powers of Congress and the role of the courts—all of which serve to preserve and protect individual liberty. These timeless truths about political power, the structure of government and the protection of individual liberty are still the foundation of our political institutions, and those public officials who exhibit an ignorance or disregard for these truths do not live up to their own oath of office, much less to the Founders' heralded principles.

The single best source for the exposition of the principles underlying the Constitution of the United States of America is the collection of essays known as *The Federalist Papers.* Written by Alexander

Hamilton, James Madison and John Jay but published under the pseudonym Publius, the essays represent a cogent, thorough and wide-ranging defense of the Constitution produced at the Constitutional Convention in Philadelphia in 1787 and that, in most important respects, is still with us today. Hard as it may be to believe from a contemporary vantage point that has witnessed the Constitution's impressive durability and warm embrace by the overwhelming majority of Americans, the ratification of the Constitution was anything but a sure thing, and the Publius-authored essays were designed to persuade the citizens of the important state of New York to support ratification.

For political leaders like Madison and Hamilton, the ratification of the Constitution was vital to the preservation of the republic. The American Revolution had been the seminal event in the lives of the Founding Fathers and ushered in what many saw as a new, glorious era of liberty, yet the years following the Revolution witnessed what John Quincy Adams called "this critical period" in which America was "groaning under the intolerable burden of accumulated evils."[2]

The impotence of the federal government under the Articles of Confederation and the dysfunction of many of the state governments, highlighted by the armed insurrection of indebted Revolutionary War veterans led by Daniel Shays in Massachusetts, alarmed many political leaders and helped lead to the convening of the Constitutional Convention. "No morn ever dawned more favorably than ours did," George Washington wrote to James Madison, "and no day was ever more clouded than the present! Wisdom and good examples are necessary to rescue the political machine from the impending storm."[3] Alexander Hamilton's choice of the pseudonym "Publius" as the pen name for *The Federalist* was thus quite appropriate: just as Publius Valerius Publicola put the teetering Roman Republic on a sounder, more republican foundation, the new Constitution was the necessary antidote to the nation's political ills, and promised to secure the principles of the American Revolution for the United States, its Founders, and their posterity.

Today, *The Federalist Papers* are most commonly thought of as a collection of great philosophical tracts that lay out the American science of politics. Though justified, this sometimes obscures the fact that the essays were written with the more immediate goal of ratification in mind. That the essays succeeded in this more proximate objective was apparent at the time to no less a source than the hero of the Revolution and the American Cincinnatus, George Washington. Writing to Hamilton a month after New York narrowly voted to ratify the Constitution, Washington noted that he had "read every performance which has been printed on one side and the other of the great question lately agitated (so far as I have been able to obtain them) and, without an unmeaning compliment, I will say, that I have seen no other so well calculated (in my judgment) to produce conviction on an unbiased Mind, as the *Production* of your *triumvirate*."[4]

The immediate tactical victory of ratification was important to Washington because he firmly believed the Articles of Confederation had been inadequate to the task of securing the American Revolution. The new Constitution would allow Americans to take advantage of the "opportunity afforded the United States of becoming a respectable Nation,"[5] and, potentially, a beacon of liberty of historical significance. At the same time, Washington also understood that the handiwork of Hamilton, Madison and Jay represented a brilliant description of, and trenchant philosophical justification for, the new, enduring American republic. Referring to *The Federalist Papers*, Washington wrote to Hamilton: "That Work will merit the Notice of Posterity; because in it are candidly and ably discussed the principles of freedom and the topics of government, which will be always interesting to mankind so long as they shall be connected in Civil Society."[6] Even Thomas Jefferson, who did not attend the Convention in Philadelphia and was cagey about whether he even supported the Constitution's ratification, deemed the essays to be the "best commentary on the principles of government which ever was written."[7]

When one considers the extraordinary talent and intellect of Madison and Hamilton (John Jay made only minimal contributions to the series because he fell ill shortly after the series debuted), it is not surprising that *The Federalist Papers* have remained a political *tour de force*. To this day, Alexander Hamilton stands as one of the preeminent examples of upward mobility in all of American history. He was born in destitute circumstances to an unmarried mother in the British West Indies—John Adams snidely referred to him as the "bastard son of a scotch pedlar." Hamilton had little prospects for success. As a young teenager, he lamented "the grovelling and conditions of a clerk…to which my fortune &c. condemns me," and even wished "there was a war" so that he could elevate his station in life.[8] Few would have expected that when Hamilton set sail for America in the early 1770s, he was setting forth on a path of extraordinary achievement and political ascendancy: studying at King's College in New York, serving as aide-de-camp to General George Washington during the Revolutionary War, facilitating the convening of the Constitutional Convention, writing the lion's share of *The Federalist* essays, leading the pro-Constitution forces at the New York ratifying convention, setting the standard for the office of the Secretary of the Treasury, and devising a far-reaching financial plan for the new Republic. When his life was prematurely snuffed out by Aaron Burr in 1804, he stood as the dominant intellectual force in the Federalist Party, towering over his colleagues by such an extent that his death all but ended the existence of the party as a force in American politics. He is undoubtedly one of the greatest American statesmen never to serve as president.

Although the Constitution was not ideal by his lights, Hamilton resolved to lead an intellectual charge in favor of its ratification. He thus recruited his friend and fellow Convention delegate James Madison and the reputable and erudite John Jay to assist him in penning the series of essays that came to be known as *The Federalist.* As Hamilton biographer Ron Chernow points out, Hamilton and Madison churned out a voluminous collection of essays under an enormous time crunch: the first of the many state ratifying conventions was already scheduled to take place within a couple of months, leaving Hamilton and Madison little time to do anything but expound upon the knowledge they already possessed. As if this did not make the task difficult enough, Hamilton had to juggle his contributions around a full-time law practice that demanded a large chunk of his time.[9]

For Hamilton, overcoming these suffocating constraints on his time was absolutely imperative, for he doubted whether America could survive under the ineffectual Articles of Confederation. He also viewed the debate over the Constitution to have far-reaching implications for the future of self-government and individual liberty. "It has been frequently remarked," Hamilton wrote in the first installment of *The Federalist*, "that it seems to have been reserved to the people of this country, by their conduct and example, to decide the important question, whether societies of men are really capable or not of establishing good government from reflection and choice, or whether they are forever destined to depend for their political constitutions on accident and force."[10] The stakes could not have been higher.

Hamilton was wise to enlist the services of James Madison in his venture. No American of that time period spent as much time studying and thinking about constitutional first principles than the able Virginian, and it is not surprising that, during the 1780s, Madison led the charge in favor of creating a new federal government. He has been called the Father of the Constitution because he was the leading intellectual force at the Constitutional Convention, and his political writing as Publius in *The Federalist* continues to this day to epitomize the American science of politics. By the time of the Convention in 1787, Madison had already established himself as an apostle of religious freedom; his "Memorial and Remonstrance" against a religious tax in Virginia helped to inform the First Amendment's prohibition on a federal establishment of religion, and remains a frequently cited source in Supreme Court opinions regarding the meaning of the religion clauses of the First Amendment.

After the launching of the new ship of state in 1789, Madison was the preeminent member of the House of Representatives, a true legislative tactician responsible for, among other things, authoring the Bill of Rights and ushering the amendments through Congress. As a Jeffersonian republican, he served as the Secretary of State in the administration of his fellow Virginian during the early 1800s, and, of course, he served two terms as president in his own right. Perhaps no figure in the nation's history is as synonymous with American constitutionalism as is James Madison.

It is certainly true that the Constitution was born out of a debate between some of the most able political thinkers in American history, and therefore reflects compromises over a number of important issues ranging from the powers of Congress to the role of the courts. When they left Philadelphia in the summer of 1787, no Convention delegate believed that the Constitution was perfect. An aged Benjamin Franklin, the era's most celebrated American not named Washington, acknowledged that the Constitution was not free of faults but felt that the situation was sufficiently dire to prompt the delegates to put aside such reservations for the sake of the country. "Thus I consent, Sir, to this Constitution," Franklin wrote in a speech read aloud to the Convention by his Pennsylvania colleague James Wilson, "because I expect no better, and because I am not sure, that it is not the best." Franklin urged the Convention delegates to support the Constitution without equivocation, declaring that "the opinions I have had of its errors, I sacrifice to the public good. I have never whispered a syllable of them abroad. Within these walls they were born, and here they shall die."[11] Hamilton and Madison heeded Franklin's call to make the best possible case for the Constitution when they wrote *The Federalist*; had they been preoccupied with personal misgivings about the Constitution, it is unlikely that the writings they produced would have been the monuments of American political thought that have become.

In spite of the philosophical disputes and sectional divisions, the power struggles and the cultural differences, the delegates somehow managed to devise a system of government that would soon become the envy of the world. Perhaps the delegates had a sense of this before the ink was even dry on the Constitution. As James Madison recorded in his Convention notes, while the final delegates were signing the Constitution, Benjamin Franklin looked towards the president's chair and observed to his colleagues the presence of a painted sun. He had, "often and often in the course of the Session, and the vicissitudes of my hopes and fears as to its issue, looked at that behind the President without being able to tell whether it was rising or setting: But now at length I have the happiness to know that it is a rising and not a setting Sun."[12]

After months of discussion and debate, the delegates had produced a plan of government that had the chance to lift the nation out of its prevailing difficulties and cement the achievements of the American Revolution. Though much work was yet ahead of the American people, the framework of government so tirelessly and eloquently advocated by Hamilton and Madison in *The Federalist* served and continues to serve as the foundation upon which a more perfect union is built.

****

Barack Obama and his allies in Congress have prompted millions of Americans to demand a return to first principles, and it is no secret that those principles are most conspicuously enshrined in the Constitution of the United States. While the rights to life, liberty and the pursuit of happiness articulated in the Declaration of Independence are, as Jefferson famously wrote, self-evident truths, it is not always clear from the face of the Constitution *why* the Constitution's creators framed our basic institutions in the manner that they did. *The Federalist* provides the *why*. It explains and expounds upon the Constitution's philosophical foundations and reveals the Founders' outlook on a number of critical issues of political theory. As such, it gives us a view of republican government and individual liberty from the most basic perspective: as constitutional creators, the Framers were writing on a slate far cleaner than any other generation in American history.

It should be acknowledged that some will regard the very notion of looking to the principles articulated by the Constitution's creators as a guidepost for evaluating the fundamental change advocated by Barack Obama to be a foolish diversion. Under this view, the Founders might have made a positive contribution in their time, but the principles they established are woefully inadequate to deal with modern political realities. For example, *New York Times* columnist Thomas Friedman has habitually lamented the resistance of the political system to the far-reaching, centralized "solutions" to a litany of problems that he sees as obviously needed, which is an implicit critique of the Constitution's auxiliary precautions that are intentionally designed to frustrate such endeavors. Incredibly, Friedman has wished that our Constitution could give way to a Chinese-style authoritarian regime "for a day," so that the ruling regime could, by fiat, "authorize the right solutions…on everything from the economy to environment."[13] Richard Cohen, a liberal columnist for *The Washington Post*, lambasted what he deemed a "fatuous infatuation with the Constitution," which, he claimed, does not deserve scrupulous adherence and which "has nothing to do with America's real problems."[14]

Hendrik Hertzberg, a progressive writer for *The New Yorker* magazine, possesses what he calls a "longstanding obsession with the obsolescence of our eighteenth-century political and electoral hydraulics (such as the separation of powers and the lack of a single government accountable to a national electorate)."[15] Ezra Klein, a progressive writer for *The Washington Post*, doesn't see the contributions of the creators of the Constitution to be particularly noteworthy and admits that "veneration about the Founders occasionally perplexes" him.[16]

Others cite the personal flaws of the Founding Fathers and the society they were born into as a reason to deemphasize, if not reject, all of their political insights, even if unrelated to any of their identified flaws. Since the Founders failed to abolish the institution of slavery in their time, so the argument goes, the Founders' conception of government should not necessarily command a great deal of respect from our generation of Americans. For example, during the bicentennial celebration of the drafting of the Constitution in 1987, Thurgood Marshall, the Supreme Court justice and legal giant who brilliantly mounted the legal offensive against racial segregation, spoke out against the original Constitution and the men who created it. "Nor do I find the wisdom, foresight, and sense of justice exhibited by the Framers particularly profound," Marshall stated, for "the government they devised was defective from the start."[17] Under this view, it is misguided at best to look back to a generation of leaders who, in framing a Constitution that did not abolish slavery, failed to live up to the ideals they espoused. For someone like Marshall, this failure overshadows the numerous and long-lasting political achievements embodied in the structural foundations of the government that have nothing to do with the institution of slavery.

Such criticism misses the mark for three reasons. First, it is unlikely that the delegates to the Convention could have framed a constitution that abolished slavery and that would have actually been ratified—a view shared by strongly anti-slavery delegates like Alexander Hamilton and Benjamin Franklin. Slavery had been a fact of life throughout human history, and had existed in Britain's American colonies for 150 years before the Convention at Philadelphia in 1787. In certain southern states, slave labor was the backbone of the entire economy, and immediately abolishing slavery would have represented an enlightened but also a monumental change—a revolution far more socially, politically and economically momentous than the American Revolution itself.

This is why there was no real chance that the Convention would abolish the peculiar institution of slavery. Some of the notorious compromises that demonstrated a toleration of slavery, such as the "federal ratio," which allowed the slave-holding states to count 5 slaves as the equivalent of 3 free citizens (the free states did not want slaves counted at all because they did not want the political power of slave states to be enhanced), were even thought to be necessary to ensure ratification. Hamilton, a counselor to the New York Manumission Society, later lamented that without such a compromise "no union could possibly have been formed."[18] Similarly, Benjamin Franklin, who served as president of the Pennsylvania Abolition Society, declined to read a letter to the Convention delegates from the Society that denounced slavery on religious and republican grounds. Franklin did not want to derail the Convention by further inflaming the delegates over the issue of slavery, and believed that the United States could not last without a new federal government, for, as he wrote in his final Convention speech, "our States are on the point of separation, only to meet hereafter for the purpose of cutting one another's throats."[19] For anti-slavery delegates like Hamilton and Franklin, abolition of slavery would be a moot point if a failure to erect a functioning government snuffed out the ideals of the American Revolution in their infancy; then, the future of all Americans, the free as well as the slave, would eventually be as serfs to a despotic government.

The second reason why it is an error to dismiss the Framers' wisdom is because the philosophical foundations of the Constitution are incompatible with slavery. At the Convention, slavery opponents, such as Pennsylvania delegate and New Yorker Gouverneur Morris, lambasted the institution. Morris said he "would never concur in upholding domestic slavery. It was a nefarious institution – It was the curse of heaven on the States where it prevailed." In debating the status of slaves for the purpose of calculating popular representatives, Morris was incensed "that the inhabitant of Georgia and S. C. who goes to the Coast of Africa, and in defiance of the most sacred laws of humanity tears away his fellow creatures from their dearest connections and damns them to the most cruel bondages, shall have more votes in a Government instituted for protection of the rights of mankind, than the Citizen of Pa or N. Jersey who views with a laudable horror, so nefarious a practice."[20]

Supporters of slavery had no way to justify the existence of slavery in a nation predicated on individual liberty. South Carolina's John Rutledge meekly argued that, " if slavery be wrong, it is justified by the example of all the world," apparently not comprehending that America was charting a new course in human history, or understanding the "radical change in the principles, opinions, sentiments, and affections of the people" that John Adams said was the "real American revolution."[21] The mere fact that slavery's continued existence in the United States was an uneasy one is a testament to the philosophical inconsistency of America's liberty-protecting Constitution with the institution of slavery. Though it was not immediately abolished, slavery was doomed to fail in a nation whose Constitution embodied such philosophical truths.

Finally, and perhaps most importantly, the Constitution was created despite the existence of slavery, not because of slavery. Indeed, the vast bulk of what was accomplished in Philadelphia simply had nothing to do with slavery. Political innovations such as checks and balances, an independent judiciary, and an energetic but republican executive represent sound features of representative self-government; had the Convention delegates created a constitution that affirmatively banned slavery throughout the entire country, one would still want to see these very same innovations included in that constitution. The philosophical justifications articulated in *The Federalist* for maintaining military power, for protecting the rights of private property, for producing a good administration, and for maintaining limitations on the scope and power of government stand as bedrock principles of the American constitutional tradition—and remain relevant to this day.

It is difficult to take seriously those who characterize the contributions of the Founding Fathers as anything other than monumental achievements. Can anyone plausibly contend that a constitutional convention headed by modern-day political figures like Nancy Pelosi, Barney Frank and Harry Reid could have produced a document even remotely comparable in excellence to the one that the delegates to the Constitutional Convention produced in Philadelphia? Would any of our contemporary legislative tacticians have been able to devise and pass a slew of amendments as great as the Bill of Rights? These questions are not meant to single out members of today's ruling class—American history does not yield a single instance in which a collection of political leaders accomplished a similarly-impressive collection of feats as those achieved by the Founders. From twentieth century progressives to contemporary naysayers, those who have criticized the Constitution and its creators have failed to articulate an alternative, but equally compelling, vision for self-government, much less witness that vision enshrined in a workable written constitution. In creating the Constitution and the Bill of Rights, the Founding Fathers erected a framework that secured the American Revolution, laid a foundation for future prosperity, and provided protection for individual liberty that would soon become the envy of the world—a truly historic string of achievements.

The Constitution is the focal point of American political life, providing the federal government its sole source of authority and safeguarding many of the God-given rights that Americans cherish. Not surprisingly, the oath that members of Congress take before taking their seats reflects the preeminence of the Constitution: "I do solemnly swear that I will support and defend the Constitution of the

United States against all enemies foreign and domestic; that I will bear true faith and allegiance to the same; that I take this obligation freely, without any mental reservation or purpose of evasion; and that I will faithfully discharge the duties of the office on which I am about to enter. So help me God." Failure to live up to this oath, be it through purposeful disregard or blissful ignorance, represents a failure to keep faith with the Founding Fathers, and with the enduring principles to which they pledged their lives, their fortunes and their sacred honor.

Given the Constitution's central importance to the nation, it would be impossible to effect a fundamental transformation of the United States without also transforming the principles and values that underlie America's foundational document. These principles and values represent the timeless, enduring political truths that inform the basic institutions of the American Republic. The reaction against the policies of Obama and his congressional allies by a large number of Americans has been motivated by their sense that the transformational change instituted in the nation's capital betrayed those principles and values, and by their fear that the Republic was being unmoored from her limited government roots.

This may be a function of seeing certain aspects of that "change" agenda, such as the unprecedented provision of the health care overhaul that forces individuals to purchase health insurance, as being unconstitutional, though it would be a mistake to see the protests as being so narrowly targeted. Instead, it is better to view the fierce opposition engendered by Obama's attempt to transform the United States as stemming from a recognition that Obama's political project amounts to a rejection of the basic political outlook—an ethic of constitutionalism—relied upon by the Founding Fathers when they created the Constitution. On issue after issue—economic policy, the role of the courts, political leadership, and foreign affairs, among others—Obama and his congressional allies have chartered a course that is alien to the Republic's philosophical foundations. And it is because of their attempt to transform America that these self-described "change" agents ignited a prairie fire of political opposition throughout the country that would make the Constitution's creators proud.

PART TWO

NOTES ON POLITICAL INFLUENCES ANCIENT AND MODERN

3

JAMES MADISON UNIVERSITY

As the 2008 presidential campaign drew to a close, Barack Obama held a much-publicized campaign rally at a college in Harrisonburg, Virginia, which lies in the heart of the Shenandoah Valley and is home to traditionally Republican voters. As the media noted in eager anticipation of a Democratic electoral victory, Obama stood a good chance of being the first Democratic candidate to win Virginia since Lyndon Johnson carried it in 1964. That he was campaigning on Republican turf so late in the game suggested that Obama had the political winds at his back and the presidency within reach. Claiming to be the first presidential candidate to stump in Harrisonburg since Democrat Stephen A. Douglas campaigned there against Abraham Lincoln during the election of 1860, he couched his candidacy in historic terms, portraying himself as the fulfillment of the American ideal and "a testimony to this country." Yet, Obama nevertheless declared the urgent need "to come together and change this country." Obama's notion of "change" included the repudiation of President George W. Bush but was by no means limited to that end; he saw his election as portending a transformation in the very fundamentals of the United States of America.[1] A victory in Virginia would make it a near certainty that Obama's next stop would be 1600 Pennsylvania Avenue, giving him the opportunity to usher in the far-reaching change that he coveted.

Viewing Obama's trip to Harrisonburg through the red state/blue state prism that had by that point been endlessly belabored, the media characterized the potential for Obama to win a state traditionally inhospitable to liberal Democrats as the major story of the late-October campaign rally. What also was reported, but not in any way highlighted at the time, was the venue for the Harrisonburg event:

James Madison University. Few noticed the irony in the candidate who evinced a design to fundamentally change the country making a clarion call for such change at a university bearing the name of the intellectual driving force of the foundational institutions of American political life. But this is hardly surprising. With the whiff of an Obama victory in the air, journalists for major media outlets like *The New York Times* and *The Washington Post* were not about to raise issues that might cause voters to take a more critical look at their preferred candidate. No major candidate in the modern media age had been less thoroughly scrutinized than Barack Obama, and most journalists showed little interest in investigating, much less highlighting, a number of aspects about Obama's politics and philosophy that might have doomed other, less favored candidates, such as the radical political views he espoused as a young man and his associations with a number of unsavory characters from the Illinois political machine.

The kid glove treatment given to Obama by the media was brought into comic focus less than a week before the election. On October 30, 2008, Charlie Rose of PBS interviewed former news anchor Tom Brokaw about the presidential campaign generally and Barack Obama specifically:

> ROSE: He is principally known through his autobiography and through very aspirational speeches.
>
> BROKAW: Two of them!
>
> ROSE: What do we know about the heroes of Barack Obama, like the books?
>
> BROKAW: …Yeah, It's an interesting question. I don't know what books he's read.
>
> BROKAW: We don't know a lot about Barack Obama and the universe of his thinking about foreign policy.

> ROSE: I don't know what Barack Obama's worldview is.
>
> BROKAW: No, I don't, either.
>
> ROSE: I don't know how he really sees where China is.[2]

These admissions by Brokaw and Rose represent a devastating critique of the media's performance during the presidential campaign. As *Time*'s Mark Halperin noted after the election, the media's work constituted "extreme bias, extreme pro-Obama coverage."[3]

Much of this bias was due to the fact that Obama's left-of-center politics and worldview corresponded nicely with the political orientation of most rank-and-file journalists, and they wanted a president, unlike George W. Bush, who they could identify with and whose progressive policies they would support. Had the media not been so invested in an Obama victory, Obama's visit to Harrisonburg could have served as a reason to examine Obama's desire to transform America, and whether he sought to transform it into something that would be unrecognizable to Founding Fathers like James Madison.

As the namesake of the Harrisonburg-based University, Madison is not necessarily the Founding Father that looms largest in the consciousness of the average American. Unlike George Washington, he has no claim to be the father of his country, as he played but a small role in the American Revolution. Unlike his friend and political mentor Thomas Jefferson, he cannot claim authorship of the Declaration of Independence and was not the leader of the nation's first political party. Unlike Benjamin Franklin, he was not an international superstar whose political achievements represented a mere fraction of his lifetime exploits. Instead, James Madison is synonymous with American constitutionalism, the man who, while not the sole author of the Constitution, was at least its chief architect, and who authored the Bill of Rights while serving in the House of Representatives during the Washington administration.

In this respect, Madison occupies a fundamentally different and, in some respects, unsettled place in the American imagination. While nothing can change the fact that Washington founded a republican nation when he could have made himself a king, that Jefferson articulated the permanent truths that justified a revolution, or that Franklin achieved fame in science and politics, Madison's accomplishments are continually up for grabs, directly related to the extent to which the Constitution is embraced by Americans. A transformational project that unmoors the nation from its philosophical and constitutional foundations represents an attack not just on America's political traditions but also on Madison's place in history. In this respect, Barack Obama must realize his transformational triumph at the expense of James Madison.

The balance of this book will be dedicated to examining the divergence between the policies and philosophies embraced by Barack Obama, as well as his allies in Congress, and the principles and enduring truths that the Constitution's creators relied upon when they framed America's foundational document. This divergence will be even clearer when viewed against the backdrop of the major sources of influences that have shaped the political outlook of Obama and the American Founders. When James Madison arrived in Philadelphia for the Constitutional Convention, he brought with him a thorough knowledge of republican government, and was well-versed in a wide array of political, philosophical and religious sources. As the Rose-Brokaw dialogue demonstrated, the media did little to investigate what motivated Barack Obama's attitudes, yet this does not change the fact that Obama brought with him to the Oval Office a number of mature beliefs, which were the product of a political socialization quite narrow in scope. Just as the constitutional road paved by the Framers represents the logical application of their basic philosophical assumptions and worldview, so too does the transformational project of Barack Obama embody the cramped set of philosophical beliefs that have shaped his political persona.

4

THE PHILOSOPHY OF "CHANGE"

"This is as openly a radical background as any significant American political figure has ever emerged from, as much Malcolm X as Martin Luther King, Jr."[1] So wrote Benjamin Wallace-Wells, a reporter for *Rolling Stone*, the music and culture magazine that champions stridently left-wing political views, in an approving profile of then-Senator Obama's political influences. Wallace-Wells wrote the piece shortly after Obama announced his presidential candidacy in February 2007, when Obama was considered a long shot candidate. He had been in the Senate for a mere two years, and was competing against Senator and former First Lady Hillary Clinton, who was the clear choice of the Democratic Party establishment and regarded by the political media as the prohibitive front-runner.

Perhaps for this reason, and in stark contrast to the media's favored treatment of Obama during the general election, a handful of left-leaning journalists were willing to offer unfiltered assessments of the intellectual and personal influences that had shaped the young Senator, as they were not yet invested in his victory—and in shielding him from past associations, such as his relationship with Reverend Jeremiah Wright, a Chicago pastor with radical, anti-American views, that could harm his electoral prospects.

The article in *Rolling Stone* originally carried the title "The Radical Roots of Barack Obama," but, as the primary season heated up and Obama proved to be a viable candidate, the title of the article was mysteriously changed to "Destiny's Child."[2] Wallace-Wells relied mostly on Obama's relationship with Reverend Wright to praise the radical nature of Obama's roots, but Wright is just one of a number of influences that shaped Obama's political outlook. Unlike the Constitution's creators, who were influenced by a wide range of sources from classical antiquity to Enlightenment theorists, from the common law to their religious faith, as well as an encyclopedic knowledge of history, Barack Obama is the product of the modern political left. He has traveled exclusively in extremely homogenous political environments—the prevailing philosophy in these circles relishes central planning, champions the redistribution of wealth, and avoids, if not outright rejects, any firm connection to the dreams of the Founding Fathers.

When he first walked on the national stage at the 2004 Democratic National Convention, Obama introduced himself to the country as a symbol of national unity, the unique product of a racially-mixed, intercontinental union between a white Kansan and a black Kenyan, a man who had no use for the "spin masters and negative ad peddlers who embrace the politics of anything goes" in a nefarious effort to "divide us." Though acknowledging America's "famous individualism," Obama struck a collectivist theme, which he characterized as the "fundamental belief—I am my brother's keeper, I am my sister's keeper—that makes this country work." He paid tribute to the greatness of America by proclaiming that, as the product of an "improbable love" between a Kansan and a Kenyan, "in no other country on earth, is my story even possible."[3]

The speech was a stupendous success. Obama delivered it with deftness and projected the image of a post-partisan, racially-diverse candidate with national appeal. That Obama connected with a vast swath of voters from across the country was an impressive political achievement for someone, like Obama, who is the product of a narrow set of left-of-center political influences that are hardly rooted in the nation's founding principles.

Virtually every major influence in his life is readily identifiable with leftist politics. He has called his mother "the dominant figure in my formative years....The values she taught me continue to be my touchstone when it comes to how I go about the world of politics." Stanley Ann Dunham was born in Wichita, Kansas during World War II, and Obama has frequently touted this fact as a way to wrap himself in the values of the American Heartland. There is, however, little evidence that Dunham embraced those values, and quite a bit to suggest that she rejected them. For one thing, Dunham flatly rejected religion, particularly organized churches. "She touted herself as an atheist, and it was something she'd read about and could argue," recalled Maxine Box, the best friend of Dunham in high school in Seattle, WA. "She was always challenging and arguing and comparing. She was already thinking about things that the rest of us hadn't."[4] In *Dreams From My Father,* Obama described his mother as "a lonely witness for secular humanism."[5]

Dunham embraced a vision of America and the world that eschewed traditional notions of faith and morality in favor of leftist politics. She seemed to relish those ideas and philosophies that represented a direct attack on the prevailing ethos of American society. "If you were concerned about something going wrong in the world, Stanley would know it first," according to former classmate Chip Wall, who described her as a "fellow traveler," which is a moniker typically used to describe communist sympathizers.[6] Wall noted that her belief system involved a strong critique of America: "The press is dumbed down, education is dumbed down, people don't know anything about geography or the rest of the world."[7] One of her high school teachers noted that she questioned the basic premises of post-WWII American society, including the Cold War, asking questions such as "What's so good about capitalism? What's wrong with communism? What's good about communism?"[8] As a free spirit, she was not about to be bound by what she saw as the domineering political, cultural and religious constraints of Eisenhower-era American society.

Given Dunham's left-of-center, secular humanist outlook, it is not surprising that her son was not engaged with religion as a young man. Some have claimed Obama to have been a Muslim as a child, but until he joined Reverend Jeremiah Wright's Trinity United Church in the 1980s, Obama showed little regard for *any* religion. He had attended an Islamic school for two years while in Indonesia, but he also went to Catholic school for two years. Nothing seemed to sink in—he was reprimanded by a teacher for making faces during Koran studies, and during prayer time at the Catholic school he would "close my eyes, then peek around the room. Nothing happened. No angels descended." In Chicago, when a fellow community activist and Catholic named Will told him about his catechism, Obama "nodded, deciding not to ask what a catechism was....I felt that way now, listening to Will; my silence was like closing my eyes."[9] Due to both the influence of his mother and his personal choice, Obama's formative years were decidedly irreligious. As we will see, not only was his political philosophy formed before he began practicing religion, but it was his political activism in Chicago that drove him to embrace the politicized Christianity practiced by Reverend Jeremiah Wright.

As a left-wing anthropologist uninterested in conforming to prevailing American mores, Dunham probably didn't give much thought to a permanent life for herself on the American mainland. Yet, according to Obama, she understood the "chasm that separated the life chances of an American from an Indonesian. She knew which side of the divide she wanted her child to be on."[10] Accordingly, after Obama spent several years with Dunham and her husband, Lolo Soetero, in Indonesia, Dunham sent her son back to Hawaii to live with her parents. Obama described his grandparents as "vaguely liberal,"[11] and before they moved to Hawaii they attended services at East Shore Unitarian Church in Bellevue, Washington—a decidedly left-leaning congregation that was known as the "Little Red Church on the Hill" for its political bent.[12]

It is not clear to what extent these grandparents served as influences for Obama's political worldview. *Dreams From My Father* suggests that Obama's grandfather thought that Obama needed the type of tutelage that he was incapable of providing, and arranged a mentorship for Obama with someone Obama describes as "a poet named Frank," who is better known as Frank Marshall Davis, an African-American communist writer with bitterly anti-American views. Davis was a truly radical figure. He lambasted the Truman administration for, of all things, the Marshall Plan that helped rebuild the defeated nations following World War II, complaining that American "actions at home and abroad are making American democracy synonymous with oppression." He "watched with growing shame for my America as our leaders have used our golden riches to re-enslave the yellow and brown and black peoples of the world." To Davis, the Marshall Plan was a "device" to maintain "white imperialism."[13]

Obama appreciated Davis' tutelage, later writing that he "was intrigued by old Frank, with his books and whiskey breath and the hint of hard-earned knowledge behind the hooded eyes." When Obama was preparing to attend college at Occidental in California, Davis warned him about "leaving your race at the door," and about how "they'll train you so good, you'll start believing what they tell you about equal opportunity and the American way and all that shit."[14]

"It made me smile," Obama wrote in *Dreams*, "thinking back on Frank and his old Black Power, dashiki self. In some ways, he was as incurable as my mother, as certain in his faith, living in the same sixties time warp that Hawaii had created."[15] When Obama hit the ground in Chicago as a community organizer years later, he "imagined Frank in a baggy suit and wide lapels, standing in front of the old Regal Theater, waiting to see Duke or Ella emerge from a gig."[16] Davis' mentorship did not necessarily replace the mythical figure of his father as a male role model, but it certainly mattered to Obama. He certainly would not have discussed Davis in *Dreams From My Father* had Davis' counsel failed to make an impact on him.

Though his father was never a physical presence in Obama's life, Obama was very much his father's son—his mother once told him that "your brains, your character, you got from him."[17] Barack Obama Sr. was a Harvard-educated political economist who left his infant son and American wife, returned to his native Kenya, and embarked on a quest to remake Kenyan society after an era of colonial rule. Obama's mother described Obama Sr. to her son as a larger-than-life figure, a man that "led his life according to principles that demanded a different kind of toughness, principles that promised a higher form of power."[18] Despite Obama Sr.'s absence, Obama, through the stories told by his mother, nevertheless developed an idealized image of his father as "the brilliant scholar, the generous friend, the upstanding leader," and, perhaps for this reason, Obama dedicated his first autobiography, which he wrote when he was in his early thirties, to the dreams he received from his father, undertaking what he called "a very personal journey to piece together my father's story and figure out who he was."[19] This journey even included a personal voyage to Africa because "it was into my father's image…that I'd packed all the attributes I sought in myself."[20]

Obama Sr. was, in fact, hardly a prototypical role model. Not only did he callously leave Obama and his mother behind to pursue his own ambitions, but he was also a serial womanizer and polygamist who fathered children with multiple women, a drunkard who killed himself when, in an inebriated stupor, he drove his car into a tree. He was supposed to be one of Kenya's brightest lights, a superior intellect who would employ his Western education towards remaking the continent following the age of colonialism. But Obama Sr. never achieved the political success he craved, ending his life, in his son's words, as a "defeated, lonely bureaucrat."[21] Obama recognized these shortcomings, and saw his father as a tragic figure who squandered his prodigious talent. "For all your gifts," Obama emotionally told his father at his African gravesite, "the quick mind, the powers of concentration, the charm—you could never forge yourself into a whole man by leaving [the past] behind."[22] That his father ultimately failed in his life's endeavor did not deter Obama from romanticizing his father, for though the man was flawed, Obama considered his cause to be just. "A man's either trying to live up to his father's expectations or make up for his father's mistakes," Obama has said. "In my case, both things might be true."[23]

As the title *Dreams From My Father* suggests, Obama's first autobiography leaves little doubt that Obama has received some level of inspiration from Barack Obama Sr. This is driven home in a poignant scene in which Obama cries at his father's grave, and in which Obama pledges himself to pursue his father's dreams:

> With my tears finally spent, I felt a calmness wash over me. I felt the circle finally close. I realized that who I was, what I cared about, was no longer just a matter of intellect or obligation, no longer a construct of words. I saw that my life in America—the black life, the white life, the sense of abandonment I'd felt as a boy, the frustration and hope I'd witnessed in Chicago—all of it was connected with this small plot of earth an ocean away, connected by more than accident of name of the color of my skin. The pain I felt was my father's pain.[24]

Obama had previously been influenced by his father's dreams; when he became a community organizer after graduating from college, Obama felt "that there was something to prove…to my father."[25] At the gravesite, he pledged himself to succeed where his father had so miserably failed.

But while *Dreams From My Father* demonstrates that Obama has taken the dreams of his father as his own, it tells us preciously little about the content of the dreams that he received from Barack Obama Sr. It is clear that Obama did not receive any type of spiritual inspiration from his father, who was born a Muslim but had shunned all forms of religion by the time Obama was born. This fact is sometimes lost in the political whispers intimating that Obama holds his father's Muslim faith. Barack Obama Sr.'s true faith was not a Muslim faith but a political faith in the power of the state to engage in central planning, and it was this secular humanist faith in the power of government that inspired his son. To Obama's grandmother Sarah, Obama Sr.'s political dreams represent the backbone of Obama's political career. During the 2008 presidential election she told *Newsweek* that "this son is realizing everything the father wanted—fighting for people, the dreams of the father are still alive in the son."[26]

As we will see, Obama developed an antipathy towards private business, and found his life's calling in political activism, as an agent for so-called "redistributive change," the goals of his activism reflecting some of his father's most cherished beliefs. In "Problems Facing Our Socialism,"[27] a 1965 essay written for the *East Africa Journal* and one of the most important public acts of his life, the elder Obama offered a sharply critical review of the objectives and policies of the post-colonial Kenyan government. The political outlook of Obama Sr. rejected American mainstays such as private property rights and a limited role for government. Obama Sr. differed with the Kenyan plans not because such plans embraced socialism but because they did not go far enough to elevate public control over private land, to redistribute income throughout society, and, in his words, to "force people to do things they would not do otherwise." This even included "restrict[ing] the size of farms that can be owned by one individual throughout the country." Although ostensibly seeking to promote economic growth in Kenya, Obama's policy proscriptions targeted the goal of "find[ing] means which we can redistribute our economic gains to the benefit of all and at the same time be able to channel some of these gains to future production," though he did not endorse any policies that would actually foster private sector economic growth.[28]

Obama Sr.'s redistributive goal was also an anti-colonial goal rooted in returning the wealth created during the colonial era to those Obama Sr. regarded as its rightful owners, the native Africans. When the Kenyan policy paper questioned whether nationalization of private enterprises would hinder economic growth, Obama Sr. rejected such a concern, arguing that "it is the African who owns this country" and that the African government should "control the economic means of growth in this country." For Obama Sr., a free economy was inherently suspect because it "is individual private enterprise and business that tends to encourage accumulation," and this allows economic gains to be realized by those whom Obama Sr. held in contempt. It is, according to Obama the elder, better "to bring standardized use and control of resources through public ownership," which would enable "the equitable distribution of economic gains that would follow."[29]

Though Obama Sr. wanted to erase the vestiges of colonialism from Kenya, his policy prescriptions were by no means limited to that anti-colonial end. Obama Sr. saw a limitless role for the national government, so much so that he advocated an income tax rate of 100%. "Theoretically," he wrote, "there is nothing that can stop the government from taxing 100 per cent of income so long as the people get benefits from the government commensurate with their income which is taxed." He regarded the notion that such confiscatory tax rates could be counterproductive as "a fallacy," dismissing concerns about squashing economic incentives for work, savings and investment, and not even considering the enormous incursion on individual liberty that the deprivation of all income would represent.[30] As we will see, this type of analysis is something that Alexander Hamilton, who was, ironically, articulating an economic philosophy for a post-colonial order in America, directly repudiated when discussing the Constitution's taxing power in *The Federalist Papers*. For now, suffice it to say that this heavy-handed brand of government intervention is inimical to the basic tenets of American political theory which require limitations on government power and respect for private property rights.

Obama Sr.'s fervent support for unbridled government power was equaled by a resolute belief in the competence of central planning and bureaucracies. Although finding numerous faults and negative consequences with private enterprise, Obama the elder glossed over and in some instances outright ignored any ill-effects or unintended consequences of government activism, and certainly did not acknowledge that there are certain things that are beyond the capacity of government to do.

This is perhaps best illustrated by Obama Sr.'s discussion of encouraging foreign tourism, in which he chided the Kenyan Government for not paying any attention to "making [tourism] cheap so as to include those who are not rich. At the present time, the cost of living is too high for tourists." He complained that "hotels charge exorbitant rates" and lamented that there were "no price controls" so that those who were not rich could "afford to come to Kenya as tourists," which Obama intimated would allow for more tourism and, presumably, more economic benefits for Kenya itself. "The government," he demanded, "ought to do something about this."

Putting aside the implicit rejection of the role played by market forces in determining the price of tourism, it is striking that Obama Sr. saw government's role not in helping to create conditions that attract tourists, but in setting the prevailing rates by fiat. That he did not recognize such controls would be doomed to failure speaks volumes about his boundless faith in the capacity of centralized public power. It is this faith in the ability of government to decree a society into prosperity that epitomizes the essence of Obama Sr.'s philosophy, and this represents a rejection of much of what the Founders believed to be indispensable principles of good government and a just society. Nevertheless, this belief in transformational change through centralized public power, rather than any type of religious faith (Muslim or otherwise), is what Obama inherited from his father.

Before arriving in Chicago as a community organizer, Obama gravitated towards radical politics more in line with his father's socialism than with the principles underlying the Constitution. In *Dreams From My Father*, he recounts that when he was a student at Occidental College in California, he deliberately sought out "Marxist professors and structural feminists and punk rock performance poets" and spent his nights in the dorm discussing "neocolonialism, Franz Fanon, Eurocentrism, and patriarchy."[31] These are not the topics of discussion that one consumed with the Founding Fathers and their principles would typically relish. Indeed, America and her Founders are usually seen as villains of monumental proportions by those who embrace such left-wing outlooks.

But because "there were thousands of so-called campus radicals, most of them white and tenured and happily tolerated," Obama wanted to be more than just another radical face in the crowd, and thus sought additional ways to distinguish himself from "bourgeois society's stifling constraints."[32] Dr. John C. Drew, a grant-writing consultant and former Marxist who knew Obama when Obama attended Occidental, recalls Obama "arguing a straightforward Marxist-Leninist class-struggle point of view, which anticipated that there would be a revolution of the working class, led by revolutionaries, who would overthrow the capitalist system and institute a new socialist government that would redistribute the wealth." Dr. Drew further recalled that Obama thought "that wealthy people were exploiting others. That this was the secret of their wealth, that they weren't paying others enough for their work, and they were using and taking advantage of other people. He was convinced that a revolution would take place, and it would be a good thing."[33] This notion of the inherently exploitive nature of a free enterprise economy is very much in tune with his father's disdain for private property, and would be an implicit assumption underlying some of candidate and President Obama's controversial policies and statements.

As a collegian, first at Occidental College in Los Angeles and then at Columbia University in New York City, Obama shared the political orientation of the campus left, and even embraced the left's faddish cause célèbres. He wrote an article for Columbia's *Sundial* campus magazine titled "Breaking the War Mentality," which lauded two leftist student groups for their dedication to the nuclear freeze movement and, Obama wrote, for their quests "to foster awareness and practical action necessary to counter the growing threat of war." Writing during a time when President Ronald Reagan was rebuilding the nation's military power, confronting the Soviet Union, and propelling America to an eventual victory in the Cold War, Obama noted the groups "share an aversion to current government policy," are "visualizing the possibilities of destruction and grasping the tendencies of distorted national priorities, [and] are throwing their weight into shifting America off the dead-end track."

Employing the tried and true language of campus leftists, Obama described this type of campus organizing activity as "lay[ing] the foundation for future mobilization against the relentless, often silent spread of militarism in the country." Obama and his fellow campus activists had a fundamental philosophical disagreement with President Reagan: while Reagan (and, as we will see, the creators of the Constitution) believed that military strength served to deter foreign conflict, the campus radicals thought that reducing American strength would cause other nations to forego conflict, thus purportedly leading to a more peaceful world.

Although Obama portrayed himself as supportive of the goals of the freeze movement, he also questioned whether the goals of the movement were too tame and unlikely to bring about the type of wholesale changes in national policy that he fervently advocated. "The narrow focus of the Freeze movement as well as academic discussions of first versus second strike capabilities," Obama wrote, "suit the military-industrial interests, as they continue adding to their billion dollar erector sets." Obama wondered "whether disarmament or arms control issues, severed from economic and political issues, might be another instance of focusing on the symptoms of a problem instead of the disease itself." One of the student activists disagreed. "We do focus primarily on catastrophic weapons," Freeze-proponent Mark Bigelow told Obama. "Look, we say, here's the worst part, let's work on that. You're not going to get rid of the military in the near future."

Obama saw at least some value in an approach that targeted major weapons platforms. As Bigelow pointed out to him, the "Freeze is one part of a whole disarmament movement. The lowest common denominator, so to speak." The massive reductions in the American military sought by campus activists would be a boon for those looking to drastically increase social welfare spending. For Bigelow, "this may dispel the idea that disarmament is a white issue, because how the government spends its revenue affects everyone." It was, in fact, this prospect for greater domestic, non-military spending that appealed to Obama, for he saw the need to reorient America's national priorities away from national defense, which had traditionally been the core function of the federal government, towards greater federal involvement in domestic economic issues, including (and, as we will see, especially) as a force for the redistribution of wealth. In language alien to anyone not well-versed in the discourse of the campus left, Obama concluded his article by postulating that the "most pervasive malady" of the "American experience" has been "that elaborate patterns of knowledge and theory have been disembodied from individual choices and government policy." Accordingly, he hoped that leftist student groups would serve as a corrective to the "twisted logic of which we are today a part."[34]

While at Columbia, Obama attended socialist conferences at New York's Cooper Union—ironically, the site of Lincoln's 1860 speech in which he embraced American constitutional conservatism—and further developed an antipathy toward private business.[35] He described his short stint working at a small consulting firm in Manhattan as being a "spy behind enemy lines," as if working in private industry was inherently immoral. Occasionally, Obama experienced glimmers of a life spent as a "captain of industry, barking out orders, closing the deal, before I remembered who it was I told myself I wanted to be and felt pangs of guilt for my lack of resolve." It was as if he felt himself reneging on the dreams received from his father.

But he resented the lack of racial diversity in the corporate world. The only other black faces in the company, he claimed, were the secretaries and security guard. Interestingly, they didn't seem to share Obama's aversion to private industry, and indeed looked forward to him rising through the ranks of the company to become, one day, the chief executive. When Obama told an African-American security guard named Ike that he planned on leaving the company to become an organizer, Ike told him flatly that he was wasting his talent and that he "can't help folks that ain't gonna make it nohow, and they won't appreciate you trying. Folks that wanna make it, they gonna find a way to do it on they own." Obama was undeterred. He wanted to work "closer to the streets," as a community organizer, for "change." [36]

Change was the buzzword of Obama's 2008 presidential campaign, but it was not a new slogan for him. It is something that he has been trumpeting since his time as a community organizer. "Change won't come from the top," Obama would tell his college classmates, "change will come from a mobilized grass roots."[37]

Yet the concept of change is an elusive one. One thing that is certain is that the concept of "change" was one of the bedrock principles of the community organizing movement that Obama so eagerly embraced after graduating from Columbia, and this movement is central to Obama's political worldview. As his wife Michelle Obama once said, "Barack is not a politician first and foremost. He's a community activist exploring the viability of politics to make change."[38]

But what specific type of change does the community organizer seek? In the authoritative source for community organizing, *Rules for Radicals*, self-described radical Saul Alinsky stressed the need for an organizer to have an "ideology of change" that is flexible enough to accommodate a number of different circumstances and to mask the true radical intentions of the organizer. As reporter Ryan Lizza noted in a sympathetic profile of Obama in the liberal *New Republic*, though Obama spends more than 150 pages in *Dreams From My Father* discussing his community organizing days, "there's little discussion of the theory that undergirded his work and informed that of his teachers. Alinsky is the missing layer of his account."[39] Under Alinsky's theory, maintaining a certain amount of flexibility enables devotees such as Obama to "organize for power…get it and use it" to, among other things, effectuate a redistribution of wealth.

Alinsky asserted that "the failure to use power for a more equitable distribution of the means of life for all people signals the end of the revolution."[40] As Alinsky dispenses mostly tactical advice, there is very little beyond this clarion call for income and property redistribution in *Rules for Radicals* that would flush out the stubborn details of Alinsky's revolutionary program. Like a true agent for change in the Alinsky tradition and unlike, say, an openly militant Marxist, Obama remained, at least insofar as one can tell from reading *Dreams of My Father,* flexible about the details of his political agenda beyond the basic imperative of redistributive change.

While Obama's adherence to the Alinsky "ideology of change" tended to obscure any detailed political positions beyond his more general redistributive goals, it nevertheless revealed much about his broader philosophical outlook. Unlike the Founders, Alinsky rejected the idea of timeless truths. He argued that the organizer "does not have a fixed truth—truth to him is relative and changing; everything to him is relative and changing. He is a political relativist."[41] In his chilling dedication to *Rules for Radicals*, Alinsky even rejected perhaps the most time-honored distinction, that between good and evil:

> Lest we forget at least an over-the-shoulder acknowledgment to the very first radical: from all our legends, mythology, and history (and who is to know where mythology leaves off and history begins—or which is which), the first radical known to man who rebelled against the establishment and did it so effectively that he at least won his own kingdom—Lucifer.[42]

Alinksy believed that people were motivated by pure self-interest, and that values and ideals mattered little. His goals were blatantly materialistic: *Rules for Radicals*, he wrote, is a "revolutionary handbook…for the Have-Nots of the world regardless of the color of their skins or their politics."[43] And he made no bones about the fact that his organizing "had only one reason for being—that is, organization for power in order to put into practice or promote" his materialistic ends.[44]

The curious thing about Alinsky is that while he stressed the need for an organizer to eschew fixed truths and take the world as he finds it, his worldview rested on an assumption of a static, class-based society. "Mankind," he declared in *Rules for Radicals*, "has been and is divided into three parts: the Haves, the Have-Nots, and the Have-a-Little,

Want Mores." The Haves are "on top…with power, money, food, security and luxury. They suffocate in their surpluses while the Have-Nots starve." Although they are the fewest in number, they "want to keep things as they are and are opposed to change." "The Have-Nots, on the other hand, "are chained together by the common misery of poverty, rotten housing, disease, ignorance, political impotence, and despair." In between these two poles lies the middle class, the so-called Have-a-Little, Want Mores, whom Alinsky describes as "social, economic, and political schizoids" since they are "torn between upholding the status quo to protect the little they have, yet wanting change so they can get more."[45]

According to Alinksy, the key to bringing about a true political and social revolution was to dissipate "man's illusion that his own welfare can be separate from that of all others. As long as man is shackled to this myth, so long will the human spirit languish." This, incidentally, is a theme that Obama would embrace as president, on issues ranging from health care to job creation. Alinsky asserted a philosophy of the interconnectedness of man, a "world where no man can have a loaf of bread while his neighbor has none. If he does not share his bread, he does not sleep, for his neighbor will kill him." Thus, Alinsky proposed to harness the self-interest of those who "have" as a way to enlist their support for his redistributive agenda, for "he is beginning to learn that he will either share part of his material wealth or lose all of it."[46]

The underlying assumption of Alinsky's worldview is that there exists a fixed amount of wealth in society; the rich accumulate wealth at the expense of others, and the only way to make society more equitable is to take this wealth and redistribute it to the "Have-Nots," who are, to Alinsky, the rightful owners of the wealth in the first place. Under this view, the plight of the so-called lower classes is attributable to the greed of society's "Haves," who control an inordinate percentage of the nation's economic pie and selfishly hoard their wealth, leaving little, if any, economic opportunity for those at the bottom.

More than three decades after the initial publication of *Rules For Radicals*, then-Senator Barack Obama, in his second autobiography, assigned blame to the "Haves" for a number of societal problems in terms eerily similar to Alinsky. In the *Audacity of Hope*, Obama wrote that "the problems of poverty and racism, the uninsured and the unemployed…are also rooted in societal indifference and individual callousness—the desire among those at the top of the social ladder to maintain their wealth and status whatever the cost, as well as the despair and self-destructiveness among those at the bottom of the social ladder."[47]

Alinsky was an atheist, yet it was through the plying of the Alinksy craft as a community organizer that Obama shed his skepticism and embraced religion. As an organizer in Chicago, Obama's goals centered on the mobilization of African-Americans for redistributive change delivered through politics, and he soon realized that Chicago churches represented perhaps the most fertile ground from which a political mobilization could be launched. But Obama was warned that his irreligion would be an impediment to forging political relationships with these churches. One area pastor bluntly told him that "it might help your mission if you had a church home….It doesn't matter where, really….[The pastors will] want to know just where you're getting yours from. Faith, that is." The pastor understood and supported what Obama was trying to accomplish, and recommended that Obama talk with "a dynamic young pastor" named Reverend Jeremiah Wright, who had a strong following among politically-minded young people like Obama.[48]

Obama's relationship with Reverend Wright became an explosive issue during the 2008 presidential primaries when videos clips emerged of Wright's radical sermons. Many of these clips showed Wright making patently outrageous comments: he accused the U.S. Government of creating the HIV virus as a means to commit genocide against black people; he proclaimed that, rather than saying "God Bless America," it was more appropriate to exclaim "God Damn America" because "it's in the Bible, for killing innocent people!"; he referred to America as being a nation based on the Ku Klux Klan, calling it the "US of KKKA"; he said that the 9/11 attacks represented "America's chickens coming home to roost"—fitting medicine for a nation that bombed Hiroshima and Nagasaki during World War II; he characterized America as an "arrogant, racist, military superpower"; he compared the United States to the Al Qaeda terrorist organization; and he asserted that "racism was how this country was founded and how this country is still run."[49] Although Obama denied being present for these comments, Wright's sermons raised a concern about Obama's own outlook. After all, Obama and Wright had a close, 20-plus year relationship: Wright presided over his wedding ceremony, baptized his two daughters, dedicated his house and was "the man who led him from skeptic to self-described Christian."[50]

What was sometimes lost in the controversy that permeated the political debate at the time was the reason Wright's particular brand of Christianity appealed to Obama, the hitherto irreligious community organizer. As someone who traveled in a homogeneous political environment for virtually his entire life and as someone dedicated to organizing a "mobilized grass roots" for "redistributive change," it should not be surprising that Obama was attracted to Wright's Trinity United Church, for Wright's theology was as much a theory of political activism as it was a religious doctrine. When he first met with Wright to discuss his desire to enlist Chicago-area churches in his organizing activities, Wright even warned him that his Church might be a burden to his organizing efforts because of its perceived political radicalism.[51] This is because Wright embraced what is known as "black liberation theology," which put a premium on political activism. As Wright later explained in his *Trumpet Newsmagazine*, "there was no separation Biblically and historically and there is no separation contemporaneously between 'religion and politics'....The Word of God has everything to do with racism, sexism, militarism, social justice, and the world in which we live today."[52]

This brand of theology reinforced the already existent political philosophy that Obama had developed, and the fact that Wright's church offered more than mere piety attracted him. "Not all of what these people sought was strictly religious," Obama recalled of his first service at Trinity, "it wasn't just Jesus they were coming home to. It occurred to me that Trinity, with its African themes, its emphasis on black history, continued the role that Reverend Phillips had described earlier as a redistributor of values and circulator of ideas."[53] Obama also appreciated the collectivist perspective championed by "a church like Trinity," which "assured its members that their fates remained inseparably bound, that an intelligible 'us' still remained."[54]

It wasn't until Obama heard Reverend Wright's sermon the "The Audacity of Hope" (Obama would later title his second autobiography in honor of it) that he decided to embrace religion and join Trinity. Wright infused his sermon with political references to "Sharpsville and Hiroshima, the callousness of policy makers in the White House and in the State House." He cited a painting titled "Hope" in which a harpist appears to be situated on a majestic mountaintop, but on closer inspection there is a "valley below, where everywhere are the ravages of famine, the drumbeat of war, a world groaning under strife and deprivation." According to Reverend Wright, ours is a "world where cruise ships throw away more food in a day than most residents of Port-au-Prince see in a year, where white folks' greed runs a world in need."[55] This type of social justice bent is exactly the type of message that a community organizer fixated on redistributive change would be drawn towards; Obama later explained that Wright's Christianity "spoke to me in terms of the kind of life that I would want to lead—being my brothers' and sisters' keeper," thereby providing a religious justification for major redistributive change.[56]

After his community organizing days in Chicago, Obama continued to operate in environments that were overwhelmingly, if not monolithically, far to the left of the American political center. His first stop after organizing was Harvard Law School because he wanted to receive an education on the currency of power that he thought "would have compromised me before coming to Chicago." The things he would learn in law school could, he wrote in *Dreams From My Father*, "help me bring about real change" when he returned to to the Windy City.[57] Harvard seemed like the perfect place for this: Obama's father received an education, if not a degree, at Harvard before returning to Kenya to reengineer African society, and Harvard's leftist ideological orientation was very similar, if more elite, than the environments in which he had previously marinated.

During the late 1980s, the bitter faculty squabbles at Harvard were completely detached from the prevailing national dialogue. The debates in the nation's federal judiciary pitted conservative "originalists" who believed the Constitution possesses a stable meaning against progressives who saw the Constitution as "evolving" through judicial improvisation, yet the "debate" at Harvard seemed to be between the institutional left and the avant-garde, deconstructionist left. These academic battles pitted faculty members, deemed "conservative" at Harvard but who would, in the broader political society, be aligned with the establishment left-wing of the Democratic Party, against those considered to represent the "real" left—so called critical legal theorists—that were so radical they considered law to be "an expression of an oppressive social and economic status quo," rather than grounded on neutral principles.[58] For example, Roberto Mangabeira Unger, a critical legal theorist who taught two elective classes taken by Obama, described himself as a "leftist, and, by conviction as well as by temperament, a revolutionary."[59] Needless to say, in such an environment, the Founding Fathers are *persona non grata.*

His election to the presidency of the *Harvard Law Review* earned Obama national acclaim because he was the first African-American elected president of what is generally considered to be the most prestigious law review in the country.[60] The national reporters that covered the story naturally inquired about what the newly elected law review president planned to do after graduating from Harvard. Obama dismissed the opportunity to net a clerkship with the U.S. Supreme Court or a lucrative job with a large law firm in favor of working in the inner city to build community institutions and organizations. "I'm not interested in the suburbs. The suburbs bore me. And I'm not interested in isolating myself," he told a reporter for the Associated Press. "I feel good when I'm engaged in what I think are the core issues of the society, and those core issues to me are what's happening to poor folks in this society."[61] For Obama, the choice was clear: he would return to the South Side of Chicago and continue the work he began as a community organizer, though perhaps not only as an organizer but also as an elected official.

From the point of view of his political influences, it is interesting that Obama considered moving to Chicago's Hyde Park as a way to prevent "isolating" himself. Of course, Chicago's South Side was not isolated from the problems that affect the typical American city, and this is likely what Obama meant, even if Hyde Park is not typically considered part of the South Side. Still, the Hyde Park neighborhood in which Obama chose to live both as a community organizer and when he returned to Chicago after graduating from Harvard Law School was (and is) one of the most monolithically left-wing political communities in the United States; this says something about Obama's outlook, for he was focused on a potential political future and, at least after Harvard, he could have chosen to live and work wherever he wanted. As fellow Hyde Park resident and Obama advisor John Rogers told *USA Today*, "What better way to define what you're all about than where you choose to live and bring up your family?"[62] It would be difficult to find a neighborhood with more political homogeneity: in the 2004 presidential election, the two wards that include Obama's neighborhood and the nearby University of Chicago preferred John F.

Kerry over George W. Bush by a margin of 95%-5%.[63] This was precisely the type of environment that suited Obama.

Only in such an environment could a former Weather Underground terrorist like William Ayers be regarded as a respectable member of the community. Ayers' background is contemptible: he is responsible for numerous bombings of public buildings, including the Pentagon; he dedicated his book *Prairie Fire* to Sirhan Sirhan, the assassin of Robert F. Kennedy; he called for a communist revolution and for followers to "kill your parents"; and told *The New York Times*, in an article published (of all days) on September 11, 2001, that "I don't regret setting bombs. I feel we didn't do enough."[64] It is indisputable that Ayers has never apologized for his past crimes, and speaks of America as if it is the focus of evil in the modern world. Yet, in Hyde Park, Ayers is considered to be, in the words of one Hyde Park resident, nothing more than "an aging, toothless radical. A pussycat…[that] had a violent streak at one time" but who is now "thoroughly conventional, just [a] very nice, well-educated [person] from the neighborhood."[65] When ABC's George Stephanopoulos asked Obama about his relationship with Ayers in a televised debate during the Democratic primaries, Obama noted that Ayers was a "professor of English," which is a very respectable position in academic-centric Hyde Park.[66]

Though it is not clear to what extent he shared any of Ayers' ideas, Obama clearly had more than a passing relationship with Bill Ayers. He had a campaign meet-and-greet at Ayers' house when he launched his first campaign for the Illinois Senate, which was an opportunity for Obama to meet with some of Hyde Park's most influential leftists; he received a $200 donation from Ayers to his Senate campaign in 2001; he headed the Chicago Annenberg Challenge, which was the brainchild of Ayers, from 1995-1999; he served with Ayers on the board of the Woods Fund, a group dedicated to "social justice"; and Obama reviewed Ayers' book *A Kind and Just Parent: The Children of Juvenile Court*, which he called "a searing and timely account of the juvenile court system."[67]

Obama was quick to point out that "knowing somebody who engaged in detestable acts 40 years ago, when I was 8 years old, somehow reflects on me and my values doesn't make much sense." It may be true that a connection to Ayers tells us nothing about Obama's own personal views, and it is true that Obama has never advocated advancing his leftism through violence. But the fact that Obama had, at a minimum, a casual working relationship with someone like William Ayers tells us an awful lot about the Hyde Park circles in which he traveled. Even though he had never apologized for his crimes—and, in fact, reveled in his criminal behavior, writing that he was "guilty as hell and free as a bird…what a country"—and even though he continued to regard the United States as a terrorist state, Ayers was a member in good standing of the credentialed elite in Hyde Park, the type of academic that was particularly respected in the upper crust of the city's progressive political scene and that would habitually find himself participating in initiatives like the Woods Fund and the Chicago Annenberg Challenge. Needless to say, Hyde Park is one of the few communities in the entire country in which such a disreputable figure would be considered a respected voice on matters of public policy.

Given the almost uniformly left-of-center political environments in which Barack Obama traveled throughout his life, it is hardly surprising that, when he finally decided to throw his hat into the ring as a candidate for political office, he did so under the banner of the Democratic Party, which is the natural home for someone on the political left. Obama has said that he is "someone who is no doubt progressive," and it is the progressive impulse that has been one the party's driving intellectual forces for most of the past 100 years.[68] Today, progressivism is primarily associated with the Democratic Party, but the Republican Party has also produced prominent progressives, such as Herbert Hoover. The extent to which progressives have dominated the Democratic Party has varied over the years, but suffice it to say that candidate Barack Obama leveraged the support of the party's progressive wing to catapult him to the Democratic presidential nomination in 2008.

The origins of the progressive movement lie, first and foremost, in a dissatisfaction with the Constitution of the United States. Though progressives were eager to make wholesale revisions in the nation's governing charter, they were frustrated that most of their (supposedly unenlightened) contemporaries held the Constitution in extremely high regard. Writing in 1885, Professor Woodrow Wilson complained that "the divine right of kings never ran a more prosperous course than did this unquestioned prerogative of the Constitution to receive universal homage." Wilson, though, was delighted that his generation of political elites was the first to engage in "free, outspoken, unrestrained constitutional criticism. We are the first Americans…to entertain any serious doubts about the superiority of our own institutions as compared with the systems of Europe…[and] to think of remodeling the administrative machinery of the federal government."[69] Progressives saw the purposeful inefficiency of the Constitution, as embodied in the separation of powers and checks and balances, to be "no longer effective" in an age that they thought demanded quick, unified governmental action to meet the nation's needs.

So critical of the Constitution were members of the progressive movement that many cheered when Charles Beard's *An Economic Interpretation of the Constitution* criticized the Framers for constructing what he characterized as an undemocratic governmental system that served to protect their own economic interests. As progressive historian Richard Hofstadter noted, Beard's book attacked the heart of American civic life: "a nation of Constitution-worshippers and ancestor-worshippers was confronted a scholarly muckraking of the Founding Fathers and the Constitution itself."[70] Reducing the affection that the American people had for the Constitution and its creators would pave the way for progressive reformers to usher in a new constitutional framework, even if only through new, creative ways of interpreting the existing Constitution that would leave its form undisturbed but would nevertheless serve to transform its meaning and operation.

Progressive criticism of the Constitution was rooted in the desire to vastly expand the power and scope of the federal government. The Founding Fathers placed a premium on individual liberty when they designed the Constitution, structuring it to prevent the government from doing harm, even if this meant that positive governmental action would be inhibited. Progressives were of a different mind; they were collectivists whose philosophy subordinated individual liberty to the needs of the national government.

In *The Promise of American Life*, the prominent progressive and Constitution-critic Herbert Croly indicted the Constitution's dispersal of power and emphasis on individual freedom as the major roadblocks to "a candid, patient, and courageous attempt to advance the social problem towards a satisfactory solution" through government action, which he acknowledged was "flagrantly socialistic."[71] According to Croly, the only way this problem could be solved was by "reviving the practice of vigorous national action for the achievement of a national purpose."[72] Indeed, the "nationalizing of American political, economic, and social life" necessarily pointed towards "a more scrupulous attention to existing Federal responsibilities, and the increase of their number and scope."[73]

Rather than reconfigure the actual constitutional structure, progressives like Woodrow Wilson proposed to fundamentally transform the very nature of a written constitution. The Founding Fathers considered the Constitution to be fundamental law with a stable meaning, but progressives dismissed this supposedly mechanical, Newtonian view of the Constitution in favor of a Darwinian outlook that saw the nation's governing blueprint as a "living" document. The Constitution, Wilson argued, "is not a mere lawyers' document...[but] a vehicle for life, and its spirit is always the spirit of the age."[74] "No living thing," Wilson continued, "can have its organs offset against each other as checks, and live. On the contrary, its life is dependent upon their quick cooperation, their ready response to the commands of instinct or intelligence, their amicable community of purpose.[75]

Because the "living" Constitution rested in large part on the opinion and practice of each generation, Wilson sought to transcend checks and balances by altering the manner in which Americans viewed the Constitution. The public would need to look past the "scheme of congressional supremacy," as Wilson labeled the actual structure of the Constitution, and see the presidency as the most legitimate source of national political authority, thereby enabling more federal action.[76] Then the people needed to turn to "a man who understands his own day and the needs of his country, and who has the personality and the initiative to enforce his views both upon the people and upon the Congress."[77] The result would be a vast increase in the size, scope and power of the federal government, and an evisceration of the constitutional safeguards carefully designed by the Founding Fathers to protect individual liberty.

One of the upshots of this progressive impulse is the need for a small group of wise individuals to plan and administer the ever-expanding menu of federal initiatives. Progressives tended to frown upon the rough and tumble of politics in favor of the implementation of ostensibly nonpartisan "solutions" devised by experts. An example that captured the progressive impulse of Wilson's time was an awful novel, *Philip Dru: Administrator*, written by Edward Mandell House, who Woodrow Wilson described as his "second personality," and as someone whose "thoughts and mine are one."[78] House considered American institutions such as the

Constitution to be deeply flawed, and thus dedicated the novel to "to the unhappy many who have lived and died lacking opportunity, because, in the starting, the world-wide social structure was wrongly begun."[79] In the book, Philip Dru leads a revolt against the government and assumes the position of Administrator (i.e., dictator) of the United States; he then organizes a commission of five lawyers to devise the "correct" policies, and he implements them by executive fiat, claiming they will benefit the many instead of the few. This has been a longstanding progressive dream, and can be seen today, for example, in the expressed desire of *New York Times* columnist Thomas Friedman that America suspend its constitutional republic and adopt China's totalitarian regime for a day so that controversial policies advocated by wise men like Friedman can be adopted by dictatorial decree.

Obama certainly shares the progressive affinity for the notion that superior government lies in empowering experts to devise (and then impose upon the public) comprehensive "solutions" to pressing national problems. When, as president, Obama was asked by a reporter about a number of unsavory "deals" that had been engineered in Congress to help secure passage of Obama's massive and controversial health care law, he replied that he "would have loved nothing better than to simply come up with some very elegant, academically approved approach to health care, and didn't have any kinds of legislative fingerprints on it, and just go ahead and have that passed." But he lamented the fact that is "not how it works in our democracy. Unfortunately, what we end up having to do is to do a lot of negotiations with a lot of different people." As columnist George F. Will pointed out, by lamenting that he could not simply impose a plan—devised, of course, by academics—on the American people, Obama, the self-described progressive, showed himself to be Woodrow Wilson's kindred spirit, a president disenchanted with the limitations on government's power that Madison and his brethren so effectively built into the Constitution.[80] Indeed, at one point, Obama even told people close to him "that it would be so much easier to be the president of China."[81]

Though he projected an image of a cool, cerebral centrist during the presidential campaign, many of President Obama's policy initiatives charted an unabashedly leftward course; his first two years in office represented the most liberal governance the nation has seen in nearly half of a century. Indeed, unlike other modern Democratic presidents such as Bill Clinton and Jimmy Carter, who both grew up in southern states and developed a familiarity with political thought beyond left-wing progressivism, Obama's entire background and experience has been rooted in the philosophy of the political left, and his worldview reflects this cramped intellectual upbringing.

With this in mind, it is not surprising that Obama's transformational project represents a decided break from the principles relied on by the Founding Fathers when they created the Constitution. How could he keep faith with the philosophy of the Constitution's creators when that philosophy conflicts with the set of beliefs ingrained into him by the various sources of influence in his life, from the dreams of central planning he received from his father to the redistributionist credos of the likes of Saul Alinsky and Jeremiah Wright? Even if he were inclined to embrace the nation's founding principles, his embedded belief system renders him incapable of recognizing the Founders' achievements or building on their success. He seeks transformational change because that is all that he knows. He is a prisoner of his own narrow political worldview.

5

THE PHILOSOPHY OF LIBERTY

It was "really an assembly of demigods," Thomas Jefferson marveled in a letter to John Adams.[1] He was describing the collection of 55 delegates to the Constitutional Convention that descended on Philadelphia in the summer of 1787, most of whom had already established national reputations and some, like George Washington and Benjamin Franklin, who had gained international fame. These delegates brought to the Convention a number of different political outlooks and represented a number of divergent interests. Some were thoroughly republican, others were less so. Some hailed from states with purely agrarian economies, others from states with a burgeoning commercial bent. Some believed that an independent executive was the fetus of monarchy, others deemed executive energy essential for the effective administration of the federal government.

At the same time, the delegates who descended on Philadelphia in 1787 did so within the context of a basic agreement on a number of important first principles regarding politics and the role of government. Authoritative references such as the common law, the writings of philosophers like John Locke and Montesquieu, and the Bible all represented sources of common currency among the delegates. The prevailing influences on the constitutionalists of the Founding Era serve as an important window into the philosophy that underlies their constitutional creation, for the Constitution they produced is a reflection of the operating assumptions they brought with them to the Convention—assumptions about the nature of political power, individual liberty, and the very purpose of government.

Perhaps more than any other delegate, James Madison embodied the intellectual currents of the times. He brought to Philadelphia a deep knowledge of the full spectrum of philosophical, political, economic and religious strands of thought running through the Convention. Madison received a classical liberal arts education at Princeton, where he gained an insight into human affairs through the comprehensive study of the histories of ancient Greece and Rome, developed a view of the individual's place in political society based on classical liberal political philosophy, and devoured the writings of the likes of Trenchard and Gordon, Plato, Aristotle, Hobbes, Machiavelli, and Montesquieu—all of which he processed within the context of a Christian tradition that stressed the importance of conscience and human dignity, but also recognized the depravity of human nature.[2]

Before he attended the Constitutional Convention, Madison studied the design and practices of federal systems throughout history, from the confederacies of ancient Greece to the Swiss Confederation and the United Provinces of the Netherlands. The result of this study was a lengthy paper titled "Notes on Confederacies Ancient and Modern," which reviewed the configuration of every confederacy in history, detailing their respective operations and identifying the defects that lead to their demise. When Madison entered Independence Hall in the summer of 1787, he was bringing with him a body of knowledge of extraordinary breadth, knowledge that would serve as an important foundation from which the delegates would debate the new plan of government.

This vast knowledge base was influenced by a number of different sources. First, religion played a large role in 18th century American society, and delegates like Madison were very much products of a religious worldview. Most of the delegates had attended college; unlike elite American universities of recent history, colleges during the 18th century steeped their programs of study in religious doctrine and practice. At Yale, which counted 4 of its graduates among the Convention delegates, religion was a central justification for the very existence of the institution—Congregationalist ministers unhappy with the liberal religious bent of Harvard founded the school in 1701 so that "Youth may be instructed in the Arts and Sciences [and] through the blessings of Almighty God may be fitted for Publick employment both in Church and Civil State."

While at King's College (later Columbia University) in New York, Madison's colleague Alexander Hamilton studied in a heavily religious environment: chapel before breakfast each day, evening prayers upon the ringing of the prayer bells after dinner, and the attendance of two services on Sundays were all requirements. Like everything he did,

Hamilton pursued the study of religion with a noticeable energy and intensity. Robert Troup, a friend of Hamilton at King's College, noted that he had "often been powerfully affected by the fervor and eloquence of his prayers. He had read many of the polemical writers on religious subjects and he was a zealous believer in the fundamental doctrines of Christianity."[3]

Religious faith provided a baseline from which many of the Founders studied and understood the world around them. Though Madison was so knowledgeable about the Bible that he tested out of his first two years of Biblical studies at Princeton, his other studies were informed by a religious worldview. The lectures of Princeton's James Witherspoon, Madison's foremost professorial influence, expounded upon the fundamentals of political liberty and classical republicanism within the context of New Light Presbyterianism. Witherspoon taught that the seminal work of a political theorist like John Locke, who advocated a theory of government premised on a social compact and natural rights, had to be understood as being subordinate to God's law. "All men, at all times, are related to God," Witherspoon instructed. "They are made by him, and live by his providence."[4]

This was a view widely shared by the delegates. For example, writing on the eve of revolution, Alexander Hamilton noted that the centrality of God was an immutable fact of life, proclaiming that the "sacred rights of mankind are not to be rummaged for, among old parchments, or musty records. They are written, as with a sun beam, in the whole volume of human nature, by the hand of divinity itself; and can never be erased by mortal power."[5]

The God-given rights possessed by each individual are not necessarily respected in a primitive state of nature, so the social compact represented an invaluable means, not to bestow rights upon the people, but to protect rights that the people already possessed. The infringement of these rights represents an illegitimate exercise of power and a usurpation of God's basic command. The religious baseline that served as the foundation for the study of preeminent thinkers like Montesquieu, as well as ancient philosophers and legal theorists like Sir William Blackstone, represents a critical component of the intellectual currency relied on by the Founders when they arrived in Philadelphia and is reflected in the underlying principles of the Constitution.[6] Whereas the community organizer Barack Obama would embrace Christianity as an outgrowth of his political activism, the political outlook of the Constitution's creators flowed from their foundational belief in a supreme God that endowed individuals with certain basic rights.

Madison and other Founders saw God as not simply the creator and supplier of rights but also as an active force on America's behalf. Religion had been an important aspect of the American Revolution. Other than strident revolutionaries, members of the clergy were perhaps the main champions of a God-inspired natural rights philosophy, and it was the American clergy, the so-called "Black Regiment," that King George III blamed for inciting the colonial revolt against Britain. Many members of the Founding generation saw divine inspiration in the improbable victory over Great Britain achieved by the American people. "It is impossible for the man of pious reflection not to perceive in it," Madison observed about the Constitution in *The Federalist* No. 37, "a finger of that Almighty hand which has been so frequently and signally extended to our relief in the critical stages of the revolution."[7]

That God was on America's side was underscored at the Constitutional Convention by none other than Benjamin Franklin. As the Convention wore on and some began to fear that the delegates would not be able to agree on a governing charter, the aging Franklin, who was by far the most prominent Convention delegate other than Washington, rose to address the delegates:

> How has it happened, Sir, that we have not hitherto once thought of humbly applying to the Father of lights to illuminate our understandings? In the beginning of the Contest with G. Britain, when we were sensible of danger we had daily prayer in this room for the divine protection.- Our prayers, Sir, were heard, & they were graciously answered. All of us who were engaged in the struggle must have observed frequent instances of a superintending providence in our favor.
>
> To that kind providence we owe this happy opportunity of consulting in peace on the means of establishing our future national felicity. And have we now forgotten that powerful friend? or do we imagine that we no longer need his assistance? I have lived, Sir, a long time, and the longer I

> live, the more convincing proofs I see of this truth- that God Governs in the affairs of men. And if a sparrow cannot fall to the ground without his notice, is it probable that an empire can rise without his aid?[8]

Though he never embraced a particular religion, let alone an organized church, and was certainly a product of Enlightenment rationalism, Franklin still urged the delegates to enlist God's aid in their quest to memorialize the American Revolution with a written constitution. Once the Constitution was ratified and the new ship of state launched, George Washington insisted that God's hand would continue to guide the new nation: "America, under the smiles of a Divine Providence, the protection of a good government, and the cultivation of manners, morals, and piety, cannot fail of attaining an uncommon degree of eminence, in literature, commerce, agriculture, improvements at home and respectability abroad."[9]

Religion had an even more concrete link to the constitutionalism practiced by the Philadelphia delegates: it helps explain why the delegates believed it appropriate to bind themselves and their posterity to a set of principles through a written document. From the early-17th century, the Protestant dissenters that populated much of colonial New England embraced the notion of a priesthood of all believers, the idea that everyone should be reading and interpreting the Bible on their own rather than receive guidance through Church structures or hierarchies. Under this view, while members of the clergy serve a leadership role and are more learned than the average believer, they do not have any real teaching authority.

However, simply because everyone has the right and, indeed, the duty, to read and interpret the Bible does not mean that this will be done correctly. These dissenters thus believed that the most reliable way to guard against the dangers of individualistic and sinful interpretation of the Bible was for the community to deliberate and decide such matters. To carry out the task of living in accordance with the proper interpretation of the Bible, many of these communities formed congregations based on written religious covenants that reaffirmed the basic truths of God's laws. For instance, the Salem Covenant of 1636 declared that "We Covenant with the Lord and with one another; and go beyond our selves in the presence of God, to walk together in all his waies, according as he is pleased to reveal himself unto us in his Blessed word of truth."[10]

This use of religious covenants soon spawned the use of written covenants to order the political affairs of the community. These colonists took the mechanisms used to create and maintain their congregations and applied them to local self-government. Just as certain fundamental Christian truths bound a congregation, so too did civil society operate within the confines of certain inviolable principles that tied together the political community. Because the use of religious covenants was second nature to the early American colonists, they may not have even fully grasped the implications of the application of the religious covenant model to the political realm. But this innovation was profound, for it ingrained the notion that an enduring constitutionalism was a desirable way to structure's the nation political institutions and protect individual freedom.[11]

Without the influence of religious covenants, this would not necessarily have been an obvious insight to someone thinking about political first principles in the 1780s. For one thing, the best example of a liberty-protecting constitution, the heralded British mixed constitution, was not even a single written document but was instead a conglomeration of statutes, common law, and political tradition. The mere notion of memorializing the basic principles and arrangements of government into a single document was certainly a divergence from the British practice, whose free-floating "constitution" was not susceptible to easy consultation by the citizenry.

Perhaps even more importantly, the right of one generation to bind subsequent generations is far from self-evidently correct as a matter of basic political theory. Sure, there are certain timeless, fundamental principles that must be honored in any constitution, but there is a lot of room for debate regarding the best means to enshrine and give effect to these principles. The creation of a written constitution that is binding on future generations, even if avenues of amendment are available, creates restrictions on the ability of these generations to construct what they deem to be desirable institutions and may hinder their ability to learn from past experience.

Yet, of the delegates who attended the Convention in Philadelphia, not one of them questioned their generation's ability to pre-commit their posterity to a certain political course. Without decades of colonial experience applying the religious covenant model to political charters, it is unthinkable that the notion of enduring constitutionalism would have appeared to be as natural to the delegates as it did. As Madison remarked in *The Federalist* No. 53, this "important distinction so well understood in America between a Constitution established by the people and unalterable by the government, and a law established by the government and alterable by government, seems to have been little understood and less observed in any other country."[12] Americans like Madison understood this distinction so well because they framed the Constitution against the backdrop of more than a century of constitutional practice originally inspired by written religious charters that pre-committed future generations to certain fundamental truths. The adoption of a binding, written constitution, while not reflective of the practices of any other nation in the world, was, for the Framers, an inherently conservative act that institutionalized, on a continental scale, this distinctively American style of constitutionalism.

Though the form of their constitutionalism had been developed over decades of practice, the substance of the Constitution framed by the delegates depended on a number of important theoretical justifications, and this is where Enlightenment thinking figured prominently. As Alexander Hamilton noted in *The Federalist* No. 9, "the science of politics...like most other sciences, has received great improvement. The efficacy of various principles is now well understood, which were either not known at all, or imperfectly known to the ancients."[13]

Most importantly, Constitution creators like Madison embraced classical liberal theory as articulated by the philosopher John Locke. The most famous phrase of the Declaration of Independence—"We hold these truths to be self-evident, that all men are created equal, that they are endowed by their Creator with certain unalienable Rights, that among these are Life, Liberty and the pursuit of Happiness"—was a close approximation of the natural rights trilogy of life, liberty and property that Locke outlined in the *Second Treatise of Government.* And the Lockean notion that the legitimacy of government depends not on royal bloodlines but on the consent of the governed provided the American revolutionaries with the intellectual basis to assert a break from Great Britain.

By the time of the Constitutional Convention, Locke's classical liberalism was a common philosophical touchtone for the delegates. One critically important aspect of Lockean liberalism was the centrality of the right to private property. As a matter of first principle, every individual possesses a fundamental right to his labor, and is entitled to the fruits of that labor. According to Locke, this insight creates a responsibility for government to protect these fruits: "Thus *Labour,* in the Beginning *gave a Right of Property.*"[14] For Madison, any acceptable constitution needed to be capable of protecting the property of its citizens. "Government is instituted to protect property of every sort; as well that which lies in the various rights of individuals," he observed. "This being the end of government, that alone is a *just* government, which *impartially* secures to every man, whatever is his *own.*"[15]

Madison's Locke-inspired formulation is flatly inconsistent with the anti-property rights, state-centric philosophy articulated by the likes of Barack Obama Sr. While Madison and his colleagues considered government-mandated wealth redistribution to be unjust, advocates of debilitating wealth redistribution like Barack Obama Sr. consider the government, rather than the individual, to have the first claim of right to property under its jurisdiction, even to the point that a tax rate of 100% is justifiable.

Classical liberal theory also held that the power of government needed to be limited and individual liberty respected. To maintain the limited nature of the government, Locke argued that it was critical that government's major functions be separated into distinct, individual departments. In one of the first acts of the Convention, Madison and his brethren took Locke's basic premise and, utilizing the theories of the French philosopher Montesquieu that expanded on Locke's basic observation, voted to create a federal government with three separate branches of government: legislative, executive and judicial. To Madison and other Convention delegates, the accumulation of legislative, executive and judicial power in a single source represented the textbook definition of tyranny.

This separation (along with the auxiliary checks that Madison and other delegates included in the Constitution) was also designed to prevent government power from expanding at the expense of individual liberty. As we will see, the Framers deliberately created a system that erred on the side of preventing harm from government, even if this made it more difficult for the government to do desirable things. In contrast, the political sources that influenced Barack Obama—the dreams he received from his father, the radical professors that attracted him in college, and the progressive impulse that he championed as a candidate—all elevated the power of the state over the freedom of the individual, thereby subordinating the interests of the individual to the interest of the collective, as they defined it.

Few thinkers influenced delegates like Madison as much as Locke and Montesquieu, yet others were important. Americans rightfully see 1776, the year that the American colonists signed the Declaration of Independence, as an important year in the history of individual liberty. But the Declaration of Independence was not the only epic monument to freedom produced in 1776, for that same year also witnessed the publication of *An Inquiry into the Nature and Causes of the Wealth of Nations* by the Scottish philosopher and economist Adam Smith. The *Wealth of Nations* is a brilliant exposition of free enterprise and a devastating assault on the concept of mercantilism, which was the most prominent economic theory of the 18th century. Under a mercantilist theory, the wealth of the state was the focal point of national policy, and even measures that harmed individual citizens, such as tariffs, were deemed desirable if they were in the best interests of the empire. Mercantilism assumed that wealth was fixed; since a nation gained wealth only at the expense of another, there existed little reason to institute policies that would foster the creation of new private wealth. Instead, government habitually intervened in the economy to skew the allocation of capital in a way that best aggrandized its own national wealth.

Through the employment of concepts such as the division of labor, Smith demonstrated that new wealth could be created rather than merely transferred from one nation to another, thereby exposing the fallacy of the mercantilist notion that wealth was a zero sum game. He also illustrated how habitually interventionist government policies did not lead to the most efficient allocation of capital. According to Smith, allowing individuals to pursue their own self-interest leads to a better employment of resources, because "it is not from the benevolence of the butcher, the brewer, or the baker, that we expect our dinner, but from their regard to their own self-interest. We address ourselves, not to their humanity but to their self-love, and never talk to them of our own necessities but of their advantages." This better promotes the public good with respect to economic growth and individual opportunity, thereby fostering ends that are not even intended by the individuals acting based on self-interest. It is as if there is an invisible hand. Unlike a mercantilist theory, the free enterprise system does not aggrandize the wealth of the state so much as further the freedom of the individual, who is able to pursue his economic affairs in the way that best suits his situation. And, yet, this will yield more national wealth than even the most robust mercantilist system.[16]

Smith's work reinforced the inclination of Madison and his colleagues to restrict the powers of government to limited, enumerated functions. Madison was a student of Adam Smith, as well as other Scottish Enlightenment thinkers like David Hume. George Washington's personally signed copy of *The Wealth of Nations* from 1789 is to this day preserved at a rare book library in Princeton, New Jersey.[17]

But it was Alexander Hamilton, not Madison or Washington, who was the preeminent economic thinker among the Founding Fathers, and Hamilton incorporated insights from Smith's work into his own understanding of political economy, championing the division of labor, citing the advantages of increasing the means of transportation, and touting the need to leave industry alone so that it will find its most useful and profitable employment.[18] Though Hamilton did not agree with Smith on everything, he and other delegates subscribed to enough of Smith's theory that they created a constitution that left the bulk of decisions about capital allocation to private decision making.

Delegates like James Madison were not content to rely purely upon political theory, and they relied heavily on the lessons of history in evaluating certain ideas. "Experience is the oracle of truth," Madison wrote in *The Federalist* No. 20. "And where its responses are unequivocal, they ought to be conclusive and sacred."[19] The Founders, accordingly, looked to sources ancient and modern for guidance regarding political institutions and individual liberty, as well as for inspiration in fostering public virtue, integrity, and a resistance to corruption.

As they debated constitutional first principles, the Framers often invoked historical examples from classical antiquity. They possessed not a mere passing acquaintance but a thorough understanding of the major ideas, practices and individuals that dominated ancient times. Plutarch's *Lives of the Noble Greek and Romans* was one of the most widely read works of the era, and George Washington never tired of the exhibition of public virtue contained in Joseph Addison's "Cato," even requesting a performance of the play for his troops during a brutal winter in Valley Forge during the Revolutionary War. These eras seemed to contain a treasure trove of lessons that the Framers could use to make sense of their own political times.

The lessons were numerous: the extinguishment of its people's liberty at the hands of Philip II of Macedon illustrated the perils of weakness and decentralization in Ancient Greece; Sparta's defeat of Athens revealed the pure democracy of Athens to be too unstable, and too susceptible to faction, to serve as a suitable example for an American republic; Sparta's national military strength was something that one could appreciate, but its totalitarian, rigid collectivism was utterly at odds with the American Revolution's emphasis on individual liberty; the early Roman Republic demonstrated the prevalence of the great political virtues needed to sustain a great republic, while its fall provided the Founders with numerous examples of the diseases that can infect a popular form of government.[20]

As the political debates of the post-Revolution period heated up, the Founders frequently invoked classical antiquity as a means of buttressing their arguments. The heroes of ancient times demanded respect from political leaders of all stripes. In his *Defence of the Constitutions of the United States*, written before the Convention in 1787 (which he did not attend), John Adams rested his support for a government with three independent branches on the views of the great Roman constitutionalist Cicero. "As all the ages of the world have not produced a greater statesman and philosopher united than Cicero," he declared, "his authority should have great weight."[21] At the Convention, Madison criticized the so-called New Jersey Plan, which called for a weak federal government, as being inadequate to establish a stable, well-functioning republic. To support his critique, Madison cited the weakness of the confederacy of Ancient Greece: "Philip of Macedon," he said, "with little difficulty, destroyed every appearance of it."[22]

Madison was obsessed with squeezing as much knowledge out of history as possible. He wasn't satisfied with a thorough knowledge of classical antiquity so, in "Notes on Confederacies Ancient and Modern," he personally examined in detail a number of confederacies such as the Lycian Confederacy, the Amphyctionic Confederacy, the Achaean Confederacy, the Helvetic Confederacy, the Belgic Confederacy, and the Germanic Confederacy. He noted the internal configuration of each confederation, and also identified the key vices that had lead to each confederation's demise. So, for example, Madison observed how, in the Belgic Confederacy, "the difficulty of procuring unanimity has produced a breach of fundamentals in several instances—Treaty of Westphalia was concluded without consent of Zealand &c D'Albon & Temple," which Madison thought tended "to alter the constitution." Madison was leaving nothing to chance; he left no intellectual stone unturned because he knew that the future of human liberty rested on what the delegates accomplished in Philadelphia.

By the time he arrived at the Convention, he had also diagnosed the maladies that seemed to be afflicting America during the 1780s. In "Vices of the Political System of the United States," Madison identified 12 main problems with the nation's political apparatus, many of which related to the weakness of the federal government under the Articles of Confederation, such as the inability of the federal government to raise revenue. But he also noted the troubling defects in the operations of many of the state governments. He criticized states for their "luxuriancy of legislation," and worried about individual liberty suffocating under a copious body of laws that he characterized as "a nuisance of the most pestilent kind."

Worse, Madison saw the "injustice" of many state laws as even "more alarming not merely because it is a greater evil in itself, but because it brings more into question the fundamental principle of republican Government, that the majority who rule in such Governments, are the safest Guardians both of public Good and of private rights." Madison knew that one of the Convention's foremost tasks was to construct a republican form of government capable of "restrain[ing the majority] from unjust violations of the rights and interests of the minority."[23]

The notes that Madison compiled in anticipation of the Convention show the thoroughness of his study and the breadth of his knowledge. Unlike Obama, Madison did not confine his intellectual pursuits to the study of only a small leftward slice of political thought; instead, he scoured the annals of history in an attempt to identify those fundamental political principles that had stood the test of time and that could serve as a sturdy foundation for the American constitutional experiment. It would not be out of the question to suggest that, when he walked through the doors of the Constitutional Convention, James Madison possessed a greater knowledge of political, republican and constitutional principles than any political leader that had ever walked the face of the earth.

6

ANCIENT AND MODERN

James Madison was a freedom man. Barack Obama is a government man. This doesn't mean that Madison was an anarchist who didn't believe in government or that Obama is a totalitarian who doesn't believe in freedom. For his part, Madison was a main catalyst for the Constitutional Convention because he felt that the federal government under the Articles of Confederation was too weak to perform the limited but necessary functions of an effective national sovereign. Accordingly, he sought to frame a new constitution that equipped the federal government with sufficient authority to discharge its core duties, such as the defense of the nation, its people, and their property. He thought government was an evil made necessary by the defects in human nature, and he worried as much about anarchy bred by too little government as he worried about the despotism that too much government power would guarantee. In neither case would individual liberty survive. It didn't matter to Madison whether oppression occurred at the hands of a mob or a single tyrant. More than anything else, Madison's Constitution was designed to secure the desired end of liberty.

Barack Obama is no Madisonian. Sure, he sees value in certain aspects of individual liberty. For example, he spoke out forcefully in favor of the right of a Muslim group to build a mosque near Ground Zero in Lower Manhattan, even though the issue didn't involve the federal government and even though few, if anyone, disputed the right of the group to build the mosque. Obama stressed "that Muslims have the same right to practice their religion as everyone else in this country….This is America, and our commitment to religious freedom must be unshakable."[1] But individual freedom is not the central animating principle of his political conscience. Indeed, he has criticized what he considers America's "strong bias towards individual action," declaring that America "must unite in collective action [and] build collective institutions" while minimizing the importance of "individual actions, individual dreams."[2] He has even argued that the protection of individual freedom by government is much less important than the taxpayer-financed economic benefits dished out by government, telling the annual convention of the National Association for the Advancement of Colored People that "it matters little if you have the right to sit at the front of the bus if you can't afford the bus fare; it matters little if you have the right to sit at the lunch counter if you can't afford the lunch."[3]

Obama's transformational project represents an attempt to reorient the nation away from its traditional focus on individual liberty and towards his collectivist vision. This should not be surprising, as Obama has a different philosophical starting point than Constitution creators like Madison. In addition to mastering the philosophical principles articulated by some of the world's greatest thinkers, Madison studied history to identify the flaws that have plagued popular governments because he wanted to be sure that he and his brethren created a constitution that effectively protected the freedom of the individual. He knew that most republics throughout history had failed spectacularly, and he wanted to capitalize on his opportunity to confound history by creating a durable, liberty-protecting constitution. The breadth of Madison's influences stand in stark contrast to Barack Obama's very narrow set of political influences, most all of which embrace the need for government to plan and execute collective schemes that redistribute wealth—the biological father who advocated a tax rate of 100%, the organizing father whose writings explained how to get the power necessary for effectuating redistribution, the spiritual father who indicted American greed as the root of all of society's ills.

Madison placed individual liberty at the heart of his political philosophy because he believed that each individual is endowed by the Creator with certain inalienable rights, such as life, liberty and the pursuit of happiness. Government has no inherent value, and is entitled to wield no authority beyond that authority delegated to it by the people; it thus has to be limited to its delegated functions, lest it infringe upon the people's authority. Obama has frequently mentioned "inalienable rights" without acknowledging the role of the "Creator," including omitting the mention of the Creator when reciting the Declaration of Independence on more than one occasion,[4] and it is clear that his political philosophy is not something that grows out of his religious faith; rather, his religious faith buttresses his pre-existing collectivist vision.

Obama has been criticized, on religious grounds, for his expressed view that "my individual salvation is not going to come about without a collective salvation for the country," and it is certainly true that the notion of collective salvation is foreign to traditional Christian thought.[5] But these critics misunderstand Obama, for he is not asserting a collective religious salvation so much as a collective political salvation, a national utopia in which enlightened political leaders, like himself, bring about, through the coercive power of government, the "redistributive change" that he craves. Like his father, this is his true foundational faith.

This vision elevates the prerogative of the government over the dreams and liberty of the individual, reflecting the major influences of Obama's life, influences that are wildly divergent from the liberty-centric influences that made an impact on Madison and his Convention colleagues. As we will see, Obama has, in a number of different contexts, failed to keep faith with the Founding Fathers and the principles that they espoused, but, given his political socialization, this should not be too surprising. He never had faith in their beliefs and principles in the first place.

PART THREE

"WICKED PROJECTS"

7

"SPREAD THE WEALTH AROUND"

During the final weeks of the 2008 campaign, an encounter between Barack Obama and a plumber from Ohio named Joe Wurzelbacher (aka "Joe the Plumber") became an important symbolic event, if ultimately unsuccessful in influencing the outcome of the election. At a campaign stop near Toledo, Wuzelbacher confronted Obama about his plan to raise marginal income tax rates on small business owners, which Wurzlbacher, who was about to purchase his own plumbing business, viewed as punishing his success. Obama gave a long-winded answer that delineated the minute details of his tax plan—the dividing line between "the rich" and "not rich" appeared to be earning $250,000 in income, though it was not clear why—but finished by saying that "when you spread the wealth around it's good for everybody."[1]

As Americans have traditionally viewed government's taxing power as a means of raising the revenue necessary for the operation of the government rather than as a mechanism for redistributing wealth, this response raised questions about Obama's views of taxation, giving John McCain an issue on which he could at least try to resurrect his campaign.

These questions were reinforced when, during the final week of the campaign, an interview surfaced of Obama speaking about judicially-mandated wealth redistribution during his state senate days. In the interview, Obama criticized the civil rights movement for being too focused on litigation strategies that sought to obtain legal relief through the courts, rather than trying to effect "redistributive change" through democratic political activism. According to Obama, the Supreme Court, under Chief Justice Earl Warren, had succeeded in mandating recognition of the right to vote and abolishing segregated lunch counters, but it "never ventured into the issues of redistribution of wealth and sort of basic issues of political and economic justice in this society and to that extent as radical as people try to characterize the Warren Court it wasn't that radical."

Responding to a caller who asked whether it was "too late for that kind of reparative work and is [the court] the appropriate place for reparative economic work to take place," Obama responded that he was "not optimistic about bringing about major redistributive change through the courts." He did not have a philosophical objection as much as a practical concern—the "court is not very good at it and politically it is hard to legitimize opinions from the court in that regard." Obama took for granted that there should be a redistribution of wealth; the only question was how to bring such about such "redistributive change."

As one might expect of someone whose political influences put a premium on collectivism, Obama expressed dissatisfaction with the Warren Court's failure to revise the traditional understanding of the Constitution as a protector of individual liberty. The Warren Court, he said, "didn't break free from the essential constraints that were placed by the Founding Fathers in the Constitution, at least as it's been interpreted." Obama lamented that the Court continued to see the "Constitution [as] a charter of negative liberties," which establishes prohibitions on government's power that serve to protect freedom, but which "doesn't say what the federal government or state government must do on your behalf." In other words, the Founders' Constitution doesn't provide for constitutionally mandated wealth redistribution.[2]

A re-interpretation of the Constitution as mandating so-called "positive rights," which is a euphemism for a wide variety of taxpayer-financed welfare payments designed to equalize economic outcomes, seriously confuses the basic purpose of the Constitution. The federal government created by the Constitution was charged with discharging limited but important functions necessary for a society in which individual liberty is respected. Obama's characterization of the Constitution as a "charter of negative liberties" obscures that there is already a "positive" aspect of the Constitution—but this lies not in redistributionist economic guarantees that must be provided to individuals by government at the expense of other citizens, but in what duties government must undertake, such as providing for the common defense, that benefit the public as a whole.

As we will see, the Constitution's creators saw a free society as one in which equality of economic outcomes is impossible—the "faculties" of acquiring property can never be equal since they involve an individual's natural talent, discipline, initiative and capacity for risk-taking. They rejected providing mandates for wealth redistribution in the Constitution because such mandates necessarily erode the individual liberty that the document was designed to safeguard. By bemoaning the failure of the Warren Court to effect, through unbounded interpretive creativity, a transformation of the very nature of the Constitution, Obama revealed himself to be an anti-Madisonian, one who views government's ability to mandate "redistributive justice," rather than to protect individual liberty, to be the primary measuring stick of our political institutions.

Though the interview did not damage Obama enough to slow his inevitable march to electoral victory, it served as yet another telling glimpse into the ideological commitments of a candidate promising to bring "fundamental change" to the United States. Of course, Obama's heavily-scripted presidential campaign never intentionally raised the issue of redistribution of wealth. The public radio interview was not released by his campaign and the confrontation between Obama and Joe Wurzelbacher had not been planned. That the Obama campaign would refrain from raising such an issue was a matter of practical politics: a Gallup poll taken in June of 2008 found that Americans opposed government-mandated wealth redistribution by a margin of 84% to 13%.[3]

Obama's views on redistributing wealth had also percolated above the surface during a televised debate against Senator Hillary Clinton during the Democratic presidential primaries. The debate moderator, Charles Gibson from ABC News, confronted Obama about his plan to double the tax rate on capital gains, and pointed out that in the past, when the capital gains tax rate was reduced, revenue to the government actually increased (due, no doubt, to the fact that such reductions enhanced incentives to realize various types of capital gains). If the government will be able to raise more revenue through a lower tax rate, Gibson queried Obama, "then what is the justification for raising the rate?"

Obama, speaking extemporaneously, responded that he was willing to raise capital gains tax rates "for purposes of fairness." In other words, even if the rate increase would deplete revenue to the government, Obama would still be willing to go through with the increase. Obama reasoned that the rate on capital gains was less than the prevailing rates on individual income, so the increase in the tax rate contributed to "fairness" in that different types of financial gains would be treated more equally, never mind that a lot of capital gains are realized from initial capital investments that have already been taxed as income. Obama's response to Gibson's question suggested that Obama held an ideological view of the taxing power that envisioned the use of taxation not simply or even to raise revenue but to implement what Obama refers to as "distributive justice."[4]

An assumption underlying Obama's view of the government's power of taxation is that reductions in tax rates are indistinguishable from government spending. During the presidential campaign, Obama criticized the incumbent administration for "spending $300 billion on tax cuts for people who don't need them."[5] Referencing the tax reductions of the previous administration, President Obama told a joint session of Congress that a "surplus became an excuse to transfer wealth to the wealthy."[6] Reductions in tax rates, though, don't transfer wealth but merely allow individuals to keep more of the income that they have earned; this distinguishes tax cuts from many federal spending programs, which confer a benefit on individuals irrespective of their contributions (unlike, say, Social Security, which requires individual taxpayer contributions or medical disability benefits for wounded veterans, which have clearly been earned by the recipient).

John Locke argued, and the Founding Founders agreed, that property was inherently a function of the personal labor of the individual, yet Obama regards the personal income and property retained by individuals as a courtesy of the state. Rather than a system in which individuals determine, through the machinery of democracy, how much of their money the government is permitted to take, the Obama persuasion sees the government as having plenary control of the nation's resources and the ability to decree how much individuals can keep. Under Obama's view, the redistribution of wealth is much less problematic as a philosophical matter. Since the government has the first claim on income and property, its choice to enact a spending scheme is indistinguishable from "spending" tax receipts via reductions in tax rates.

In any event, when Obama assumed the presidency, he did so after running a campaign in which any aims at redistributing wealth had, for the most part, been intentionally muted. Rather than run on an aggressive program of wealth redistribution, Obama centered his campaign around popular themes such as middle class tax reductions and a rejection of the historically unpopular President George W. Bush; to the extent that he advocated higher tax rates, these higher tax rates would apply to "the wealthy" who were, he claimed, scheming the system and not paying their fair share.

Yet, as we have seen, his political and social influences almost invariably held up wealth redistribution as the primary goal of political life—the distant father who rejected the very notion of private property, the Marxist professors he gravitated towards in college, the radicalism of Saul Alinsky whose tactics he employed as a community organizer. He had also, prior to the campaign, consistently bemoaned "constraints" on power, whether it was constraints that inhibited his desired "change" as an organizer or the constitutional constraints imposed by the Founding Fathers from which he ruefully noted the Warren Court had failed to break free. Now he found himself in a position of great power, not simply in the formal power of the presidency but in the fact that he stood at the head of the largest Democratic electoral wave in more than a generation. Far from being a constraint on his power, the commanding liberal legislative majorities in both houses of Congress would be the most potent enablers of his agenda.

The centerpiece of Obama's "change" agenda was a federal overhaul of the nation's health care system. As a candidate for the U.S. Senate, Obama voiced support for a so-called single-payer health care system, which would abolish private insurance and make the federal government the sole funding source of health care. "I happen to be a proponent of a single-payer universal health care program," Obama told an AFL-CIO labor union conference. "I see no reason why the United States of America, the wealthiest country in the history of the world, spending 14 percent of its Gross National Product on health care cannot provide basic health insurance to everybody." This would be a coercive, highly redistributionist scheme. Obama made it perfectly clear that such a system would override the existing health care arrangements of every American; he delightfully characterized the essence of the system to be "everybody in, nobody out," regardless of whether citizens are happy with their current health care. Though such a sentiment thrilled the leftmost flank of the Democratic Party, Obama acknowledged that "we may not get there immediately."[7]

Perhaps because he knew that a Canadian-style single-payer health system was extremely unpopular, Obama strategically distanced himself from the idea, labeling it an "extreme" proposal. Yet, after assuming office, he quickly made reconfiguration of the nation's entire health care apparatus, which comprises 16% of the entire U.S. economy, his top priority, even as many complained that he was neglecting what the public considered to be the much more pressing issue of the national economy, which Obama himself described as a crisis and as the worst economy since the Great Depression. During the presidential transition, incoming White House chief of staff Rahm Emanuel told *The Wall Street Journal* that one should "never let a crisis go to waste…[because it is an] opportunity for us to do things that you could not do before."[8]

Rather than justify his health care overhaul based on the need to redistribute wealth, Obama—consistent with Saul Alinsky's advice—defended it as a middle-class reform necessary to protect those who already have health insurance from further increases in monthly premiums and from insurance company malfeasance. To the extent that his proposal would divert money and resources from taxpayers to provide health insurance to those who did not have it (even if by choice), Obama eschewed "redistributive justice" as the rationale for this, instead asserting that increased coverage would reduce costs because taxpayers would no longer have to pick up the tab for visits to the emergency room by the uninsured. Thus, his reform would, he argued, save taxpayers money. Even though some, such as *Washington Post* columnist Robert Samuelson, convincingly dismissed this as flatly untrue, Obama never deviated from his justification of health care as a good deal for American taxpayers, and never tried to sell the proposal as a mechanism for wealth redistribution.[9]

In spite of the consistent public opposition to the health care bill, the passage of ObamaCare was, predictably, heralded as an achievement of historic proportions by members of the Washington press corps and historians who view history through the lens of a left-of-center, progressive perspective. Under this view, the march towards a larger government with expansive bureaucracies is the "right" side of history, regardless of the unintended consequences of such government expansion and irrespective of the erosion of individual liberty that such expansion entails. Initially justified by Obama as a needed remedy for the problem of rising health care costs that hurt members of the middle class, the post-passage euphoria revealed a different, more controversial justification for a federal overhaul of the health care system: the redistribution of wealth.

In fact, both politicians and journalists trumpeted the prospect that the health care law would redistribute wealth. "This is also an income shift," Montana Senator Max Baucus, a Democrat, said. "It's a shift, a leveling toward lower-income Americans. The wealthy are getting way too wealthy." Baucus believed that the health care law "will help address that maldistribution among all Americans."[10] Howard Dean, the former Vermont governor and presidential candidate, argued in a television interview that the health care overhaul needed to be viewed in the context of the "question…in a democracy, what is the right balance between those at the top and…those at the bottom?" Presumably, elites in government will be charged with determining the "right" balance. If the balance "gets out of whack, as it did in the 1920s, and it has now, you need to do some redistribution. [The health care law] is a form of redistribution."[11] David Leonhardt, a left-of-center economics writer for *The New York Times*, wrote that "every major aspect of the health bill pushes in the…direction" of wealth redistribution. To Leonhardt, this helps explain "why Mr. Obama was willing to spend so much political capital on the issue, even though it did not appear to be his top priority as a presidential candidate."[12] To many politicians and journalists supportive of the Obama agenda, ObamaCare was the crown jewel of his presidency not in spite of the fact that it redistributed wealth but because of the fact that it redistributed wealth.

If there was any doubt about whether ObamaCare was designed as a mechanism to redistribute wealth, Obama's recess appointment of Dr. Donald Berwick to head the Centers for Medicare and Medicaid Services removed it. Senate Republicans had wanted to give Berwick a hearing because they wanted to air his views on health care and the redistribution of wealth, but Obama recess appointed Berwick because he did not want to shine a spotlight on Berwick, lest his views be used to feed the narrative that the health care overhaul was designed for redistributive justice rather than for reducing the cost of health insurance. This was a smart political calculation by Obama, for Berwick has aggressively championed government-run health care schemes that are deliberately designed to redistribute wealth. In a speech in England celebrating the 60th anniversary of Britain's government-run national health care program, the National Health Service (NHS), Dr. Berwick praised NHS for its centralization of authority, refusal to allow for consumer choice, and tendency to redistribute wealth to the government's chosen recipients. "Any health care funding plan that is just, equitable, civilized and humane," Berwick told his British audience, "must—must—redistribute wealth from the richer among us to the poorer and less fortunate. Excellent health care is by definition redistribution." Berwick acknowledged that such a system requires a vast government bureaucracy that crowds out individual decision making, but he regarded this as a positive attribute of a government-run system, rejecting the idea that "consumer choice among an array of products with competitors' fighting it out leads to the health care system that you want and need." Without pervasive government control of individual health care decisions, Berwick worried that the result would be an "unaccountable system play[ing] out in the darkness of private enterprise."[13] As a U.S. Senate candidate, Obama had strongly supported a purely government-run, single-payer system similar to the British or Canadian models; his recess appointment of Donald Berwick represented a down payment on his ultimate dream of a massive, highly redistributionist nationalized health care system.

ObamaCare was far from the only example of Obama and his congressional allies wielding political power in the service of redistributing wealth, as the bankruptcy of one of the "Big Three" American automakers, Chrysler, illustrated. Like the other automakers in the United States, Chrysler had been embarked on a financially unsustainable path for many years, due in part to enormous legacy costs, when the financial crisis of 2008 pushed the industry to the brink of total collapse.

During his final month in office, President George W. Bush approved an emergency bailout of Chrysler (as well as General Motors), which was designed to keep the company afloat for a few months—enough time for Chrysler to devise a business plan for long-term profitability and to postpone a final resolution of the company's future until his successor took office. As the months wore on and as it became increasingly clear that a viable plan to turn around the failing company was unlikely to emerge, the Obama administration injected itself into the bankruptcy negotiations, pushing for a sale of Chrysler that subordinated the company's secured creditors—who loaned money to Chrysler on the promise that they would receive priority in getting paid in the event of a bankruptcy—to the United Auto Workers, an unsecured creditor but a politically favored ally of Obama.

When the secured creditors balked at this scuttling of traditional bankruptcy rules, President Obama denounced them as a "small group of speculators" who "endanger Chrysler's future by refusing to sacrifice like everyone else."[14] The pressure put to bear on the so-called "holdout" creditors was unrelenting, eventually prompting them to abandon their claim of priority over the UAW. Thomas Lauria, a financial contributor to Democratic candidates but also a lawyer for some of the creditors, told *The Wall Street Journal* that this "overarching sense of political pressure remained out there until the end."[15]

The behavior of the federal government in trying to force the hand of secured creditors raised a number of eyebrows. For one thing, far from being rapacious "speculators," Chrysler's secured lenders included a wide-array of institutions that included not just financial companies but also the University of Kentucky, the retirement fund of Kraft Foods, and the Bill and Melinda Gates Foundation.[16] In other words, the subordination of these secured debts to the health pension system of the United Auto Workers did not just elevate union retirees over banks and hedge funds but also over other retirees whose pension plans loaned money to Chrysler in the (previously settled) expectation that they would receive priority over the unsecured creditors. Second, the government's push to favor the UAW over the secured creditors violated a bedrock principle of American bankruptcy law, the so-called "absolute priority rule," which requires that secured lenders—who contract to loan money at a lower price in exchange for their place at the front of the repayment line—receive payment for what they are owed before any unsecured creditor gets paid anything. Finally, the proposal pushed by the government—the new Chrysler would split ownership between a trust for union retirees and Italian automobile manufacturer Fiat—represented a transfer of wealth from secured bondholders to a labor union that supports Obama with both money and votes. The administration's actions prompted Michael Barone, the author of the *Almanac of American Politics* and the nation's preeminent political analyst, to characterize the Chrysler saga as "bailout favoritism and crony capitalism" that equated to "an episode of Gangster Government."[17]

A less visible but equally instructive example of Obama marshalling public power to redistribute wealth to his favored constituencies concerns his executive order that federal agencies be "encouraged" to consider requiring project labor agreements (PLAs) when awarding federal contracts for construction projects. The order asserted enhanced efficiency and cost-savings as potential justifications for requiring a PLA, even though most objective analysts consider union construction projects to be more costly and more prone to work stoppages than a non-union project.

One of the supposed goals of the prodigious $814,000,000,000 stimulus was "shovel-ready" infrastructure projects, but many critics, understandably, wondered how the PLA policy contributed to putting Americans back to work, given that the overwhelming majority (and perhaps as many as 85%) of construction workers are not members of a union. By requiring a PLA, a government agency may discourage prospective bidders who utilize non-union workers from even bidding on a project, thereby foreclosing the chance that those non-union workers are given the chance for gainful employment. This makes the price of construction projects increase at the very time when the federal government's budget deficit should be prompting political leaders to make every effort to protect taxpayers.

By putting a presidential thumb on the scale in favor of unionized construction workers, Obama was helping to divert to his union allies potentially billions of dollars in construction contracts on public projects. Given that a number of studies have demonstrated that PLAs increase the costs to taxpayers by as much as 20% due to a combination of a less competitive bidding process and the enhanced costs of working with unions and their inefficient work rules, the use of a PLA does not simply direct to unions taxpayer dollars that would have been spent anyway; the additional surcharge imposed on taxpayers, due to the use of a PLA, transfers wealth from taxpayers, most of whom are far less affluent than the typical union boss, to a politically favored constituency.

What is more, when non-union workers participate in a project governed by a PLA, these workers are typically bound by rules that require upwards of 6% of their paychecks to be placed into a union pension fund. Since the vesting schedule for drawing union pension benefits is invariably longer than the duration of the project, these non-union workers will never recover anything from the fund. By mandating that all project workers contribute to the union fund, the PLA serves as a mechanism to redistribute wealth from active, non-union workers to woefully underfunded pension plans that service retired union employees. This type of rank favoritism—the utilization of the levers of power to direct private resources towards political allies—represents the lifeblood of Obama's program of "redistributive change."

Obama also sought to redistribute wealth through intervention in the home mortgage market. His proposal, which was defeated in the Senate due to bipartisan opposition, allowed bankruptcy judges to reduce the principal on an indebted homeowner's mortgage. Of course, proponents of the measure characterized it as a way to punish, in the words of Rhode Island Democratic Senator Sheldon Whitehouse "greedy, stubborn and unreasonable" banks (some of whom received TARP bailout funds) and reward hard-working Americans facing foreclosure through no fault of their own.[18] Such a characterization was hardly an entirely accurate portrayal of the economic upheavals wrought by the steep decline in the American housing market; after all, many banks (particularly community and mid-sized banks) did not receive TARP funds, and some homeowners knowingly entered into mortgages they could not afford.

Be that as it may, the Obama "cramdown" proposal was explicitly pitched as a justified transfer of wealth from unpopular bankers to debt-ridden homeowners. In practice, though, the costs of the cramdown would have been borne by other homebuyers—banks would increase their borrowing costs to account for the possibility of a cramdown on the mortgage and to recoup lost revenue from other loans reduced by bankruptcy judges, serving to redistribute wealth from prospective homebuyers to delinquent homeowners. Mortgage agreements are legally-enforceable instruments, and the after-the-fact abrogation of such an agreement represents an attempt by government to renege on the rule of law in order to punish disfavored constituencies. Like the government intervention in the Chrysler bankruptcy, the cramdown proposal demonstrated the willingness of Obama and his congressional allies to set aside established notions of contractual arrangements in the service of redistributing wealth to their chosen recipients, even if such redistribution comes at the expense of a stable, predictable system of rules that is a prerequisite for economic risk taking.

The centerpiece of Obama's purported effort to "fix" the global climate, the cap and trade energy proposal, represents a means to redistribute a massive amount of wealth. The goal of the plan is to increase the cost of carbon-based energy to force consumers and businesses to utilize more costly, less efficient forms of purportedly "clean" energy. But since most, if not all, of these alternative sources of energy are not readily available at reasonable prices, the proposal would impose substantial new costs on average Americans. As then-presidential candidate Obama explained to the progressive editorial board of *The San Francisco Chronicle*, his cap and trade system was designed so that "electricity rates would necessarily skyrocket....Because I'm capping greenhouse gases, coal power plants, natural gas, you name it—whatever the plants were, whatever the industry was, they would have to retrofit their operations. That will cost money. They will pass that money onto consumers."

Obama reveled in the fact that cap and trade would also stymie the creation of new plants powered by fossil fuels. "If somebody wants to build a coal-powered plant, they can," Obama said. "It's just that it will bankrupt them because they're going to be charged a huge sum for all that greenhouse gas that's being emitted."[19] Obama's plan to make "clean energy the profitable kind of energy" rests on making traditional forms of energy so prohibitively expensive that hitherto uneconomical forms of energy are transformed into the least costly available option—even at a substantial cost to individual citizens, businesses and the overall economy.

Although a cap and trade regime would have a negligible effect on global temperatures, it would extract a huge amount of revenue from already strapped American taxpayers. Analysis from the Obama administration concluded that the system would generate $200,000,000,000 per year in revenue, with the average cost for an American household of roughly $1,700, though other estimates pegged the cost at more than $3,000 per household. According to Obama, these funds are "dollars that we can invest in solar, wind, biodiesel and other alternative energy approaches," yet there is no guarantee that the money will even be spent on clean energy "investments," much less that any such "investments" will actually yield dividends.

What is certain is that the enactment of a cap and trade system will redistribute an enormous amount of wealth: Americans who live in regions of the country that rely heavily on fossil fuels for baseload energy, that require energy to moderate the climate, or that have a strong manufacturing base will all be disproportionately affected. As many of the people in these affected areas are far from wealthy, the net result will be a transfer of wealth from low- and middle-class energy consumers to favored recipients of federal largesse, such as politically connected, if unprofitable, "green" energy companies.[20]

While he acknowledged that his cap and trade system would pass on substantial costs to the average energy consumer (and therefore act as a hidden tax), Obama nevertheless repeatedly promised during his presidential campaign that he would not raise taxes on anyone other than the so-called "rich." He said that "no family making less than $250,000 a year will see *any* form of tax increase."[21] Yet, he instituted a number of measures that contradict this pledge, including a stiff tax hike on cigarettes, which disproportionately affects those earning less than $250,000, a levy on indoor tanning, and a number of taxes contained in ObamaCare (on medical devices, health savings accounts, and catastrophic medical expenses) that are either directly borne by, or will be passed onto, consumers.

Given the vast scope of Obama's ambitions for a "transformation" of American society and government, it could hardly be otherwise, especially since the "rich" already account for a disproportionate share of federal tax receipts. In the absence of a rapidly expanding economy (which Obama's redistributionist and other policies inhibit) to get the level of tax receipts that can satisfy his thirst for federal government activism, Obama has to extract a higher level of taxation from low- and middle-income taxpayers. Indeed, Obama even refused to rule out the imposition of a value-added tax (VAT), which is a European-style sales tax that hits consumers of all stripes but, being assessed at each stage of production, is "hidden" from plain view since the tax is built into the price of the good.[22]

This flurry of redistributionist activity, as well the proposals that portended even more, gave pause to a number of Obama's political supporters. Perhaps because Obama was not vocal about the redistributionist nature of his policies during the campaign, many of the biggest supporters of candidate Barack Obama hailed from the highest levels of American finance. During the 2008 election season, he received almost $1,000,000 in campaign contributions from individuals affiliated with investment titan Goldman Sachs, and raised far more money from major financial institutions than did his GOP rival, John McCain.

Yet, after experiencing two years of a hyperactive federal government, many of these erstwhile supporters started to reevaluate their view of Obama. Daniel S. Loeb, a hedge fund manager, Democrat, and one of Obama's biggest supporters during the 2008 campaign, raised a number of eyebrows when he sent a letter to his investors that lambasted Obama for pursuing policies that were, essentially, un-American. Citing Thomas Jefferson's admonition that the "sum of good government" is to "leave men free to regulate their own pursuits of industry and improvement," and "not take [from] the mouth of labor the bread it has earned," Loeb attributed the prevailing economic weakness to "an increasingly worrisome landscape of new laws and proposed regulations that are perceived by many market participants to promote 'redistribution' rather than growth, and are contrary to free market ideals." This seemed to Loeb to be contrary to America's first principles. "As every student of American history knows," he wrote, "this country's core founding principles included non-punitive taxation [and] Constitutionally-guaranteed protections against persecution of the minority."

The philosophy of "redistributive change," which Obama has embraced his entire life, seemed to be the common thread that united his approach to economic and property rights issues. For Loeb, this led to policies "designed to fracture the populace by pulling capital and power from the hands of some and putting it in the hands of others." For example, he criticized Obama's credit card regulations because they barred banks from raising interest rates on borrowers who are delinquent on their revolving credit obligations. Loeb sensibly explained that the "effect of this legal prohibition has been to force the banks to raise the interest rate paid by *all* borrowers, to compensate for losses they are now being forced to take on delinquent borrowers. The effect is a redistribution of wealth from people who pay their debts on time to those who do not."[23]

Obama, though, was undeterred. At a televised town hall meeting in September of 2010, Obama fielded a question from an audience member that drew national attention. The questioner, Velma Hart, an enthusiastic supporter of Obama during the election, rebuked him for the sluggish economy, telling Obama that she was "exhausted of defending you, defending your administration, defending the mantle of change that I voted for, and deeply disappointed with where we are." Obama was visibly taken aback by the comments, and gave a rambling response in which he tried to enlighten Hart about his policies, including the new credit card regulations that prohibit interest rate increases on delinquent, revolving credit balances.[24] But as Daniel Loeb pointed out, these regulations will cause credit card companies to raise interest on *all* borrowers; as there is no indication that Velma Hart was delinquent on her obligations, it stands to reason that she would be hurt, not helped, by the changes Obama trumpeted.

Obama's response to Hart also touched on other initiatives such as the federalization of student loans and health insurance mandates regarding preexisting conditions for children, but he did not explain how his policies would engineer a recovery in the private economy. This is because he sees government spending, not capital investment, as the main catalyst for economic growth. At a meeting of the President's Economic Recovery Advisory Board, Harvard economist Martin Feldstein urged Obama to postpone increasing income tax rates for all earners, including those making more than $250,000 per year, who Obama has habitually criticized as "wealthy." Obama questioned whether the postponement of the scheduled tax increase would do anything to spur economic growth. "If we were going to spend $700 billion," Obama said, "it seems it would be wiser having that $700 billion going to folks who would spend that money right away."[25]

This yet again evinced Obama's belief that a reduction of tax rates is tantamount to government spending. He thinks government is entitled to the income that its citizens earn. Under this view, reducing tax rates doesn't allow people to keep more of what *they* earn, but instead confers a benefit on the recipient by "spending" the government's money on the taxpayer. But it also showed Obama to labor under the belief that an economic recovery is driven by government spending, rather than business investment. Then-House Speaker Nancy Pelosi, Obama's primary legislative deputy, even went so far as to suggest that food stamps are one of the most effective economic stimulants, claiming that each dollar spent in food stamps pumps $1.75 into the economy.[26] The notion that higher tax rates might serve as a disincentive to risk taking and investment matter little to Obama, and this indifference to economic incentives dovetails nicely with his general passion for redistributive change.

All told, the Obama approach to the economy and property rights rests heavily on political considerations: what group to punish, what behaviors to require, and what outcomes to engineer. Rather than emphasize policies that create an environment where people can create wealth or otherwise enhance their own circumstances, Obama champions "redistributive change," shorthand for government activism that transfers resources among different classes of citizens through the force of law. As Obama explained to *The New York Times*, while he understood the need "to grow the pie," it was more important "to make sure that prosperity is spread across the spectrum of regions and occupations and genders and races."[27]

It would be a mistake to infer that Obama's notion of "spreading" prosperity means simply taxing the rich to provide public assistance for the poor. After all, Obama's redistributionist credo encompasses the extraction of union dues from a non-union (and likely, lower-paid) construction worker to subsidize a union fund under a PLA. Obama calls for the imposition of a de facto energy tax that disproportionately afflicts the middle class and the proceeds of which get redistributed by the government to fund the pet projects of political elites. And he imposed a federal overhaul of 16% of the nation's economy under the guise of improving health care for the middle class but which was later celebrated as a mechanism through which to redistribute wealth. As we will see, Obamanomics represents a dramatic departure from the nation's founding principles.

8

"The First Object of Government"

As legend has it, Benjamin Franklin once said that "when the people find that they can vote themselves money, that will herald the end of the republic." Franklin and other Founding Fathers believed that respect for individual property rights was the *sine qua non* of a free society, and regarded the so-called "leveling spirit," which seeks to equalize property through government action, as a danger that American institutions needed to check. When James Madison penned "Vices of the Political System of the United States," his pre-Convention diagnosis of the ills of American politics following the American Revolution, he bemoaned the "injustice" of the laws being promulgated by a number of state legislatures, laws which upset individual property rights based on the whims of a factious legislative majority. These laws worried Madison because "their injustice betrays a defect still more alarming: more alarming not merely because it is a greater evil in itself, but because it brings more into question the fundamental principle of republican Government, that the majority who rule in such Governments, are the safest Guardians both of public Good and of private rights."[1] How to craft a government based on popular consent that did not devolve into popular majorities voting themselves the property of others was one of the main concerns for Madison and his colleagues at the Constitutional Convention.

Most Convention delegates wanted to create a more powerful federal government, but wanted to do so in a way that protected individual liberty and private property rights; in fact, the protection of liberty and property was the reason they sought a more energetic federal government. Madison noted that as the delegates "were now digesting a plan which in its operation wd. decide forever the fate of

Republican Government we ought not only to provide every guard to liberty that its preservation cd. require, but be equally careful to supply the defects which our own experience had particularly pointed out."[2] One of the defects that Madison consistently identified was the unjust state laws that seemed to be proliferating at a rapid pace, especially those laws which tended to undermine the rights of property. "No agrarian attempts have yet been made in this Country," Madison told the Convention, "but symptoms of a leveling spirit, as we have understood, have sufficiently appeared in a certain quarters to give notice of the future danger. How is this danger to be guarded agst. on republican principles?"[3]

For his part, Alexander Hamilton "concurred also in the general observations of (Mr. Madison) on the subject, which might be supported by others if it were necessary." Derided by his adversaries as a "bastard," Hamilton was not a scion of a wealthy family, and, as an upwardly mobile achiever of historic proportions, he understood that equality of economic outcomes was inconsistent with a free society. "It was certainly true," Madison recorded Hamilton telling the delegates, "that nothing like an equality of property existed: that an inequality would exist as long as liberty existed, and that it would unavoidably result from that very liberty itself." The key, then, was to construct a government with "due stability and wisdom," one that could prevent the redistribution of wealth through the political process, lest the very notion of republican government "be disgraced & lost among ourselves, disgraced & lost to mankind for ever."[4]

The Framers wanted to construct a system of government that fostered the public good and provided protection for the minority, but knew that this was no easy task. "The instability, injustice, and confusion introduced into the public councils," Madison argued, "have, in truth, been the mortal diseases under which popular governments have everywhere perished." He acknowledged that many of the Revolutionary Era state constitutions represented valuable improvements on popular governments both ancient and modern, but pointed out that "complaints are everywhere heard from our most considerate and virtuous citizens, equally the friends of public and private faith and of public and personal liberty, that our governments are too unstable, that the public good is disregarded in the conflicts of rival parties, and that measures are too often decided, not according to the rules of justice and the rights of the minor party, but by the superior force of an interested and overbearing majority." To Madison, the "increasing distrust of public engagements and alarm for private rights which are echoed from one end of the continent to the other" were obvious "effects of the unsteadiness and injustice with which a factious spirit has tainted our public administration." Madison had studied virtually every popular government in recorded human history prior to attending the Convention, and his verdict was clear: unless a new constitution was implemented, the governments of the United States were traveling down the well-worn path to destruction.

Popular governments throughout history demonstrated a consistent inability to withstand the deleterious effects of what Madison called "faction." Madison defined a faction to be "a number of citizens, whether amounting to a majority or minority of the whole, who are united and actuated by some common impulse of passion, or of interest, adverse to the rights of other citizens, or to the permanent and aggregate interests of the community." A government could destroy faction by destroying liberty, but Madison correctly saw this as wildly excessive, for it undermined the basic premise of a republican government. Nor could faction be tamed by giving every citizen the same interests. As long as liberty prevails, man will be free to form different opinions and to exercise their various individual faculties, "from which the rights of property originate."[5]

The nation was founded on the belief that all men were created equal, but this concept was understood by the Framers to mean equality of opportunity and equality before the law, not equal economic outcomes. In fact, Madison considered "the first object of government" to be the "protection of these faculties," which Madison saw as a prerequisite for a free society. This protection results in the "possession of different degrees and kinds of property," and "from the influence of these on the sentiments and views of the representative proprietors ensues a division of the society into different interests and parties." Just as it would be foolish to attempt to cure faction by eradicating liberty, so too would it make no sense to attempt to give everyone the same interests, as the unequal acquisition of property that inevitably stems from liberty will render this impossible.[6]

Madison concluded that the problem was endemic to the human condition—the "latent causes of faction are thus sown into the nature of man." Differing views about religion and government, as well as attachment to certain ambitious leaders, have, he wrote, "divided mankind into parties, inflamed them with mutual animosity, and rendered them much more disposed to vex and oppress each other than to co-operate for their common good." As a general matter, the tendency for "mankind to fall into mutual animosities" over a number of different issues is strong, "but the most common and durable source of factions has been the various and unequal distribution of property." Those who own property and those who do not form distinct interests in society, and other differences, such as between creditors and debtors, fall under a "like discrimination."[7]

The problem with this recognition is that, in a republican form of government in which popular majorities rule, the very people who represent these different interests will be the same people who will be the driving force behind legislative action. Madison used the example of apportioning taxes as being tailor-made for the "predominant party to trample on the rules of justice. Every shilling with which they overburden the inferior number is a shilling saved to their own pockets."

Popular pressure to redistribute wealth or otherwise undermine the rights of property will be ever present. When a majority pursues an unjust end, the republican principle offers no relief to the injustice, nor any guarantee that "the public good and private rights" will be secured. Erecting a system on republican principles capable of controlling the effects of faction represented, for Madison, the "great desideratum for which alone this form of government can be rescued from the opprobrium under which it has so long labored and be recommended to the esteem and adoption of mankind."[8]

Madison distinguished a republic from what he called a "pure democracy," which he defined as a system in which citizens "assemble and administer the government in person." In the latter, there is nothing to check the obnoxious passions of the majority from running roughshod over the minority; thus, "such democracies have ever been spectacles of turbulence and contention; have ever been found incompatible with personal security or the rights of property; and have in general been as short in their lives as they have been violent in their deaths." He ridiculed "theoretic politicians" that "erroneously supposed that by reducing mankind to a perfect equality in their political rights, they would at the same time be perfectly equalized and assimilated in their possessions, their opinions, and their passions." Since Madison regarded the protection of individual liberty and the different faculties of acquiring property that inevitably flows from such liberty as the primary object of government, the pure democracy could not serve as a bulwark against the abuses of faction.[9]

Madison pulled no punches about specifying the particular types of faction that a republican form of government needed to guard against. "A rage for paper money, for an abolition of debts, for an equal division of property, or for any other improper or wicked project," he concluded, "will be less apt to pervade the whole body of the Union than a particular member of it, in the same proportion as such a malady is more likely to taint a particular county or district or an entire State." It was not that Madison merely objected to legislative abolition of debts or government-mandated redistribution of wealth as a matter of policy, which, of course, he did. Abolishing debts through political action, for example, may provide temporary relief to an overburdened debtor, but (among other things) the demoralizing effect it has on creditors undermines a critical component of the economy, thereby harming the public good. Madison, though, also viewed these "wicked projects" as inimical to fundamental notions of justice and individual liberty. As a matter of first principle, the republic needed to be constructed to prevent such projects from ever coming into being.[10]

The enduring protection for private property rights portended by the Constitution represented one of the major selling points trumpeted by the Federalists during the ratification debates. In *The Federalist* No. 85, the final essay by Publius, Hamilton urged support for the Constitution based in part on the "additional securities to republican government, to liberty, and to property, to be derived from the adoption of the plan under consideration."

Chief among these securities was the "precautions against the repetition of those practices on the part of the State governments which have undermined the foundations of property and credit, have planted mutual distrust in the breasts of all classes of citizens, and have occasioned an almost universal prostration of morals."[11] This is a far-reaching indictment of politically engineered redistributive schemes: according to Hamilton, such schemes not only undermine the nation's economic foundations, but also foster political division and corrode the basic social fabric.

Long after the Constitution was ratified and more than a decade after he retired from public life, Madison gave a speech to the Virginia Constitutional Convention in which he invoked first principles in justifying the need for a constitution to contain protections for individual liberty and private property. "It is sufficiently obvious," Madison told the Virginia delegates, "that persons and property are the two great subjects on which Governments are to act and that the rights of persons, and the rights of property, are the objects, for the protection of which Government was instituted." In words that could have been included in John Locke's *Second Treatise on Government*, Madison advised the delegates that these "rights cannot well be separated. The personal right to acquire property, which is a natural right, gives to property, when acquired, a right to protection, as a social right."[12] Madison considered the protection of property rights to be an enduring requirement of good government, a necessary corollary to the protection of individual liberty. He designed the Constitution to guard against the legislative-mandated redistribution of property, and his advice to his fellow Virginians in 1829 is proof positive that he considered such a safeguard to be an important and necessary aspect to any constitution.

By stressing the need to guard against politically inspired "leveling" of property, the Founders were not trying to protect a static class of elite property owners—they wanted to establish a new order for the ages that fostered upward mobility in society. They were creating a republican government to secure the principles of the American Revolution (hence the use by Hamilton of the pseudonym "Publius"). "It is evident," Madison wrote in *The Federalist* No. 39, "that no other form would be reconcilable with the genius of the people of America; with the fundamental principles of the Revolution; or with that honorable determination which animates every votary of freedom to rest all of our political experiments on the capacity of mankind for self-government." Madison penned essay No. 39 to illustrate that the new Constitution was, in fact, republican; and he offered as "the most decisive…proof…of the republican complexion of the system…its absolute prohibition of titles of nobility, both under the federal and the State governments."

Such a provision may seem quaint from a vantage point more than two hundred years later, but nipping even the pretense of aristocracy in the bud was an important statement of the national character. The Framers did not expect everyone to achieve great things or amass impressive fortunes, but they did expect that those from humble beginnings would be able to climb their way to the upper strata of society based on talent, initiative and merit.

Perhaps because the Constitution's creators wanted to foster upward mobility, Anti-Federalists attacked the Constitution as being an aristocratic document designed to protect the "wealthy." The Anti-Federalist writer "Montezuma" penned a satirical essay "in favor" of the Constitution in which he purported to speak for "the Aristocratic party of the United States, lamenting the many inconveniences to which the late confederation subjected the well-born, the better kind of people, bringing them down to the level of the rabble—and holding in utter detestation that frontispiece to every bill of rights, 'that all men are born equal.'" Montezuma argued that the Constitution was needed "for the purpose of drawing a line between such as we think were ordained to govern, and such as were made to bear the weight of government without having any share in its administration," and happily submitted "to our friends in the first class for their inspection, the following defense of our monarchical, aristocratical democracy." Montezuma "celebrated" the typical roster of Anti-Federalist objections: the undemocratic nature of the Senate, the ability of the executive to veto a popularly passed law, the vast reach of federal judicial power, and the lack of a bill of rights. To Montezuma, this was a constitution of the wealthy, by the wealthy and for the wealthy.[13]

Alexander Hamilton was hardly a member of the so-called "well-born," and he flatly dismissed such criticisms as utter nonsense. In discussing the Anti-Federalist critique of allowing Congress to choose the time and manner of federal elections, Hamilton ridiculed the "objects of the preference with which [opponents of the Constitution] endeavor to alarm us, those whom they designate by the description of the 'wealthy and the well-born.' These, it seems, are to be exalted to an odious preeminence over the rest of their fellow-citizens." The notion that the power to choose the places of election implied an ability of the new government to favor the so-called "wealthy and well-born" struck Hamilton as preposterous—are such characters, he asked rhetorically, "confined to particular spots in the several States?" The only true way of "securing to the rich the preference apprehended [is] by prescribing qualifications of property either for those who may elect or be elected," and the Constitution deliberately eschewed such requirements.[14] Hamilton saw the Anti-Federalist argument to be a cheap attempt at stoking divisions within the body politic for purely partisan gain.

Hamilton had nothing but contempt for criticisms of the Constitution resting on blanket assertions that the Constitution favored the wealthy. In his final installment of *The Federalist*, Hamilton declared that the "perpetual changes which have been rung upon the wealthy, the well-born, and the great have been such as to inspire the disgust of all sensible men."[15] Hamilton, whose ascendancy from a downtrodden existence in the Caribbean to the pinnacle of American government was unequaled in his day, understood the difference between a hereditary (or otherwise artificial) aristocracy and a free society in which individuals from a wide range of backgrounds have the ability to succeed, even spectacularly, just as he did. Given his humble beginnings, Hamilton would have never been able to excel as he did in the military, or rise to the top of national politics, if he was a British subject; he knew that America offered him, and would offer generations to come, a unique opportunity for upward mobility. As Thomas Jefferson later remarked to John Adams, there should always be those who rise to the commanding heights in society based on "virtue and talents," but this is wholly different from a system that perpetuates artificial distinctions based on rank, wealth or birth.

The prospect of upward mobility was what separated the American republic from other governments of the era. Unlike a system premised on familial privilege or the pageantry of rank, Hamilton observed in *The Federalist* No. 36 that, in America, there were "strong minds in every walk of life that will rise superior to the disadvantages of situation and will command the tribute due to their merit, not only from the classes to which they particularly belong, but from the society in general."

Hamilton thought that those elected to federal office would generally come from certain segments of society, such as large landowners or lawyers, because of their faculties and economic independence. But Hamilton thought this was a natural phenomenon, and rejected any notion that the Constitution should foster artificial privilege: "the door ought to be equally open to all; and, I trust, for the credit of human nature, that we shall see examples of such vigorous plants flourishing in the soil of federal as well as of State legislation."[16]

Throughout *The Federalist Papers*, Publius makes reference to the enterprising spirit of the American people; Hamilton, Madison and Jay knew that Americans were a people on the rise. In *The Federalist* No. 8, Hamilton highlighted "the industrious habits of the people of the present day, absorbed in the pursuits of gain and devoted to the improvements of agriculture and commerce" as a primary difference with the ancient republics of Greece. The vibrancy of the nation's commerce, invigorated by the introduction and circulation of precious metals, could produce economic dividends throughout society. As Hamilton noted, "the assiduous merchant, the laborious husbandman, the active mechanic, and the industrious manufacturer—all orders of men look forward with eager expectations and growing alacrity to this pleasing reward of their toils."[17] He observed in *The Federalist* No. 11 that the enterprising spirit was not limited to a few individuals but was part and parcel of the national character, and that this "adventurous spirit, which distinguishes the commercial character of America, has already excited uneasy sensations in several of the maritime powers of Europe." Those nations with colonies in America "look forward to what this country is capable of becoming with painful solicitude."[18]

Hamilton's justification of the Constitution's power of taxation underscores the basic outlook of the Constitution's creators with respect to wealth redistribution. Hamilton was obsessed with the ability of the federal government to raise a consistent stream of revenue—"a nation," he wrote in *The Federalist* No. 12, "cannot long exist without revenue"—and was so schooled in modern modes of finance that later, during his time as President Washington's Secretary of the Treasury, the House of Representatives abolished its Ways and Means Committee, choosing to rely solely on him for its financial knowledge.[19]

Interestingly, although he rejected the propriety of redistributing wealth throughout society, Hamilton believed that wealthy people should contribute more in taxes than those in the so-called lower classes. He argued in *The Federalist* No. 36 that tax policy "must naturally tend to make it a fixed point of policy in the national administration to go as far as may be practicable in making the luxury of the rich tributary to the public treasury in order to diminish the necessity of those impositions which might create dissatisfaction in the poorer and most numerous classes of society." This way, the government's interest in preserving its own revenue will coincide with what Hamilton called a "proper distribution of the public burdens and tends to guard the least wealthy part of the community from oppression." However, unlike Barack Obama, who advocated increases in tax rates as a matter of distributive justice (even if, as Charles Gibson pointed out, a decrease in revenue was likely) Hamilton conceived of the taxing power as a means of raising revenue necessary to meet the general public obligations of the federal government. His goal was national greatness, not redistributive change.[20]

In fact, Hamilton was very sensitive to the manner in which taxation affected economic behavior and incentives and was not interested in punishing people for their success. In *The Federalist* No. 35, he cited the need to have federal representatives with a thorough knowledge of political economy so that they will be unlikely "to resort to oppressive expedients, or to sacrifice any particular class of citizens to the procurement of revenue." Such measures could be as economically unsound as they are unjust. Hamilton instead thought that it "might be demonstrated that the most productive system of finance will always be the least burdensome."

It is with this principle in mind that Hamilton argued for imposts, duties and excises on consumption since "they contain in their own nature a security against excess." He rejected the notion, popular among progressives like Obama, that increasing the tax rate will necessarily increase the revenue to the public treasury, warning that if "duties are too high, they lessen the consumption; the collection is eluded; and the product to the treasury is not so great as when they are confined within proper and moderate bounds." Unlike modern presidents such as John F. Kennedy and Ronald Reagan, who both reduced marginal income tax rates across the board for reasons similar to those articulated by Hamilton, Obama pays little, if any, attention to economic incentives; such concerns simply get in the way of his quest for redistributive justice.[21]

Hamilton appreciated consumption taxes because their voluntary nature provided an additional security to the taxpayer. With a consumption tax, "the amount to be contributed by each citizen will in a degree be at his own option, and can be regulated by an attention to his resources. The rich may be extravagant, the poor can be frugal; and private oppression may always be avoided by a judicious selection of objects proper for such impositions." This was important to Hamilton because he viewed the use of the taxing power to punish disfavored constituencies as both unwise and unjust. Since his goal was not to punish taxpayers in service of legislating a false economic equality, Hamilton supported tax policy that imposed minimal burdens on individuals, understanding that as taxation became more burdensome the revenue to the government would not necessarily increase accordingly. He based his arguments on the propriety of providing revenue for the government to discharge its core functions rather than a desire to redistribute wealth to the favored constituencies of federal legislators—especially since the latter tended to undermine the former.

These principles were put to the test shortly after the launching of the new ship of state in 1789, when Hamilton, as Secretary of the Treasury, had to make a number of recommendations regarding the discharge of the nation's Revolutionary War debt. One controversial recommendation from his *Report on Public Credit* involved the manner in which to honor the domestic public debt, much of which had been originally held by veterans of the Revolutionary War. Some, including Hamilton's constitutional ally and *The Federalist* contributor James Madison, argued that the government should discriminate between the original holders of the public securities and those who lawfully purchased them. Under this view, the original holders needed to share in any appreciation of the securities since many of them were forced by desperate circumstances to sell their notes at pennies on the dollar. As this argument went, the purchasers were essentially speculators who stood to make huge profits at the expense of the taxpayer if they received full reimbursement for notes they bought at a fraction of the face value.

"After the most mature reflection on this force of this argument," Hamilton rejected "the doctrine it contains, as equally unjust and impolitic, as highly injurious, even to the original holders of public securities; as ruinous to public credit." As a matter of justice, Hamilton noted that the whole point of making notes assignable to third parties is so the holder can sell it at whatever price the market will bear, and the bona fide purchaser will be safe in the sale. By discriminating against a purchaser in favor of the original holder, the government would be effectuating a "breach of contract; in violation of the rights of a fair purchaser." Hamilton rebuffed any notion that the buyer is "chargeable with having taken undue advantage. He paid what the commodity was worth in the market and took the risks of reimbursement upon himself." What is more, Hamilton noted that discrimination against the buyer violated the express provision of

Article VI of the Constitution that "Debts contracted and Engagements entered into, before the Adoption of this Constitution, shall be as valid against the United States under this Constitution, as under the Confederation."[22]

For Hamilton, a violation of not just basic notions of justice but also a specific provision of the Constitution would have disastrous policy implications. Discrimination in favor of the original owners undermined the security of transfer of public securities, thereby reducing the quality of the debt and hindering the new nation's ability to borrow money. Also, the "breach of faith" that such an action entailed reduces the value of the security and causes lenders to raise premiums on the money they lend, both of which demoralize the state of public credit. Finally, many of these purchasers bought the securities during a time when the "hazard...was far from inconsiderable."[23] Whereas the selling of the debt reflected a pessimistic view of the nation's circumstances, the purchase of the bond was a bet on America's future. Rewarding such risk taking was not simply consistent with fostering sound public credit but was also the moral and honorable thing to do.

Hamilton saw his plan to fund the domestic national debt to be a straightforward application of the principles he articulated, with Madison's assistance, in *The Federalist Papers*, and he was shocked when his former colleague opposed his funding plan in the House of Representatives. Massachusetts Congressman Theodore Sedgwick was also perplexed by Madison's "discrimination" proposal, wondering "what merit will the Government possess if we strip one class of citizens, who have acquired property by the known and established rules of the law, under the specious pretence of doing justice to another class of citizens?" Madison disputed that he was proposing any such thing, but acknowledged that he "had been animadverted upon for appealing to the heart as well as the head," and that "in great and unusual questions of morality, the heart is the best casuist."[24]

In truth, Madison's attempt to blunt Hamilton's funding plan had less to do with the redistribution of wealth than it did with the plan's cultural ramifications. By creating an environment in which securities could be freely traded, Hamilton was setting the stage for America to mature into a modern financial power—something that threatened the Jeffersonian vision of a virtuous republic of rural yeoman that Madison had by that time embraced. Perhaps because Madison was focused on this cultural concern and not the sound principles articulated in *The Federalist*, the House of Representatives decisively rejected his "discrimination" plan by a vote of 36-13.

Madison's opposition to funding the debt represents the exception that proves the rule regarding the prevailing views of property rights during the formative period of American constitutionalism. The Framers considered the protection of individual liberty to be the primary object of government. Understanding that individuals possessed different "faculties" for acquiring property, they presupposed that an equality of property could never exist in a free society. Since the lawful acquisition of property is a function of an individual's liberty, a government that leveraged the power of the state to redistribute, or "level," wealth throughout society necessarily undermined the very liberty that it was constructed to safeguard.

Founding Fathers like Madison and Hamilton saw property as originating from the labor the individual, not from the benevolence of the state. When Barack Obama characterizes a reduction in tax rates as representing a "transfer" of wealth, he is implicitly arguing that the government has the first claim of right on the property produced by individuals. Under this view, it is only because of the institutions and rules established and maintained by government that individuals are able to acquire property; thus, when the government reduces tax rates, it is "giving" additional income to individuals that *it* is primarily responsible for producing. This view turns the philosophy underlying the Constitution on its head. It is not the only aspect of Obamanomics to do so.

9

OBAMANOMICS AND AMERICAN CONSTITUTIONALISM

A philosophical chasm separates the views of Barack Obama from the views of the Founding Fathers with respect to the redistribution of wealth. While James Madison warned, as a matter of first principle, against "wicked projects" like those that legislatively extinguished valid debts, Obama championed a cramdown proposal that would have empowered judges to reduce the principal on home mortgages, thereby redistributing the costs to other borrowers. Obama habitually demonizes tax reductions that "transfer" wealth to "the wealthy," yet Hamilton, who himself believed that economic policy should be constructed to capitalize on the extravagance of the affluent, nevertheless expressed contempt for those that resorted to general attacks on "the wealthy" as a substitute for making principled arguments. Of course, Hamilton and other Constitution creators believed the fruits of one's labor belonged to the individual, not the government, rendering nugatory Obama's notion that a reduction in taxes is akin to a "transfer" of wealth from the government to the taxpayer.

Obama put the full coercive force of the United States government behind a subordination of Chrysler's secured creditors to the unsecured debts of the administration-aligned United Auto Workers union; Hamilton characterized a much more benign "discrimination" proposal as "equally unjust and impolitic, as highly injurious, even to the original holders of public securities; as ruinous to public credit." Hamilton envisioned a tax system that incentivized productive behavior, that was not unduly burdensome and that focused on raising revenue for the government. Obama, in contrast, embraced an approach to the taxation of capital gains that both discouraged risk taking and portended less revenue for the government, but, because such an approach punished those who had capital gains to be realized, contributed to his goal of redistributive justice.

While the Framers strived to construct a system of government that prevented government-mandated wealth redistribution, Obama is intent on "spreading the wealth" using the power of the state. Indeed, Obama seems to desire wealth redistribution as much to punish high-earners as to "help" his chosen recipients for government largesse. During a speech in Quincy, Illinois, Obama declared that "at a certain point you've made enough money"—an implicit endorsement of the notion that government has a role in determining (and perhaps enforcing) the upper limits of acceptable success.[1] Tellingly, this admonition was not included in his prepared remarks, yet Obama saw fit to add it at the very point in his written speech that specifically disavowed punishing people for success. Like his disquisition on raising the capital gains tax to impose "fairness" or his impromptu back-and-forth with Joe the Plumber regarding the need to redistribute wealth, Obama's extemporaneous remark about people making "enough money" is part of a pattern: when he goes off-script, Obama falls back on the redistributionist instincts that have been ingrained in him by virtually all of the major influences throughout his life. These statements reveal Obama to subscribe to a static conception of the economy in which the success of one must come at the expense of another. Under this Malthusian view, whenever an individual or business achieves economic gains, the government must redistribute some of those gains back to those who did not share in the profits; with a fixed economic pie, the risk-taking few cannot be permitted to procure a disproportionate share for themselves.

Constitution creators like Hamilton rejected Obama's vision of the economy and property rights, especially the notion of a static, fixed-sum economy in which profits were realized at the expense of others. They studied thinkers like Adam Smith and understood the dynamism of a free enterprise economy, and generally repudiated statist philosophies like mercantilism that rested on flawed premises and failed to foster economic growth. They put a premium on individual liberty, but did not labor under any illusions that freedom bred no problems. "True liberty by protecting the exertions and talents of industry, and securing to them justly acquired fruits," Hamilton observed, "tends more powerfully than any other cause to augment the mass of national wealth and to produce the mischiefs of opulence."

But the opulence that freedom makes possible is not a sufficient basis to justify limitation and redistribution of wealth via the power of the state, especially considering the need to respect liberty and the benefits provided by economic growth. Acknowledging the negative effects of opulence, Hamilton wondered how a free society could prevent this while remaining free, asking rhetorically "shall we therefore on this account proscribe liberty also?" It is far better simply to come to terms with the fact that "every good [man] enjoys shall be alloyed with ills, that every source of his bliss shall be a source of his affliction—except virtue alone."[2] Unlike Obama, who seeks to socially engineer a synthetic equality of outcomes through central planning, the Founders' belief in individual liberty presupposed that a society based on equality before the law would be inconsistent with equality of property, money and possessions.

****

A public opinion poll taken in July 2010 by the polling firm of highly partisan Democrat James Carville found that 55% of likely voters considered Barack Obama to be a socialist. This was newsworthy because it suggested that many Americans considered Obama to hold radical views. At the same time, there is significant disagreement in America on what constitutes socialism, so it is not entirely clear whether those polled possessed a common understanding of the term. The textbook definition of socialism is the government ownership of the means of production, and there has been much to suggest that Obama has moved America towards socialism: taking over troubled automobile manufacturer General Motors, maintaining ownership of large financial institutions like Citibank, and transforming the health care system in such a way that a purely government-run, single-payer system is inevitable.

At the same time, Obama also resisted nationalizing some large financial institutions such as Bank of America, despite pleas from leftist commentators that he do so. Furthermore, the scope of Obama's ambitions with respect to the expansion of government and the redistribution of wealth requires a steady stream of tax revenue from a growing private sector, which a socialist economy would inhibit rather than foster. As Margaret Thatcher famously quipped, the problem with socialism is that, eventually, you run out of other people's money. Transforming America into a truly socialist state would likely require suffocating government constraints and a curtailment of the democratic prerogatives of the people—there is no reason to think that Obama is politically inept enough to think such an outcome would be acceptable to anyone but a small minority of leftist ideologues.

Whatever the label, Obama's project is the transformation of the United States from a constitutional republic that limits government power and protects individual liberty to a system that subordinates liberty to the power of the state and its collectivist goals. This will require an even larger federal government and massive rules and regulations that, as Alexis de Tocqueville noted in *Democracy in America*, might not equate to a traditional tyranny but that will degrade individuals nonetheless. In this scheme, government would not own everything, but entrepreneurs and private business would operate as a matter of political grace, not as a matter of right, and would be expected to pursue certain priorities (such as electric cars) that the government deems worthwhile, even when such priorities are not economically efficient.

A business which acts in a way that conflicts with the government's political agenda will do so at its peril. For example, when aircraft manufacturer Boeing announced it would open a production facility in Charleston, South Carolina, Obama's National Labor Relations Board filed a complaint against Boeing, one of America's largest exporters, because the facility, unlike the Boeing plants in Washington State, will not be unionized. This represented a startling use of government power to stifle private decision making.

This project is very much in keeping with what Obama championed in his 2001 Chicago public radio interview about the Warren Court and the redistribution of wealth. It represents a shift from a constitution that limits government's power as a means of protecting individual liberty to an ever-present government that serves as the primary regulator of most aspects of American life and, thus, possesses the first claim on the wealth that is generated in the private sector. Within this context, Obama's frequent admonition about making sure that businesses live up to "their responsibility to create American jobs" makes perfect sense. He doesn't see job creation as incidental to the goal of businesses large and small to become and remain profitable; he sees businesses as having a responsibility to serve his collectivist vision, creating jobs based on social and political imperatives rather than in accordance with business viability. This is the economic vision of the community organizer, not the limited government constitutionalist.

Obama's fiscal policies are motivated by ideological ambition rather than sound economic theory. Obama eschewed a business-friendly economic policy, yet also failed to faithfully follow the Keynesian economic theories that have exerted a stranglehold on the liberal academy and the Democratic Party for generations. When Obama signed the $814,000,000,000 economic stimulus package at the beginning of his presidency, it seemed like he was reading from the Keynesian playbook, applying liberal counter-cyclical deficit-spending to prop up the economy in the midst of an economic downturn. But, as the economy continued to struggle deep into 2010, Obama rejected the Keynesian dictum that taxes should not be raised during a recession by refusing to support postponing the increase in the top marginal income tax rate scheduled to take effect in January 2011. Even as many warned that such an increase could be a blow to an already fragile economy, Obama continually refused to entertain postponement of the tax increase, characterizing such forbearance as "spending" $700,000,000,000 on "millionaires and billionaires." Following the "shellacking" that his Democratic Party received in the 2010 midterm elections, Obama was forced to accept a compromise with Republicans in Congress that postponed, for two years, the scheduled increase in tax rates for all levels of earners. Nevertheless, he expressed such disgust at the deal that it was clear that he viewed his inability to raise marginal tax rates as a major source of regret.

This reaction left little doubt that Obama's true passion was for government-mandated redistribution of wealth rather than a growing economy in which economic gains are not equally shared. During the 2010 midterm election campaign, with his public approval rating mired in the doldrums, Obama delivered a bitterly partisan speech in Parma, Ohio in which he expanded on his vision of centralized planning and redistributive justice. He touted historical American values of personal responsibility and hard work, but he spoke of these values in terms of a "country that rewards responsibility; a country that rewards hard work; a country built on the promise of opportunity and upward mobility…That's what we Democrats believe in—a vibrant free market, but one that works for everybody."[3] Then-House Speaker Nancy Pelosi was explicit that this required government action to reduce income inequality, saying that the "disparity is about ownership and equity. It's all about fairness in our country."[4]

Economic "rewards" have historically been understood to be a function of the private market. Obama, though, sees the government as the central economic clearinghouse, rewarding what he deems good behavior and punishing those whose success he considers ill-gotten or excessive. In fact, he has said that successful people achieve their success not through hard work, risk taking or perseverance but because they have "won life's lottery."[5] If success is simply random, then it follows that policy initiatives such as reductions in tax rates are conferring an undeserved benefit on those already enjoying arbitrarily generated wealth. Obama said he supports tax cuts for "folks in the middle class" because they are "more likely to spend their tax cut on basic necessities," which he considers an acceptable use of a tax break. This allows Obama to showcase his purported amenability to tax cuts and to appear willing to consider policy alternatives other than more spending, but his willingness to relinquish control over taxpayer money is purely contingent upon the taxpayer spending his money in the manner in which Obama approves.

For Obama, the government is not merely the power broker that serves to redistribute wealth and benefits generated by the private sector; it is the primary driver of the economy. This is why, in the midst of debilitating budget deficits brought about through his unprecedented spending binge—according to the Congressional Budget Office, the stimulus carried a price tag of $100,000,000,000 *more* than the cost of the entire Iraq war through 2010—Obama ruled out spending reductions, which he calls "investments," because more government spending "will grow our economy in the future."[6] Whether Obama really believes American economic prosperity to be the result of government central planning rather than private innovation and entrepreneurship is unclear, but it is clear that this economic philosophy fits comfortably with Obama's desire to use the levers of political power to redistribute wealth.

This view of the economy should not come as a big surprise, as it is very much in keeping with Obama's life-long distrust of private enterprise. In *Dreams From My Father*, Obama described his brief stint working for a Manhattan-based "consulting house" as akin to being a "spy behind enemy lines." He spurned a career in private industry in favor of community organizing, and commended himself for not "allowing my ambitions to travel a narrower, more personal course, so that in the end I might have taken [a] friend's advice and given myself over to stocks and bonds and the pull of respectability."[7] Like his distant father, who advocated the abolition of private property and spoke favorably of a 100% tax rate, Obama considers the pursuit of profit to be impure, as if financial success is achieved by exploiting others.

As president, Obama has expressed views similar to those he outlined in *Dreams From My Father*. In a commencement day address to the graduates of Arizona State University, President Obama urged graduates to do as he did and reject "the formulas for success that have been pedaled so frequently in recent years." Obama criticized the prevailing view of career advancement: "You're taught to chase after all the usual brass rings; you try to be on this 'who's who' list or that top 100 list; you chase after the big money and you figure out how big your corner office is; you worry about whether you have a fancy enough title or a fancy enough car. That's the message that's sent each and every day." But, he said, this "displays a poverty of ambition—that in fact, the elevation of appearance over substance, of celebrity over character, of short-term gain over lasting achievement is precisely what your generation needs to help end." Obama instead urged graduates to pursue careers in the community service and non-profit sectors.[8]

This negative view of financial success is yet another instance of Obama not being in tune with the views of the Framers. Alexander Hamilton commended the "the industrious habits of the people of the present day, absorbed in the pursuits of gain and devoted to the improvements of agriculture and commerce," and noted how "all orders of men look forward with eager expectations and growing alacrity" to what he called the "pleasing reward of their toils." In contrast to Hamilton, Obama criticized those individuals—including debt-burdened college graduates—who seek financial gain in lieu of advancing his progressive vision; to him, such people display a "poverty of ambition."

Hamilton took comfort in the "adventurous spirit" that distinguished "the commercial character of America" to such an extent that other, more powerful nations would be sure to notice. Obama considers private commerce as inherently exploitive and sees the wealth-creating "adventurous spirit" to lie not in the fabric of the American people but in the government, its spending and its bureaucracy. This is a wholesale reformulation of the basic philosophy relied on by the Founders when they created the Constitution. From leveraging government power to redistribute the wealth of the nation's citizens to conceiving of taxation as a punishment rather than as a mechanism to raise revenue, Obama's economic worldview represents an outright rejection of the basic, time-honored principles that the Framers espoused. The transformation he seeks is largely what they sought to prevent.

PART FOUR

REPUBLICAN GOVERNMENT

10

LEGISLATIVE INCOMPETENCE

In *The Federalist* No. 68, Alexander Hamilton declared that the "true test of a good government is its aptitude and tendency to produce a good administration."[1] Even a government erected on purely republican principles will amount to little if the government does not perform competently. This is because, as Hamilton wrote two essays later, "a government ill executed, whatever it may be in theory, must be, in practice, a bad government."[2] Throughout *The Federalist*, Hamilton and Madison argued that the Constitution was structured in such a way that it would lead to much more effective government—due to competent executive administration as well as to the superior institutional arrangements that would breed wise lawmaking. In the process of making these arguments about the Constitution, Publius offered a number of dicta about what makes for good governance, and these admonitions stand as strong rebukes to the operation of the federal government in the age of Obama.

The prospect of a good federal administration was one of the driving forces behind the work of the Convention delegates. Constitution creators such as Benjamin Franklin and George Washington agreed with Hamilton's assertion in *The Federalist* No. 15 that "there are material imperfections in our national system under the Articles of Confederation and that something is necessary to be done to rescue us from impending anarchy." The shortcomings of the Articles were pervasive: the government failed to pay the debts owed to foreigners acquired during the Revolution; foreign powers flouted the nation's territorial integrity, yet there was no means by which America could "resent or repel the aggression"; the nation's public credit was virtually nonexistent; commerce was lackluster; and the nation's bumbling administration elicited so little respect from other nations that "our ambassadors are the mere pageants of mimic sovereignty." The situation was so dire that, Hamilton continued, "we may indeed with propriety be said to have reached almost the last stage of national humiliation." The Articles of Confederation represented an unquestionably deficient administration; it was, Hamilton lamented, nothing more than a "shadow of a federal government."[3]

The ineptitude of the Articles of Confederation could not be countenanced for much longer, as the liberty of the people would inevitably fall prey to the impending tumults spawned by that incompetence. If there is one thing upon which the Constitution's creators could all agree, it was that history did not evince a lot of comforting examples of stable, well-administered republican governments. "It is impossible to read the history of the petty republics of Greece and Italy," Hamilton bristled at the beginning of *The Federalist* No. 9, "without feeling sensations of horror and disgust at the distractions with which they were continually agitated, and at the rapid succession of revolutions by which they were kept in a state of perpetual vibration between the extremes of tyranny and anarchy." From this stormy political history, "advocates of despotism have drawn arguments, not only against the forms of republican government, but against the very principles of civil liberty."[4]

It is often forgotten that, when the Founding Fathers came of age, many European elites argued that enlightened despotism was the best form of government. In *The Federalist* No. 45, Madison characterized this view as the "impious doctrine in the old world that the people were made for kings, not kings for the people."[5] The Founders rejected this as inconsistent with the genius of the American Revolution as well as their own colonial experience, which was heavily incubated in self-government, and strove to build a solid, durable republican edifice that would safeguard individual liberty.

At the time of the Constitution's creation, Founders like Madison and Hamilton worried that the federal government would not, at least at first, command superior affections from the people. Madison counseled in *The Federalist* No. 46 that the "change can only result from such manifest and irresistible proofs of a better administration as will overcome all of their antecedent propensities."[6] The new Constitution would *earn* the federal government the respect of the people by providing an effective administration.

One innovation designed to enhance the effectiveness of the federal government was the principle of representation, which James Madison referred to in *The Federalist* No. 63 as the "pivot" on which the American state governments move.[7] Under the American system of government, the people do not decide issues themselves; instead, the people choose individual representatives to decide society's political questions on their behalf. Because representation was a central part of the Constitution, Publius sketched out a number of theories about how the ideal representative would function and how this would contribute to effective governance. As we will see, the contrast between the principles underlying the Madisonian view of representation and the behavior of the representative in the age of Obama is quite striking.

As an initial matter, the representative needed to be intellectually proficient. Madison observed in *The Federalist* No. 53 that no one "can be a competent legislator who does not add to an upright intention and a sound judgment a certain degree of knowledge of the subjects on which he is to legislate."[8] Hamilton thought that the ranks of elected federal officials would be swelled with members of what he called the "learned professions"—lawyers, doctors and scientists, among others. It is these types of individuals "whose situation leads to extensive inquiry and information," which makes it more likely that the representative will "be a competent judge" of the prevailing views emanating throghout the public, thereby producing wise policy.[9] The representative needed to be well equipped to handle the critical issues of the day, from taxation and finance to war and negotiation.

It goes without saying that a working knowledge of the Constitution is an obligatory attribute for an elected federal official. "The propriety of a law in a constitutional light," Hamilton decreed in *The Federalist* No. 33, "must always be determined by the nature of the powers on which it is founded." Since government officials must "judge, in the first instance...the proper exercise of [federal] powers," knowledge of and dedication to the boundaries contained in the Constitution is critical in ensuring that the federal government stays within its proper constitutional orbit, thereby maintaining in fact what is intended in theory: a limited government that does not invade the liberty of the people.[10] Also, for the purposes of a good administration, the legislator needed to govern in accordance with constitutional limits because as the government takes on more responsibility outside its constitutional mandate, it becomes less likely that it will produce the competent administration deemed by people like Hamilton and Madison to be so vital to a successful republic.

Legislators in the era of Obama fall far short of the minimal standards of competence demanded by Hamilton and Madison. Incredibly, as the debate over ObamaCare illustrates, some federal representatives demonstrate a stunning ignorance of, and even a lack of regard for, the Constitution. When asked by a constituent what provision of the Constitution empowers Congress to force an individual to buy health insurance, Rep. Phil Hare, a Democrat from Illinois, cut him off by saying that he doesn't "worry about the Constitution on this to be honest" because, in his estimation, giving tax dollars to those without health insurance was a laudatory endeavor. Incensed by the response, the constituent lambasted Hare for placing his personal political ambitions ahead of the Constitution he swore to uphold. Later, Rep. Hare's office offered a clarification of the congressman's remarks; he did not mean that it was not necessary to follow the Constitution, but he simply believed that mandating individuals to purchase health insurance was constitutional. This explanation, though, is belied by the congressman's rejoinder to his constituent, for when he was accused of disregarding the Constitution, he replied that he believed the Constitution "says we have the right to life, liberty and the pursuit of happiness."[11]

Unfortunately for Hare, the phrase "life, liberty and the pursuit of happiness" is the most famous phrase from the Declaration of Independence, but is not in the Constitution. That a sitting member of the United States Congress would not know the difference between the two most important documents in the history of the Republic is itself a sad commentary on the state of the nation's political leadership. Shockingly, when told that he confused the Constitution with the Declaration, Hare replied that it "doesn't matter to me. Either one."[12]

The incident showcased Hare's fundamental misunderstanding of the very nature of constitutional government. When Thomas Jefferson penned the Declaration of Independence, he channeled John Locke and cited the rights to "life, liberty and the pursuit of happiness" as inherent, God-given rights which no legitimate government could infringe upon. Far from asserting an affirmative source of authority for government action, the citation of "self-evident" truths represents Jefferson's legendary attempt to draw a line in the sand, emphatically rebuking the British autocrat George III for so brazenly crossing the acceptable limits of governmental authority.

Jefferson's natural rights statement in the Declaration of Independence represents the essence of individual liberty, and serves as an intellectual foundation for the entire American experiment. It is also anything but a grant of power from the people to the government—yet this seemed to escape Rep. Hare. When his constituent questioned him about what provision of the Constitution gave Congress the right to force citizens to purchase health insurance, Hare's answer suggested that he considered the Declaration of Independence to confer a regulatory power upon Congress.

This represents a fundamental misconception of the source from which federal power is derived. The Constitution has no residual power; it is purely a creation of the people, whom the Constitution's creators believed to be the only true fountain of legitimate authority. The only authority possessed by the federal government is that authority which the American people have specifically granted to it under the Constitution. This is why, whenever Congress passes legislation, it can only act on the basis of one of the enumerated powers contained in Article I of the Constitution. If Congress acts in a way that is not justifiable on the basis of one of these powers, then it is usurping the power of the people. Hare's answer to his constituent suggests that he has not given a lot of thought to these issues, much less that he actually understands them. Suffice it to say that if perhaps the most far-reaching and, potentially, economically burdensome piece of legislation in the nation's history did not prompt him to consider the constitutional basis of his legislative action, he is not much concerned with the Constitution, or with his oath of office.

But perhaps Rep. Hare deserves points for at least trying to answer the question. The same cannot be said for Senator Kay Hagan, a Democrat from North Carolina, who voted for ObamaCare but could not even offer an explanation as to the source of authority that gave Congress the power to force individuals to buy health insurance. In an interview on a North Carolina radio station conducted several weeks after Congress passed and the president signed the overhaul, Hagan dodged a question about what provision of the Constitution empowers Congress to force people to buy a product. She gave a series of purported "answers"—she said she believed that it would reduce the deficit and that those without health insurance cause health care costs to increase—that were completely non-responsive to the specific question asked of her. She then abruptly and awkwardly ended the interview without even acknowledging the question about the Constitution, much less citing the constitutional basis for her vote in favor of the Obama health care overhaul.[13]

The justification most often put forward for Congress' authority to impose an individual mandate on all Americans is that the mandate flows from the power of Congress, enumerated in Article I, Section 8 of the Constitution, to regulate commerce among the states. Although the interstate commerce clause had not generally been invoked by Congress to regulate purely local economic activity for more than 100 years after the Constitution's ratification, progressives in the early-20th century began to assert an extremely broad construction of the clause that permitted Congress to regulate any economic behavior so long as the cumulative effects of purely intrastate activity exerted a "substantial effect" on interstate commerce. During Franklin D. Roosevelt's presidency, the Supreme Court endorsed this view, sustaining the power of Congress to regulate the growing of wheat as a means of propping up wheat prices, even wheat grown by a farmer for subsistence. The Court held that even if "activity be local, and though it may not be regarded as commerce, it may still, whatever its nature, be reached by Congress if it exerts a substantial economic effect on interstate commerce."[14]

Although the individual health care mandate is a step beyond even this expansive interpretation, it is telling that members such as Hare and Hagan are incapable of articulating this more expansive view; instead, they offer either no justification or a faulty explanation for their support for the federal overhaul. Interestingly, in what only can be considered an act of poetic justice, Illinois voters voted Hare out of office in November 2010—in a district gerrymandered to ensure a Democratic congressman, no less.

The health care debate revealed additional reasons to question whether today's representatives are measuring up to the standard envisioned by the Framers. Although left-of-center politicians and commentators hailed the passage of the Obama-backed health care legislation as a victory for so-called social justice (because the law served to redistribute wealth) *after* it was passed by Congress, for more than a year the Obama administration and its congressional allies tried to pitch their reform proposal as a middle-class reform that would *reduce* the budget deficit. To support their seemingly incongruous assertion that a new federal health care entitlement would reduce the nation's already mushrooming budget deficit, ObamaCare supporters trumpeted the analysis by the ostensibly non-partisan Congressional Budget Office (CBO), which showed that over a ten-year period, the proposal would reduce the budget deficit by several hundred billion dollars.

The forecast was premised on flawed assumptions. When the CBO "scores" a tax or spending proposal, it takes the information provided to it without questioning any of the underlying assumptions. It is, therefore, easy to generate a favorable CBO score if the goal is simply to get a score for its own sake rather than to determine how the proposal will actually work in practice. Left-of-center congressional leaders and the Obama administration utilized this tactic to generate a score they could use as proof that the health care proposal would reduce the deficit. With this in mind, they structured their submission to the CBO so that ten years' worth of tax receipts were measured against only six years of expenditures, and also assumed an unrealistically steep reduction in Medicare reimbursements for medical providers, even though most understood that a restoration of this funding reduction would follow the passage of the health care overall. Of course, as is customary with CBO analyses, there was no attempt by the CBO to question any of the obviously unrealistic assumptions of the proposal.

Nor was there an attempt to forecast the cost to the taxpayer of the health care overhaul in light of the established fact that the costs of other government health care programs have been greatly underestimated. When he proposed Medicare in the 1960s, President Lyndon Johnson gave assurances that the program would cost roughly $500 million per year—which, adjusted for inflation, is roughly $3.5 billion in 2009 dollars—yet by 2009 the annual cost of Medicare was over $500 billion.[15] The actuary who conducted the initial analysis of Medicare's projected costs acknowledged that, even after discounting for factors such as enhanced benefits and higher inflation that could not have been foreseen, the Medicare estimate still dramatically understated the actual costs.[16] One could also look to the United Kingdom's experience with its National Health Service—its costs ran almost 40% more than projected in its very first year.[17]

Given the track record of cost estimates for health care programs of this kind and the CBO's failure to take this into account, the cost projections for the Obama health care overhaul were incomplete at best and disingenuous at worst. And yet, even if the CBO had dutifully considered the history and used full-proof assumptions, it is still far from clear that the CBO estimate would warrant a legislator's reliance, because, as the CBO itself acknowledges, its reports typically do not accurately forecast economic and budget activity.[18]

Still, for a legislator inclined to expand government's reach over the American health care system for ideological reasons, the CBO numbers provided a useful talking point to trumpet to those constituents who might recoil from using the federal government for "redistributive change." Since the CBO scored the proposal to reduce the deficit over the first ten years, these members of Congress could say that the overhaul represented a chance to save the United States and its budget from rising health care costs. That a politician would cynically use the CBO report to earn support from deficit-conscious voters for a health care proposal actually predicated on redistributive justice can hardly be seen as surprising.

What is surprising and perhaps more alarming, at least from the perspective advanced in *The Federalist Papers* regarding the need for competent federal legislators, is that some supporters of the health care overhaul appear to have supported it because they actually believed it represented a deficit reduction tool. As chronicled by *The Washington Post*'s Cici Connolly, the Obama administration urged wavering members of Congress to support the overhaul because it would be a potent way to curb the budget deficit. "You ran because you care about the deficit," White House Chief of Staff Rahm Emanuel told Rep. Melissa Bean, a Democrat from Illinois. "This is north of $1 trillion in deficit reduction." Bean agreed that the bill's effect on the deficit was of paramount importance. "Melissa," Emanuel challenged her, "name me once in the last six years you voted for a bill with more deficit reduction."[19]

Connolly's account is a behind-the-scenes look at the negotiating and cajoling that took place on the eve of the health care vote outside of the public view, so it is unlikely that Emanuel would have made those arguments to Bean if he believed she considered the claims of deficit reduction to be mere convenient cover for legislators who supported the health care law based on ideological commitments. In the end, Bean supported the proposal because, she said, "for fiscal conservatives like myself, this is a win."[20] Unfortunately for Bean, her constituents did not buy her outlandish claims; they unceremoniously voted her out of office in 2010.

There are a number of reasons why a legislator would support the federal health care overhaul, from seeking the redistribution of wealth to wanting the federal government to provide "health security" to all Americans, but it is difficult to see how a legislator with a strong grasp of the federal budget, economics, or history would actually think that instituting a federal health care entitlement would reduce rather than enlarge the budget deficit. Not only will the new taxpayer-funded entitlement require increased federal spending, but the bill is structured in such a way that it will likely increase health care premiums, thereby requiring even more taxpayer funding. By prohibiting insurers from charging higher premiums to policy-seekers who are already sick and by setting the penalty for those who do not purchase insurance at a lower level than the typical annual insurance premium, there is nothing preventing someone from waiting until sickness strikes before seeking insurance.

For an insurer, the only way to stay solvent in such a situation is to raise premiums; besides punishing the average holder of a private health insurance policy, this will require greater federal subsidies to those getting health insurance through the federal program. Of course, this will be occurring in the face of an unprecedented spike in federal spending from 2008 to 2010, and against the backdrop of existing entitlement obligations that will continue to eat up an ever-increasing share of the federal budget. It is one thing for a left-of-center legislator to think that the benefits of the federal health care overhaul will be worth the added stress on the budget; it is quite another to believe that the federal entitlement will relieve that stress.

Proof of the absurdity of seeing the health care overhaul as a way to reduce the budget deficit came in short order following the passage of the law. In April 2010, the month following its enactment, chief Medicare actuary Richard Foster, hailed by Democrats during the Bush administration as a model of objectivity, issued a report analyzing in detail the cost implications of the law. The report contradicted the assertion, made repeatedly by President Obama and his congressional allies, that the overhaul would reduce health care costs for individuals, families and government. Foster's report found that even considering tax increases and assuming unrealistic future Medicare cuts, the money required to fund the new federal entitlement will increase the federal government's net health care spending by more than $300,000,000,000. What is more, new fees and taxes on medical devices will "generally be passed through to health consumers in the form of higher drug and devices prices and higher premiums."

Perhaps most troubling, the report concluded that the overhaul will cause roughly 14 million Americans to lose their employer-based health insurance coverage, thereby obligating the federal government to pledge even more taxpayer money to paying out health insurance subsidies.[21] One study even suggested that roughly 30% of employers would drop their employee health plans due to the costs associated with ObamaCare, which would cause the bill's cost to increase almost $1,000,000,000 more than forecasted by the CBO.[22] The bottom line is that any legislator who supported the Obama health care overhaul based on the belief that it would reduce the budget deficit betrayed the basic notions of legislative competence that Madison and Hamilton deemed requisite in a well-functioning republic.

In January of 2011, the Intercollegiate Studies Institute released the results of its survey measuring the knowledge of American civics by members of the public. The public did poorly, but, as has been the case in past surveys, elected officials represented the one identifiable group that did worse than the public as a whole. The results are dismaying: only 49% of elected officials could name the three branches of government, only 46% knew that Congress possesses the power to declare war, and only 57% grasped the function of the Electoral College. At first blush, it seems odd that a group of individuals who swear an oath to support and defend the Constitution would lack a basic knowledge of its functions.[23] However, after witnessing the performance of elected officials such as Phil Hare, who failed to grasp the difference between the Declaration of Independence and the Constitution, and Melissa Bean, who actually believed that the creation of a new federal health care entitlement would relieve stress on the federal budget, such results are much more understandable. The results merely confirm what the age of Obama has exhibited for all to see.

11

"VOLUMINOUS AND INCOMPREHENSIBLE"

In *The Federalist* No. 62, James Madison bemoaned what he called "mutability in the public councils" that "is inconsistent with every rule of prudence and every prospect of success." The deleterious effects of a "mutable policy" are so "calamitous" that they undermine the rule of law, which "poisons the blessings of liberty itself." Being able to choose one's leaders will have little benefit if the "laws be so voluminous that they cannot be read; or so incoherent that they cannot be understood." By crafting lengthy, incomprehensible laws, legislators muddied the rule of law and drove a wedge of separation in between the government and its citizens. The Constitution, Madison hoped, would serve as an antidote to this ruinous mutability by virtue of, among other things, a Senate that would be a stabilizing force in government and a repository for knowledge about maintaining fidelity to the true object of government: the happiness of the people. "No government, any more than an individual," Madison concluded in *The Federalist* No. 62, "will long be respected without being truly respectable; nor be truly respectable without possessing a certain portion of order and stability."[1]

The same "calamitous" effects that troubled Madison are a staple of today's Congress, where thousand-plus page bills are the norm. It is difficult to maintain that these bills are the handiwork of legislative excellence, as most members do not even read them, most of which are briskly jammed through Congress. The health care overhaul, running more than 2,000 pages, represents exactly the type of voluminous and incomprehensible legislation that Madison criticized for undermining self-government. Critics of the law lambasted members of Congress for passing a law that they themselves did not actually read, and many legislators forthrightly admitted that they did not read the entire bill, even though they maintained that they understood and supported its contents. Senator Max Baucus, a Montana Democrat hailed as one of the chief authors of the legislation, told a constituent that it would be a "waste" of his "time to read every page of the healthcare bill. You know why? It's statutory language....We hire experts."[2]

Soon after President Obama signed the bill into law, though, the Congressional Research Service issued a report warning that the overhaul could have unintended consequences for the personal health care coverage of members of Congress, requiring senators, representatives and their respective staffs to forego their current federal employee benefits in favor of participation in insurance exchanges created by ObamaCare. But since the insurance exchanges were not scheduled to start for several years and since the law appeared to strip members of Congress of their current benefits immediately, the report noted that the law might have unintentionally left members of Congress with no available health care coverage. A reporter for *The New York Times* wondered: "if they did not know exactly what they were doing to themselves, did lawmakers who wrote and passed the bill fully grasp the details of how it would influence the lives of other Americans?"[3]

The so-called economic "stimulus" bill represents another telling example of this type of legislative malpractice, for that bill, which carried a $814,000,000,000 price tag, representing the largest domestic spending bill in the nation's history, received legislative approval the day after the language of the bill was publicly revealed, making it next to impossible for a member of Congress to have actually read the lengthy legislation. In fact, New Jersey Democratic Senator Frank Lautenberg admitted that he did not "think anyone will have the chance to [read the entire bill]."[4]

This is remarkable given the enormous amount of taxpayer money at stake. According to the Congressional Budget Office, the stimulus bill represented roughly $100,000,000,000 more in taxpayer money than what was appropriated for the war in Iraq during the entire period of 2003 through 2010.[5] Madison worried about *the people* not being able to read voluminous laws, but probably never imagined that *legislators* would not even bother to read the laws before they imposed them on the people.

By voting on the stimulus without first closely inspecting the legislation, many members of Congress failed to be true guardians of the public's money. The stimulus was pitched by President Obama as a necessary prescription to "immediately jumpstart job creation and long-term growth," particularly through funding for "shovel-ready" infrastructure projects. He promised that his stimulus would be "an economic recovery plan that is free from earmarks and pet projects."[6] Nevertheless, the stimulus bill contained a litany of pet projects that had virtually no connection to creating jobs or economic growth; the very type of pork-barrel projects that appropriators can most safely enact into law when they are assured of minimal public scrutiny.

Whatever their overall merits, it is clear that some of these projects lacked any obvious stimulative qualities, such as:

- $50,000,000 for the National Endowment for the Arts,
- $300,000,000 to "combat" violence against women,
- $4,000,000,000 for "neighborhood stabilization,"
- $1,000,000,000 for "community development" block grants,
- $650,000,000 for digital television conversion, and
- $90,000,000 to educate so-called "vulnerable populations" about the analog-to-digital switch.

From the $1,000,000,000 for census programs over and above existing appropriations to the $350,000,000 for computers at the Department of Agriculture, many of the spending initiatives seemed to be aimed at stimulating the federal government more than the private economy. And some provisions were, at least when viewed in combination with other stimulus provisions, just plain odd; for example, the stimulus allocated $200,000,000 to the National Aeronautics and Space Administration (NASA) to study global warming, but also earmarked $87,000,000 to the Coast Guard for a polar ice-breaking ship.[7] Obama's promise of the stimulus being free from non-stimulative pork projects was plainly erroneous, and any member of Congress who actually read the bill could have readily discerned this obvious fact.

The vote on the stimulus bill occurred against the backdrop of a promise made by members of Congress to post the language of the bill on the internet for at least 48 hours before taking a vote on the measure. The leadership in the House of Representatives did not, however, post the full bill until late in the evening on the day before the floor vote, rendering a full reading of the bill virtually impossible for members of Congress. The reason for the promise to post the bill on the internet was less so that legislators could read it and more so that the public could review the bill, comment upon the respective provisions, and inform their representatives of their views.

Interestingly, when he analyzed the defects of the Pennsylvania state constitution in *The Federalist* No. 48, Madison criticized the Pennsylvania legislature for passing a "great number of laws…violating, without any apparent necessity, the rule requiring that all bills of a public nature shall be previously printed for the consideration of the people." Pennsylvania had the public posting provision because it represented "one of the precautions chiefly relied on by the [Pennsylvania] Constitution against improper acts of the legislature." The mandate that pending legislation be made public stood as a tool by which the people could restrain their elected officials from violating the Constitution and acting in violation of the public good. When voluminous and incomprehensible laws are passed without any input from the public, the blessings of liberty become, as Madison warned, poisoned.

Seen in this light, the broken promise made by congressional leaders to post the stimulus bill online for a certain period of time before conducting a vote deprived the people of a critical opportunity to scrutinize the legislation and to influence the process. By posting the bill on the internet late in the night before the vote, Congress made it next-to-impossible for even the most diligent citizen to read and analyze such a huge bill, much less to express an opinion about the measure to a federal representative. What is more, the complex and convoluted nature of the stimulus served to conceal any special deals and unsavory measures that inevitably found their way into such a bill. This is especially true because the bill was posted as a so-called "scanned" PDF document that could not be searched on a computer like a normal document. Without this convenience, an average citizen had virtually no chance to identify the projects that represented a dubious use of taxpayer funds, and/or that had no relation to economic stimulus.

Madison shrewdly diagnosed an equally deleterious effect of voluminous, incomprehensible laws: "the unreasonable advantage it gives to the sagacious, the enterprising, and the moneyed few over the industrious and uninformed mass of the people." Every new regulation concerning economic activity or taxation promulgated by the legislature "presents a new harvest to those who watch the change, and can trace its consequences; a harvest, not reared by themselves, but by the toils and cares of the great body of their fellow-citizens." To Madison's consternation, this represented a "state of things in which it may be said with some truth that laws are made for the *few*, not for the *many*."[8]

One comical example of this occurring in the age of Obama stemmed from a stimulus provision that granted substantial tax credits—as much as $5,500—for the purchase of vehicles running on electric power. Since Congress wrote the tax credit in a way that included even diminutive road-worthy vehicles, this provision created a burgeoning market for new golf carts, as dealers and consumers rushed to capitalize on this obscure stimulus provision. One dealer in Central Florida known as the Golf Cart Man ran an advertisement on the internet that blared: "GET A FREE GOLF CART. Or make $2,000 doing absolutely nothing!" This was no joke, but instead referred to an offer in which a buyer purchases a golf cart for $8,000, takes a $5,300 tax credit, leases it back to Golf Cart Man for $100 a month over a 27 month period, and retains an option to sell the cart back to Golf Cart Man for $2,000. As the Golf Cart Man says, "this means you own a free Golf Cart or made $2,000 cash doing absolutely nothing!!!"

The number of carts that an individual can buy was not limited under the stimulus, providing an incentive for some to buy multiple golf carts, take the federal credits, and then re-sell the carts at a profit. Because these profits are realized on the backs of the taxpayer, it is precisely the type of situation that Madison warned about—a "state of things in which it may be said with some truth that laws are made for the *few*, not for the *many*." Of course, the sellers and purchasers of taxpayer-subsidized golf carts were behaving in a way that is perfectly legal; it is the special tax provisions instituted by Congress and approved by Obama that penalize the taxpaying many in favor of the sagacious few.[9]

Madison further noted that voluminous and incomprehensible laws breed an uncertainty that hurts the economy by demoralizing risk taking and investment. Lacking confidence in government's ability to maintain stability in policy and administration, there is less reason to pursue useful undertakings, the "success and profit of which may depend on a continuance of existing arrangements." As Madison sensibly observed, what "prudent merchant will hazard his fortunes in any new branch of commerce when he knows not but that his plans may be rendered unlawful before they can be executed?"[10] Madison's observation appears to have gone unheeded by the Obama administration and its legislative deputies in Congress, as the uncertainty generated over the implementation of "change" caused many private businesses to flinch from pursuing new investments or new expansion. Gargantuan bills such as the overhaul of the health care system and a reformulation of financial regulations, the prospect for higher tax rates as well as higher energy costs due to the so-called cap and trade global warming proposal and the not unreasonable belief by many businessmen that President Obama personally dislikes business and views profits as inherently suspect all contributed to this uncertainty, and prevented the economy from breaking through the prevailing malaise as soon as it otherwise could have.

The debate over the federal health care overhaul cast an enormous cloud over businesses large and small throughout the first year of the Obama administration. Then-House Speaker Nancy Pelosi's statement that "we have to pass the bill so that you can find out what is in it" had the effect of underscoring, in startling terms, the notion that nobody really knew what was in the health care bill. Already mired in a lengthy recession with access to loans restricted due to the hangover from the financial crisis, many small and medium-sized businesses were paralyzed with uncertainty over how the remaking of a sizable part of the American economy would impact their business costs.

The owner of a chain of auto parts stores in Virginia, W. Michael Brown, scaled back the number of new employee hires for his new stores due to an inability to forecast his potential costs in the midst of so many political questions. "There's so much trepidation out there," Brown told *The Wall Street Journal*. "The thing I'm struggling with is how the potential government takeover of health care coupled with impending taxes will impact my company." Carl Redman, vice president of an Oregon-based electrical contracting business, had plans to expand the company's warehouse, thereby enabling the company to expand operations, but ultimately decided not to go forward with the expansion. "We pulled the plug," he said. "I made the decision based on all the unknowns. I didn't think it would be wise to make the expenditure because I don't know if I will need the money to pay for something else."[11] Madison's insight about the paralyzing effect of uncertain policy seems prescient in light of the reaction of many job creators to the "change" debated and enacted in Washington, D.C.

The enactment of the health care law did not erase this uncertainty. Many small business owners were confused about how the 2,000-plus page law would be implemented, and how the implementation would affect their ability to expand, or even to make a profit. "I don't think anyone really, really knows how it's going to affect them," said Butch Porter, a principal at a Virginia-based financial firm. "There are a lot of open-ended questions."[12] Patty Briguglio, owner of MMI Public Relations in Raleigh, NC, provides her 20 employees with a $2,400 annual allowance rather than provide them with a group health plan because "it's less expensive than a group plan because I have a young work force." But she worried about whether the federal overhaul would force her to offer a group plan. "What's going to happen? Are they going to force me to buy a group plan that will cost me more? Should I stop growing so I can get more tax incentives?"[13]

It is not hard to see why the enactment of the federal health care overhaul has failed to reduce uncertainty, as the 2,000-plus page law left a large number of critical questions unanswered, delegating many of these questions to executive branch agencies. In fact, ObamaCare creates more than 150 new federal offices, agencies and programs—many of which will be implemented by and/or report to a number of existing agencies such as the Department of Health and Human Services (HHS), the Government Accountability Office (GAO), the Treasury Department, the Center for Disease Control (CDC) and the Centers for Medicare and Medicaid Services (CMS).[14] How these bureaucracies will interpret and implement the vast and complicated health care law will have enormous ramifications for individual citizens as well as the American economy, yet the number of important questions intentionally left unanswered in the bill and the sheer magnitude of the new health care bureaucracy means that it is difficult to determine when and how these questions will be answered.

The one thing that is clear is that federal bureaucrats will have a wide berth of discretion to administer the health care colossus. For example, ObamaCare delegates authority to the Secretary of HHS to take discretionary action in hundreds of different instances, and empowers the Secretary to define the minimal "essential" health benefits that all Americans will be forced to maintain, which will have enormous implications for the cost of insurance. This means that businesses and individuals who, in Madison's words, are inclined to "hazard" their fortunes will have no choice but to do so against the backdrop of hundreds, if not thousands, of forthcoming bureaucratic decisions that could have a palpable effect on their endeavors.

The enactment of the Obama health care law implicated yet another of the Framers' admonitions about good government: democratically enacted laws should not exempt members of the governing class or their pet constituencies from their effect. In *The Federalist* No. 57, Madison explained that the Constitution was constructed in such a way that legislators, and here he speaks specifically of House members, "can make no law which will not have in its full operation on themselves and their friends, as well as on the great mass of society." This serves as "one of the strongest bonds by which human policy can connect the rulers and the people together. It creates between them that communion of interests and sympathy of sentiments, of which few governments have furnished examples; but without which every government degenerates into tyranny." Madison didn't think that American legislators would make artificial discriminations in favor of themselves and their favored constituencies because, on the one hand, the genius of the Constitution as whole, and, one the other hand, "the vigilant and manly spirit which actuates the people of America—a spirit which nourishes freedom, and in return is nourished by it."[15]

In other words, to the extent that the Constitution does not prevent such discriminatory laws, the people will exercise disapproval of the obnoxious behavior of legislators through their collective political voice as channeled through the ballot box.

Perhaps not surprisingly given the volume and complexity of the legislation, ObamaCare contained instances of the governing majority indulging a number of obnoxious discriminations in favor of themselves and their favored constituencies. Initially, many opponents of the federal overhaul were concerned that members of Congress would create a number of new rules and regulations that would undermine the quality and accessibility of care for many Americans but that would not apply to the health plans utilized by the members. As it turns out, the true authors of the bill, the congressional staffers working for the relevant House and Senate committees, did exempt themselves from participation in the insurance exchanges in which many Americans will be forced. The bill requires that members of

Congress and their staffs participate in the insurance exchanges, but, in its devilish details, defines "staff" to include only "full-time and part-time employees employed by the official office of a Member of Congress, whether in Washington, DC or outside of Washington, DC," which excludes those staffers employed by a congressional committee rather than an individual member.[16]

Thus, the committee staffers, the very people who designed the health care overhaul and presumably understood and supported the law, declined to mandate their own participation in the bill, a disturbing sign that raises the question of whether the overhaul will reduce the quality of health care for those now subject to its dictates. The refusal of the authors of the health care overhaul to receive their personal health care under the bill is hardly surprising, as a substantial number of Americans worried that the overhaul would have a negative impact on their own health care.[17]

Because of this prevailing view, the Obama administration and its allies in Congress found it necessary to cut a number of special deals to make the overhaul more acceptable to wavering members of Congress and politically favored constituencies. One special favor advanced by Democrats concerned a proposed compromise with union officials over the so-called "Cadillac tax"—a 40% levy included in the Senate health care bill that applied to pricey health insurance plans. This tax was opposed by unions because they feared that the tax would hit the generous health benefits of many union members. Yet, rather than scrap the tax in its entirety, Democrats cut a deal with union bosses that exempted from the tax, for five years, health care plans stemming from collective-bargaining agreements, including the health plans of state and local government employees.

This proposal represented rank discrimination against non-union health care plans in favor of the plans of those unions that represent the lifeblood of the Democratic Party's political base.[18] Even the left-leaning editorial board of *The Washington Post* was flummoxed by the preferential treatment for Obama's political allies and was left to wonder how such treatment could possibly be considered fair.[19]

Ultimately, the notion of creating a special exemption for union health care plans was so patently offensive to proper lawmaking that it had to be dropped at the last minute; the fact that such a special deal was even entertained by the Obama administration speaks volumes about the extent to which the governing class rejects the Madisonian dictum of just lawmaking.

If the Cadillac tax exemption for unions was the only special consideration proposed by Obama and his congressional allies then it might be possible to dismiss it as an aberration. Unfortunately, the legislative gamesmanship that accompanied the health care overhaul's passage through Congress produced a number of special provisions that represented political bribery for certain members of Congress. To secure the vote of Senator Mary Landrieu, a Democrat more liberal than her home state of Louisiana, Senate Majority Leader Harry Reid inserted a special provision that singled out Louisiana for a huge increase, as much as $300,000,000, in federal matching funds for Medicaid expenditures. Not surprisingly, the legislative language did not mention Louisiana specifically but instead provided that "certain states recovering from a major disaster" would be eligible for the funding. This criteria was constructed in such a way that only Louisiana qualified for the additional funds. The provision was, no doubt, written in this fashion to camouflage the special deal from the public's opprobrium. Nevertheless, the deal soon garnered the nickname the "Louisiana Purchase."

Another wavering Senator, Nebraska's Ben Nelson, a purported moderate Democrat from the conservative state of Nebraska, also received a special favor in return for his vote in favor of the health care overhaul. Since a key ingredient of ObamaCare is the expansion of Medicaid, which requires states to foot part of the bill, the Senate version of the overhaul provided a boon to Senator Nelson by obligating the federal government to pick up Nebraska's entire Medicaid expenses in perpetuity. Dubbed the "Cornhusker Kickback," the special deal was so unseemly that even voters in Nebraska were outraged at the special treatment their state was due to receive. "The last few days have made Nebraskans so angry that now it's a matter of principle," Nebraska Gov. David Heineman said. "The federal government can keep that money."[20] The public outrage over Senator Nelson's sweetheart deal was so strong that, eventually, the special status for Nebraska was removed from the bill during the "reconciliation" process, but by this time Senator Nelson had already cast the decisive health care vote in the Senate and, hence, the kickback had performed its desired function.

The passage of ObamaCare did not end the special favors; the enormous law delegated so many important questions to bureaucratic decision making that opportunities for favoritism still existed. Several months after Obama signed the bill into law, a conglomeration of federal agencies issued an interim rule defining the circumstances under which an existing health care plan remains exempt from the litany of rules and mandates contained in the ObamaCare legislation, which make insurance more expensive. Existing plans are "grandfathered" in, and thus not subject to the new rules, but when "an employer or employee organization enters into a new policy, certificate, or contract of insurance after March 23, 2010...then that policy, certificate, or contract of insurance is not a grandfathered health plan."[21]

An employer that switches insurance carriers, even if switching to a similar but cheaper plan, loses "grandfather" status and gets subjected to the full catalogue of health care mandates and regulations. Curiously, the interim rule exempted union health care plans from the restriction on "grandfather" status. Unlike an employer of non-union employees, a union could switch to an entirely new group health care plan and remain fully exempt from the costly mandates of ObamaCare. This is a huge boon for Obama's union allies, but a potentially devastating burden on those not fortunate enough to be a favored constituency of the ruling class.

The legislative malpractice that has characterized the day-to-day operations in the nation's capitol and drawn the ire of the public is exactly the type of behavior that the Founding Fathers designed the Constitution to combat. Madison warned of laws too voluminous to read and to incomprehensible to understand, yet the Nancy Pelosi-Harry Reid Congress churned out bills running thousands of pages without batting an eye; bills that were not read by many members of Congress and which contained a litany of questionable elements. The need for laws to apply to both members of Congress and their supporters, which Madison deemed an essential aspect of a just government, gave way to a system in which committee staff exempt themselves from health care mandates and Democratic politicians provide preferential treatment to the health care plans of the unions that support them. In the words of James Madison, "this is a state of things in which it may be said with some truth that laws are made for the *few*, not for the *many*."[22]

12

THE PEOPLE'S REPRESENTATIVES

"It is a misfortune incident to republican government, though in a less degree than to other governments," James Madison observed in *The Federalist* No. 62, "that those who administer it may forget their obligations to their constituents and prove unfaithful to their important trust."[1] During the long debate over the health care overhaul, with public opinion polls consistently showing strong disapproval of the proposed law, many of the political opponents of President Barack Obama and the Pelosi-Reid Congress accused the governing class of betraying the trust of the people by pursuing a federal takeover of the health care system in spite of the wishes of their constituents. Before the final vote in the House of Representatives, Republican John Boehner pilloried his liberal colleagues for failing "to listen to America…and fail[ing] to reflect the will of our constituents." He warned them that "in a democracy you can only ignore the will of the people for so long and get away with it."[2]

Defenders of the Pelosi-Reid-Obama health care push argued that compliance with public opinion was not the touchstone of effective representation; instead, they said that political leaders needed to make good policy, even in defiance of the public's views. Pennsylvania Governor Ed Rendell, a Democrat, cited as an analogy the so-called Iraq troop "surge" initiated in 2007 by President George W. Bush, which was enormously unpopular when announced but soon proved to be the right policy. Rendell argued that "we are not elected to just put our finger to the wind, take a public opinion poll and do what exactly the prevailing mood is at the time. We're elected to use our own judgment to try to figure out what's best in the long run for people we represent."[3]

Rendell's defense of Obama and his congressional allies raised the question of whether the pursuit of large, far-reaching pieces of legislation in the face of stiff public opposition is consistent with, or a divergence from, the conception of representation as articulated by Hamilton and Madison in *The Federalist.*

As a general matter, the essays in *The Federalist* plainly reject the notion that elected officials should do nothing more than implement the prevailing strand of public opinion. Instead of serving as a delegate that merely reflected the views of the public, an elected official needed "to refine and enlarge the public views." As Madison explained in his celebrated *The Federalist* No. 10 essay, republican government is premised on the filtering of public opinion "through the medium of a chosen body of citizens, whose wisdom may best discern the true interest of their country and whose patriotism and love of justice will be least likely to sacrifice it to temporary or partial considerations."

Madison even suggested that, under a scheme of representation, it might be that the "public voice, pronounced by the representatives of the people, will be more consonant to the public good than if pronounced by the people themselves, convened for that purpose." While a "pure" democracy would have no defense to the spirit of faction, a representative government could serve to discipline, if not tame, the disease from which so many popular governments had perished.[4]

The theory of representation as articulated by James Madison rests on the notion of the elected official as a trustee rather than as a delegate. This distinction was most famously highlighted by Edmund Burke in his "Speech to the Electors at Bristol," in which Burke admonished his constituents that he felt himself bound to vote against their wishes if he judged such vote to be what the public good required. To be sure, Burke believed that the representative needed "to live in the strictest union, the closest correspondence, and the most unreserved communication with his constituents. Their wishes ought to have great weight with him; their opinion, high respect; their business, unremitted attention." In the event that the interest of the representative conflicted with the interest of his constituents, "it is his duty to sacrifice his repose, his pleasures, his satisfactions, to theirs; and above all, ever, and in all cases, to prefer their interest to his own." However, the representative should not sacrifice his "unbiased opinion, his mature judgment, his enlightened conscience" to his constituents, for "these he does not derive from [their] pleasure; no, nor from the law and the constitution. They are a trust from

Providence, for the abuse of which he is deeply answerable." The representative owes his constituents "not his industry only, but his judgment; and he betrays, instead of serving [his constituents], if he sacrifices it to [their] opinion."[5]

But Burkean though they were, it would be a mistake to conclude that the Framers were hostile to allowing public opinion to play a role in policymaking. In *The Federalist* No. 63, Madison contended that while the "people can never willfully betray their own interests…they may possibly be betrayed by the representatives of the people."[6] Acknowledging the potential for representatives to act contrary to the public good, Hamilton identified the "restraints of public opinion" as being one of the "two greatest securities [the people] can have for the faithful exercise of any delegated power." Indeed, when discussing the presidency, Hamilton identified the need for the public to exert a constraining influence on elected officials as a reason to support lodging the executive authority in a single individual; otherwise, the constraints "lose their efficacy, as well on account of the division of the censure attendant on bad measures among a number on account of uncertainty on whom it ought to fall."[7] Thus, while an elected official must exercise individual judgment per the dictum of Edmund Burke, public opinion serves as a way to blunt the effects of these judgments when they are not properly calculated to serve the public interest.

Constitution creators like Hamilton and Madison wanted the government's policies to rest not on every passing fancy of public opinion but instead on the durable, reflective desires of the public. "The republican principle demands that the deliberate sense of the community should govern the conduct of those to whom they intrust the management of their affairs," Hamilton wrote in *The Federalist* No. 71. "But it does not require an unqualified complaisance to every sudden breeze of passion, or to every transient impulse which the people may receive from the arts of men, who flatter their prejudices to betray their interests."

Hamilton was concerned that the public could be led by demagogues to support measures that, while superficially appealing, tended to be corrosive of the public good. He knew that the people sometimes erred but "the wonder is that they so seldom err as they do, beset, as they continually are, by the wiles of parasites and sycophants, by the snares of the ambitious, the avaricious, the desperate, by the artifices of men who possess their confidence more than they deserve it, and of those who seek to possess rather than to deserve it." In situations in which the public passions diverge from the public good, "it is the duty of the persons whom they have appointed to be the guardians of those interests, to withstand the temporary delusion, in order to give them time and opportunity for more cool and sedate reflection."[8]

When discussing the presidency, Hamilton derided those "who would be inclined to regard the servile pliancy of the Executive to a prevailing current, either in the community or in the legislature, as its best recommendation." Advocates of this view "entertain very crude notions, as well of the purposes for which government was instituted, as of the true means by which the public happiness may be promoted." In this respect, the Founders distinguished between a "prevailing current" of popular opinion and those public views that represent the "cool and deliberate sense of the community."[9] Public opinion based on deliberation and reflection "ought, in all governments, and actually will, in all free governments, ultimately prevail over the views of its rulers."[10] The prerogative of an elected official to refine, to enlarge, and even, in certain instances, to reject the views of the public was not unlimited; in a republican form of government, the enduring sense of the community is superior to the personal ambitions of any elected leader.

For our purposes, it is clear that Framers like Hamilton and Madison would frown upon those elected officials who channel their actions to follow every blip in public opinion polls. The public's views on certain issues can change dramatically over a short period of time, and the wise representative will be impervious to sudden (and usually fleeting) changes in opinion, focusing instead on making sound policy judgments. In this regard, the assertion that a representative needs to function as a mirror that reflects the views of his constituents without any attempt to "refine and enlarge the public views" is not consistent with the philosophy of representation outlined in *The Federalist.* At the same time, those public views that endure over time are of an entirely different character than a mere passing political fancy, and the representative does owe a due regard for these more enduring public desires.

With these principles in mind, Rendell's defense of the push for an unpopular health care overhaul is not fully consistent with the views articulated by Madison and Hamilton in defense of the Constitution. As a general matter, Rendell is right that the representative should not be beholden to every shift in public opinion. The mere fact, for example, that a public opinion poll illustrates public opposition to a particular policy such as the health care overhaul does not, in and of itself, mandate that a member of Congress oppose it. If a legislator like Nancy Pelosi honestly construed public disapproval of the health care bill to be nothing more than a "transient impulse," then it follows that bucking the polls to support ObamaCare could be characterized as an act of Burkean legislative statesmanship, an example of legislators withstanding what Hamilton called a "temporary delusion" in order to vindicate the public interest. This no doubt is how the vote was portrayed by President Obama and congressional leaders.

But this view is mistaken. Obama tried to pitch the health care debate as the culmination of a century-long struggle to vindicate the power of the people over various "special interests"—a view resting heavily on the questionable assumption that the progress of history is a steady, inexorable march towards more centralized government power and less individual freedom. He cited a number of presidents dating back to Theodore Roosevelt who supported some sort of a nationalized health care system as proof that a federal overhaul of the health care system was long overdue. And while Obama's framing of the health care debate in this fashion meshed nicely with a number of progressive assumptions about history and politics, it tended to undermine the argument that members of Congress were merely resisting a temporary public opposition to the overhaul. It wasn't just that, for the better part of a year, polls showed that the public rejected the Obama health care proposal. Instead, it could be argued that the American people have consistently opposed a national health care system for the past *century*; had the public manifested a prolonged desire for such an initiative, it would have been enacted long before anybody ever heard of Barack Obama.

In spite of this durable public opposition, congressional leaders like Nancy Pelosi and Harry Reid as well as President Obama placed their own personal political ambitions—the health care overhaul was, in the words of Vice President Joseph Biden, a "big f---ing deal"—over the clearly expressed desires of the American people. This was not something that the Founders failed to contemplate. As Hamilton acknowledged in *The Federalist* No. 71, "representatives…seem sometimes to fancy that they are the people themselves." While the "restraints of public opinion" were not strong enough to overcome the commanding legislative majorities enjoyed by President Obama and his congressional allies, the American people have the opportunity to render a direct a judgment on the health care overhaul via the medium of elections. Their initial judgment, expressed via the 2010 midterm elections, represented a decisive rebuke to those who orchestrated the enactment of ObamaCare. The 2012 presidential election will, perhaps, serve as the final verdict on whether the elected officials that bucked the public's views did so with propriety or with recklessness.

13

"MANIFEST AND IRRESISTIBLE PROOFS"

The giddiness amongst members of the chattering classes that greeted Barack Obama's election was not entirely due to the historic nature of Obama's candidacy or even to the left-of-center political outlook that Obama shared with the overwhelming majority of coastal elites. According to a catalogue of political pundits and television talking heads, Obama was going to bring a unique blend of intelligence and competence to the presidential chair—a welcome correction to what they deemed to be the intellectual deficiencies and ineptness of the incumbent chief executive, George W. Bush.

In an interview on the Don Imus radio program shortly after the 2008 election, Michael Beschloss, a liberal historian, asserted that Obama's "I.Q. is off the charts...[one] cannot say that he is anything but a very serious and capable leader." Beschloss marveled at how fortunate Americans were to be blessed with such a historical rarity because "our system doesn't allow those people to become president, those people meaning *that* smart and *that* capable." Obama was, Beschloss gushed, "probably the smartest guy ever to become president"—smarter than American luminaries like Thomas Jefferson, James Madison and Abraham Lincoln. Upon further questioning, Beschloss admitted that, in fact, he had no idea what Obama's I.Q. actually was, but this relevant detail did not matter, for the jury of commentators had already deliberated and rendered their verdict: Obama was historically and unbelievably smart.[1]

Obama's prodigious intellect seemed to be matched only by his extraordinary dexterity. Following Obama's electoral victory, *The San Francisco Chronicle* celebrated what it called Obama's "campaign that radiated hope and resonated competence."[2] Obama framed his candidacy as representing a strong antidote to what he characterized as the serial mismanagement practiced during the George W. Bush administration, from shooting wars abroad to the response to Hurricane Katrina at home. During the primary season, he made a celebrated campaign stop in New Orleans to highlight the Katrina issue, and said that, if elected president he would "restore competence to the White House and rebuild trust between Washington and the citizens who were impacted by Katrina."[3] *Time* magazine named Obama as its Person of the Year in 2008 "for showing the competence that makes Americans hopeful that he will" fulfill his *Time*-approved, left-of-center agenda.[4]

Both Obama and his supporters were supremely confident in his ability to execute the office with deftness and intelligence. In fact, few Obama loyalists or supportive journalists even considered the possibility that a former community organizer without any executive experience would have a difficult time riding what Harry S. Truman described as the presidential tiger. Incredibly, the source of concern seemed to be that the presidency might be *too meager* of a challenge for a man of such prodigious ability. Terry Moran from ABC News was in awe of the fact that, "in some ways, Barack Obama is the first president since George Washington to be taking a step down into the office….I mean, from visionary leader of a giant movement, now he's got an executive position that he has to perform in."[5]

After Obama assumed office, *Newsweek*'s Evan Thomas was struck by how Obama seemed to be transcending the presidency: "I mean, in a way, Obama's standing above the country, above—above the world, he's sort of God."[6] To Obama loyalists like fellow Chicagoan and advisor Valerie Jarrett, the fact that Obama left weak-kneed journalists amazed at his intellectual and political prowess was hardly a surprise. Obama "knows exactly how smart he is," Jarrett recounted. "He has been bored to death his whole life. He's just too talented to do what ordinary people do."[7]

This near messianic view of Obama was not confined to left-leaning journalists and Obama sycophants, but was shared by elites throughout the world, including members of the Norwegian Nobel Committee, which is in charge of awarding the Nobel Peace Prize. That committee awarded the 2009 Nobel Peace Prize to President Obama, despite the fact that he had been in office for a mere 12 days before the nomination deadline and despite the fact that he had not registered any concrete foreign policy achievements. The headline of an article written by Jennifer Loven, a reporter for the Associated Press, asked a question that captured the thoughts of many upon hearing news of the award: "He Won, But for What?"[8] Peter Beinart, a liberal writer for *The Daily Beast*, dismissed the award as unjustified: "I like Barack Obama as much as the next liberal, but this is a farce."[9]

But the Nobel Committee, like the Valerie Jarretts and Evan Thomases of the world, never worried that Obama would not be up to the job of being a towering, transcendental figure for the ages. "Only very rarely has a person to the same extent as Obama captured the world's attention and given its people hope for a better future," the committee said. "His diplomacy is founded in the concept that those who are to lead the world must do so on the basis of values and attitudes that are shared by the majority of the world's population."[10] Since Obama's greatness was so self-evident, there existed little reason to require him to go through the trouble of earning the award.

These accounts of an ultra-competent, politically dexterous and historically great Obama painted a picture of someone tailor-made for the presidency established by the Framers. They envisioned a federal government administered far better than the government under the Articles of Confederation, a government that could execute what Alexander Hamilton called "extensive and arduous enterprises for the public benefit." Executive competence would be matched by legislative excellence; lawmakers would pass wise laws that reinforced rather than counteracted the blessings of liberty upon which the government was founded. As the leader of the Democratic Party as well as the broader "hope and change" movement, political pundits certainly expected Obama to use his competence and intelligence to shepherd progressive bills—aimed at igniting an economic recovery, controlling health care costs and reducing the planet's temperature—through an overwhelmingly Democratic Congress with which he would have a close working relationship. Indeed, one of Obama's main selling points was that business as usual in Washington was no longer acceptable; he would lead his legislative allies in Congress in a new era of legislative statesmanship. It did not take long, though, for Obama to confound the Founders' expectations through executive and administrative incompetence.

The questionable actions of lawmakers—from writing incomprehensible laws to disregarding long-standing public opinion—are clearly troubling from a Madisonian perspective, and these nefarious practices have not been counterbalanced by what Madison referred to as "such manifest and irresistible proofs" of a competent administration. From efforts to blunt home mortgage foreclosures to implementation of major pieces of legislation like the economic stimulus, the federal government has repeatedly failed to produce the good administration that Hamilton argued the Constitution would deliver. Hamilton envisioned a federal government that would increasingly earn the respect and confidence of the people as it "further…enters into those objects which touch the most sensible chords and put in motion the most active springs of the human heart," including enforcing the rule of law and protecting the people from external attacks and from internal convulsions.[11]

Perhaps because the age of Obama has witnessed the federal government undertake such a large number of huge projects, the federal administration has failed to execute these diverse undertakings in an effective fashion. The upshot is a chronically ineffective government that fails to engender the same level of respect and admiration that Hamilton believed the Constitution portended.

If there was a single factor that set the stage for the election of Barack Obama, it was the crash of the American housing market, which was the catalyst for both the 2008 financial crisis and the broader economic recession. Within a month of taking office, Obama unveiled a federal mortgage relief program designed, he said, to "arrest the downward spiral" in the housing market and prevent the crisis from further "unraveling" the middle class.[12] The program, which raised the ire of CNBC reporter Rick Santelli and prompted him to call for organizing tea parties to protest Obama's policies, proved to be an abject failure.

According to congressional overseer Elizabeth Warren, the Treasury Department was "still fighting to get its foreclosure programs off the ground" more than a full year after the program's enactment. Indeed, one-third of the 1.24 million borrowers had already dropped out of the program. *The New York Times* noted that the mortgage relief program served to instill false hope in a number of heavily indebted homeowners, who continued to make payments in a futile attempt to keep their homes, only to end up in foreclosure after having squandered their income on the payments.[13] "Re-default signals the worst form of failure" for the program, Warren noted. "Billions of dollars of taxpayer dollars will be spent and families will nonetheless lose their homes."[14] *The Times* further observed how this ineffective intervention by the federal government served to delay the "wrenching yet cleansing process" necessary for the housing market to recover its bearings. With so few homeowners benefitting from the plan, many economists dismissed the plan as a failure that actually did more harm than good.

Obama's main political prescription for the nation's economic downturn was, of course the $814,000,000,000 economic stimulus, and its implementation showcased a chronically ineffective federal establishment. Obama heralded the stimulus as a boon for a "clean energy" economy that would ignite an economic recovery; the stimulus even included $500,000,000 to help workers train for so-called "green jobs." But this proved to be nothing more than fanciful speculation, as even Obama's allies acknowledged. "Spending on renewables is slow to get out of the door. Leaks to foreign companies is an inadequate driver of jobs and growth and may not create a strong exporting industry," said Samuel Sherraden, an economic analyst at the progressive New America Foundation. Peter Morici, a business professor at the University of Maryland, dismissed the green stimulus funding as having been "squandered" because "large grants to build green buildings don't generate many new jobs, except for a few architects." Although the "subsidies for windmills and solar panels created lots of jobs in China," they did not lead to strong job growth in America.[15]

Given the primacy that Obama placed on "green jobs," it was odd when the Bureau of Labor Statistics, which is responsible for developing and implementing the collection of new data on green jobs, placed a notice of solicitation of comments in the *Federal Register* in March 2010 (more than a year after the enactment of the stimulus) regarding the definition of a "green job." Billions of stimulus dollars had already been allocated for "green jobs," yet the Bureau's notice admitted there is no widely accepted standard definition of "green jobs" and hoped that reader suggestions could help the Bureau formulate a working definition. Incredibly, by the time of the notice, the Department of Labor had already publicly announced a number of purportedly successful "green jobs" initiatives: $100,000,000 in green jobs training through the stimulus, $150,000,000 in "Pathways Out of Poverty" training grants for green jobs, $190,000,000 in state energy sector partnership and training grants for green jobs. Thus, at the very same time the Department of Labor was doling out millions if not billions of dollars in taxpayer funds for "green jobs," they lacked a definition of what constituted a "green job."[16]

The confusion over "green jobs" raised the question of whether the federal government's scorekeeping regarding the stimulus program was even remotely accurate. Not surprisingly, there was much to suggest that reports detailing the "success" of the stimulus were anything but correct. Obama touted the website www.recovery.gov as the citizen's tool to track where and how money from the stimulus was being spent and the number of jobs it created. But many observers were perplexed when the website started to post data from the stimulus that showed how the funds were being spent in New Hampshire: $1,471,518 going to New Hampshire's 6th congressional district, $1,033,809 to its 4th congressional district and $124,774 to the 27th congressional district. In addition, according to recovery.gov, the New Hampshire congressional district "00" received $194,537,372 in stimulus funding and saw 2,893.9 jobs created. The problem with these figures is that none of these congressional districts actually exist. All told, various watchdog groups identified a whopping 440 phantom congressional districts mentioned, at one time or another, on recovery.gov.[17]

The stimulus statistics also included phantom zip codes. A New Mexico watchdog group identified a number of questionable claims from recovery.gov about stimulus spending and job creation in their state. The website claimed that the stimulus spent $373,874 in zip code 97052 (0 jobs created), $36,218 in zip code 87258 (5 jobs created), and $100,000 in zip code 86705 (0 jobs created). None of these zip codes correspond to a zip code in New Mexico—or in any other state.[18]

Many of the claims made by the government regarding stimulus-created jobs represented patent absurdities. In June 2009, the federal government purchased, using $1,047 of stimulus money, a riding lawnmower to cut the grass at a national cemetery in Fayetteville, Arkansas. Later, the recovery.gov website asserted that this particular purchase helped save or create 50 jobs—a claim that a spokesman for the Toro Company, the seller of the lawnmower, dismissed as false. An order of work boots (at a cost of $890) from a Kentucky shoe store was said to have created nine jobs, while a so-called "Basketball System Replacement," secured via a contract funded with $7,960 of stimulus money, was claimed to have produced three new jobs. The bureaucracy's unbelievable claims about stimulus jobs call into question whether any claims made by the government regarding jobs created—to say nothing of the much more elusive concept of jobs "saved"—by the stimulus have any credibility, and whether the impact of the huge spending bill will ever be able to be accurately measured.[19]

Unfortunately, the problems with the stimulus were not limited to shoddy accounting practices; ineffectiveness also permeated its implementation. The Social Security Administration, for example, sent stimulus payments of $250 to roughly 89,000 individuals who were either dead or in prison. Although approximately 41,000 of the erroneous payments were returned, the stimulus did not contain a provision that empowered the government to retrieve funds that had been mistakenly remitted to the dead and incarcerated, so the remaining payments might not be recovered.[20] Also disconcerting was the report from the City Controller of Los Angeles that the $111,000,000 of stimulus funds received by the city created or saved a mere 55 jobs. At $2,000,000 per job, this was hardly an effective use of taxpayer money, and the City Controller acknowledged that the government needed to do a "better job cutting the red tape and putting Angelenos back to work."[21]

Most disappointing of all, though, was the failure of the stimulus to jumpstart the economy through spending on infrastructure projects. In fact, it was this area of infrastructure projects that revealed Obama to be far from the all-knowledgeable, ultra-competent chief executive that supporters and awe-struck journalists had portrayed him to be during the campaign and the early days of his administration. Obama touted the infrastructure spending contained in the $814,000,000,000 stimulus proposal as a critical component of his strategy to jump start job creation. In an interview on *Meet the Press* during the presidential transition period, Obama asserted that, throughout the country, a large number of so-called "shovel-ready" projects were ready to get underway. "When I met with the governors all of them have projects that are shovel-ready, that are going to require us to get the money out the door, but they've already lined up the projects and they can make them work."[22] By pumping billions in taxpayer money into "shovel-ready" projects, Obama claimed that the stimulus would reinvigorate the economy and help stem the tide of private sector job losses, while, at the same time, making a number of internal improvements that were long overdue.

While this perhaps sounded good in theory, these efforts were repeatedly frustrated by bureaucratic hurdles, such as a union-backed provision that mandated wage levels for weatherization projects. In

Detroit, it took more than a year after the enactment of the stimulus to clear bureaucratic roadblocks before any stimulus-funded weatherization projects even got started; 18 months after the stimulus, less than one-third of homes targeted for weatherization with stimulus funds had been weatherized.[23] Also disconcerting was the fact that the vast majority of recipients of roughly $7,200,000,000 in stimulus grants for the expansion of high-speed internet services had not, by August of 2010, even started to lay cables. *The Wall Street Journal* reported that most of the recipients were "still busy with pre-construction work, such as environmental assessments, local approvals to attach fiber to utility poles, permits for rights of way and hiring subcontractors."[24] This is the antithesis of "shovel-ready." Not surprisingly, the promised wave of new private sector jobs never materialized.

In the face of the well-documented failure of the stimulus' infrastructure spending to provide an immediate boost to the economy, Obama made a stunning admission during an interview with a reporter for *The New York Times*. Looking back on the first two years of his presidency, he said that one of the "tactical lessons" that he learned was that "there's no such thing as shovel-ready projects" when it comes to public infrastructure spending.[25] As the economy continued to sputter into mid-2011, Obama even joked about the failure of the stimulus, remarking that "shovel-ready was not as shovel-ready as we expected."[26]

Prior to becoming president, Obama served eight years in the Illinois legislature and four years in the United States Senate; during this time, he apparently never had a moment to investigate whether it was feasible to rely on public works spending to provide short-term economic stimulus. Instead, he blindly put his faith in "shovel-ready" projects as a needed panacea for the sluggish economy without having any appreciation for the cumbersome bureaucratic and regulatory hurdles that such projects must surmount. He promised a new era of government accountability and competence, yet his signature economic initiative showcased the very type of government ineptitude that Americans have grown to detest but also to expect.

This ineptitude was brought into alarming focus during the attempted cleanup of the oil attacking the shoreline of America's Gulf Coast due to the Deepwater Horizon disaster. As the deepwater well could not readily be capped, the federal government took the lead in mitigating the effects of the ongoing spill. Rather than effectuate a swift, streamlined response, the government responded in a haphazard fashion, failing to break through copious red tape and to coordinate overlapping bureaucracies. This resulted in more environmental damage than would have occurred if the response had been competently executed.

During the months immediately after the spill, there was no clear and effective command structure instituted to combat the spill. "The information is not flowing," Senator Bill Nelson, a Democrat from Florida said. "The decisions are not timely. The resources are not produced. And as a result, you have a big mess, with no command and control." This lack of an effective command structure proved to be a major problem given that the spill response involved not just BP and the federal government, but also a number of state governments and local officials. When, for example, local parishes in Louisiana wanted to take action to prevent damage to their coast and wetlands, approval from the murky command structure could take weeks, even for a simple request. "You would throw it into the dark black hole and it might not ever come back," Ralph Mitchell, the public safety director for Terrebonne Parish, described his requests for shore-protecting boom.[27] This confusion outraged James Carville, a hyper-partisan Democratic political strategist and native of Louisiana, prompting him to rip the Obama administration for the government's inability to fight the spill. Carville admonished Obama that, "man, you got to get down here and take control of this and put somebody in charge of this thing and get this thing moving. We're about to die down here."[28]

Without a clear line of authority, the early cleanup effort became mired in red tape and paralyzed by bureaucracy. With the spill being so vast, the need for skimmers to clean up oil from the surface of the gulf was obvious. However, of the skimmers located in the United States, only a fraction of them were initially deployed to the Gulf of Mexico. "We want all the skimming vessels in the world deployed," Plaquemines Parish President Billy Nungesser said. "This is an oil spill bigger than anything we've ever seen. It's a national disaster. We're at war. If you were at war and in charge, would you deploy everything you had to win the war?" The problem stemmed from federal legal and regulatory hurdles that required oil spill cleanup vessels to be stationed in various parts of the country in the event of spills in those locations; in other words, these skimmers could not be sent to alleviate an actual, ongoing cataclysmic oil spill in the Gulf of Mexico because of the remote possibility of an oil spill elsewhere. On June 28, 2010, the U.S. Coast Guard and the Environmental Protection Agency finally issued a joint emergency temporary interim rule suspending certain federal regulations so that additional skimmers could relocate and respond to the Gulf oil disaster—but this was a full 70 days after the initial spill.

It proved to be equally cumbersome to enlist the assistance of foreign skimmers in the cleanup effort. *The New Orleans Times-Picayune* reported how the French oil spill response company, Ecoceane, volunteered a number of oil-collection boats but was rejected by BP and the Coast Guard—despite the fact that local officials habitually complained about the lack of vessels involved in the cleanup. The company's chief executive, Eric Vial, claimed that the major impediment was the Jones Act, a maritime law dating back to 1920 designed to promote American shipping interests by restricting the use of foreign vessels in American ports. "We could have sent boats earlier, but we wanted to make sure that if we sent our boats, they could be used in the U.S., because of the Jones Act," Vial said in an interview translated from French. The government claimed that Jones Act waivers were not required to use foreign ships to help combat the spill, yet Ecoceane ultimately sold nine company boats to a private contractor in Florida so that they would no longer be subject to the Jones Act and, hence, could be readily deployed to the Gulf of Mexico. Vial criticized the response to the crisis, saying that "whether it's BP or the U.S. government, they may have created too many administrative steps and barriers that are making the whole process much lengthier."[29]

Other regulatory burdens seemed unintelligible in light of the damage being caused by the gushing oil well. Shortly after the initial spill, the Dutch government offered additional technological support, in the form a so-called sweeping arm system that has proven effective in combating large oil spills, to both BP and the United States government. This offer, though, got bogged down in the bureaucracy and was not acted on for more than one month. *The Christian Science Monitor* noted that the delay stemmed from the fact that the Environmental Protection Agency (EPA) initially rejected the sweeping arm system based on EPA discharge regulations requiring that 99.9985 percent of returned water be oil-free—a sensible regulation when the object is to prevent clean water from being polluted but which makes no sense in the context of a massive oil spill. "'One size fits all' doesn't work for all oil spills. This is a monster," Bruce Johnson, professor emeritus of oceanic engineering at the United States Naval Academy said. "If you could suck up 80 percent of the oil and discharge 5 percent, you are still catching 75 percent, which is infinitely more than they are currently doing." That the EPA was not capable of immediately distinguishing between a catastrophic oil spill cleanup mission and run-of-the-mill pollution served to further highlight the bureaucratic ineptitude that plagued the federal response.[30]

For his part, President Obama accepted responsibility for the cleanup effort, yet seemed more interested in leveraging the oil spill to push a costly and unpopular cap and trade energy bill through Congress. In his first address to the nation from the Oval Office, Obama admonished his fellow citizens that "we can't afford not to change how we produce and use energy, because the long-term costs to our economy, our national security and our environment are far greater." Channeling White House Chief of Staff Rahm Emanuel, who said one should never let a crisis go to waste, Obama argued that the Deepwater Horizon disaster demonstrated the urgent need to increase the cost of carbon-based energy in an effort to force businesses and individuals to utilize hitherto more expensive and less efficient forms of "clean" energy. But this struck many as inappropriate given that the oil was still spewing into the Gulf of Mexico from the Deepwater Horizon well. "President Obama said today he is going to use the gulf disaster to immediately push a new energy bill through Congress," comedian Jay Leno observed. "I got an idea....How about first using the Gulf disaster to fix the Gulf disaster?"

****

A Gallup poll taken in September of 2010 found that an astounding 72% of Americans had a negative view of the federal government. The reason for this view is due to its inefficiency, size, and incompetence—the most common specific responses provided by poll respondents described the government as "too big," "confused," and "corrupt."[31] Gallup also found that most Americans think that the federal government has too much power and that government takes on too much.[32] Not surprisingly, the percentage of Americans who feel this way has increased since Barack Obama assumed the presidency. Though Obama sported an approval rating near 70% when he was inaugurated, by October of 2010 a startling 56% of Americans disapproved of his job performance.[33] Only 18% of Americans approved of the performance of the Congress.[34] The upshot of this is inescapable: Americans find the federal government to be massive, costly, cumbersome and ineffectual, and most blame the leading political practitioners in the age of Obama for its dismal performance.

The legislative malpractice and administrative incompetence that have characterized the age of Obama are likely major reasons for such views. Madison and Hamilton's belief that the "cool and deliberate sense of the community" should ultimately prevail in a free society has been scuttled in favor of a view that delights in rejecting, not merely the temporary fluctuations in public opinion properly eschewed by a representative's Burkean judgment, but also the enduring, clearly expressed public views of the people. Rather than effectively touching "the most sensible chords and put[ting] in motion the most active springs of the human heart" so as to "conciliate the respect and attachment of the community," the federal government habitually proved itself to be "ill executed," botching mundane tasks like defining a "green job" as well as major undertakings such as cleaning up oil in the Gulf of Mexico.

Some would say that such criticism fails to appreciate the difference between Madison's time and the current era, that governing complex systems like health care cannot be done short of gargantuan pieces of legislation, that many of the special deals involved in securing big laws represent the price of "getting things done," that the voters often do not know what's in their best interest, and that the litany of bureaucratic mistakes is nothing that wouldn't afflict any large organization. All of this, while fashionable in certain circles, is highly questionable, and rests on the same anti-Founding Fathers viewpoint that has characterized progressive thought for more than a century. These practices are, in fact, corrosive of the principles underlying the Constitution and, as Madison warned, "serve to poison the blessings of the liberty the Constitution was designed to protect."

The performance of Obama and his congressional allies represents a reformulation of the notion of self-government as understood by the Constitution's creators. In this configuration, the people are blindly governed by voluminous, unintelligible laws that a reasonable person cannot understand, the particular interests favored by the governing class are arbitrarily given preferential treatment, and everything is implemented by an all-encompassing yet serially incompetent federal establishment. Perhaps this is to be expected in the age of Obama, an age in which the federal government is hyper-active and policymakers seem unconcerned with traditional notions of limited government. Nevertheless, the purveyors of this dysfunctional form of constitutionalism have a serious James Madison problem.

The performance of the federal government has proven the rosy predictions regarding Obama's dexterity as a chief executive to be woefully off the mark. Obama ran against the incompetence displayed by George W. Bush in his response to the hurricane that battered the Gulf Coast, yet the environmental damage inflicted upon the same Gulf Coast by the Deepwater Horizon oil spill was made worse by the bumbling bureaucracy that Obama directs. He promised that the stimulus bill would be free of earmarks, but the $814,000,000,000 monstrosity that he signed into law contained a cornucopia of legislative pet projects wholly unrelated to economic growth. He also touted the stimulus as heralding increased economic growth due to "green jobs," though the Department of Labor could not define a "green job" and even some liberals acknowledged that such jobs—however defined—are not an effective means of economic stimulus. Perhaps most embarrassingly, he claimed that "shovel-ready" infrastructure projects funded by stimulus money would ignite private sector job creation, but then admitted that "there's no such thing as shovel-ready" when it comes to public works. It would be one thing if the stimulus proved to be an effective policy measure that ignited a recovery, but that certainly did not happen, though the shoddy scorekeeping makes it difficult to evaluate the true extent of its failure.

Most fair-minded observers recognized that the initial characterization of Obama as being practically overqualified for the presidency was mistaken, but many did not hold Obama accountable for his missteps, choosing instead to blame the "system." One lengthy piece in the left-leaning *Vanity Fair* magazine that took an inside look at the Obama White House wondered if our government is "dysfunctional" and "beyond repair?"[35] For their part, White House aides complained that the nation's political apparatus is "not on the level," and questioned whether it was even possible for a modern president to succeed.[36] This is akin to the Norwegian Nobel Peace Prize Committee blaming Obama's failures in foreign affairs on the dysfunction of modern international relations. After all, if someone possessing talents so prodigious that he has been driven to boredom cannot engineer a competent administration or extinguish legislative chicanery from the lawmaking process, then it *must* be the system that is at fault.

PART FIVE

"FEW AND DEFINED"

14

LIMITED AND ENUMERATED

Within a very short time after Barack Obama came to power, it became readily apparent that the former community organizer and University of Chicago law professor was resurrecting the era of big government, which had been pronounced dead by Democrat Bill Clinton in 1996. Less than sixty days into the Obama presidency, a headline in *U.S. News and World Report* declared that "Under President Obama, Big Government is Back." The new president seemed to be embarking on what David Leonhardt, the left-of-center economics writer from *The New York Times*, approvingly characterized as a "generational shift in how Washington operates," a flurry of federal activity that rivaled "any other since the New Deal in scope or ambition." The cover of *Newsweek* magazine even proclaimed that "We Are All Socialists Now."

The first budget Obama submitted to Congress represented the opening salvo in his campaign to embark on a new age of federal government activism, which he claimed was needed to "transform" the American economy in the 21st century. Justifying his support for an expanded government geared toward remaking large portions of American society, Obama asserted that "at this particular moment, government must lead the way"—an endorsement of wholesale central planning that, at least since the Reagan Revolution, had hitherto been unthinkable. The boldness of Obama's prescriptions for greater federal involvement in education, energy and health care (as well as the higher taxes needed to fund these ambitions) left many liberal journalists and talking heads enthusiastic about the new president's designs to "sweep away" the last vestiges of "Reagan ideas."[1]

Although few considered this sprint towards a more powerful and pervasive federal government to be anything other than what it was, Obama attempted to deny the obvious. In his Inaugural Address, he tried to obscure the fact that his policy agenda would expand the power and scope of the federal establishment, characteristically implying that criticisms of his policies for embracing big government were focused on what he regarded as the tired debates of the past. "The question we ask today," he exclaimed, "is not whether government is too big or too small, but whether it works." Yet, the question that he said deserved to be posed—whether government "helps families find jobs at a decent wage, care they can afford, a retirement that is dignified"—was constructed in such a way that the answer could only lead to extensive federal involvement in everyday life.[2]

In his first address to a joint session of Congress in February 2009, he pitched a flurry of new initiatives that required increased federal government activism, but claimed he was doing so "not because I believe in bigger government. I don't. Not because I'm not mindful of the massive debt we've inherited. I am."[3] And when the federal government took the leading role in determining the fate of two major but debt-laden U.S. auto companies, General Motors and Chrysler, Obama feigned disinterest in having the government so intimately involved in managing private industry. "I don't want to run auto companies, and I don't want to run banks," Obama told journalists during an April 2009 press conference. "I've got two wars I've got to run already. I've got more than enough to do."[4]

But Obama did not focus the first year of his presidency on conducting the wars in Iraq and Afghanistan. He did not even make a decision on an Afghanistan strategy until the end of 2009, despite repeated protestations as a candidate that George W. Bush was neglecting what he considered to be a necessary war. Instead, he devoted his efforts to engineering a transmogrification of the nation's health care system, which vastly increased government's power. Not only did the Afghanistan conflict not preoccupy Obama, but, incredibly, he even tailored his Afghanistan strategy in a way that best helped with the passage of ObamaCare. *The New York Times* quoted one Obama adviser as saying that "our Afghan policy was focused as much as anything on domestic politics. [Obama] would not risk losing the moderate to centrist Democrats in the middle of health insurance reform and he viewed that legislation as the make-or-break legislation for his administration."[5]

Though elected in large part due to voter backlash stemming from the financial crisis that erupted in the midst of the general election campaign, Obama employed his political power, which the commanding Democratic majorities in Congress buoyed, in service of the long-standing legislative wish lists of liberal interest groups and left-of-center politicians. During the postelection transition period, incoming White House Chief of Staff Rahm Emanuel foreshadowed the path that the new administration would take when he proclaimed that "you never want a serious crisis to go to waste." That is, Emanuel said, the economic crisis "provides the opportunity for us to do things that you could not do before." Seen in this light, Obama's assertion that his preoccupation with the nation's military conflicts made him lack any interest in wielding government power over a vast swath of the domestic American economy rings utterly hollow.

From forcing individuals to buy health insurance to firing the chief executive officer of General Motors, Obama expanded the authority of the federal government into vast swaths of American life. It was this avalanche of big government policies that served as the catalyst for the tea party-inspired political opposition to Obama and his allies in Congress. These citizens were driven to activism because they saw government expanding beyond traditional constitutional limitations, rendering explicit constitutional prohibitions, like the Tenth Amendment, a dead letter.

Perhaps not surprisingly, some of Obama's allies saw this opposition as intellectually perplexing. Rep. Jan Schakowsky, an Illinois Democrat, ridiculed those who "quote from the Constitution" and proclaim "that government's powers are derived from the consent of the governed." Such foolish machinations regarding limited government are, Schakowsky scoffed, akin to wild conspiracy theories; invoking, by analogy, those who irrationally claim that the September 11 attacks were perpetrated by the U.S. Government, Schakowsky characterized those who "embrace the tenth amendment" as being "tenthers."[6] Schakowsky was incredulous that the people had the temerity to question the political designs of the ruling class, especially by citing purportedly antiquated constitutional doctrines like federalism. Whereas Obama tried to deny that he was an apostle of big government, Schakowsky tried to deny that, even from a constitutional perspective, unconstrained government was in any way remarkable. However, there is what James Madison called a "host of proofs" that, when they debated and wrote the Constitution, the Framers possessed the very concerns regarding expansive government that Schakowsky dismissed as irrational. The Founding Fathers were the original "tenthers."

Indeed, it is an understatement of not inconsiderable proportions to say that James Madison was of a different mind than Rep. Schakowsky regarding the need to have constitutional limitations on the authority of the federal government. To Madison, the power of the federal government was derived solely from the consent of the governed, and the government's authority was precisely limited to those enumerated powers granted to it by the people via the Constitution. Writing in *The Federalist* No. 22, Madison recommended the ratification of the Constitution because "the fabric of the American empire ought to rest on the solid basis of THE CONSENT OF THE PEOPLE," who are the "pure, original fountain of all legitimate authority."

The Articles of Confederation were never adopted by the American people, but had been ratified by state legislatures, and Madison saw this as undermining the legitimacy of the Articles. Since the Constitution possessed no inherent authority beyond those powers delegated to it by the people, its authority needed to be legitimized in conventions convened specifically for the purpose of considering the ratification of the Constitution.

Unlike Schakowsky, Madison understood that a government based on popular consent implied limitations on the power and scope of the government, and he considered the limited nature of the Constitution to be one of its defining aspects. In *The Federalist* No. 45, he famously characterized the government created by the Constitution as one of limited and enumerated powers: "The powers delegated by the proposed Constitution to the federal government are few and defined. Those which are to remain in the State governments are numerous and indefinite."

The federal government's powers related to big-picture issues like "war, peace, negotiation and foreign commerce," for which federal taxes "will, for the most part, be connected." In contrast, the powers reserved by the people to themselves and their state governments "will extend to all the objects which, in the ordinary course of affairs, concern the lives, liberties, and properties of the people, and the internal order, improvement, and prosperity of the State."[7] The constitutional design was emphatically a federal system, which Madison considered to be a "double security" for the rights of the people.

Framers like Madison placed a premium on the protection of individual liberty, and thus understood that government power needed to be carefully circumscribed, lest it be allowed to erode the freedom of the people. At the same time, the mere fact that the delegates decided to meet in Philadelphia demonstrated the necessity of creating a new federal government (the delegates were charged with *revising* the Articles of Confederation, but they quickly moved to scrap the Articles and begin anew) that contained sufficient powers to discharge the various functions—from defending against foreign threats and regulating interstate commerce to honoring war debts and raising revenue—that the Articles of Confederation had proven incapable of fulfilling. The key task was to construct a government that facilitated these necessary functions while, at the same time, remaining constitutionally limited to such functions.

To this end, the Constitution did not create a government with a roving authority to legislate in every aspect of American life; it empowered the federal government to perform key tasks but left most issues to the people and to the states. "If the new Constitution be examined with accuracy and candor," Madison explained in *The Federalist* No. 45, "it will be found that the change which it proposes consists much less in the addition of new powers to the Union, than in the invigoration of its original powers."[8]

Publius stressed throughout *The Federalist Papers* that the Constitution created a government of limited and enumerated powers, and the nation's First Congress reaffirmed this basic principle when it passed the Tenth Amendment: "The powers not delegated to the United States by the Constitution, nor prohibited by it to the States, are reserved to the States respectively, or to the people." The Tenth Amendment was not something that the creators of the Constitution deemed necessary to include in the original document because it simply confirmed what they already knew to be true: the Constitution created a government possessing only limited, explicitly specified powers.

It was this notion of government containing limited and enumerated powers that counseled the delegates *against* including a bill of rights in the original Constitution. The lack of a bill of rights was one of the most potent arguments advanced against the Constitution by Anti-Federalists, who worried that the new federal government lacked sufficient safeguards for individual liberty. Alexander Hamilton responded to these critics by invoking the limited nature of the Constitution: while such bills of rights were typically "abridgments of prerogative in favor of privilege" regarding kings and their subjects, a "minute detail of particular rights is certainly far less applicable to a Constitution like that under consideration, which is merely intended to regulate the general political interests of the nation, than to a constitution which has the regulation of every species of personal and private concerns." For Hamilton, not only were bills of rights "unnecessary in the proposed Constitution," they "would even be dangerous" because they "contain various exceptions to powers which are not granted," thereby providing "a colorable pretext" for government to claim more authority than which was actually granted to it by the people.[9]

Hamilton used the example of the "liberty of the press" to illuminate his limited government argument. The Constitution contained no enumerated power that permitted federal regulation of the press, so an affirmative statement that the government cannot restrain the "liberty of the press" served to "furnish, to men disposed to usurp, a plausible pretense for claiming that power." In other words, the creation of a protection for press freedom created a "clear implication that a power to prescribe proper regulations concerning it was intended to be vested in the national government," which was flatly untrue.

Hamilton described this as creating "numerous handles which would be given to the doctrine of constructive powers." While a bill of rights may prevent the government from invading certain specific objects, these prohibitions provide a pretext for legislators to act in areas that, while not in conflict with provisions of the bill of rights, are beyond the scope of the government's enumerated powers. Thus, the price for the protection of certain rights is expanded government power beyond the objects enumerated in the Constitution, which was inconsistent with the intent of the Framers and the structure of the Constitution.[10]

Hamilton was somewhat annoyed by the protestations against the Constitution based on its lack of a bill of rights. For one thing, it was not necessarily true, as the original Constitution contained a number of restrictions on government's power, such as prohibitions against bills of attainder, ex post facto laws, and titles of nobility, as well as affirmative protection for certain rights, such as the right to a trial by jury in criminal cases. Perhaps even more significantly, the primary purpose of the Constitution was the protection of individual liberty. "The truth is, after all the declamations we have heard," Hamilton noted, "that the Constitution is itself, in every rational sense, and to every useful purpose, a bill of rights."[11]

The Constitution was designed to instill the federal government with enough authority to fulfill those necessary functions that the incompetent Articles failed to discharge; such incompetence enhanced the prospect of the new nation succumbing to a liberty-destroying anarchy, which was anathema to the Founders, particularly Hamilton. At the same time, the Constitution was also designed to set limits on that authority and to do so in such a way that its internal configuration, such as the separation of powers and the numerous blocking mechanisms possessed by each branch, prevented the erosion of individual liberty by the federal establishment.

To help engineer the ratification of the Constitution, Federalists like James Madison agreed that the addition of a bill of rights would be one of the first orders of business of the new government. Today, it is almost unthinkable that the Constitution did not contain the Bill of Rights when it was produced by the Constitutional Convention. It is, after all, the Bill of Rights, and not the structural mechanisms contained in the document, that most Americans consider to be the Constitution's primary protections for individual liberty. Modern observers almost uniformly side with the Anti-Federalists who demanded the inclusion of a bill of rights in the Constitution over those, like Hamilton, would deemed a bill of rights unnecessary in a government of limited and enumerated powers.

Though we can never know for sure the extent to which the Bill of Rights has facilitated the expansion of the power of the federal government beyond those powers enumerated in the Constitution, the spectacle of modern politicians publicly confessing a desire to shut down news organizations (the politician was West Virginia Senator Jay Rockefeller and he specifically named the Fox News Channel) demonstrates the prescience of the Anti-Federalists. In other words, even assuming, as Hamilton argued, that the identification of certain rights has provided "numerous handles" with which to augment federal power beyond its proper scope, the protections in the Bill of Rights represent such indispensable bulwarks against the infringement of fundamental, God-given rights that the absence of such protections would expose the liberty of the American people to innumerable dangers. That Hamilton was mistaken about the need for a bill of rights should not, though, obscure the power of his analysis regarding the limited nature of the Constitution. He would not have had *any* basis to argue against the addition of a bill of rights were it not for the fact that the Constitution emphatically and unequivocally created a government whose powers were few, defined and limited.

15

OBAMA AND THE DEMISE OF LIMITED GOVERNMENT

As a presidential candidate, Barack Obama downplayed the idea that he was a big government liberal eager to remake the nation's health care system in a way that significantly expanded government's power and influence. Obama even ran television ads that positioned his health care plan as a reasonable alternative to what he considered the "extreme" position of a government-run health care system requiring higher taxes. As for the question of whether the federal government should mandate that individuals purchase and maintain health insurance, Obama flatly rejected the idea, and he ridiculed Hillary Clinton for advocating an individual mandate. "If a mandate was the solution," Obama stated in an interview on CNN, "we could try that to solve homelessness by mandating that everybody buy a house."[1] During a debate against Clinton, Obama also cited the experience of Massachusetts, which required its citizens to purchase health insurance, as demonstrating that an individual mandate did not work—and even, he argued, left some people "worse off."

But what *candidate* Obama dismissed as an extreme big government health care overhaul that high-handedly forced people to buy coverage, *President* Obama embraced as essential to the expansion of coverage, the curtailment of increases in insurance premiums, and (incredibly) the reduction of the budget deficit. As he tried to do during a speech to a joint session of Congress in 2009, Obama characteristically attempted to portray his efforts to remake the nation's health care system as a sensible middle ground between "a single-payer system like Canada's, where we would severely restrict the private insurance market and have the government provide coverage for everyone" and "end[ing]the employer-based system and leav[ing] individuals to buy health insurance on their own."[2] Nevertheless, the final product produced by members of Congress, signed by Obama, and hailed by both as an achievement of historic proportions cannot be characterized as anything less than a vast expansion of the federal government: the legislation spanned more than 2,000 pages, created more than 100 new federal bureaucracies, and carried a price tag of more than $1,000,000,000,000.[3]

The provision mandating Americans to purchase private health insurance, which is identical to the provision that Obama criticized during the presidential campaign, is unprecedented in the nation's history. Though the specter of the federal government mandating that individual citizens purchase a product from a private company as a condition of citizenship struck many as a troublesome, and constitutionally problematic, expansion of the federal government's power, most supporters of the overhaul dismissed such concerns out of hand.

Then-House Speaker Nancy Pelosi reacted incredulously when a reporter asked her to identify the source of authority in the Constitution that empowered Congress to force individuals to buy private health insurance, wondering whether the reporter was seriously questioning her authority to regulate even the inactivity of the American people. Pelosi's San Francisco Bay area colleague Pete Stark, an abrasive congressman with hard-left views, brushed off criticism from his constituents that the federal government was going too far; the federal government, he explained, "can do most anything in this country."[4] Senator Mark Warner, a Virginia Democrat, suggested that the health care overhaul did not require a firm basis in the Constitution: "there is no place in the Constitution that talks about you ought to have a right to get a telephone," Warner told a skeptical constituent, "but we have made those choices as a country over the years."[5]

Some supporters of the individual mandate acknowledged the need to justify it on both policy and constitutional grounds. At a town hall meeting in which he received a number of critical questions from constituents regarding the constitutionality of the pending health care bill, Senator Ben Cardin, a Democrat from Maryland, asserted that "Congress has the power to legislate for the general welfare of the United States," and that a federal overhaul of the health care system, including the individual mandate, fit squarely within this purported grant of constitutional authority.[6] Under Cardin's view, Congress has the authority to legislate in virtually any area so long as it does so to promote what it deems to be the "general welfare." As the concept of the "general welfare" is inherently nebulous and insusceptible of principled application, the implication of the Cardin theory of legislative power is that the federal government has no real limitations on its power beyond those contained in the Bill of Rights. It is a government with a general grant of power subject to certain enumerated exceptions rather than a government of purely enumerated powers.

This theory is at variance with the text, history and structure of the Constitution, and was specifically rejected by Constitution creators such as James Madison. The Constitution contains no blanket power that permits Congress to legislate in service of what it deems the "general welfare," which is a phrase that appears in the Constitution's Preamble ("we the People of the United States, in Order to form a more perfect Union, establish Justice, insure domestic Tranquility, provide for the common defence, promote the general Welfare....") and in Article I, Section 8 ("The Congress shall have the Power to lay and collect Taxes, Duties, Imposts, and Excises, to pay the Debts and provide for the common Defence and general Welfare of the United States....").

The Preamble does not grant authority to any institution established by the Constitution but, instead, merely explains why the people are delegating certain powers to the federal government in the articles that follow. The mention of the "general welfare" in Article I, Section 8 can more plausibly be said to invest Congress with broad authority to legislate in service of what it considers the "general welfare," since Article I, Section 8 is the section of the Constitution that vests affirmative legislative powers in the Congress. Nevertheless, such an interpretation is misguided; rather than create an unlimited bastion of government power, the "general welfare" clause qualifies the taxing and spending powers specifically identified in that same clause. Thus, Congress has the power to lay and collect taxes, but can only do so to the extent that such taxes support the "general welfare."

This is, at any rate, the explanation that James Madison offered when he described the powers that flow from the "general welfare" clause. As Madison recounted in *The Federalist* No. 41, opponents of the Constitution criticized the "general welfare" language on the grounds that it "amounts to an unlimited commission to exercise every power which may be alleged to be necessary for the…general welfare." He dismissed the complaint as resting on a fanciful interpretation that is inconsistent with the structure of the Constitution, as there would be little reason to enumerate certain powers if they were by definition included in a freestanding power to legislate in support of the general welfare. "Nothing is more natural nor common," Madison explained, "than first to use a general phrase, and then to explain and qualify it by a recital of particulars."[7]

Later, in a letter to James Robertson, he explained that he "always regarded [the words 'general welfare'] as qualified by the detail powers connected with them. To take them in a literal and unlimited sense would be a metamorphosis of the Constitution into a character which there is a host of proofs was not contemplated by its creators."[8] As Madison explained to Edmund Pendleton, if "Congress can do whatever in their discretion can be done by money, and will promote the General Welfare, the Government is no longer a limited one, possessing enumerated powers, but an indefinite one subject to particular exceptions."[9] Those politicians that see Congress as having unlimited power to legislate in support of the general welfare (and thus sufficient authority to force citizens to purchase a product) act in direct defiance of the interpretation of the "general welfare" clause, to say nothing about the overall philosophy of limited government, articulated by Madison during and after the debates concerning the creation and ratification of the Constitution.

Other supporters of the health care mandate tried to draw an analogy with the requirements to carry car insurance that state governments have imposed on their citizens. In an article in *The Washington Post* confidently declaring that "Like Car Insurance, Health Coverage May Be Mandated," reporter Cici Connolly detailed how, under an Obama-style health care overhaul, "the medical system of the future would put responsibility for health coverage first and foremost on every adult" in the same way that drivers are required to carry automobile insurance. She observed how "it is striking that such a wide and diverse coalition has formed around the individual mandate," as "labor unions, economists, the medical industry, big business, some prominent Republicans and Obama all support the requirement," which, Connolly asserted, "has its roots in the conservative philosophy of self-reliance." Connolly's article, though, did not grapple with any constitutional objections to the individual mandate. The fact that, in her view, such a "wide and diverse coalition" supported the mandate, and the fact that a similar mandate had already been enacted in Massachusetts several years earlier, meant that the prospect for an individual mandate was limited by the political will of elected officials, but not by the limited nature of the Constitution.[10]

If one takes the limited nature of the Constitution seriously, critical distinctions between a state mandate to carry car insurance and a federal requirement to purchase health insurance are readily apparent. For one thing, as many critics of the individual mandate correctly pointed out, no state requires its citizens to buy car insurance based simply on existing within the borders of the state. Instead, insurance is mandated as a condition of driving an automobile on public roads within state borders; since driving is a privilege that citizens are free to refrain from exercising, there is a ready avenue to avoid the forced maintenance of car insurance. Additionally, such insurance is mandated to protect not the driver but *other* motorists; states generally do not require motorists to carry insurance that covers damage to their own person or automobile.

More importantly, if less discussed during the high tide of the health care debate, car insurance mandates are enacted and enforced by state governments, while the health care individual mandate is a federal requirement. Since the states have residual authority—Madison described their powers as "numerous and indefinite"—they necessarily have a broader scope of regulatory authority, an authority that can reach a number of issues pertaining to the health, safety and welfare of the people. In contrast, the federal government, both in its basic structure and as reaffirmed by the Tenth Amendment, contains no reserved powers; it is solely a creation of the powers specifically delegated by the people and enumerated in the Constitution. Putting aside the differences between car insurance and health insurance, the mere fact that a state government can require a citizen to purchase insurance does not mean that the federal government can do the same thing, especially in the absence of a power enumerated in the Constitution.

This was self-evident to the creators of the Constitution, yet it seemed to be completely lost on many of the politicians and journalists eager for the enactment of a federal overhaul of the health care system. A case in point was the constant reference to the health care law instituted by Massachusetts in 2006, which contained a provision mandating that Massachusetts citizens carry health insurance. For a reporter like Cici Connolly, the "Massachusetts experience with an individual mandate has provided a model" for supporters of a federal mandate to emulate, and she noted that the mandate seemed to be popular in the Bay State. "I don't see people revolting over having to have a driver's license or insurance to drive a car," Connolly quoted MIT economist Jonathan Gruber, who helped design the Massachusetts law, as saying. "And we haven't seen it with the mandate."[11]

To supporters of Obama-style federal health care reform, the fact that the Massachusetts health care bill was signed into law by Governor Mitt Romney, a Republican, further demonstrated that an individual mandate at the federal level was unobjectionable—as if a Republican endorsement of a state mandate immunized an analogous initiative from federal constitutional infirmity. Leaving aside the wisdom of an individual mandate on the state level (which is, undeniably, a substantial incursion on individual liberty), one could believe that a state may force its citizens to buy a particular type of health insurance and, at the same time, maintain that the federal government may do no such thing. Yet, this basic Madisonian premise seemed to be consistently overlooked in the yearlong debate over ObamaCare.

Some considered the federal individual mandate to be an unexceptional exercise of federal authority, and tried to analogize it to federal mandates used in other contexts. Senator Jack Reed, a Rhode Island Democrat, was asked by a reporter what provision of the Constitution permitted Congress to force citizens to buy health insurance. "Let me see," Reed replied. "I would have to check the specific sections. So, I'll have to get back to you on the specific section. But it is not unusual that the Congress has required individuals to do things, like sign up for the draft."[12] At first blush, Reed makes a sensible point: if Congress has the power to draft an otherwise unwilling individual and send that person to fight, and possibly die in a war, why could it not force that same individual to buy a product, which represents a far less potent use of federal power?

The Constitution provides the answer. On the one hand, the Constitution contains no obvious enumerated power that permits Congress to mandate the purchase of a product, as even a broad interpretation of the Article I power to "regulate Commerce…among the several States" implies regulation of affirmative economic activity of some kind, not merely inactivity. On the other hand, Article I, Section 8 of the Constitution contains an explicit grant of authority to Congress to "raise and support Armies"; in *Arver v. United States*, the Supreme Court sensibly upheld (against constitutional challenge from draftees in World War I) the power of Congress to institute a draft under this enumerated power. It thus cannot be said that because the Constitution vests Congress with certain potent powers, like the power to raise armies, it also must allow Congress to force citizens to take other actions, such as buying a product, that are arguably less intrusive but not firmly grounded in any Article I power.

Other proponents of the mandate, such as MSNBC's Chris Matthews, even tried to analogize the federal health care mandate to the Civil Rights Act of 1964, which prohibited racial segregation in "public accommodations," such as restaurants and hotels. Such an attack represented a delicious opportunity for left-leaning elites like Matthews, as it provided a vehicle for attacking opposition to the mandate while also insinuating that opponents of ObamaCare were bigots. Congress passed the Civil Rights Act pursuant to the Commerce Clause, and Matthews tried to liken the law's mandate to serve all customers regardless of race to ObamaCare's mandate that all individuals purchase health insurance in the private market. If Congress can force a restaurant owner to serve black customers, Matthews asked, then why can't it force someone to purchase health insurance?

The comparison was inapposite because the Civil Rights Act did not force anybody to participate in commerce; it merely placed a condition on those who already made the decision to operate a commercial establishment. Those who did not want to operate, say, a hotel in the manner that Congress decreed were free to exit the business altogether. But the individual who objects to the mandate to purchase health insurance has no similar recourse; that person cannot readily cease the offending activity because the offending behavior is simply existing within the United States without maintaining the government-mandated insurance coverage.

It is clear that many members of Congress were either confused or indifferent about the constitutional basis for the individual mandate, but what about Obama? Although he lambasted Hillary Clinton for championing a mandate during the presidential primaries, he defended it as president on Commerce Clause grounds: forcing citizens to maintain coverage would affect interstate commerce because it would purportedly contribute to lowering insurance premiums.

Obama was adamant that the mandate and the monetary penalty imposed against those who fail to purchase coverage was not a tax but a regulation, which allowed him to insist that he was not reneging on the central promise of his campaign; namely, that individuals earning less than $250,000 per year would see no tax increase of any kind. Obama said he "absolutely" rejected the notion that the mandate was a tax, and those who tried to characterize it as a tax were taking a position that was not simply wrong, but also illegitimate. Yet, when a number of states brought a constitutional challenge against the individual mandate following the enactment of the federal overhaul, the Obama administration supplemented the Commerce Clause justification with the argument that the mandate fell within the power of Congress to lay and collect taxes—a power that is generally regarded as broader than the power to regulate interstate commerce.

Given his adamant position that the mandate was not a tax, this was embarrassing for Obama, and it is unlikely that the argument would have been advanced unless there existed some apprehension about whether the power of Congress to regulate interstate commerce represented sufficient authority to force someone, otherwise intrastate and inactive, to engage in a commercial transaction. No Congress has ever forced citizens to buy a commercial product as a requirement of citizenship, and no court has ever upheld such an expansive interpretation of the Commerce Clause. It is understandable why Obama would want to advance a less novel argument in favor of his most cherished legislative achievement.

The ultimate constitutional fate of the individual mandate will have profound implications for the future of limited government. If the federal government establishes its authority to regulate even the inactivity of the American people simply because such inactivity can affect the health insurance market, then no discernible limitation on the regulatory power of the federal government will exist. After all, on a daily basis, virtually *every* decision that an individual makes, such as deciding what to eat or choosing not to exercise, influences an individual's health. Under attenuated reasoning similar to that used to justify the mandate, it can easily be argued that such decisions tangentially affect the health insurance market and the health care system. Surely, if the federal government mandated that all citizens under the age of 50 run five miles and consume 4 cups of fruits and vegetables per day, the health of the citizenry would be enhanced, thereby putting a downward pressure on health insurance rates, which affect interstate commerce.

That such a regulation seems preposterous is no justification for the individual mandate. When Madison defined the federal government as one with "few and defined" powers, he was articulating constitutional limitations that presupposed that some elected officials would attempt to expand government's power beyond its intended scope. With this in mind, for all the negative aspects of ObamaCare the proliferation of bureaucracy, the added stress on an already hemorrhaging federal budget deficit and the adverse effect on patient care, it is the individual mandate that is the most pernicious.

The Constitution's Commerce Clause has already been expanded to cover conduct beyond what the Framers understood to be the outer limits of the power. For more than half a century, Congress, buoyed by a compliant judiciary, has asserted the authority to regulate *any* economic activity, including purely local, intrastate activity, on the theory that the cumulative effect of such activity "substantially affects" interstate commerce, thereby exposing it to federal supervision. However, the regulation of *in*activity represents an assertion of power even more far-reaching in scope. If it can be said that a refusal to buy a commercial product is subject to congressional regulation because such inactivity exerts a substantial effect on interstate commerce, then the federal government will have a residual police power, enabling it to regulate in any area not in conflict with the Bill of Rights and other explicit constitutional prohibitions. The limited Constitution will have finally fallen prey to what James Madison called "the gradual innovations of an unlimited government," which will be a severe blow for individual liberty.

16

First, Do No Harm

Winston Churchill once remarked that democracy was the worst form of government—except for all of the others that have been tried. James Madison and his brethren were of a similar mind with respect to the republican form of government that they established on the American continent. They believed that a government based on popular consent was the best hope for mankind, but they knew that a popularly elected government that lacked structural safeguards and limits on its power was not desirable. As Madison noted in *The Federalist* No. 48, "an *elective despotism* was not the government we fought for."[1] The American Revolution was not fought to perpetuate particular municipal establishments, but instead so that the "people of America should enjoy peace, liberty and safety," and Madison and his fellow Convention delegates crafted the Constitution with the expectation that it would provide a solid foundation from which their compatriots could pursue happiness in a free society. At the same time, Madison was under no illusion about the limits of positive good that government could be expected to produce and was fully cognizant of the dangers that concentrated government power posed to individual liberty. The government needed to serve important functions but also be carefully limited in its scope, rendering it incapable of injecting itself into every aspect of American life.

Madison struck this limited government chord in *The Federalist* No. 55, where he defended the House of Representatives as a "safe depository for a limited and well-guarded power of legislating for the United States." In the course of his defense, as was common for political writers of the period, Madison referenced the common experience of the American Revolution to buttress his argument in favor of the House, highlighting the structure and operation of the Continental Congress, the national legislature during the revolt against the British. Writing about the representatives of the Continental Congress, Madison remarked that during "the whole course of the war they had the fate of their country more in their hands than it is to be hoped will ever be the case with our future representatives."[2]

Constitution creators like Madison wanted the new government to have the power to discharge the functions necessary for maintaining an ordered, constitutional republic that protected individual liberty. But they also demanded that government be limited such that it could not exert an all-encompassing influence on the lives of the American people. Though no doubt having its place, politics in the nation's capital should not, once a stable constitutional foundation is established, be the determining factor in the success or failure of America or its citizens. Madison's hope that the proposed federal Congress would never hold the fate of the nation in its hands contains an underlying hostility to the notion of far-reaching centralized government planning, a hostility that is in direct conflict with a modern Congress that churns out individual pieces of legislation running thousands of pages and affecting an enormous amount of personal behavior with impunity.

Within a short time after Obama assumed office, the idea that the Constitution's creators intended to construct a limited government that reserved most issues to the people and the states would have struck an observer unfamiliar with the Constitution's foundations as unintelligible. In the age of Obama, federal government activism is regarded as *the* indispensable ingredient in American success, and the primary vehicle through which economic prosperity is achieved. Vice President Joe Biden went so far as to claim that "every single great idea that has marked the 21st century, the 20th century, and the 19th century has required government vision and government incentive."[3] Massachusetts Congressman Barney Frank flatly acknowledged that "we are trying on every front to increase the role of government."[4]

As Madison noted in *The Federalist*, the Framers did not want an intrusive federal government capable of exercising a pervasive negative influence on the livelihood of its citizens. They wanted, instead, a Hippocratic government that would do no harm. As a candidate, Obama said that "our government should work for us, not against us. It should help us, not hurt us."[5] This seemed to ally Obama with Madison, and during the debate over the health care bill, Obama repeatedly stressed that his efforts to overhaul the health care system would not negatively affect those who were content with their health care, flatly declaring that "if you like your plan, you can keep your plan."

Yet, as details of the new law began to be digested by employers, it became clear that the new legislative behemoth set in motion a number of major changes that jeopardized the current employer-based plans of millions of Americans. The law requires that all but the smallest businesses provide health insurance to their employees or pay an annual fine of $2,000 for each employee; the uncharitable "grandfather" regulations (which are, not incidentally, far more favorable for union health plans) means that this fine will, in most instances, be less expensive than the cost of maintaining health plans made more expensive due to the cornucopia of new federal mandates.

Caterpillar, a large manufacturer of construction equipment, estimated that it could reduce its health care costs by 70% if it terminated its employee health plans and paid the federal penalty; communications giant AT&T said it would be liable for $600,000,000 in federal fines if it decided to discontinue insuring its employees—a huge savings from the $2,400,000,000 billion price tag of providing health plans under ObamaCare mandates.[6] Though the Obama administration began issuing "waivers" to large companies so that they would retain their employee health plans, the law's onerous burdens, if enforced, will lead to individuals losing their health plans through no fault of their own.

ObamaCare was also hailed as a boon for children since it contained a provision that barred health insurers from denying coverage to children with preexisting health conditions. Obama said his health law would "end the worst practices of insurance companies" because "insurance companies will be banned forever from denying coverage to children with preexisting conditions."[7] Then-House Speaker Nancy Pelosi beamed that families were ecstatic that "no longer will their children be denied coverage because they have a pre-existing condition." Senator Tom Harkin said that the child coverage "guarantees are not a promise. They are part of the law right now. And we are not going to let them take it away from the American people."

Though this sounded noble, the law had the effect of undermining insurance coverage for children. By mandating that insurers take on more risk than is economically justifiable, ObamaCare forced insurers either to absorb financial losses or else increase premiums for all policies. As constructed, the law provided an incentive for parents to refrain from purchasing coverage until their child developed an illness, thereby skewing the pool of potential policyholders towards those children requiring the most expensive medical treatment.[8]

Because of this, just as the new child insurance mandates were set to take effect, a number of major health insurers decided to cease offering child-only plans rather than comply with the mandates. Of course, the law was designed to enhance access to health insurance policies for children with preexisting conditions, which, according to the Department of Health and Human Services, represented between 31,000 and 72,000 children—a small fraction of children with preexisting conditions, much less children as a whole.[9] That a number of insurers fled the market rather than comply with ObamaCare is a testament that the law failed to deliver as advertised with respect to preexisting conditions. Perhaps more troubling, the law also reduced access to affordable child-only policies for the overwhelming majority of children, thereby doing affirmative harm to a large number of families and children despite its good intentions.

Perhaps it should not be a surprise that the law demonstrated such perverse effects so soon after its enactment. Government officials lack the competence to centrally plan one-sixth of the American economy without generating a litany of unintended consequences. What is more, the actual bill that passed was not originally intended to become law. It was only when Massachusetts elected Republican Scott Brown in a special election for the U.S. Senate seat vacated by the death of Ted Kennedy that the Democrats knew that they would not be able to muster 60 votes in the Senate for a Nancy Pelosi-style health care bill. Notwithstanding its convoluted design, the Senate bill, which received 60 votes in the Senate before Brown's election, was the only plausible means by which a health care overhaul could be implemented. It became ObamaCare due to dire political necessity.

It is noteworthy that the bill did not include a provision allowing Americans to purchase health insurance across state lines, which could lower insurance rates through enhanced competition. While Obama justified the bill as a way to reduce insurance premiums, his refusal to entertain more consumer choice in health care is telling evidence that the true goal of ObamaCare was less about cost of insurance premiums than about government control of health care, and, by extension, individuals. Many understood that this progressive fantasy would not happen overnight. According to Congressman John Dingell, "it takes a long time to do the necessary administrative steps that have to be taken to put the legislation together to control the people."[10] But there can be no mistake that expanded government control of individuals was an animating principle of the ObamaCare legislation.

In fact, by enacting a 2,000-plus page bill that created more than 100 new bureaucracies, Obama was doing more than any president in 50 years to expand the power, reach and size of the federal government. From a progressive perspective, ObamaCare's primary achievement was to establish the federal government as the most potent force in American health care, thereby reducing private health care companies to quasi-public utilities, and laying the foundation for the creation of a purely government-run, Canadian-style health care system by the next generation of progressive "reformers."

Led by ObamaCare, Obama implemented a number of initiatives that increased Government's supervisory control over the American economy. The prospect of a number of large companies, such as McDonald's, dropping their employer-based health care plans due to the onerous mandates in ObamaCare necessitated the issuance of a number of "waivers" from the law's provisions. This meant that many American companies had a new business partner: the Secretary of Health and Human Services, to whom a business must appeal for a waiver. This politicization of basic business decisions regarding employee health benefits is substantial and leaves smaller companies without the financial wherewithal to maintain a fleet of lobbyists in the nation's capital at a competitive disadvantage.

Certainly, those businesses and unions that provide political support for Obama will invariably receive the requested administrative grace. For example, the Obama administration granted a waiver to New York City's United Federation of Teachers union—even though the union lobbied publicly on behalf of ObamaCare and its onerous mandates. Incredibly, within one year of the law's enactment, the number of waivers granted by the administration exceeded 1,000.[11] Discredited New York City Congressman Anthony Weiner, who previously bragged about having been the author of ObamaCare (even boasting that "the bill and I are one"), also inquired about obtaining a waiver for New York City.[12] To be sure, absent repeal of the law, waivers from ObamaCare will be the mother's milk of lobbying, a lucrative reprieve from the vast ocean of ObamaCare's administrative bureaucracy. In June 2011, the Obama administration indicated that it would cease the waiver program by the fall of 2011 but would allow businesses and entities who received waivers to keep them, thereby placing an even greater premium on the ability to curry favor with the federal health care bureaucracy.

The waivers were not the only example of the Secretary of Health and Human Services exerting a pervasive influence on the private economy. After the enactment of ObamaCare, many companies raised health insurance premiums in response to the myriad of mandates imposed on the insurance market by the new law. When the companies justified the rate increases to their customers, they pointed to the new law's provisions as the reason. In response, Secretary Kathleen Sebelius rebuked the companies for disseminating what she considered "misinformation," and promised that there would be "zero tolerance" for such criticism. She warned that "we will not stand idly by as insurers blame their premium hikes and increased profits on the requirement that they provide consumers with basic protections."[13]

Sebelius even issued a threat: companies that continued to criticize ObamaCare would be barred from participating in the insurance exchanges due to be launched at some point in the future. Even by ObamaCare standards, this projection of government power was startling—buoyed by a 2,000-plus page colossus that invested vast authority in her office, Kathleen Sebelius used her power to intimidate private businesses for engaging in speech she didn't like. This illustrates the progressive impulse to centralize authority in bureaucratic arrangements at its apogee.

The bullying of private industry by Secretary Sebelius was part and parcel of the *modus operandi* of the Obama administration. Under Obama, the federal government exercised a roving review authority over the business decisions of a number of large companies. After Obama provided additional taxpayer funds to union-heavy General Motors, he nixed the initial recovery plans put forward by the former auto giant and criticized the proposed price of the Chevy Volt, an "electric" car. Obama also "asked" the company's chairman and CEO, Rick Wagoner, to step down from his position. Wagoner dutifully obliged. According to *Politico*, Obama ran Wagoner out of the company because Wagoner was "considered responsible for increasing GM's focus on trucks and SUVs," which Obama opposed. Obama further admonished GM that it needed to be "realistically designed to weather the storm and to emerge at the other end much more lean, mean and competitive than it currently is."[14]

Obama also orchestrated a bankruptcy of GM that favored his political allies, the United Auto Workers union, over the company's secured creditors. *The Washington Post* described the actions of the Obama administration as "coming dangerously close to engaging in financial engineering that ignores basic principles of fairness and economic realities to further political goals."[15] This included pressuring the bondholders to accept a 10% equity stake for their $27,000,000,000 while, at the same time, bestowing upon the UAW's retiree health care fund a 39% stake for its $10,000,000,000.

Incredibly, Obama claimed that his administration was not calling the shots when it came to GM. At the bankruptcy announcement, he stated, "What we are not doing—what I have no interest in doing—is running GM." In the future, he promised that "when a difficult decision has to be made on matters like where to open a new plant or what type of new car to make, the new GM, not the United States government, will make that decision."[16] But as *The Wall Street Journal* pointed out, the administration had already assured the mayor of Detroit that the company would keep its headquarters in the city, which is precisely "one of those decisions typically not made by people who are busy not running the company."[17]

As a young man, Obama saw his brief stint working for a private company in New York as akin to his being "a spy being behind enemy lines," and, sure enough, he rejected a career in business to work as a community organizer in pursuit of redistributive change. In *Dreams From My Father*, Obama did confess that, for a brief moment, he envisioned himself as a captain of industry, barking out orders and closing deals. He probably never guessed that, by eschewing such a career in favor of a political quest for redistributive justice, he would one day be given the opportunity to run an automobile company as a government official. Though ironic, this gave Obama a greater ability to effectuate redistributive change than he ever had as a community organizer, and he zealously employed this authority in service of his union allies and to redistribute wealth. The politicization of the high levels of American industry is the organizer's dream come true.

This pervasive government authority is a far cry from the limited Constitution heralded by Madison, Hamilton and Jay. In *The Federalist* No. 14, Madison emphasized how federal authority was "limited to certain enumerated objects, which concern all the members of the republic, but which are not to be attained by the separate provisions of any."[18]

Under Obama, the government's power is not so limited but instead permeates basic, hitherto private decisions, such as whether to retain employee health benefits and whether to retain a business executive. The assumption of greater supervisory authority over a whole host of American endeavors, though purportedly done to "solve" problems, provides government with the means to exert a deleterious influence on the economy, harming the livelihood of some of its citizens, such as those who lose employer-based health care plans. Under the Constitution, as originally understood, the federal government was never supposed to have this all-encompassing influence on the daily lives of the citizenry. The decidedly negative character of such an influence is yet another testament to the wisdom of the Founding Fathers, who knew that the conversion of a limited Constitution into an unlimited government would have severe consequences for individual liberty.

Irrespective of constitutional limitations, Framers like Madison and Hamilton appreciated the limits of what government could do to solve problems, and thus considered confining the scope of government's power to certain limited objects to be prudent. Although Hamilton is commonly referred to as a champion of expansive government, since he wanted to build and maintain a strong military and to create a framework for a modern financial system, he had no interest in creating anything remotely like the modern nanny state. Hamilton believed that the federal government should exercise its enumerated powers in a robust fashion, but he saw little reason for the federal government to intrude into petty issues, especially those which were not befitting the attention of a talented statesman like himself.

In *The Federalist* No. 17, he dismissed the possibility that ambitious federal officials would desire to usurp traditional state functions because "commerce, finance, negotiation, and war seem to comprehend all the objects which have charms for minds governed by that passion." Indeed, Hamilton wrote, "the attempt to exercise [state] powers would be as troublesome as it would be nugatory; and the possession of them, for that reason, would contribute nothing to the dignity, to the importance, or to the splendor of the national government."[19] Though he saw an energetic government as a positive good, Hamilton understood that injecting the federal government into trivial issues undermined its effectiveness and diminished the esteem in which it is held by the citizenry.

In contemporary times, few issues garner the ire of the American public—and corrode the public's respect for the government—more than wasteful federal spending, and Obama has overseen the federal government waste money in a prolific fashion. One thing that irritated a lot of Americans was the millions of taxpayer dollars spent on the signs erected near construction projects funded by Obama's stimulus. These signs were by no means necessary to facilitate the projects, but were merely taxpayer-funded advertisements for the $814,000,000,000 stimulus bill. Most typically exclaimed "Putting America Back to Work: Project Funded by the American Recovery and Reinvestment Act."

Though Obama promised to watch every stimulus expenditure like a hawk, his own Recovery Accountability and Transparency Board acknowledged that it didn't have "any idea, nor does the board, on how much has been spent" on stimulus signs.[20] Unfortunately for Obama, the taxpayer-funded stimulus signs did little to enhance public esteem for his stimulus. Instead, the signs stood as yet another example of the federal government failing to respect the beleaguered American taxpayer.

The stimulus signs were not the only example of Obama using public resources to tout his purported political achievements. After Obama secured ObamaCare's enactment, the lingering public dissatisfaction with the law, particularly among senior citizens, represented one of the chief dangers to the electoral prospects of Obama's Democratic Party. One of the tools he used to combat this dissatisfaction was a television advertising campaign, featuring actor Andy Griffith, which touted the benefits of ObamaCare to senior citizens. Costing the taxpayer $3,184,000, the ads deployed the sheriff of Mayberry to tell seniors that, "our new health-care law sure sounds good for all of us on Medicare" and "like always, we'll have our guaranteed [Medicare] benefits." According to FactCheck.org, the latter statement was not even true because ObamaCare cut benefits for those Medicare beneficiaries in private Medicare Advantage plans.[21] Even putting aside the factual inaccuracies, the commercials were nothing more than transparently pro-ObamaCare propaganda purchased with taxpayer money.

Another taxpayer-funded public relations campaign backed by Obama involved his wife's "Let's Move" initiative seeking to reduce childhood obesity, which resulted in sweeping new federal regulation of school nutrition. Obama thought that the campaign had "enormous promise," and Michelle Obama was confident that "this problem can be solved." *The New York Times*, though, warned the First Lady that she "must be careful not to cast herself in the role of the food police, chiding parents about how they feed their children."[22] She had, after all, instructed voters during the presidential campaign that "Barack Obama will require you to…come out of your isolation, that you move out of your comfort zones….And that you engage. Barack will never allow you to go back to your lives as usual, uninvolved, uninformed."[23] Given that the Constitution contains no basis for the president to force people to move out of their "comfort zones," let alone prohibit people from remaining uninvolved in politics, this is a vision for a government armed with potentially debilitating regulatory authority.

Though she insisted that she was not advocating a big government solution to the childhood obesity problem, the child nutrition bill she championed empowered the federal government to regulate—and even ban—certain types of food sold during school bake sales and other fundraisers. Mrs. Obama said that the bill was needed because, "We can't just leave it up to the parents."[24] Margo Wootan, a member of the Center for Science in the Public Interest (as well as a political donor to Hillary Clinton), justified the regulatory expansion by bemoaning that "these fundraisers are happening all the time. It's a pizza sale one day, doughnuts the next….It's endless." She claimed that the restriction, and even prohibition, of such fundraisers by the federal government actually *enhances* parental choice regarding child nutrition. Schools, Wootan said, needed a "strong nudge" from the federal government to make them govern their affairs in a way that passes muster with experts like her.[25]

The establishment, support and regulation of primary and secondary education is quintessentially a state and local function; there is no enumerated power in the Constitution that gives the federal government carte blanche authority to regulate dietary choices made by students. From a Hamiltonian perspective, regulation of the snack habits of elementary school children is precisely *not* the type of issue which the federal government should usurp for itself.

Under this Hamiltonian view, such an incursion is troublesome because the expansion does nothing to enhance the respect that citizens have for the federal establishment. Instead, it is an intrusive, nanny state regulation that implicitly communicates to citizens that they are incapable of handling local issues in their own communities. Certainly, the political class is in no position to make any such judgments, especially considering that this same political class proved incapable of discharging its own core functions (by the time Congress passed the school food regulations in December of 2010, they had not passed *any* appropriations bill for a fiscal year that began the previous October).

Initiatives like the stimulus road signs, the Andy Griffith commercials, and the federal school bake sale regulations all highlight critical distinctions between the limited Constitution envisioned by the Founding Fathers and the all-encompassing government championed by Obama. Hamilton wanted a government that served vital functions in a manner that earned it the veneration of the people, yet Obama used the government in a way that garnered the people's contempt. Some, of course, objected to the stimulus, health care overhaul and regulation of culinary choices as a matter of policy; such disagreement is part and parcel of ordinary politics. Many citizens, though, also recoiled at the fact that the government was absorbing functions properly belonging to state and local government, and was even undertaking actions, such as airing partisan commercials with taxpayer funds, that should not be done by government at all. This objectionable governing ethos may be a lot of things, but faithful to the founding ideal of limited government is not one of them. Its implications for individual liberty are profound.

17

GOVERNMENT AS SCHOOLMASTER

Reflecting on his time spent observing American politics and society, the French political thinker Alexis de Tocqueville tried to identify the threats to liberty most likely to affect democratic societies like the one he so carefully examined in the United States. Although he appreciated the danger posed to individual freedom by a single tyrant capable of arbitrarily depriving individuals of life, liberty and property, he thought that any type of despotism established in an American-style society "would probably have a different character. It would be more widespread and milder; it would degrade men rather than torment them." To Tocqueville, this "type of oppression which threatens democracies is different from anything there has ever been in the world before," and oft-repeated concepts like "tyranny" seemed, from his 19th-century vantage point, to be inadequate descriptions of this threat.

Tocqueville described the emergence of a centralized government power that, while superficially benevolent, slowly but relentlessly exerts more power over the lives of its citizens, undermining individual liberty at every step of the way. This authority "gladly works for their happiness but wants to be the sole agent and judge of it." It is a central aspect of their daily lives, as it "provides for their security, foresees and supplies their necessities, facilitates their pleasures, manages their principal concerns, directs their industry, makes rules for their testaments, and divides their inheritances." At this point, Tocqueville asks, "why should it not entirely relieve them from the trouble of thinking and all the cares of living?"

As the government expands its reach into ever-increasing aspects of society, it necessarily "restricts the activity of free will within a narrower compass, and little by little robs each citizen of the proper use of his own faculties." Although it serves what appears to be a paternal function, its goal is not to prepare its "charges for a man's life, but on the contrary, it only tries to keep them in perpetual childhood." In such a situation, Tocqueville did "not expect their leaders to be tyrants, but rather schoolmasters."

As government-as-schoolmaster places restrictions on individual liberty, it proceeds further to exert stifling constraints on the whole of society. "It covers the whole of social life with a network of petty, complicated rules that are both minute and uniform," which Tocqueville saw as creating a barrier "through which even men of the greatest originality and the most vigorous temperament cannot force their heads above the crowd."

Unlike a traditional tyranny, this "does not break men's will, but softens, bends, and guides it; it seldom enjoins, but often inhibits action; it does not destroy anything, but prevents much from being born; it is not at all tyrannical, but it hinders, restrains, enervates, stifles, and stultifies so much that in the end each nation is no more than a flock of timid and hardworking animals with the government as its shepherd." Yet, because this burgeoning centralization is the product of an elected government, the people do not see this trend as a threat to their freedom, and, in fact, console themselves by the fact that the schoolmasters under which they live are the schoolmasters of their choosing. Tocqueville characterized it thusly: "each individual lets them put the collar on, for he sees that it is not a person, or a class of persons, but society itself which holds the end of the chain."

The net result of this is a strange, and uneasy, coexistence between the sovereignty of the people and what Tocqueville called "administrative despotism." On the one hand, the citizens exercise an important prerogative in national affairs due to the ability to elect their leaders. On the other hand, in the everyday instances in which "plain common sense is enough," the elected schoolmasters "hold that the citizens are not up to the job," and augment their own power at the expense of the liberty of the individual.

This "subjugation in petty affairs," though it does not drive citizens to despair, "slowly stifles their spirits and enervates their souls," which in turn "leads them to give up using their free will." Disturbingly to Tocqueville, the people "are turned alternatively into the playthings of the sovereign and into his masters, being either greater than kings or less than men." He considered it "difficult to imagine how people who have entirely given up managing their own affairs could make a wise choice of those who are to do that for them," as "one should never expect a liberal, energetic, and wise government to originate in the votes of a people of servants." Tocqueville derided the notion of a "constitution republican in its head and ultramonarchical in all its other parts" as "an ephemeral monstrosity." Such an arrangement "is not good enough for me," he concluded. "I am much less interested in the question who my master is than in the act of obedience."[1]

Tocqueville appreciated the limitations on government power contained in the Constitution, and, during his time in America, he marveled at the absence of federal government influence on American society. Nevertheless, demonstrating a great deal of prescience (which he did in other contexts as well, such as predicting the Cold War between the United States and Russia), Tocqueville indentified the rise of a suffocating administrative state—a soft tyranny—as the most ominous threat to liberty in America.

The rise of the administrative state in the 20th century, which created a plethora of independent, seemingly self-sustaining agencies and vastly expanded the scope of federal power, represents a shift towards the type of petty supervisory state that Tocqueville feared. Some of these agencies, such as the Occupational Health and Safety Administration (OSHA), assumed the authority to issue rules and regulations regarding a large number of rudimentary, common sense issues, such as how to climb a ladder, which presupposed extraordinary incompetence throughout the citizenry. All told, between 1935 and 2010, the United States Code grew from a single volume containing less than 2,500 pages of statutes to thirty volumes of statutory law. And, by 2010, 225 volumes were required to house the 35,367 pages of dense, fine-print regulations that comprise the Code of Federal Regulations.[2]

The existence of this large administrative edifice was something Obama sought not to curtail but to expand and empower. The 2,000-plus page ObamaCare law represents the most dramatic expansion of the regulatory state in a generation and, perhaps, in all of American history. It not only created more than one hundred new bureaucracies, but it also instilled the Secretary of HHS with vast administrative and regulatory authority; according to journalist Philip Klein, the 2,000-plus page behemoth contained 700 references to what the secretary "shall" do, 200 instances in which the secretary "may" do, and 139 provisions wherein the secretary "determines."[3]

There is simply no way that a reasonably diligent citizen will be able to keep tabs on, much less influence, this new bureaucratic leviathan. Towards the end of 2010, Sebelius (and Medicare administrator Donald Berwick, the redistribution of wealth advocate and unconfirmed recess appointment) signed a 347-page, 118,072-word "rule" designed to implement parts of ObamaCare affecting Medicare programs, which represented the smallest parts of ObamaCare.[4] These bureaucratic "rules" are not only extraordinarily lengthy (the "rules" implementing the major new parts of ObamaCare will be significantly longer), but are also written in an almost indecipherably dense language, a maze of bureaucratic jargon that can mystify even the most diligent of readers unversed in such lingo.

This new regulatory authority is something that the incumbent secretary, Kathleen Sebelius, has already wielded with a vengeance, and is something that, absent repeal of the law, future bureaucrats will employ to exert a pervasive influence over the health care decisions of virtually every American. As *National Review*'s Rich Lowry noted, the evolution from "we the people" to "the secretary may" represents the triumph of progressive central planning over the republican ideals of the Founding Fathers.[5]

Obama was undeterred by this divergence from the limited government ethos of the Constitution's creators and, in fact, extended the authority of the federal government beyond even the broad statutory language of the ObamaCare law. At the end of 2010, the administration announced a new policy regarding the use of end-of-life planning in the Medicare program. The policy provides monetary incentives for doctors who advise patients about end-of-life medical care, including the creation of an advance directive that memorializes the patient's desire to forego aggressive life-sustaining treatment; such forbearance, if replicated by citizens throughout the nation, has the potential to make government's health care spending programs more economical.[6]

This was a curious decision because a similar provision, known infamously as Section 1233, was initially included in the ObamaCare legislation, but had to be dropped amid a chorus of complaints that, in the context of a health care overhaul destined to lead to price controls and rationing of care, it represented the beginning of a march toward government-sponsored "death panels." Though controversial, these concerns were not foolhardy. After all, when Barack Obama was asked by a citizen whether consideration should be given to the "spirit" of an individual in determining the appropriateness of end-of-life care, he responded by rejecting such a notion, surmising that a senior citizen might be "better off not having the surgery but taking the pain killer." Obama's response, though crude, demonstrated an understanding of the fact that, once the government politicizes the entire health care system, it will inevitably be forced to find ways to reduce the consumption of medical care, because such consumption has a direct effect on its finances. It is, then, unlikely that the government decreed the new end-of-life counseling policy based on a belief that the policy will lead to greater consumption.

By placing a thumb on the scale in favor of foregoing expensive life sustaining treatments, the federal government will be injecting itself into the life-and-death personal decisions of its citizens. James Madison hoped that the Congress would never have the fate of the entire country in its hands, but probably never envisioned the specter of unelected bureaucrats imposing a state-sponsored "nudge" in favor of terminating end-of-life medical treatment. The fact that such a policy was promulgated by the bureaucracy without any legislative authorization whatsoever is, from a Madisonian, rule of law perspective, equally troubling.

The need for government to push end-of-life counseling is something that the Congress considered and rejected. What, exactly, was the point of having the political and legislative debate over "death panels" in the summer of 2009 if such a policy could simply be inflicted on the people at the whim of unaccountable administrative agencies? Perhaps because there was no valid answer, the administration was forced to rescind the regulation.[7]

ObamaCare did, though, contain a provision which created a 15 member board, known as the Independent Payment Advisory Board (IPAB). The health care law invested these unelected members with the authority to draft "legislative" proposals regarding the rationing of medical care; incredibly, these proposals have the force of law unless Congress proposes equally large spending reductions or votes to override the IPAB proposal. This represents a dramatic shift away from a government based on democratic accountability and towards the type of pervasive administrative state that fancies itself superior to the people, a government that—consistent with progressive anticonstitutionalists like Woodrow Wilson—elevates bureaucratic prerogative over fundamental principles like the separation of powers.

Though the most conspicuous, ObamaCare is just one example of the overbearing regulatory state in the age of Obama. In December of 2010, the Federal Communications Commission issued so-called "net neutrality" rules that, for the first time, claimed for government the right to substantively regulate the operation and management of the Internet—even though the rules were adopted without the contents of the order being published for public comment. Earlier in 2010, news reports revealed that the Food and Drug Administration planned to set legal limits on the amount of salt in food products—even though the agency was not given any specific authority from Congress to make such far-reaching changes. Not to be outdone, the Environmental Protection Agency announced that it considered carbon dioxide emissions to be a threat to the public, presaging the imposition of economically debilitating regulations—even as the effort to enact costly "cap and trade" legislation to "combat" global warming stalled in Congress. In each of these instances, vast swaths of personal conduct—communications, consumption of food, and use of energy, respectively—are dramatically affected, yet these significant changes are being done not through legislation, but by administrative fiat.

This bureaucratization of politics blurs the lines of political accountability, thereby sapping the ability of the citizen to hold elected officials politically responsible. To be sure, when Congress enacts a law that delegates broad discretion to administrative agencies, citizens are free to voice their displeasure at the ballot box. But it is very difficult to expect the citizenry to wade into the minutia of 2,000-plus page bills; typically, citizens respond to the law in operation rather than the law as it exists on the books.

When a bureaucrat like Kathleen Sebelius issues regulatory edicts that have not been affirmatively authorized by Congress, the citizen cannot directly hold her politically accountable, but, instead, is forced to seek redress, indirectly, through the legislative branch. As members of Congress cast hundreds of votes on a wide range of controversial issues, the citizen will most naturally render a judgment on a member of Congress based not on the policies of an administrative agency but on the member's deeds. Thus, the legislator can effectively immunize himself from responsibility by subcontracting out the messy details of the legislative enterprise to unelected administrators, who are themselves immune from political accountability. Such is the state of things in the era of Kathleen Sebelius, Administrator.

For his part, Barack Obama did not seem to care that this vast bureaucratic authority undermined the ability of the people to govern themselves. He characterized American citizens who expressed concern about the vast expansion of government as being "teabag, anti-government people,"[8] and he rebuked them for saying "that all of government is inherently bad" because "it ignores the fact that in our democracy, government is us." Obama tried to paint anyone who questioned the expansion of government being effectuated by his transformational design as being opposed to *any* government, which was a way to marginalize opposition to his policies and to paint such critics as lawless, which he did by insinuating (at a commencement address at the University of Michigan) that criticism of government can incite violence.[9] This is, of course, a straw man, as opposition to specific government actions does not equate to opposition to the legitimacy of the entire government. In fact, many of the so-called "tea-bag, anti-government" people derided by Obama demonstrated strong support for a number of government functions, such as the United States Armed Forces and veterans programs, even as they protested Obama's expansionist policies.

Obama never engaged with those who raised concerns about the pace and scope of "change," but such concerns are entirely legitimate. For one thing, the creation of hundreds of new administrative agencies with vast discretion to issue "rules" (or, in the case of IPAB, "legislative proposals") cuts strongly against the Constitution's command that all legislative powers are vested in Congress. Since the federal government is purely a creature of the powers delegated by the people to it under the Constitution, the vesting of broad, quasi-legislative authority in the executive branch represents a troubling departure from the system of separated powers that the Founding Fathers considered a necessary condition for the preservation of liberty. To be sure, Congress can assign responsibilities to administrative agencies in the executive branch, but these responsibilities cannot be so extensive and so unconstrained that unaccountable bureaucrats like Sebellius have vast discretion to legislate and impose voluminous "rules" on the American people under the guise of "administration."

The Constitution also structures the government in a way that intentionally limits the ability of the federal government to "solve" problems. As Toqueville explained, "a central power, however enlightened and wise one imagines it to be, can never alone see all the details of the life of a great nation....Such a task exceeds human strength." Though the statesman might pursue what Alexander Hamilton called "extensive and arduous enterprises for the public benefit," such opportunities are relatively few in number, and concern projects of continental dimension rather than social engineering. The conceit that underlies many of the policies of Obama and his allies is that virtually any issue, from the waistline of children to the temperature of the earth, is ripe for intervention of expert (and progressive) central planners. It isn't just that these issues are beyond the capability of these central planners to "solve," which they are; the Constitution is configured with numerous internal mechanisms designed to prevent the government from doing harm because the Founding Fathers presupposed that such centralized designs would, more often than not, exert a deleterious influence on the people.

What does the expansion of central planning say about the American character in the age of Obama? As Tocqueville predicted, the central planners premise their designs on the inability of Americans to govern their own affairs in a wide variety of contexts. No longer can parents be expected to feed their children without the Secretary of Agriculture exercising supervision of their child's snack habits; no longer can citizens seek access to the internet free from the regulatory arm of government, which promises its actions are need to ensure "net neutrality"; no longer can citizens be trusted to manage their energy consumption without the implementation of a suffocating regime of regulations in place to override any decisions that deviate from the government's bureaucratic wisdom.

It is not clear to what extent the American public is supportive of this potentially stifling set of restrictions, but surely this more closely resembles the nation of timid animals that Tocqueville feared than the dreams of the Constitution's creators. Far from a nation in which "subjugation in petty affairs" is the defining characteristic of the political order, the Founding Fathers conceived of a republic in which such blind obedience represented the antithesis of the national character. As James Madison observed in *The Federalist* No. 57, the new nation was conspicuous for "the vigilant and manly spirit which actuates the people of America, a spirit which nourishes freedom, and in return is nourished by it."[10]

Part Six

Judicial Authority and the Politics of Empathy

18

LAWS AND MEN

Americans take pride in an old saying that ours is a "government of laws, and not of men." Though not contained in either the Declaration of Independence or the Constitution, the maxim stands for the idea that the liberty and livelihood of the individual should be subject to the rule of law, not the arbitrary and unrestrained dictates of individuals. Through the voracious study of political thinkers like Locke and Montesquieu, the Framers came to believe that one of the most indispensible ways to guard against such an abuse of authority is the division of the major functions of government—legislative, executive, and judicial—into separate departments.

And so it was with this important principle in mind that John and Samuel Adams drafted one of the most heralded provisions of the Massachusetts Constitution of 1780:

> In the government of this commonwealth, the legislative department shall never exercise the executive and judicial powers, or either of them: the executive shall never exercise the legislative and judicial powers, or either of them: the judicial shall never exercise the legislative and executive powers, or either of them: to the end it may be a government of laws and not of men.

By dispersing power among three different and competing branches of government, John and Samuel Adams, as well as other constitution-writers during the Revolutionary War period, made a deliberate choice to make the protection of individual liberty the paramount object of government—even at the expense of government efficiency.

Political thinkers like James Madison understood that, whatever the form, the concentration of power in any one source, even if not an executive source, could be disastrous. "The accumulation of all powers, legislative, executive, and judiciary, in the same hands," Madison argued in *The Federalist*, "whether of one, a few, or many, and whether hereditary, self-appointed, or elective, may justly be pronounced the very definition of tyranny."[1]

When the delegates to the Constitutional Convention began debating the nuts and bolts of the new government, they overwhelmingly agreed that the primary functions of government should be divided among three separate departments. On May 30, 1787, one of the first actions taken by the delegates was to approve a resolution stating that a "NATIONAL GOVERNMENT OUGHT TO BE ESTABLISHED CONSISTING OF A SUPREME LEGISLATIVE, EXECUTIVE & JUDICIARY."[2]

The fact that the establishment of a tripartite system was uncontroversial, even though it represented a marked change from the Articles of Confederation, illustrates the extent to which celebrated thinkers such as Montesquieu, Hume and Locke influenced their thinking. They were willing to instill the federal government with enhanced authority if such authority was divided among the different branches.

Although important, the mere demarcation of the legislative, executive and judicial function into separate departments offered no guarantee that liberty would remain safe. "If a Constitutional discrimination of the departments on paper were a sufficient security to each agst. encroachments of the others," James Madison told the Convention delegates, "all further provisions would indeed be superfluous."[3]

However, Madison pointed out that "experience had taught us a distrust of that security; and that it is necessary to introduce such a balance of powers and interests, as will guarantee the provisions on paper." In structuring a new form of government—and here Madison was arguing in favor of a Council of Revision, which he thought could help prevent legislative domination of the government—it was important not to be content with "laying down the Theory in the Constitution that each department ought to be separate & distinct," but to "add a defensive power to each which should maintain the Theory in practice." The delegates rejected the Council of Revision, but many of the provisions adopted in Philadelphia as part of the

Constitution, from the presidential veto to the bicameral legislature, reflect Madison's concern about maintaining the separation of powers in the face of the daily operations of government.

It is in this respect that the Constitution represents an important corollary to separation of powers theory. It does more than simply separate the core powers of government; it also structures the internal functioning of government in such a way that gives each branch the wherewithal to resist encroachments by the others. The provision of political defensive mechanisms to each branch of government rests on the notion that those exercising authority will generally not do so in a purely virtuous way but will instead try to aggrandize their own authority at the expense of the other departments of the government—and, ultimately, at the expense of the people.

In his famous *The Federalist* No. 51 essay, Madison laid out the philosophy behind what we now call "checks and balances" in blunt terms: "Ambition must be made to counteract ambition." The mere existence of government is nothing if not a reflection on human nature, and the related need to pit ambition against ambition recognizes that those wielding power can never be fully trusted, for "if angels were to govern men, neither external nor internal controls on government would be necessary."

Accordingly, Madison justified the need for the "auxiliary precautions" contained in the Constitution: a bicameral legislature, a presidential veto, the division of authority between the state and federal governments—all of which operate in an extended republic in which the multiplicity of interests will make it unlikely that a self-interested faction could wield control over the entire government. By creating a system in which constitutional roadblocks operate to inhibit the exercise of consolidated authority by any single department in government, the Framers institutionalized, better than anyone could have reasonably expected, a government that rested on the rule of law rather than the caprice of individual men.[4]

It is within this context that contemporary debates about the role of the courts must be analyzed. Courts do not operate in a vacuum, and judicial decisions should be judged less on the basis of whether one likes the political outcome of a particular decision than whether the court properly exercised its judicial authority in the first place. When courts go beyond their duty and province to say what the law is, and instead try to shape the law and Constitution into what they think they should be, they are transforming a government of laws into a government of men.

Today, most Americans take the notion of judicial review for granted. If anything, many Americans, especially a disproportionate number of America's political and journalistic elite, see the courts as being the sole guardians of the Constitution. Under this view, even though they take an oath to defend the Constitution, elected officials have no duty to scrutinize the constitutionality of their actions, and are free to legislate as much as they please unless and until the courts find a constitutional infirmity with their handiwork. For instance, in 2002, when then-President George W. Bush signed a far-reaching, copious set of restrictions on campaign financing, he stated that he had constitutional concerns with a number of the restrictions, yet rather than veto the bill he punted to the courts, declaring "that the courts will resolve these legitimate legal questions as appropriate under the law."[5] Such a view tends to obscure the fact that the mere notion of judicial review was extremely controversial during the Founding Era.

The Constitution's judicial power raised the ire of a number of Anti-Federalists, including the polemicist using the pseudonym Brutus. Writing in opposition to the ratification of the Constitution, Brutus—the name is meant to evoke the Roman senator who helped kill Julius Caesar and to draw a parallel between opposition to the Constitution and opposition to Caesaresque tyranny—criticized the Constitution for giving judges the power of judicial review, which he viewed as a threat to liberty, and therefore an argument *against* ratifying the Constitution. He questioned "whether the world ever saw, in any period of it, a court of justice invested with such immense powers, and yet placed in a situation so little responsible."

This was not a judiciary, like in Great Britain, whose "determinations are subject to correction by the house of lords," but, instead, the proposed Supreme Court "would be exalted above all other power in the government, and subject to no control." Brutus scoffed at the notion that judicial decrees of the Supreme Court would not be subject to any type of review, at least in the course of the ordinary functioning of government, short of a constitutional amendment. How, Brutus wondered, will errors of this Court be corrected? And how will such judges, who serve lifetime appointments, be held accountable for their decisions? Finally, if the people have the ultimate duty to enforce constitutional limits through the ballot box, how will the people be able to hold the judiciary accountable?

It would be one thing if it could be established that judges will confine themselves to plying the purely judicial craft of interpreting the Constitution based on its plain meaning. But Brutus rejected the idea that this type of judicial modesty should be expected, and didn't believe the Constitution prevented unbridled judicial activism. He wrote that, "In their decisions they will not confine themselves to any fixed or established rules, but will determine, according to what appears to them, the reason and spirit of the constitution."

Employing a purposeful construction necessarily enlarges judicial discretion, and Brutus had no doubt that judges would use this discretion to expand the power of the courts as well as the national legislature. "Every extension of the power of the general legislature," Brutus argued, "as well as of the judicial powers, will increase the powers of the courts; and the dignity and importance of the judges, will be in proportion to the extent and magnitude of the powers they exercise." Combine this expansive authority with interpretative discretion and a judiciary not subject to popular control and the Constitution "will enable them to mould the government, into almost any shape they please." Brutus' critique of the Constitution's judicial power strikes at the heart of the idea of a government of separated, checked and balanced powers, a government based on the rule of law rather than the rule of men.[6]

Given that the notion of judicial review was still controversial, Brutus painted a terrifying picture for those contemplating supporting the Constitution. Having just revolted against excessive executive power, Americans following the Revolution discovered that legislative omnipotence could be just as dangerous to liberty. Now, the proposed Constitution raised the prospect of a judicial despotism—politically unaccountable, life-tenured judges with the power to shape the Constitution in any way they pleased and which could not easily be overruled. Was Brutus' assault on the proposed federal judicial power an exaggeration? Or did the Convention delegates, conscious about the dangers of a monarch as well as a runaway legislature, inadvertently provide for too much judicial power?

Alexander Hamilton devoted a handful of essays in *The Federalist* to answering these questions—and in the process articulated perhaps the most intellectually compelling defense of judicial review of any advanced during the ratification debates. First, Hamilton touted the fact that the Constitution provided for federal judges to hold their offices during good behavior, that is, for life. This was "one of the most valuable of the modern improvements in the practice of government," for it instilled the judiciary with the requisite firmness and independence to serve as a "barrier to the encroachments and oppressions of the representative body. And it is the best expedient…to secure a steady, upright, and impartial administration of the laws." The fact that the people had no direct say in the appointment of judges—they were nominated and, with the advice and consent of the Senate, appointed by the president—and had no way to hold life-tenured judges politically responsible was of little concern to Hamilton. This is because "the judiciary is beyond comparison the weakest of the three departments of power."[7]

In a system of separated powers, Hamilton considered the judiciary to be incapable of matching the power of the other departments, the bearer of the sword (the executive) and the commander of the purse (the legislature). The judiciary, he wrote, "has no influence over either the sword or the purse; no direction either of the strength or wealth of the society, and can take no active resolution whatever." Ultimately, it has "neither FORCE nor WILL but merely judgment; and must ultimately depend upon the aid of the executive arm even for the efficacy of its judgments." In the political battle between the branches, the courts will barely be able to defend themselves, much less "attack with success either of the other two." Nor will the judiciary be a danger to public liberty, for "as long as the judiciary remains separate and distinct from both the legislature and the executive…the general liberty of the people can never be endangered from that quarter." Whereas Brutus warned about an imperial judiciary that could operate above the Constitution, as well as the other branches, Hamilton argued that the true danger was that the "natural feebleness of the judiciary" put it in "continual jeopardy of being overpowered, awed, or influenced by its co-ordinate branches."[8]

Hamilton believed that the constitutionally-conferred firmness and independence fortified the judiciary's precarious position enough for it to discharge its core duties. Judges serve an essential function when they operate in what Hamilton called a "limited Constitution," which is one "which contains certain specified exceptions to the legislative authority," such as prohibitions on ex post facto laws and bills of attainder. Keeping government within such prescribed limits is a peculiar function of the courts, "whose duty it must be to declare all acts contrary to the manifest tenor of the Constitution void." Without courts serving such a function, the rights and privileges reserved in the Constitution would amount to a dead letter. To entertain this notion, Hamilton instructed, is not to agree that the judiciary is superior to the legislature as Brutus charged; the courts are, instead, fulfilling the modest but critical constitutionalist function of enforcing predetermined limitations on government authority.[9]

The reason why Hamilton could argue in favor of judicial review and against judicial supremacy is because the Constitution reflects an act of the people, from which all political authority flows. The enumeration in the Constitution of specific exceptions to the otherwise limited legislative authority, such as a prohibition on bills of attainder, represents an act of the people themselves. By codifying their desire that such issues should be removed from the normal political process through constitutional prohibition, the people placed limitations on the ability of future legislators to act in those areas.

This type of constitutional action by the people is qualitatively different than a run-of-the-mill legislative act, which occupies a lower plane in the constitutional orbit than the fundamental law that is the Constitution. According to Hamilton, to presume otherwise is to affirm that "the representatives of the people are superior to the people themselves," which stands the entire notion of a written constitution on its head.

Hamilton grounded the power of judicial review not in a roving, extra-constitutional authority of judges to decide every constitutional question that arises throughout the republic, but instead, more humbly, in the nature of the judicial function. "The interpretation of laws," Hamilton argued, "is the proper and peculiar province of the courts. A constitution is, and must be regarded by the judges as, fundamental law." Accordingly, the power of judicial review flows directly from the judicial duty to decide cases; when a statute and the Constitution are in conflict, the judge must give effect to the constitutional provision, "the intention of the people [preferred] to the intention of their agents." This does not elevate the judicial power above the legislative power but merely "supposes that the power of the people is superior to both." Seen in this light, a judicial decision *properly* finding a legislative act void as "contrary to the manifest tenor" of the Constitution is not antidemocratic but, rather, is a reaffirmation of the people's will as expressed in their fundamental law, the Constitution.[10]

But what if judges void laws that are not actually in conflict with the Constitution? Or what if judges erroneously allow unconstitutional laws to operate without judicial interdiction? Hamilton tried to answer these questions, which reflect the concerns expressed by Brutus that judges would possess an inordinate amount of discretion to mold the government into whatever shape they personally desired. He dismissed the notion that "the courts, on the pretense of repugnancy, may substitute their own pleasure to the constitutional intention of the legislature." This, according to Hamilton, would violate the judicial duty to "declare the sense of the law," as it would represent the "exercise of WILL instead of JUDGMENT," the "substitution of their pleasure to that of the legislative body."

But Hamilton did not point to any constitutional "auxiliary precaution" that forestalled this type of judicial legislating, merely declaring that the "observation, if it proved anything, would prove that there ought to be no judges distinct from that body."[11] Unlike members of the Congress and the president, all of whom are politically accountable to the ultimate check on power—the people—the requisites of judicial independence commanded that this most potent check be inapplicable with respect to the courts.

Perhaps because he knew that his No. 78 essay did not fully answer this question, Hamilton directly addressed the argument of Brutus in *The Federalist* No. 81. Noting that some have argued that a court will employ a purposeful construction of the Constitution "to mould into whatever shape it may think proper," Hamilton rejected the charge as constitutionally unfounded. There is, he argued, "not a syllable in the plan under consideration which *directly* empowers the national courts to construe the laws according to the spirit of the Constitution, or which gives them any greater latitude in this respect than may be claimed by the courts of every state."

The courts had to subordinate the acts of the legislature to the acts of the people as embodied in the plain meaning of the Constitution, and Hamilton acknowledged that judges who go beyond this function usurp authority not their own. The mere prospect that judges can abuse their authority was not a sufficient reason to indict the proposed Constitution, for this same line of argument would "serve to condemn every constitution that attempts to set bounds to the legislative discretion."[12] If the courts cannot be charged with deciding constitutional cases, then the very notion of written constitutions would be rendered, as Chief Justice John Marshall would say more than a decade later, nothing more than "absurd attempts on the part of the people to limit a power in its own nature illimitable."[13]

Because he thought the judiciary was so weak, Hamilton dismissed the prospect that the courts would actually encroach on the other branches. Judges could, no doubt, misconstrue and contravene the law and Constitution, "but they can never be so extensive as to amount to an inconvenience, or in any sensible degree to affect the order of the political system." This is so because judges lack the ability to enforce their decisions by force, and the scope of judicial authority is contingent on what cases happen to come before the courts.

What is more, Hamilton theorized that courts would not dare to usurp the legislative prerogative in the face of "the important constitutional check which the power of instituting impeachments...would give to [the legislature] upon the members of the judicial department." Judges simply would not risk embarking on a "series of deliberate usurpations on the authority of the legislature" if such actions would "hazard the united resentment of the body intrusted with it, while this body was possessed of the means of punishing their presumption by degrading them from their stations." According to Hamilton, "this alone is a complete security."[14]

The disagreements between Hamilton and Brutus strike at the heart of the separation of powers, at the idea that the Constitution represents a government of laws and not of men. It should first be noted that both Hamilton and Brutus rejected the notion that judges can properly construe the Constitution, in the words of Brutus, "not only according to the natural and ob[vious] meaning of the words, but also according to the spirit and intention of it." Once judges free themselves from the lawyer's task of construing a statute against the Constitution's plain meaning, they are no longer exercising the judicial function but instead are legislating their will in place of the will of the elected representatives—all the while perverting the people's will as expressed in the Constitution.

This agreement raises the question of whether the Constitution guards sufficiently against judges who "legislate from the bench," that is, judges who interpret the law and Constitution based on their personal beliefs rather than in accordance with its settled meaning and on the basis of objective interpretive principles. Brutus did not think that the Constitution contained sufficient safeguards because he viewed the impeachment power, which can be wielded against a federal judge for "treason, bribery and other high crimes and misdemeanors," as insufficient to cover garden-variety judicial mistakes not stemming from wicked or corrupt motives. This is problematic because when judges void valid legislative acts on the basis of a mistaken view of the Constitution it creates an artificial rigidity in the political arena—a rigidity which cannot be overcome short of an amendment to the Constitution, which is, for obvious reasons, difficult to enact. Hamilton was willing to live with judicial mistakes because of the important function that the independent judiciary served in the overall constitutional scheme. For Hamilton, the combination of the feebleness of the judiciary and the specter of impeachment was enough to keep judges from willfully discarding the judicial role in favor of legislating from the bench.

While Brutus expressed real concerns about excessive judicial power, his support for an American version of Parliamentary supremacy is, as Hamilton shows, ultimately ill suited to a nation utilizing a written constitution. By allowing the legislature to overrule the constitutional judgments of the courts, Brutus' view of the judicial power would necessarily lead to a legislative power unrestrained by effective constitutional limitations. To be sure, the people would have the ability to exercise a political check on legislative excursions beyond the enumerated powers in the Constitution. But the political will of the people, not to mention the president, will sometimes be supportive of the very legislative overreaches that the Constitution forbids. In these instances, the judgment of the courts to void a law that conflicts with a provision of the Constitution constitutes the final check on legislative usurpation, as well as a vindication of the ultimate will of the people as expressed in the fundamental law. In this respect, the proper exercise of judicial review enhances the republican character of the government and fortifies the supremacy of the Constitution.

To the extent that the Constitution does not provide for sufficient checks on judicial legislating, is there any other way that judges can be confined to the judicial sphere? All officeholders, but judges in particular, have a responsibility to discharge their duties in a way that respects and reinforces the diffusion of power over the separate departments. Although much of the Constitution was premised on officeholders pursuing their own personal and institutional interests at the expense of the other branches and levels of government, the creation and perpetuation of an ethic of self-restraint is particularly relevant to the so-called " least dangerous," but also least accountable, branch.

In his Farewell Address, President George Washington admonished political leaders "to confine themselves within their respective Constitutional spheres; avoiding the exercise of the Powers of one department to encroach upon another. The spirit of encroachment tends to consolidate the powers of all the departments in one, and thus to create whatever the form of government, a real despotism." There could be no doubt, Washington reminded the nation, that the value of separate departments "has been evinced by experiments ancient and modern....To preserve them must be as necessary as to institute them."[15]

This is not to say that the Constitution is free of errors and cannot be modified; if and when a change is needed, Washington advised to "let it be corrected by Amendment in the way which the Constitution designates. But let there be no change by usurpation; for though this, in one instance may be the instrument of good, it is the customary weapon by which free governments are destroyed. The precedent must always greatly overbalance in permanent evil any partial or transient benefit which the use can at any time yield."

Even if, in acting beyond the confines of the Constitution, government officials provide tangible benefits to the public, Washington warned that such actions would only serve to sow the seeds of future oppression. Ours is a government of laws and not of men, and the exercise of public authority in this superficially beneficial way is no justification for elevating the rule of men over the rule of law. The constitutional oath of office requires honoring the separation of powers that prevents a government premised on the latter from devolving into the former. Thus, Washington's admonition, although directed to officials of every branch, has a peculiar relevance to the conduct of judges, and to their capacity to restrain themselves from enlarging the judicial vortex beyond the confines of the Constitution.

19

ACTIVISM AND ABDICATION

Modern disputes over the role of the courts and judicial activism take a much clearer focus when viewed against the backdrop of the Hamiltonian conception of judicial review. Although the notion that judicial activism represents a cancer on the body politic is widely shared, there is significant disagreement over what type of judicial actions constitute extra-constitutional activism. For some, the extent to which a judge engages in judicial activism is directly proportional to the number of cases in which that judge votes to strike down a democratically enacted law. Others claim that failure to adhere to precedent, even in constitutional cases and even by the Supreme Court, is the hallmark of a judicial activist. The problem with such characterizations of judicial activism is that neither is firmly rooted in the nature of judicial review as espoused by the Constitution's creators.

The twin touchstones of Hamiltonian jurisprudence are, first, that judges must subordinate a statute to the Constitution when a conflict between the two exists, and, second, that judges exercise "neither force nor will but merely judgment." Accordingly, the frequency with which a judge finds a legislative act to be void as a violation of the Constitution tells us very little about whether that judge is properly serving the judicial function. If, for example, Congress were to pass a flurry of bills of attainder, it would stand to reason for Hamilton that these acts, which are plainly repugnant to the Constitution, must be voided by the courts. Striking down a large number of patently unconstitutional laws in this fashion is not an activist contravening of the will of the people but is an assertion of the superiority of the will of the people—as expressed in the Constitution—over the will of their elected representatives, whose actions are circumscribed by the Constitution. One cannot draw conclusions about judicial activism without scrutinizing the individual cases in which the judge votes to strike down such laws.

Nor can adherence to precedent be the focal point of determining judicial activism. Hamilton, to be sure, argued that to "avoid an arbitrary discretion in the courts; it is indispensable that they should be bound by strict rules and precedents which serve to define and point out their duty in every particular case that comes before them." But Hamilton made this argument within the context of illustrating the intellectually taxing nature of the judicial craft, which he thought underscored the need to have judges serve for life, since only a small number of individuals "unite the requisite integrity with the requisite knowledge." And he was making his argument with an eye towards the soon to be created district and intermediate appellate courts as much as he was the supreme judicial tribunal, and the decisions of the latter served as binding precedent upon the former. The Supreme Court's prior precedents do not bind subsequent decisions of the Supreme Court itself, so a justice on that court might very well encounter instances in which a law and precedent appear to be at variance with the Constitution. At a minimum, Hamilton would not expect a member of the Supreme Court to foreclose the possibility of reversing a precedent if that precedent was contrary to the Constitution. Hamilton's conservatism and desire for stability in the law might weight the scales against taking such an action, but vindication of the Constitution requires overruling a prior precedent in certain circumstances.

From the perspective of *The Federalist Papers*, judicial activism occurs whenever a judge acts, or fails to act, in a way that relies on will instead of judgment, functioning not according to the dictates of the law and the Constitution but according to personal beliefs, philosophy, or other subjective criteria. In this respect, the duty to render a judgment, while implying at least some discretion to make a decision, requires that such judgments be based on criteria susceptible of consistent, principled application.

For Thomas Jefferson, interpreting the Constitution meant that judges needed to "carry ourselves back to the time when the Constitution was adopted, recollect the spirit manifested in the debates and instead of trying what meaning may be squeezed out of the text or invented against it, conform to the probable one in which it was passed."[1] James Madison advised that "the legitimate meaning of the

Instrument must be derived from the text itself," and that additional evidence of meaning could also be found in "the sense attached to it by the people in their respective State Conventions where it recd. all the authority which it possesses."[2] While judges can have good faith disagreements on the meaning of the Constitution, basing decisions on objective factors such as the text, plain meaning and original understanding of the Constitution serves to guard against judges injecting their personal preferences into their decisions and imposing their values on an unwitting public.

The most infamous example of a total breakdown of principled jurisprudence is the case of *Dred Scott v. Sanford*, where the United States Supreme Court declared that blacks were not citizens of the United States and were thus not recognized by the Constitution.[3] The Court also invalidated the Missouri Compromise of 1820, holding that Congress had no authority to prohibit slavery in the territories, even though the very first Congress reaffirmed the power to do so by reenacting the Northwest Ordinance of 1787 and in spite of the third section of the Constitution's fourth Article, which gives Congress the "Power to dispose of and make all needful Rules and Regulations respecting the Territory or other property belonging to the United States."

Chief Justice Roger Taney based his decision not on the text, history and structure of the Constitution but on the hitherto unknown right of "substantive" due process. He baldly declared: "an act of Congress which deprives a citizen of the United States of his liberty or property merely because he came himself or brought his property into a particular Territory of the United States, and who had committed no offence against the laws, could hardly be dignified with the name of due process of law." Seeking to "solve" the divisions in the country relating to slavery, Taney smuggled his personal views into a judicial opinion that was supposed to rest on an objective interpretation of the Constitution.

Taney's judicial legislating produced an immediate outcry. His colleague on the Supreme Court, Justice Benjamin Curtis, lambasted Taney for departing from accepted modes of constitutional interpretation in favor of the very type of purposeful construction decried by Brutus and rejected by Hamilton. "When a strict interpretation, according to the fixed rules which govern the interpretation of laws, is abandoned," Curtis wrote, "and the theoretical opinions of individuals are allowed to control its meaning, we have no longer a Constitution; we are under the government of individual men, who for the time being have the power to declare what the Constitution is, according to their own views of what it ought to mean."[4]

A candidate for the United States Senate from Illinois, Abraham Lincoln, similarly criticized the judicial activism of the decision, bemoaning that "we may ere long see…another Supreme Court decisions declaring that the Constitution of the United States does not permit a State to exclude slavery from its limits." Indeed, Lincoln argued that "such a decision is all that slavery now lacks of being alike lawful in all the States. Welcome, or unwelcome, such a decision is probably coming, and will soon be upon us. Unless the power of the present political dynasty shall be met and overthrown."[5] Lincoln rightly characterized *Dred Scott* as nakedly political: by expanding the reach of slavery through judicial fiat, Taney flouted President Washington's admonition about the need to confine the official actions of each branch of government within its proper sphere.

Judicial activism is sometimes defended on the grounds that an activist judge can "expand" individual rights, thus creating greater liberty beyond what the protections embodied in the Constitution have been traditionally understood to protect. Leaving aside the fact that judicial improvisation beyond the text, history and structure of the Constitution serves to distort the separation of powers and usurps the power of the people to act democratically, it is far from clear that this extra-constitutional approach provides adequate protection for individual liberty. Once a judge frees herself from the Hamiltonian admonition to exercise judgment but not will, she is as free to diminish rights as she is to broaden them. Just as a judicial voiding of a democratically enacted law without a sound basis in the Constitution constitutes a departure from the judicial role, the judicial failure to vindicate the Constitution against a law that does, in fact, violate the Constitution represents an abdication of the constitutional duty to decide cases under the laws and Constitution of the United States.

A modern example of judicial abdication concerned the seizure of a residence belonging to a woman in New London, Connecticut. Susette Kelo purchased a home in the city's Fort Trumbull neighborhood in 1997, but the following year the pharmaceutical company Pfizer announced that it was going to build a global research facility close by her home. This prompted the New London city council to give approval to a private, non-profit and unelected corporation to create an economic development plan for the surrounding area. The plan created by this corporation called for redeveloping 90 acres of the Fort Trumbull neighborhood to "complement the facility that Pfizer was planning to build, create jobs, increase tax and other revenues, encourage public access to and use of the city's waterfront, and eventually 'build momentum' for the revitalization of the rest of the city."[6]

Unfortunately for Susette Kelo, the plan envisioned high-rise condominiums and hotels in place of "less desirable" homes like hers, and the government was intent on using its eminent domain powers to confiscate her property, tear down her home, and allow private developers to build more "desirable" structures. Kelo refused to acquiesce to her property being transferred to a private developer against her will, and the legal dispute that followed culminated in a decision by the highest court in the land.

"Nor shall private property be taken for public use, without just compensation," declares the Constitution's Fifth Amendment (applied against state and local governments via the Fourteenth Amendment). The Framers tolerated government maintaining an eminent domain power because of the necessity for truly public projects like roads and bridges, and because, without such authority, an individual could single-handedly frustrate these legitimate public efforts. But the first Congress passed the Fifth Amendment in part so that this power would be clearly and narrowly circumscribed to those instances in which the government provides just compensation to the property owner for the taking, and takes the property for a bona fide public use. If either of these criteria is absent, the taking violates the Fifth Amendment. This restriction stands as one of the primary protections for individual rights in the Constitution.

In *Kelo v. City of New London*, the United States Supreme Court, over the vociferous dissent of four justices, abdicated its responsibility to enforce the Constitution and sustained the government's seizure of the property of Susette Kelo and her Fort Trumbull neighbors for subsequent transfer to private businesses. The Court, expanding on prior decisions that had already watered down the Fifth Amendment's protections, supplanted the "public use" requirement with a malleable, and less friendly to individual liberty, "public benefit" standard that permitted government to take private property so long as it could point to a public benefit which could be something as speculative as the prospect for increased tax revenue to the government that could result from a local development plan.

"Under the banner of economic development," Justice Sandra Day O'Connor wrote for the four dissenters, "all private property is now vulnerable to being taken and transferred to another private owner, so long as it might be upgraded–i.e., given to an owner who will use it in a way that the legislature deems more beneficial to the public–in the process."[7] As O'Connor noted, the Court did not merely narrowly construe the Fifth Amendment; it effectively deleted the "public use" limitation from the Constitution.

All five of the justices in the *Kelo* majority have rendered decisions that go beyond the text, history and structure of the Constitution to expand or create "rights" they deem worthwhile (for instance, these are also the same five justices who judicially prohibited the death penalty for the rape of a child), yet their *Kelo* decision eviscerated a protection already in the Constitution. It is one thing for a judge to seek to read constitutional protections broader than such provisions have historically been interpreted, but it is hard to see how such a broad reading should not apply to *all* constitutional protections and not just those that the judge personally embraces as a matter of political philosophy.

Likewise, a judge who constitutionalizes rights and privileges not mentioned in the document itself but then proceeds to diminish or outright ignore rights and privileges that are actually codified in the Constitution is not simply abandoning the judicial role; this judge is actually rewriting the Constitution. The result is a politically correct form of constitutionalism that tends to disfavor many rights, such as the right to private property or the right to bear arms, that many of the Founders deemed essential but that are frowned upon by some judicial elites. This is flatly inconsistent with the Hamiltonian judicial function. In fact, it represents the realization of Brutus' fear that judges would mold the Constitution into whatever shape they saw fit. Perhaps not surprisingly, this is precisely the type of jurisprudence that Barack Obama has championed.

20

NOT OF LAWS BUT OF MEN

One of Barack Obama's main weaknesses as a presidential candidate was his thin resume. He had been in the U.S. Senate for barely two years before he officially announced his presidential candidacy and he lacked any identifiable executive experience. His service in the Illinois legislature was accurately characterized by political opponents like Hillary Clinton as an undistinguished tenure during which he habitually voted "present" (he did so on 129 occasions) to avoid taking a stand on politically sensitive issues. To help counteract this lack of experience, supporters pointed to Obama's experience as a lecturer on constitutional law at the University of Chicago Law School, which allegedly illustrated Obama's understanding of, and fealty to, the Constitution—something, progressives insisted, that was sorely lacking under the administration of George W. Bush. "It certainly is an advantage that he really knows the Constitution of the United States," said Cass Sunstein, a colleague at the University of Chicago who President Obama appointed as his regulatory czar. "I don't know if we have had a president that knows as much about the founding document as he does."[1]

This is a truly remarkable claim. After all, our first president, George Washington, served as the President of the Constitutional Convention in 1787 and established a number of important constitutional precedents during his two terms in office; our fourth President, James Madison, was the driving force behind the Constitution's creation, made legendary contributions to *The Federalist Papers*, and authored the Bill of Rights; our sixteenth president, Abraham Lincoln, defended the Constitution against the Supreme Court's *Dred Scott* activism, saved it from complete destruction, and created the foundation from which slavery could be abolished and needed amendments could be adopted.

Though Sunstein's praise for Obama's constitutional expertise was wildly exaggerated, the narrative that Obama would bring a deep knowledge of the Constitution with him to the Oval Office became widely accepted during the presidential campaign. News reports noted that Obama stood out as a student when he was at Harvard Law School, was elected president of the *Harvard Law Review* during his third year and was praised by Harvard's legendary liberal constitutional law professor Laurence Tribe as the "best student I ever had."

Supporters like Professor Tribe championed Obama as a presidential candidate uniquely qualified to appoint progressive jurists to the courts, judges "who share his view that the Constitution is a living document that has to be interpreted in light of evolving values of decency," and who would not "fool themselves into thinking they know what the Constitution's original meaning was." In a not so veiled swipe at the War on Terror policies of the Bush administration, Tribe said that Obama's judicial selections would "have a serious record of support for human rights and constitutional values, rather than justices who simply have shown their loyalty to executive power."[2]

Professor Tribe's praise for candidate Obama's constitutional acumen represented a decidedly ideological endorsement. It suggested that Obama believed that the Constitution evolved over time rather than maintained a stable meaning, and, implicitly, that judges—unelected, unaccountable and life-tenured—have both the authority and the competence to ascertain "evolving values of decency" and to identify the manner in which these values influence, affect or even change the Constitution.

This approach has a certain amount of appeal, especially for those whose political aims are continually frustrated by democratic realities: if most Americans continue to support "outmoded" policies such as, for example, the imposition of capital punishment as a penalty for the rape of a child, then why not eschew the democratic process and take the case to the courts, where judges can, with a simple judicial opinion, constitutionally prohibit the practice based on their view of the "evolving" values of decency? This empowers judges with a substantial degree of discretion in the interpretation of the Constitution, allowing such jurists to mold the Constitution in a "progressive" direction.

In *The Audacity of Hope*, Obama wrote that, in the big constitutional cases, judges must look beyond the Constitution and "take the context, history, and the practical outcomes of the decision into account."

Obama framed this approach as one in which "we are on our own, and have only our own reason and our judgment to rely on," but, in fact, it is the views of individuals in robes, not "our" collective judgment as a people, that drives this type of constitutional change.[3]

Obama contrasted his vision of the judicial role with a competing vision that Obama characterized as "assum[ing] that our democracy should be treated as fixed and unwavering." According to Obama, the adherents of this view of the courts think that "if the originalist understanding of the Constitution is followed without question or deviation, and if we remain true to the rules that the Founders set forth, as they intended, then we will be rewarded and all good will flow."

This formulation is interesting, but it is more of a straw man argument than an accurate description of the terms of the debate over the proper role of the judiciary in our democratic society bound by the Constitution. The mere existence of the Constitution presupposes that our democracy will not be "fixed and unwavering." It codifies certain fundamentals that cannot be legislatively altered, even in the face of changing social norms and passing fancies, while, at the same time, it leaves the vast bulk of issues to be hashed out in the normal political process, where democratic changes can be readily instituted. What is more, there is a reason why one would insist that the Constitution has a stable, unchangeable meaning that courts are duty-bound to respect and follow, but it is surely not, as Obama intimates, because of an expectation that "we will be rewarded and all good will flow."

Instead, this insistence is based on the need to recognize the proper province of the courts under a Constitution that consciously divides power among three separate branches, and to respect the people's will, as expressed in that Constitution. While a jurist may be able to dictate enlightened "solutions" to social problems through a free-wheeling approach to constitutional interpretation, this goes beyond the judicial function as contemplated by the Constitution, and serves to distort republican government.

Obama clearly rejects such a notion, and the judicial philosophy he has espoused is calculated towards engineering his preferred political outcomes rather than fostering respect for the separation of powers and a limited role for the courts. His view of the judiciary is inconsistent with the text, history and structure of the Constitution, is antithetical to the views expressed by Framers such as Alexander Hamilton, and is unacceptable in a nation dedicated to the rule of law.

Hamilton characterized courts as having no authority over "the strength or of the wealth of the society," yet Obama does not, as a matter of principle, object to courts acting in areas outside the scope of traditional duties, such as by redistributing wealth. In a radio interview in 2001, then-state Senator Obama opined about achieving "redistributive change" through the courts, noting that the Warren Court "wasn't that radical. It didn't break free from the essential constraints that were placed by the founding fathers in the Constitution, at least as it's been interpreted." As a result of the experience during the Warren Court era, Obama was not "optimistic about major redistributive change through the courts," but this was not due to any philosophical objection but instead to practical realities. According to Obama, the "court's just not very good at it and politically it's hard to legitimize opinions from the court in that regard."

Obama clearly supported "redistributive change," but argued that the focus should be on putting "together the actual coalitions of power through which you bring about redistributive change." Still, he made clear this was a preference born of practical necessity. When it came to using the courts to redistribute wealth, Obama, as a matter of first principle, maintained that "theoretical justifications for it [exist]. Any three of us sitting here could come up with a rationale for bringing about economic change through the courts."[4]

As this radio interview became an issue when it surfaced in the waning days of the 2008 presidential campaign, many Obama operatives tried to characterize Obama's comments as being consistent with Hamiltonian jurisprudence. Cass Sunstein, the progressive law professor who has criticized the Founding Fathers for not including social and economic "guarantees" in the Constitution, argued that Obama was not talking about "major redistributive change" in the commonly understood parlance of having a court shift wealth from economically productive citizens to recipients of the court's choosing. Instead, Sunstein argued that Obama was referencing relatively mundane issues such as education, legal filing fees, and legal representation.[5] But if this was true then why would Obama go on to stress the need to create coalitions of power to bring about redistributive change? He said it was a "tragedy" that so much focus was placed on the courts instead of on political activism, yet it seems odd that this would be so if the stakes were nothing more than a mandate on taxpayers to fund legal filing fees.

Obama campaign spokesman Bill Burton also tried to downplay the comments, saying that the interview showed that "Obama went into extensive detail to explain why the courts should not get into that business of 'redistributing' wealth."[6] This explanation fails to convey the full import of Obama's comments because Obama was not saying that courts *should* not, as a matter of first principle, redistribute wealth; Obama simply observed that the courts had not, in fact, proven to be an effective vehicle through which to redistribute wealth. As a matter of the philosophy underlying the Constitution, it is clear that Obama has no objection to a court embracing his agenda of redistributive change. In the interview, Obama never made a case in favor of a Hamiltonian judiciary that, consistent with the separation of powers and a limited Constitution, exercised "neither force nor will but merely judgment." Indeed, since his days of college activism and community organizing, Obama has been focused less on celebrating, like George Washington did, checks on power than he was on breaking free from such "constraints" to realize what he considered to be real redistributive change.

To a casual observer, it might seem awfully strange that a man who served as a lecturer on constitutional law at the University of Chicago Law School would advance positions that differed from the Framers. However, most constitutional law professors, particularly at elite law schools, do not embrace the philosophy of the Founding Fathers so much as seek ways to transcend (to them) the annoying issues of separation of powers and checks and balances, at least as far as these innovations stifle a "progressive" agenda. Also, the modern study of "constitutional law" is not really a study of the Constitution. Rather than teach the philosophical underpinnings of the Constitution as reflected in the debates at the Constitutional Convention, *The Federalist Papers*, and the actions of state ratifying conventions and the First Congress that passed and ratified the Bill of Rights (as well as the actions of subsequent Congresses and state legislatures that passed and ratified constitutional additions such as the post-Civil War amendments), constitutional law courses throughout the country generally focus on judicially created doctrines that have an at times tenuous relationship with the structural foundations of the Constitution. This inevitably leaves the impression that the Constitution means nothing more than what the Supreme Court says it means, elevating the judicial opinion above the text of the Constitution, a notion that is unproblematic to many of these professors, who regard the Constitution as quaint and in need of a more "modern" interpretation.

We have some indication that Lecturer Obama was very much in tune with this modern academic approach to constitutional instruction. The law school exams he gave his students focused not on Madisonian issues of basic constitutional power, design and function, but instead on more esoteric concepts such as "substantive due process"—the same doctrine that Chief Justice Taney invoked in *Dred Scott.* To be sure, these substantive due process cases involve important issues, including human cloning, procreation, and euthanasia. But as Obama himself noted in an exam memorandum reviewing the exam questions from one of his courses, the issues involving substantive due process give rise to "what are inescapably decisions based on policy calculation, ethical and political considerations, and the idiosyncratic values of particular justices."[7]

Thus, when judges make these decisions, they are invariably doing more than merely passing judgment on the text, history and structure of the Constitution; they are undertaking the very type of purposeful construction that both Brutus and Hamilton agreed was inappropriate. That Obama dedicated many of his exams to testing this type of free-wheeling judicial inquiry speaks volumes about his orientation towards, and tacit rejection of, the role of the courts as embraced by many of the Framers.

In the U.S. Senate, Obama articulated a view in which the role of the judge was less about interpreting the law than about siding with the "right" party in what he called the "hard cases." He justified his opposition to the appointments of then-Judges John G. Roberts Jr. and Samuel A. Alito Jr. to the Supreme Court of the United States in 2005 and 2006, respectively, on the basis of their refusal to exercise their non-judicial wills in service of Obama's preferred litigants. Obama conceded that both men represented superior legal talents, possessed impressive records and pedigrees, and could easily discharge the duties of a Supreme Court justice. But he ripped Roberts for using "his formidable skills on behalf of the strong in opposition to the weak,"[8] which Obama believed foreshadowed the outcome of Roberts' future rulings. And he chided Judge Alito for what Obama characterized as Alito's "extraordinarily consistent support for the powerful against the powerless."[9]

Obama argued that "rules of construction and interpretation" were inadequate to answer hard questions, which "can only be determined on the basis of one's deepest values, one's core concerns, one's broader perspectives on how the world works, and the depth and breadth of one's empathy."[10] To the extent that the "weak" did not prevail in the courtrooms of Judge Roberts and Judge Alito with the frequency that Obama demanded, this must be, according to Obama, a reflection of their personal hostility to the "weak" rather than a reflection of the facts of the underlying cases.

Missing from Obama's indictment of Roberts and Alito was a substantive case that Roberts and Alito had shed their judicial roles to do the bidding of the so-called "powerful."[11] It would be one thing if Obama identified a concrete case in which either of these admittedly distinguished legal minds had exercised will instead of judgment, but he did not do that so much as infer that a ruling in favor of a more "powerful" party was by definition suspect. Obama argued in favor of judges supplementing—if not abandoning—their judicial roles in favor of their "deepest values" and "empathy," an implicit rejection of the Hamiltonian judge exercising judgment rather than will.

In this respect, Obama's results-oriented critique of Alito and Roberts is not even due to the fact that they did, in fact, substitute their will for an honest judgment in a given case; Obama would be satisfied with a judge who followed his personal beliefs in support of the so-called "weak." Because they did not eschew an honest judgment and channel their personal values in favor of the constituencies Obama deems entitled to judicial support, he deemed them unacceptable as nominees to the high court.

Without analyzing the underlying issues in the cases, though, Obama's "strong vs. weak" framework tells us nothing about the judicial reasoning employed by Roberts and Alito in those cases. If a case comes before a court involving a small private company and, say, a labor union with powerful connections in the White House, which one is the weaker party? If, in fact, the union is more politically powerful than the company, and the court faithfully applies the law in a way that vindicates a legal position of the union, is such a decision legally suspect? What if a large company is being sued by a low-paid worker for a frivolous reason? If the company is making correct legal arguments, should the "weaker" party still prevail?

If one accepts the basic conception of judicial review as espoused by the Framers, to ask these questions is to answer them. Judges are charged with deciding cases under the laws and Constitution of the United States, and their authority to expound on both lies not in the superior values, empathy or philosophy of judges, but more modestly, in the nature of the lawyer's craft: the interpretation of the laws with no presuppositions regarding them.

This notion of judicial evenhandedness is not some constitutional relic from a bygone era, but is still a part of our national laws. The judicial oath, which is codified in Section 453 of Title 28 of the United States Code and which judges are required to take before assuming office, reads as follows: "I…do solemnly swear (or affirm) that I will administer justice without respect to persons, and do equal right to the poor and to the rich, and that I will faithfully and impartially discharge and perform all the duties incumbent upon me…under the Constitution and laws of the United States. So help me God." Obama's jurisprudence of personal conviction and manufactured outcomes runs directly counter to the letter and spirit of the judicial oath, which presumes judges acting in accordance with the prevailing notions of the judicial craft at the time of the Constitution's creation.

Given the sharp divergence of Obama's views of the judiciary with the views of the Framers, it is perhaps not surprising that Obama's first nominee to the Supreme Court, Sonia Sotomayor, represented a direct challenge to traditional notions of judicial fairness. In a lecture given to the University of California at Berkeley Law School in 2001, Sotomayor, a Princeton and Yale-educated Court of Appeals judge, argued that the ethnic and gender makeup of a judge should color judicial decision making. She took issue with a claim made by then-Justice Sandra Day O'Connor that "a wise old man and wise old woman will reach the same conclusion in deciding cases." Sotomayor proclaimed that "our gender and national origins may and will make a difference in our judging…whether born from experience or inherent physiological or cultural differences, a possibility I abhor less or discount less" than some of her colleagues. Going even further, she said she "would hope that a wise Latina woman with the richness of her experiences would more often than not reach a better conclusion than a white male who hasn't lived that life."[12] Sotomayor did not define what she meant by a "better" decision, but her elevation of ethnicity and gender to the forefront of judging raised the question of whether, contrary to Alexander Hamilton's guidance, Sotomayor was disposed to exercise will instead of judgment, and would do more than merely "declare the sense of the law."[13]

It is a testament to the resiliency of the Framers' conception of the judiciary that Sotomayor saw fit to distance herself from her prior views during her Senate confirmation hearings. She had assistance in this respect from the Chairman of the heavily Democratic Senate Judiciary Committee, Patrick Leahy, a liberal from Vermont, who characterized her "wise Latina" comments as stating merely that "a wise Latina woman with the richness of her experiences would reach wise decisions." But this unobjectionable statement was a material and deliberate mischaracterization that Leahy used to give Sotomayor a chance to put the best possible face on her comments. Dismissing her prior comments as "a rhetorical flourish that fell flat," she claimed that she was actually *agreeing* with O'Connor, and that she "was attempting to inspire young Hispanic, Latino students and lawyers to believe that their life experiences added value to the process," not trying to say that gender and ethnicity should influence judging.[14]

This represented an opportunistic attempt to distance herself from her prior views. In her 2001 speech she stated that when it came to O'Connor's dictum, she was "not so sure that I agree with the statement," in part because of her belief that "there is no objective stance but only a series of perspectives." Nevertheless, Sotomayor maintained this neutral posture, refusing to embrace her past views. She even directly repudiated Obama's view that judges must rely on empathy and a judge's deepest values. Sotomayor said that she "wouldn't approach the issue of judging in the way the president does….Judges can't rely on what's in their heart….It's not the heart that compels conclusions in cases, it's the law."[15]

Of course, Americans by and large still expect our judges to leave their personal views behind when they interpret the law and the Constitution because that is the only way judges can be true to the constitutional foundations of the judiciary and the separation of powers. Then-Judge Sotomayor's complete and total rejection of the Obama empathy standard is surely testament to the durable sense of the American people that judges have no constitutional basis to inject their policy views into judicial decisions.

By rejecting the president's views on using empathy as a mechanism to side with the weaker party and abandoning her prior views on ethnicity-based judicial decision making, Sotomayor greatly aided her quest for Senate confirmation. Indeed, when it comes to answering questions before the Senate Judiciary Committee, Judge Sotomayor's performance is proof that it is a wise strategy to reject an expansive, free-wheeling view of the power of the courts that has no basis in the conception of the judiciary as articulated by constitutional creators such as Hamilton.

The one person who remained unmoved by the futility in arguing for a more activist judiciary was Barack Obama, as his nominations to the federal appeals courts demonstrated. Following the confirmation and appointment of Judge Sotomayor to the Supreme Court, Obama continued to press forward with the nomination of David Hamilton, a federal district court judge who Obama had nominated to the U.S. Court of Appeals for the Seventh Circuit the previous March. Hamilton's nomination raised eyebrows due to his rulings as a district judge that critics claimed demonstrated an unwarranted leniency towards criminal defendants, a hostility to the role of religion in public life, and a willingness to disregard court precedents with which he disagrees. As even stronger evidence of his questionable judicial philosophy, critics pointed to Hamilton's approving reference to the belief "that part of our job here as judges is to write a series of footnotes to the Constitution. We all do that every year in cases large and small." Even worse, Hamilton endorsed the "empathy" standard as the centerpiece of judicial decision making, saying that a "judge needs to empathize with all parties in the case—plaintiff and defendant, crime victim and accused defendant—so that the judge can better understand how the parties came to be before the court and how legal rules affect those parties and others in similar situations."[16] These statements raised the issue of whether Judge Hamilton supported a purposeful construction of the law and Constitution, and whether he would calibrate his rulings if the law affects a litigant in a way that he deems to be unwise—behavior expressly rejected by Alexander Hamilton in *The Federalist Papers*.

In February 2010, Obama nominated a professor at the University of California at Berkeley named Goodwin Liu to the notoriously activist (and often overturned) Ninth Circuit Court of Appeals, based in San Francisco. Liu's professorial writings and political activism raised concerns about whether Liu was too much of a judicial activist even for such a reflexively activist court. In an article in the *Stanford Law Review*, Liu rejected "the prevailing view…that issues of poverty and distributive justice should be resolved through legislative policymaking rather than constitutional adjudication." In other words, he subscribed to the progressive impulse, articulated by Obama in the 2001 public radio interview, that the Constitution should be transformed from a charter of so-called "negative" liberties into a document of "positive" economic guarantees, and that the Constitution's focus should be less on what government cannot do to you than on what it must do on your behalf (and at the expense of others).

To support this, Liu advocated a free-wheeling form of judicial activism, stating that his:

> thesis is that the legitimacy of judicial recognition of welfare rights depends on socially situated modes of reasoning that appeal not to transcendent moral principles for an ideal society, but to the culturally and historically contingent meanings of particular social goods in our own society.…Judicial recognition of welfare rights is best conceived as an act of interpreting the shared understandings of particular welfare goods as they are manifested in our institutions, laws, and evolving social practices…because the shared understandings of a given society are ultimately subject to democratic revision, courts cannot fix the existence or contours of a welfare right for all time. So conceived, justiciable welfare rights reflect the contingent character of our society's collective judgments rather than the tidy logic of a comprehensive moral theory.[17]

In the midst of this thick academic jargon lies a judicial philosophy that is simply unrecognizable from the perspective of the Framers. Alexander Hamilton justified the authority of courts to void laws in conflict with the Constitution because otherwise limitations on government could not be effectively enforced; Liu sees courts as having roving authority to mandate "distributive justice" under the guise of the Constitution, which would dramatically expand government, especially the power of the courts. Of course, an important aim of the Constitution was to prevent what James Madison, in *The Federalist* No. 10, called "wicked projects" such as the redistribution of wealth. Madison, though, was concerned with unjust legislative initiatives that undermined the rights of private property and individual liberty, but could have scarcely contemplated that the federal courts would append such measures to the very Constitution designed to prevent them.

Liu's theory of judicially created constitutional welfare rights assumes that judges have the institutional capacity to engage in what he terms "socially situated modes of reasoning," but there is little reason to think that judges can, much less that they should, be arbiters of social meaning. Certainly, the creators of the Constitution did not think that judges had the institutional capacity to expound upon matters beyond the law and Constitution such as prevailing social trends. In fact, during the Constitutional Convention, delegates such as Nathaniel Ghorum argued for a limited role for the judiciary because "judges…are not to be presumed to possess any peculiar knowledge of the mere policy of public measures."[18]

As many of the delegates questioned the competence of judges to wrestle with political issues outside the strict confines of the law, the Constitution they created confined the role of the judiciary to the traditional role of interpreting the law. Liu's theory represents an attempt to provide philosophical cover for judges to indulge their political preferences in a way that enshrines those preferences into the Constitution and imposes them on an unwitting American public. Liu's desire for "distributive justice" would naturally cause him to construe social meaning and trends in a way that facilitates his political agenda. This transforms a government of laws into a government of men like Liu.

Meanwhile, despite masquerading as a constitutionalist in front of the Senate Judiciary Committee, Sonia Sotomayor quickly established herself as a progressive mainstay on the Supreme Court. She had previously rejected the Obama empathy standard as an inappropriate deviation from the judicial role, but, as Adam Liptak of *The New York Times* observed, as a justice "she has displayed a quality"—empathy—"that is alert to the humanity of the people whose cases make their way to the Supreme Court."[19]

The way she used her empathy, though, demonstrated the problems inherent with relying on such an unprincipled concept when deciding cases. In a case involving overcrowding in California prisons, Sotomayor rebuked the state for the poor conditions prevailing in the populous but underfunded prisons. "When are you going to avoid the needless deaths that were reported in this record?" she asked indignantly. "When are you going to avoid or get around people sitting in their feces for days in a dazed state?"[20] Yet, as Justice Samuel Alito pointed out, the most likely remedy—the mass release of prisoners—would likely result in a "crime wave" that inflicted a lot of harm on the public. One can only wonder why Justice Sotomayor reserved her empathy for the convicts in state prison rather than the innocent members of the public who would bear the wrath of the crime wave. But one can be certain that indulging in judicial empathy gives progressives like Sotomayor the discretion to mold their decisions in ways that suit their personal preferences.

By the time Supreme Court Justice John Paul Stevens announced his retirement in the spring of 2010, Obama was still advocating for judicial subjectivity. In a reference to his "empathy" standard, Obama championed the need for a judge to have "a keen understanding of how the law affects the daily lives of the American people," but he also demanded someone "who, like Justice Stevens, knows that in a democracy, powerful interests must not be allowed to drown out the voices of ordinary citizens." Senator Obama's opposition to the nominations of John Roberts and Samuel Alito had been rooted in his belief that both would not tilt the scales of justice in favor of the so-called "little guy," which was basically shorthand for Obama's favored litigants. And although that redistributive concern was still present in Obama's comments after the Stevens resignation announcement, Obama was focused on new concerns: the need to have Supreme Court justices that would rubber stamp his health care overhaul and the prospect that "powerful interests" could influence democratic government through what Obama deems to be excessive political speech.

This latter concern grew out of a January 2010 decision by the United States Supreme Court which struck down a federal law restricting, and in some cases prohibiting, political speech by entities organized as corporations during the run-up to a federal election. *Citizens United v. Federal Election Commission* involved a private, non-profit corporation created for the purpose of advancing the conservative political goals of limited government and a free enterprise economy. To this end, Citizens United created a movie entitled *Hillary: The Movie*, which criticized then-presidential candidate Hillary Clinton. Because the movie advocated against a candidate for federal office within the statutorily specified time period leading up to the 2008 presidential primaries, Citizens United was, it seemed, legally prohibited from distributing the movie for play on cable TV via the "On Demand" function.

At the initial oral argument before the Supreme Court, Obama's Deputy Solicitor General, Malcolm Stewart, defended the prohibition by telling the Court that, had Citizens United tried to distribute a book criticizing Hillary Clinton, its distribution could have been banned under the statute, prompting Justice Samuel Alito to declare the claim "pretty incredible" in light of traditionally understood First Amendment values.[21] The assertion by Stewart was so jarring to some of the justices that the Court set a second round of oral arguments to confirm their inclinations that the law could not withstand First Amendment scrutiny.

As Chief Justice John Roberts noted in his concurring opinion, the Obama administration's "theory, if accepted, would empower the Government to prohibit newspapers from running editorials or opinion pieces supporting or opposing candidates for office, so long as the newspapers were owned by corporations—as the major ones are."[22] Since such an outcome is inconsistent with the constitutional command that "Congress shall make no law…abridging the freedom of speech, or of the press," the voiding of the law is well within the bounds of Hamiltonian jurisprudence, an exercise of principled judgment rather than individual will.

Barack Obama did not see the decision this way. At his State of the Union Address shortly after the Court handed down the decision in *Citizens United*—and with most of the members of the Court in attendance in the front row of the House chamber—Obama lambasted the Court's unwillingness to defer to Congress' judgment. "With all due deference to separation of powers," Obama declared, "last week the Supreme Court reversed a century of law that, I believe, will open the floodgates for special interests, including foreign corporations, to spend without limit in our elections." Although critics noted that *Citizens United* did not concern the "century of law" implicating direct contributions to candidates by corporations (the prohibition of which was undisturbed by the decision) but rather a relatively recent Court decision that allowed the government to regulate independent expenditures unconnected to the campaign of an individual candidate, Obama was undeterred. He wanted Congress to make changes to the law to prevent advocacy groups organized as corporations, like Citizens United, from being able to engage in political speech during an election campaign, and began discussing the decision within the context of his next nominee to the Supreme Court.

Underlying Obama's criticism of the *Citizens United* decision is a belief that too much political speech can have a deleterious influence on American democracy. At a speech to the graduates of Virginia's Hampton University, Obama lamented to the graduates that they were "coming of age in a 24/7 media environment that bombards us with all kinds of content and exposes us to all kinds of arguments, some of which don't rank all that high on the truth meter….Information becomes a distraction, a diversion, a form of entertainment, rather than a tool of empowerment. All of this is not only putting new pressures on you; it is putting new pressures on our country and on our democracy." He continued to note that "with so many voices clamoring for attention on blogs, on cable, on talk radio, it can be difficult, at times, to sift through it all; to know what to believe; to figure out who's telling the truth and who's not."[23]

He hit on similar themes during a speech to the graduates at the University of Michigan in which he derided the "24/7 echo chamber [that] amplifies the most inflammatory soundbites louder and faster than ever before." This, Obama contended, "can send signals to the most extreme elements of our society that perhaps violence is a justifiable response"—a thinly-veiled attempt to squelch dissent by equating opposition to his policies with incitement. Contrasting today's media environment with the bygone era when Americans received their information "from the same three networks over dinner or a few influential papers on Sunday morning," Obama worried about the implications of this change, "for if we choose only to expose ourselves to opinions and viewpoints that are in line with our own, studies suggest that we will become more polarized and set in our ways"—as if the old days of a small number of news sources represented a diversity of viewpoints.[24]

Obama did not explicitly advocate for government to step in and referee the vast diversity of viewpoints in the broadcast media and on the internet, but the logic of his analysis certainly pointed in that direction. Many legal scholars and thinkers on the political left have advocated approaches, premised on similar observations as those offered by Obama, that permit the government to regulate political speech in the name of "protecting" democratic values.

For instance, Obama's head of the Office of Information and Regulatory Affairs and former University of Chicago colleague, Cass Sunstein, has, as recently as 2008, advocated combating what he deems to be "false conspiracy theories" by empowering the federal government to employ covert agents to "cognitively infiltrate…chat rooms, online social networks, or even real-space groups." Sunstein's view is that a "system of limitless individual choices, with respect to communications, is not necessarily in the interest of citizenship and self-government," and that government "solutions" to this "problem" should not be rejected on the basis of individual freedom or the First Amendment.[25]

In addition to combating conspiracy theories, Sunstein has proposed a number of initiatives that would inject the government in the business of policing and regulating a number of communications mediums, including requiring commercial broadcast stations to subsidize public affairs programming, empanelling "nonpartisan experts" to review the content of views expressed on the airwaves, mandating that internet websites present views that contrast with the views they present on their sites in the name of diversity of opinion (which was such a terrible idea that Sunstein eventually had to retract it), and even a so-called "civility check" program that would not allow "angry" emails to be sent until the elapse of a 24-hour cooling off period.

Needless to say, Sunstein has rejected the classic statement by Supreme Court Justice Oliver Wendell Holmes Jr. that the First Amendment is premised on "the free trade in ideas—that the best test of truth is the power of the thought to get itself accepted in the competition of the market, and that truth is the only ground upon which their wishes can be carried out."[26] This is important with respect to the role of the courts because an Obama judicial nominee who rejects the Holmes formulation of the First Amendment as protecting a free marketplace of ideas will be much less likely to rule that government activity that taxes, regulates or even suppresses certain political speech violates the First Amendment's protection for freedom of speech.

Seen in this light, Obama's nomination of Solicitor General and former Harvard Law School Dean Elena Kagan to the United States Supreme Court is evidence that Obama seeks judges that are deferential to government attempts to regulate political speech. In one of the major pieces of scholarship she penned as an academic, Kagan characterized First Amendment doctrine as emerging "not from the view that redistribution of speech opportunities is itself an illegitimate end, but from the view that governmental actions justified as redistributive devices often (though not always) stem partly from hostility or sympathy toward ideas or, even more commonly, from self-interest." She thus argued that government could regulate certain ideas that tilt political discourse in a certain direction so long as no improper motive was present. "If there is an 'overabundance' of an idea in the absence of direct governmental action—which there well might be when compared with some ideal state of public debate—then action disfavoring that idea might 'un-skew,' rather than skew, public discourse."

In other words, by regulating or disfavoring certain speech based on "neutral, harm-based reasons," such as through the resuscitation of the so-called "fairness doctrine," which would reduce the number of conservative voices on talk radio, the government would be "improving" political discourse through the fostering of a greater diversity of views. Kagan's article was more descriptive of how she believed First Amendment doctrine did, in fact, operate than it was prescriptive of how she thought it should operate; still, it raised the question of whether she considered speech restrictions motivated by a "benevolent" government motive to warrant less exacting judicial scrutiny.[27]

During her brief tenure as Solicitor General, she waged legal battles in favor of federally mandated speech restrictions. In arguing in support of a federal ban on visual depictions of animal cruelty, Kagan wrote that "whether a given category of speech enjoys First Amendment protection depends upon a categorical balancing of the value of the speech against its societal costs."

The Supreme Court rejected her position by a vote of 8 to 1, and Chief Justice John Roberts' opinion for the Court directly repudiated the argument Kagan advanced on behalf of the Obama administration. "The First Amendment's guarantee of free speech does not extend only to categories of speech that survive an ad hoc balancing of relative social costs and benefits," Roberts wrote. "The First Amendment itself reflects a judgment by the American people that the benefits of its restrictions on the Government outweigh the costs. Our Constitution forecloses any attempt to revise that judgment simply on the basis that some speech is not worth it."[28]

She also argued in favor of allowing the federal government to ban political speech undertaken by groups such as Citizens United. President Obama characterized the case as representing a clash between big businesses and the people, with the former capable of "drowning out" the political voices of the former. Yet, the actual group at issue in the case, Citizens United, was a grass roots advocacy organization that raised money almost exclusively from small donations from individuals. While a wealthy leftist titan such as George Soros could, as matter of constitutional right, spend an unlimited amount of his personal fortune on championing his political perspective during an election season, the supporters of Citizens United lack an effective political voice but for their ability to pool resources via a corporate organization. By seeking to enforce the ban on political speech against Citizens United, Obama wanted to tilt the political playing field in favor of ultra-wealthy elites like George Soros and against average citizens unable to compete with such elites.

Though one cannot necessarily attribute Obama's views to Elena Kagan based merely on her representation of his administration before the Court, there is evidence that Kagan's professional obligations dovetailed with her personal beliefs regarding *Citizens United.* When he announced her nomination to the public, Obama trumpeted Kagan's participation in the case as indicative of her personal philosophy. "Despite long odds of success, with most legal analysts believing the government was unlikely to prevail in this case," Obama said, "Elena still chose it as her very first case to argue before the court."[29] For Obama, Kagan's advocacy on behalf of speech restrictions counseled in favor of her as a nominee to the Court—she suited Obama's previously stated desire that a judge recognize the dangers of permitting "powerful interests" to "drown out" average Americans.

When she argued the *Citizens United* case, Kagan attempted to walk back from the alarming statement during the first *Citizens United* argument, advanced by the Obama administration, that the federal government could ban Citizens United from producing a book. Kagan did not contest the right of government to ban the book so much as suggest that the government would choose not to enforce the statute against books.

Chief Justice Roberts shot back that "we don't put our First Amendment rights in the hands of FEC bureaucrats." If, Roberts continued, "you say that you are not going to apply it to a book, what about a pamphlet?" Incredibly, Kagan responded that "a pamphlet would be different. A pamphlet is pretty classic electioneering, so there is no attempt to say that [the statute] only applies to video and not to print."[30]

The distribution of political pamphlets was the preeminent means of engaging in political speech during the Founding Era, yet Kagan's position would prohibit citizens from combining resources for the purpose of distributing political pamphlets during a federal election. Thus, at the very time that such citizens would want their voices heard, at the very instance in which they would want to express displeasure with, say, an incumbent member of Congress, the government would silence their collective voice simply because they pooled their resources to amplify their individual voices. This is quintessentially the type of political activity that the First Amendment was designed to protect.

This suggests that Obama's departure from Hamiltonian jurisprudence rests as much on anti-constitutional judicial abdication as on unconstitutional judicial activism. To be sure, Obama has articulated a philosophy of the courts that directly repudiates the views of the Framers regarding the judicial duty to "declare the sense of the law" based on judgment instead of will. As an alternative, Obama has championed judicial decision making based on "empathy" for the "weak" against the "powerful," which provides the judge with exactly the type of unchecked discretion that Brutus feared and that Hamilton rejected. This is necessarily a government of men rather than laws because the judge is supposed to tap into his personal beliefs when deciding cases and controversies, which provides philosophical cover for politicized decisions such as those that judicially mandate the redistribution of wealth.

But judicial abdication, the refusal of judges to enforce certain provisions of the Constitution, is an equally critical component to the overarching theory of the judiciary in the age of Obama. Obama's support for a government role in redistributing speech, if not through implementation of the "fairness doctrine" then through other means such as a robust localism that could undermine conservative political speech on the radio, will fare much better before Supreme Court justices that reject a "marketplace of ideas" approach to the First Amendment in favor of government regulations that purport to cure the "distortion" of political debate resulting from the unequal resources of different speakers. In addition, Obama's federal overhaul of the health care system might ultimately be decided in the courts, and Obama needs judges who think the Constitution no longer imposes meaningful limitations on the scope of Congress' regulatory power to sustain this sweeping new governmental edifice against constitutional attack.

During her confirmation hearings, Kagan left little doubt that she views the interstate commerce clause in Article I, Section 8 of the Constitution as empowering Congress with unfettered authority to regulate virtually any aspect of American life. No nominee to the Court would be willing to render an advisory opinion on a matter likely to come before the Court at a later date, so Oklahoma Senator Tom Coburn, a Republican, asked her a different and seemingly silly question: can Congress pass a law, based on the authority of the Commerce Clause, mandating every American eat three servings of fruits and vegetables every day? Kagan deemed the hypothetical to be an example of a "dumb law." But she went on to stress "that the question about whether it is a dumb law is different from the question of whether it's constitutional. And I think the courts would be wrong to strike down laws that they think are senseless just because they're senseless."[31]

Under the expansive view of the Commerce Clause that Kagan implicitly embraced, forcing Americans to eat fruits and vegetables would affect commerce because it would lead to a healthier citizenry and, presumably, lower health care costs; thus it is within the constitutional power of Congress to force people to eat the foods prescribed by the government. This exchange served as a strong indication that, if she does not recuse herself from the case, Justice Elena Kagan will rubber stamp ObamaCare without seriously questioning whether the provision requiring individuals to carry health insurance exceeds the authority of Congress to regulate interstate commerce.

It is this affirmative power that the Obama administration and allied lawmakers originally cited as the constitutional basis for the health care initiative generally and the individual mandate particularly. During the 1930s, the Supreme Court started to defer to Congress about the scope of Congress' power to regulate interstate commerce, generally refusing to scrutinize laws involving even purely local economic activity on the theory that the cumulative effect of such activity, when aggregated throughout the country, still had a "substantial effect" on interstate commerce and was therefore a valid exercise of the power to "regulate commerce...among the several states." But the Supreme Court has never approved of—and, indeed, has never been faced with—an act of Congress that forces an individual not engaged in commerce to participate affirmatively in an economic transaction.

If the Supreme Court refuses to find the individual mandate to go beyond the enumerated powers of Congress, it is hard to see how we any longer have what Alexander Hamilton referred to as "a limited Constitution." Once Congress establishes its power to force an individual to engage in a commercial transaction due to the need to "control" health care costs, there is no principled basis to prevent Congress from exerting a supervisory authority over virtually any aspect of American life, as the everyday private choices of individuals affect not just the health care market but the overall economy in countless ways. With no structural limitations on the power of Congress to regulate even wholly local *inactivity*, federal authority will be circumscribed only be the prohibitions in the Bill of Rights and other constitutional amendments.

Hamiltonian jurisprudence dictates that legislation the goes beyond the power of Congress is void because elected officials cannot exercise authority not delegated to them by the people via the Constitution. This is, in fact, what district court judges in Florida and Virginia found when they considered legal challenges to ObamaCare; recognizing the implications of the individual mandate for limited government, these judges refused to characterize inactivity as interstate commerce and, accordingly, found that Congress exceeded its constitutional authority when it passed ObamaCare.

Whether these decisions will be upheld by the U.S. Supreme Court is certainly an open question. Progressive jurists like Stephen Breyer and Ruth Bader Ginsburg have shown little inclination to enforce constitutional limits on the regulatory authority of Congress. And if Justice Elena Kagan does not recuse herself from the case, it is a near certainty that four members of the Court will vote to sustain all elements of ObamaCare, including the individual mandate. But judicial abdication in the face of the health care overhaul is not the end of the discussion. The Constitution's creators presupposed that the people would act as the ultimate constitutional safety net, enforcing the Constitution's limits through the ballot box.

The future of the Constitution as a government of limited and enumerated powers might very well survive a run of Obama-inspired judicial abdication if the people exercise their constitutional prerogative to curtail the scope of government by defeating those elected officials who have been unfaithful to constitutional limitations. This includes the former law professor who is purported to be more knowledgeable about the Constitution than any president in history but who peddles judicial theories that flout the conception of the role of the courts articulated by Founding Fathers like Alexander Hamilton.

Part Seven

Leadership

21

HUBRIS AND HUMILITY

"For the very first time in my life, I feel compelled to stand up and to speak out for the man who I believe has a new vision for America," TV superstar Oprah Winfrey told an eager crowd of Iowa voters during the run up to the 2008 Iowa caucuses. "I am here to tell you, Iowa, he is the one. He is the one!"[1] Oprah wasn't alone in heralding Barack Obama not simply as a desirable presidential candidate, but as a political leader of unique significance, an almost messianic figure who would deliver the nation to a hitherto elusive promised land. In campaigning for her husband, Michelle Obama made clear that her husband offered more than mere statecraft: "We need a leader who's going to touch our souls. Who's going to make us feel differently about one another? Who's going to remind us that we are one another's keepers? That we are only as strong as the weakest among us."[2] In Mrs. Obama's view, voters were fortunate to be presented with such a compelling candidacy, for "Barack is one of the smartest people you will ever encounter who will deign to enter this messy thing called politics."[3]

Obama deliberately cultivated the idea that he was "the One." Campaigning in New Hampshire during the primaries, Obama told his audience that, "I am going to try to be so persuasive, so that those of you who are still wavering...will suddenly come to the conclusion—a light beam will shine through—will light you up—and you will experience an epiphany—I have to vote for Barack!"[4] He claimed to be joking, but such a sentiment was strangely consistent with the broader message of his campaign. After all, his campaign trained volunteers to eschew talking to prospective voters about specific policies when campaigning for him, and instead testify about how they "came" to Obama in the same way that born-again Christians speak of "coming to Jesus." And at his campaign rallies, young supporters habitually became so overcome with emotion that they fainted in the middle of his speeches; this became so commonplace that a medical staff was required to be on stand-by at Obama rallies.[5]

The messianic posture of the Obama campaign struck many as going beyond a campaign for mere political change; Obama seemed to be offering his candidacy as a means of personal redemption. This was too much even for Paul Krugman of *The New York Times*, one of the most liberal members of the commentariat, who characterized Obama's presidential campaign as "dangerously close to becoming a cult of personality."[6] *Time*'s Joe Klein, another very liberal pundit, warned that "the message is becoming dangerously self-referential. The Obama campaign all too often is about how wonderful the Obama campaign is."[7]

Obama was unmoved by such criticism; he actually believed that he was a historically special figure. Cultivating the cult of personality that even left-leaning commentators found troubling, Obama employed the campaign refrain that "we are the ones we've been waiting for," which was an attempt to cloak his own self-reverence in humility.

During a speech in St. Paul, Minnesota, Obama went even further, casting his candidacy as one of singular historical significance and himself as a messianic figure. "I am absolutely certain that generations from now," Obama declared, "that we will be able to look back and tell our children that this was the moment when we began to provide care for the sick and good jobs to the jobless...this was the moment when the rise of the oceans began to slow and our planet began to heal!"[8] The "moment" was not anything even resembling a substantive act of statesmanship; it was merely the night he officially clinched the Democratic presidential nomination.

As someone who saw himself as a figure of planetary significance, it is perhaps not surprising that Obama decided to give a major campaign speech on foreign soil, as if he were already a head of state. He initially wanted to speak at Berlin's Brandenburg Gate, the site of Ronald Reagan's legendary "Tear down this wall!" speech, but those plans were rebuffed by German officials for being an inappropriate venue for a foreign political candidate. One advisor protested that "it is not going to be a political speech. When the president of the United States goes and gives a speech, it is not a political speech or a political rally."[9] That Obama was not yet president seemed to matter little to Obama and his advisors.

He eventually spoke in Berlin, though not at the Brandenburg Gate. The speech was as forgettable as it was typical. He criticized America for failing "to keep the promise of liberty and equality for all of our people," for making "our share of mistakes," and for times "when our actions around the world have not lived up to our best intentions." But he hailed himself as a "citizen of the world," and as someone whose "improbable" journey placed him on the cusp of global political leadership.[10] Left-leaning German crowds were happy to provide Obama a euphoric reception, as most Germans were eager to see a new American president take the place of George W. Bush. As a campaign event, it was a spectacle that was unprecedented in the history of American presidential politics.

Conservative columnist Charles Krauthammer ridiculed Obama's speech in Berlin, likening it to a foreign political candidate holding a campaign event with the Statue of Liberty as a backdrop.[11] That Obama was not even president, let alone someone who had contributed to the defeat of communism—or made a notable contribution regarding any other international issue, for that matter—made the entire spectacle a farce, yet Obama did not see anything odd about a freshman senator appropriating a foreign backdrop as a campaign prop, which says a lot about Obama's enormous self-regard. Krauthammer wondered if "there has ever been a presidential nominee with a wider gap between his estimation of himself and the sum total of his lifetime achievements?"[12]

Obama dismissed those who contended that his Berlin speech revealed his personal vanity. The adoring crowds that greeted him in Berlin seemed to vindicate his belief in himself as being a singularly important figure. When he returned from the Berlin excursion, Obama held a closed-door meeting with Democratic members of Congress, and, in the words of one journalist, "waxed lyrical" about how the trip provided further evidence of the magnitude of his candidacy. "This is the moment...that the world is waiting for," Obama told them. "I have become a symbol of the possibility of America returning to our best traditions."[13] Obama's egotism was conspicuous by the standards of presidential politics; whereas Harry S. Truman asked reporters to pray for him when he assumed the presidency because it "felt like the moon, the stars and all of the planets had fallen on" him, Obama considered himself uniquely qualified not simply to ride the presidential tiger, but to do so in a way that "healed" the planet and garnered international acclaim.[14]

The hubris exhibited by Obama's "rise of the oceans" and Berlin speeches was not an aberration; the speeches were quintessential examples of Obama's outsized sense of self. This was, after all, the same Obama who, when questioned by a reporter in 2004 about whether he was nervous in anticipation of giving the keynote address to the 2004 Democratic National Convention, invoked the Cleveland Cavaliers' superstar who dominated pro basketball during his rookie year, replying "I'm LeBron, baby. I can play on this level. I got some game."[15]

This was also the same Obama who, during the presidential campaign, utilized his own "Obama for America" pre-presidential seal—a design which *The New York Times* described as "deliberately reminiscent of the official seal of the president of the United States" but which substituted the phrase "Vero Possumus" ("Yes We Can") for "E Pluribus Unum" ("Out of Many, One").[16] Obama's use of the seal drew so much ridicule—ABC's Jake Tapper labeled the episode an example of the "audacity of hype" and wondered whether a remix of "Hail to the Chief" played for Obama[17]—that the campaign was forced to retire it.[18] And this was the same Obama who, not content to accept the Democratic nomination for president at Denver's Pepsi Center (the actual site of the Democratic National Convention), insisted on giving his acceptance speech in front of specially-designed Greek columns at Invesco Field, the Denver Broncos' football stadium, which has more than triple the capacity of the Pepsi Center (the use of which drove up the cost of the convention by $3 million).[19]

Obama's sense of self seemed to have few discernible limitations. He viewed himself as possessing unrivaled knowledge about virtually all aspects of politics and government. As he told one of his campaign aides during a job interview, "I think that I'm a better speechwriter than my speechwriters. I know more about policies on any particular issue than my policy directors. And I'll tell you right now that I'm gonna think I'm a better political director than my political director."[20] During the search to replace White House Chief of Staff Rahm Emanuel, Obama remarked, in all seriousness, "You know, *I'd* make a good chief of staff."[21] When Senator Harry Reid complimented then-Senator Obama on a speech that he had given, Obama replied "I have a gift, Harry."[22] Though Reid, incredibly, tried to characterize Obama's response as humble, it is doubtful that anyone with a healthy dose of humility would have said anything more than, simply, "thank you." And when Obama announced his presidential candidacy, he did so in front of the Springfield, Illinois state house so as to conjure up comparisons with the canonical Illinois rail splitter, Abraham Lincoln. He invoked Lincoln throughout the speech, and tried to draw parallels between Lincoln and himself, even referring to Lincoln as a "tall, gangly, self-made Springfield lawyer" as a way to liken his own thin physique and legal training to the occupation and build of Lincoln.[23]

Assumption of the presidency did little to humble Obama. Early in his presidency, when he paid an official visit to London's Buckingham Palace to meet Queen Elizabeth II, Obama gave the Queen an iPod containing, among other things, recordings of his own speeches and photographs of his inauguration.[24] Whereas his predecessor had maintained in the Oval Office a valuable bust of former British Prime Minister Winston Churchill, a loan from Prime Minister Tony Blair following the September 11 attacks, Obama unceremoniously returned the bust to British officials, even though they offered to extend the loan and even though he could have relocated the bust to another part of the White House. This was widely considered to be a snub of America's closest ally.

When lawmakers nervous about the political ramifications of enacting a massive federal overhaul of the health care system analogized the impending 2010 midterm elections to the Republican Revolution of 1994, Obama dismissed their concerns: "Well, the big difference between here and in '94 was you've got me."[25] Apparently, Obama believed that his personal aura would be sufficient to ensure victory to those members of Congress who backed ObamaCare in the face of consistently strong public opposition. Obama was such an impressive leader, so his line of thinking went, that he would be able to succeed where Bill Clinton had failed. Of course, this supposition was baseless; his party lost convincingly in the 2010 midterm elections. Not only were the vast majority of the Democratic members of the House of Representatives from competitive districts who supported ObamaCare defeated, but Obama was so politically unpopular that only a handful of these members even wanted him to campaign in their districts.

Obama's immense self-regard permeated his presidency, including its ceremonial aspects. When Germany celebrated the 20th anniversary of the fall of the Berlin Wall with an event that drew the heads of state from all European nations, Obama recorded remarks that were transmitted via video to the other world leaders. Of course, the United States had been the indispensible force in preventing the spread of communism throughout Europe following World War II, and certain Americans, from Harry Truman to Ronald Reagan, played critical roles in containing the Soviet Union and, eventually, rolling back the Iron Curtain and defeating the "evil empire." But rather than pay tribute to any of his predecessors, Obama used the opportunity to laud himself. "Few would have foreseen," Obama told the assembled crowd of dignitaries, "that a united Germany would be led by a woman from Brandenburg or that their American ally would be led by a man of African descent. But human destiny is what human beings make of it."[26]

Obama frequently marked his mere emergence on the national stage as a seminal moment in American history. Journalist Jonathan Stein, a supporter of Obama and writer for the leftist magazine *Mother Jones*, noted that, in his campaign speeches, Obama sketched American history as follows: "American Revolutionaries → Manifest Destiny → Slaves/Abolitionists → Suffragettes → the Labor Movement → the Greatest Generation → the Civil Rights Movement → Himself."[27] Stein rightly criticized Obama for suggesting that his mere election, rather than a presidential tenure in which he actually accomplished something of significance, would represent the type of enduring achievement that could rival the American Revolution or the abolition of slavery. But as far-fetched as Obama's view of history might have been during the campaign, his Berlin Wall remarks went even further. That Obama would see his own ascension to political power as in any way linked to the significance of the collapse of the Iron Curtain was, even considering Obama's penchant for self-reverence, startling.

It was this self-reverence that prompted Obama to travel to Copenhagen to address members of the International Olympic Committee, which was considering awarding the 2016 Summer Olympics to Chicago. Observers surmised that the White House must have received advanced notice that Chicago was going to be awarded the 2016 games, as an American president would not typically undertake a trip of this nature unless the groundwork had been prepared such that the success of the trip was preordained. Few thought that Obama would be willing to jeopardize the prestige of his office by risking a rejection at the hands of the I.O.C. Obama was, though, quite willing to do this because he planned to win over the I.O.C. by the sheer force of his oratorical prowess and personal charm.

Obama's presentation before the I.O.C. was preceded by a plea from Michelle Obama, who spoke about her upbringing in Chicago and how an Olympic Games in Chicago would have made her father proud. President Obama picked up on the personalized theme by declaring that his wife is a "pretty big selling point for the city" and by urging the committee to choose Chicago "for the same reason I chose Chicago nearly 25 years ago—the reason I fell in love with the city I still call home." He even touted his own election as president as a reason to choose Chicago: "Nearly one year ago, on a clear November night, people from every corner of the world gathered in the city of Chicago or in front of their televisions to watch the results of the U.S. presidential election." Though Obama claimed that the interest wasn't about him as an individual, the injection of his greatest personal triumph into a pitch for an Olympic Games seemed odd. Obama concluded his argument by telling the I.O.C. that "there is nothing I would like more than to step just a few blocks from my family's home, with Michelle and our two girls, and welcome the world back into the neighborhood."[28]

The I.O.C.'s verdict was a devastating rebuke to Obama: not only did the committee award the 2016 Olympic Games to Brazil, but Chicago's bid finished dead last in the voting. The Copenhagen gambit demonstrated Obama's vanity because Obama truly believed that his personal ability was sufficient to sway a decision from a highly politicized, international body, and because the means he chose to make his case for Chicago was a speech talking about himself and his relationship with the city. Even the hyper-liberal editorial board of *The New York Times* rebuked Obama's White House for having "a tad too much confidence in Mr. Obama's hortatory powers," and instructed Obama that, "if you're going to roll the dice, next time make sure the stakes are worth it."[29]

Obama's self-centeredness also colored how he reacted to certain events on the world stage. At the Summit of the Americas during his first 100 days in office, Nicaraguan President Daniel Ortega, a Marxist, delivered a 50-minute rant that attacked the United States for what he termed its "terroristic" policies in Central America, its attempt to topple Castro's communist regime in Cuba, and its history of "racism." Obama was present during the speech, and many looked to see how the new president would react to such a searing attack on his nation. He did not rise to the defense of his country. Instead, he highlighted the fact that many of the alleged transgressions cited by Ortega had nothing to do with him, stating that "I'm grateful that President Ortega did not blame me for things that happened when I was three months old."

This may have been Obama's way of belittling Ortega's criticism, but it was not effective—and it left the impression that Obama was only concerned about criticism of him. Criticism of the United States that properly distinguished between Obama's administration and America's "unenlightened" past—defined, apparently, as American history before January 20, 2009—did not seem to bother Obama, no matter how erroneous the charges lodged against the nation he was elected to lead.

Obama thought so highly of himself that, on more than one occasion, he undertook psychological diagnoses of the American people. The first instance of this occurred during the primaries, when Obama spoke to a well-heeled crowd at a San Francisco fundraiser about the difficulty he had winning votes from certain voters in states like Pennsylvania, where he appeared to be trailing Senator Hillary Clinton in advance of the April 22, 2008 presidential primary. Obama attributed these voters' less than favorable views of him and his urban, elite progressivism to the fact that, due to a lack of economic vitality in their states, these voters "get bitter, they cling to guns or religion or antipathy to people who aren't like them or anti-immigrant sentiment or anti-trade sentiment as a way to explain their frustrations."

Obama characterized these voters as inherently cynical about government—the very type of people most likely to reject Obama's idealistic, "hope and change" mantra, especially, he said, "when it's delivered by a 46-year-old black man named Barack Obama."[30] The remarks revealed Obama to be an almost quintessential progressive elitist, a man quick to demean the cultural practices of "lesser" Americans and quick to ascribe to such Americans dark impulses such as racism and xenophobia.

Obama received appropriate blowback for his "bitter" remarks, and one would have thought that Obama would have emerged from the controversy at least a little bit chastened. But for the man who, as one Democratic lawmaker told Peter Baker of *The New York Times*, "always believes that he is the smartest man in any room,"[31] this was apparently too much to ask. By the fall of 2010, saddled by low approval ratings and sensing that an electoral "shellacking" for his party was near, Obama attempted to explain his political predicament by offering yet another psychological diagnosis of the American electorate. Speaking at fundraiser in Boston, Obama told liberal donors that the political troubles of the Democrats was due to the inability of Americans to "think clearly" in the midst of an alarmingly weak economic recovery. Obama claimed that "facts and science and argument does not seem to be winning the day all the time" because people were scared about the economy.[32]

Charles Krauthammer, a Harvard-educated psychiatrist, mockingly referred to this as "anxiety-induced Obama Underappreciated Syndrome, wherein an entire population is so addled by its economic anxieties as to be neurologically incapable of appreciating the 'facts and science' undergirding ObamaCare and the other blessings their president has bestowed upon them from on high."[33] Obama equated Americans' disapproval of his policies with an inability to respond to facts because he refused to acknowledge that anyone could sensibly reject his policies on their merits, choosing to blame the voters rather than himself.

Of course, Obama hardly can be said to have put aside his own leftist ideology when it conflicted with "facts" and "science." His administration instituted an offshore oil-drilling moratorium in the Gulf of Mexico based on a report doctored by administration officials in a way that suggested that the engineering experts consulted by the Interior Department recommended the moratorium, which they did not.[34] And Obama has frequently cited the social, economic and environmental benefits of creating a network of high-speed rail links throughout the country, yet *Newsweek*'s Robert Samuelson has demonstrated that high-speed rail systems would not lead to "any meaningful reduction in traffic congestion, greenhouse-gas emissions, air travel, or oil consumption and imports. Nada, zip."[35]

Obama's hypocrisy in criticizing his fellow citizens for eschewing science and facts in politics when he has done the same thing demonstrates his belief that Americans who disagree with his policies are somehow incapable of rational thought. It is telling that Obama does not question those Americans that voted for him in 2008—even though fear of an economic collapse was *much* more palpable throughout the country during the fall of 2008. He sees his own election as representing the considered judgment of an enlightened electorate, a moment in time in which "hope" defeated "fear." Ultimately, Obama's clumsy attempts to offer a clinical diagnosis of the political judgments of the American people—but only when those judgments reject his agenda of transformational change—is further evidence of Obama's inflated view of his own political aptitude. Since he knows what is best for his fellow citizens, their disagreement with his policies is, in his mind, simply a case of the American people acting against what the omniscient Obama has determined to be in their best interests.

****

When the delegates to the Constitutional Convention convened in May of 1787, they knew that they were embarking on a quest to devise a constitution that not only remedied the defects of the Articles of Confederation, but also sufficiently safeguarded individual liberty, a quest that would, in their minds, forever determine whether republican government could succeed. The delegates' first order of business was to nominate and unanimously elect George Washington to serve as the Convention's president. This was important for the delegates because having the convention bear the imprimatur of Washington, the hero of the American Revolution and the most trusted man in America, added legitimacy to the Convention's handiwork. Heralded though he was, Washington did not use his election as the Convention's president as an opportunity to wax poetic about his unique historical importance. Instead, as recorded in James Madison's notes, "in a very emphatic manner he thanked the Convention for the honor they had conferred on him, reminded them of the novelty of the scene of business in which he was to act, lamented his want of better qualifications, and claimed the indulgence of the House towards the involuntary errors which his inexperience might occasion."[36]

It is almost inconceivable that, were Obama to find himself in a similarly important situation, that he would refrain from paying tribute to himself, let alone that he would explicitly acknowledge his personal shortcomings. After all, Obama has cited the greatness of his own election within the context of the fall of the Berlin Wall and his own nomination as a seminal moment in the history of the planet. For his part, Washington had every reason to hail himself as the indispensable component at the Constitutional Convention; he had not even been elected president by that point, yet he was already a preeminent national figure, a man hailed as "first in war, first in peace and first in the hearts of his countrymen." But he was not interested in basking in his own fame. He knew that the nation's political system was failing the American people, and he was willing to lend his considerable reputation to the difficult and potentially futile task of creating a new foundational governing structure. Washington provided needed gravitas to the convention, but did so in a way that focused the convention on the task of creating a good constitution rather than on himself.

It may seem unfair to compare a modern president to George Washington. As the father of our country, Washington stands as a man of such stupendous accomplishments that even the most talented of modern presidents cannot possibly prove themselves to be Washington's equal. But Washington himself observed that, when he assumed the presidency, "I walk on untrodden ground," that is, he did a great deal to establish certain customs and standards of conduct for the presidency.[37] Though no president will ever fully measure up to Washington, modern chief executives can at least be judged against the standards that he set.

Chief among the virtues that Washington brought to the presidency was a deep sense of humility, a humility that dovetailed superbly with the ethos of republican government. This humility undergirded his entire public career, especially those seminal acts of statesmanship that have made Washington a monumental figure in history. When he was elected the Commander in Chief of the Continental Army on June 16, 1775, Washington told the Continental Congress that he was "truly sensible of the high Honour done me, in this Appointment, yet I feel great distress, from a consciousness that my abilities and military experience may not be equal to the extensive and important Trust." He wanted it to be "remembered, by every Gentleman in the room, that I, this day, declare with the utmost sincerity, I do not think myself equal to the Command I am honored with." Washington accepted the commission but he insisted that "no pecuniary consideration could have tempted me to have accepted this arduous employment, at the expence of my domestic ease and happiness, I do not wish to make any proffit from it."[38] Conscious of his own limitations but willing to answer the call to service, he would serve without pay.

Washington was not necessarily the greatest military tactician, but he was a great leader and a truly indispensable force in the American drive for independence. His importance extended far beyond the military fight against the British; he single-handedly kept the American Revolution from dying in its infancy. By 1783, many of the officers in Washington's army had grown discontented with the Continental Congress, which had withheld promised payments to them and seemed unlikely to make good on their pensions. The war was all but over—preliminary articles of a peace treaty had already been signed, but word had not yet reached a group of officers meeting in Newburgh, New York.

Anonymous letters circulated among the officers that called for an unsanctioned meeting, scheduled for March 10, to discuss their grievances and that raised the possibility of a revolt against civilian authority. The military's grievances were not new: the previous year, Colonel Lewis Nicola urged Washington to join in a military insurrection and assume the position of "king" of the United States, but Washington flatly rejected such a notion. With those assembled in Newburgh primed for drastic measures, Washington was provided with another opportunity to seize power for himself.

When he got wind of the letters, Washington immediately called his own meeting to take place on March 15. Addressing the officers, he criticized the anonymous letters as being "subversive of all order and discipline," and rebuked those who would desert their country "in the extremest hour of her distress." The audience did not seem persuaded by his words. He then pulled out a letter he received from a member of Congress, but he paused before reading it aloud. The crowd grew restless.

Finally, Washington pulled out a pair of spectacles, which he was not known for wearing. "Gentlemen," he said, "you must pardon me, for I have grown not only gray but blind in the service of my country." By alluding to the years of toil and sweat that have gone into the struggle for independence, Washington forced the officers to see how a mutiny would represent an act of treason, derailing nearly a decade's worth of effort by the army and the nation. Many of the officers were reduced to tears. Talk of mutiny immediately ceased. Washington vindicated the primacy of civilian authority, and ensured that the nation's experiment with republican government would continue.[39]

The diffusing of the conspiracy at Newburgh was one of the greatest single acts in American history, yet it wasn't even the greatest act of Washington's life. His most notable feat occurred months later, on December 23, 1783, when he surrendered his sword to the Continental Congress. History was replete with examples of victorious generals, such as Caesar and Cromwell, using their military victories as a pretense to seize political power, and Washington was so beloved by his fellow countrymen by the war's end that he could have become an American Caesar. Yet, Washington stood before the Congress not to demand obedience to his rule but to resign his commission as commander in chief of the Continental Army. He noted that he resigned "with satisfaction to the appointment I accepted with diffidence, a diffidence in my abilities to accomplish an arduous task, which however was superseded by a confidence in the rectitude of our cause, the support of the supreme power of the Union, and the patronage of Heaven." He sought no position of political authority, choosing instead to "retire from the great theater of action…and take any leave of all the employments of public life." He returned to Mount Vernon in time for Christmas, content to have discharged his duties in the service of his country.[40]

Washington understood that, by snuffing out a military insurrection at Newburgh and by voluntarily relinquishing his command of the army, he would be further burnishing his own image as a national hero. He was a student of preeminent figures from classical antiquity like Cincinnatus and Cato, and modeled himself after the type of virtuous, disinterested leader who could be trusted with power, the type of individual that would forever be lionized as the "founder of a republic." He knew that by staying true to the nation's republican course, he was sacrificing the earthly wealth and power of the throne, but was availing himself of a chance to earn lasting international fame.

When word of Washington's resignation reached Great Britain, King George III remarked that declining monarchical power in favor of private retirement would make Washington "the greatest man in the world."[41] Napoleon Bonaparte, who crowned himself "emperor" and who achieved legendary military victories before suffering defeat and exile, remarked on his deathbed that "they wanted me to be another

Washington."[42] When it came to the pursuit of personal power, Washington was different, and people throughout the world knew it.

After incessant urging from some of the most prominent of his contemporaries, Washington returned to public life in 1787 to attend the Constitutional Convention. The Constitution produced by the delegates created a single, energetic executive within the context of a larger republican framework, which had hitherto been unthinkable. The revolt against King George III sowed within the American people a deep distrust in executive power, but now, less than a decade after independence was won, the delegates created a national governing framework that institutionalized a single executive, which Virginia's John Randolph considered to be the "the foetus of monarchy."[43] One major reason the delegates were willing to entertain the creation of single executive is because they knew that Washington would be the first president, and that he could be trusted with power; as Benjamin Franklin told the delegates, "the first man, put at the helm will be a good one."[44]

Unanimously elected to lead the new ship of state as the first chief executive, Washington proved himself to be both a great man and a great president. Ever true to the republican spirit, Washington discharged the presidential duties with an abiding sense of humility about both himself and the office. In his First Inaugural Address, Washington began by drawing attention not to his prodigious accomplishments but to his deficiencies, noting how:

> the magnitude and difficulty of the trust to which the voice of my country called me, being sufficient to awaken in the wisest and most experienced of her citizens a distrustful scrutiny into his qualifications, could not but overwhelm with despondence one who (inheriting inferior endowments from nature and unpracticed in the duties of civil administration) ought to be peculiarly conscious of his own deficiencies. In this conflict of emotions all I dare aver is that it has been my faithful study to collect my duty from a just appreciation of every circumstance by which it might be affected.

He also paid tribute to "that Almighty Being who rules over the universe," and asked that "His benediction may consecrate to the liberties and happiness of the people of the United States a Government instituted by themselves for these essential purposes."

Rather than recommend that the Congress pursue specific "necessary and expedient" measures at his behest and as Article II of the Constitution provides, Washington paid tribute to those who played a role in devising and adopting the Constitution. He had so much informal authority that he could have ushered through Congress, and imposed upon the nation, a whole host of his desired policies at the very outset, but he knew that the new government needed a chance to get its bearings, and was correctly concerned not to appear to be using the presidency to dominate the system. He also refused to inject himself into the touchy subject of amendments to the Constitution, which supporters of the Constitution like James Madison pledged to draft and implement following ratification, telling members of Congress that he would "give way to my entire confidence in your discernment and pursuit of the public good." He did use the end of his address to talk about himself, but only to "decline as inapplicable to myself any share in the personal emoluments which may be indispensably included in a permanent provision for the executive department." Just as he had done during the Revolutionary War, Washington wanted to serve without compensation.

As president, he was a unifying force in government who maintained his deep sense of humility. His famous Farewell Address highlighted not his accomplishments in office but his personal limitations: "I will only say, that I have, with good intentions, contributed towards the organization and administration of the government the best exertions of which a very fallible judgment was capable." He would not take credit for the remarkable strides that the new nation had made under his watch; to the extent that "benefits have resulted to our country from [his] services, let it always be remembered to your praise." He acknowledged that he might have made mistakes, but hoped that the nation would indulge them, and "fervently beseech[ed] the Almighty to avert or mitigate the evils to which they may tend."

Washington published his Farewell Address before the election of 1796, using it as a vehicle to announce that he would not stand for election to another presidential term. He explained to the nation that his decision to retire "has not been taken without a strict regard to all the considerations appertaining to the relation which binds a dutiful citizen to his country; and that in withdrawing the tender of service, which silence in my situation might imply, I am influenced by no diminution of zeal for your future interest, no deficiency of grateful respect for your past kindness, but am supported by a full conviction that the step is compatible with both." Washington could have been president for life, but instead established two presidential terms as the standard for future presidents.[45]

By retiring after two terms, Washington set an important precedent, a precedent that was honored by subsequent presidents and, soon after Franklin D. Roosevelt violated it in the 1940s, was formally added to the Constitution in the form of the 22nd Amendment's two-term limit. Washington's contributions to the American Revolution and the years following independence were vital, yet his retirement established the principle that, in a republican form of government, no man is indispensable. His cognizance of his own dispensability is something that animated his entire career, and the humility that undergirded this cognizance constituted a personal character trait of profound historical significance.

The contrast between Washington's humility and Obama's self-reverence illustrates a dramatic divergence in styles of political leadership. When he retired from the presidency, Washington had accumulated a legendary list of accomplishments: commanding a beleaguered army to stunning victory against the world's most powerful military force, surrendering command of the army to the civilian authorities following the war victory, lending critical personal support to the creation and ratification of the Constitution, and guiding the new government through its formative years as the nation's chief executive. Yet, even as he was in a position to reflect on these prodigious achievements, Washington continued to call public attention to his shortcomings, and to attribute credit for his achievements to others.

Barack Obama's achievements pale in comparison to the accomplishments of Washington. Obama gained national attention not by leading a valiant struggle against a powerful empire but by getting elected to lead a scholarly law school journal. He has been a community organizer in Chicago, a lecturer at the University of Chicago and a senator in the Illinois Legislature—all perfectly respectable but, even in combination, they are of infinitesimal importance in the broad sweep of American history. Yet, he expressed a palpable cockiness even as a lowly state senator, and made outlandish claims about his own significance as an individual, such as claiming an ability to heal the planet. He used his brief stint in the U.S. Senate not to advance and implement substantive policies but as a platform to seek higher office. One might think that a candidate seeking the presidency under these conditions would be especially conscious of his shortcomings, but Obama was not.

The juxtaposition of Obama's inflated sense of himself with George Washington's abiding humility surely makes Obama look foolish, but it also illustrates a profound political miscalculation made by Obama. Washington used his humility to earn the trust of the public and to establish important republican principles regarding political leadership. His penchant for refusing power—a demonstration of his belief in his own dispensability—was the most significant factor in his being entrusted with it.

Obama, in contrast, cultivated an image of himself as a figure of unique historical significance, which energized a large group of mostly young voters and garnered flattering media coverage by a press thoroughly enamored with his progressive politics. This, though, created expectations that were completely divorced from reality. Obama was a Chicago politician who spent his entire life in decidedly left-of-center environments and whose national achievements were virtually nonexistent, so it was absurd to think that he would be a modern-day FDR, much less that he would be a national unifying figure of Washingtonian proportions. It was, therefore, inevitable that many of Obama's erstwhile supporters would become thoroughly disenchanted when the man supposed to be "the One" was unable to transcend the nation's Madisonian-designed political apparatus and implement the full panoply of his promised progressive initiatives.

Washington was first in war, first in peace and first in the hearts of his countrymen. Few would maintain that Obama is first in war or in peace, but few can deny that he is first in his own mind.

22

THE VICIOUS ARTS

When they created the Constitution, the Founding Fathers knew that that the durability of the republic would depend not only on the efficacy of the Constitution's internal configuration, but also on the ability of the people to preserve and maintain it. With respect to the latter, it is clear that the people had an important constitutional role to play. If, to take an example used by Madison in *The Federalist* No. 44, Congress was to legislate beyond the limits of its enumerated powers, then "in the last resort a remedy must be obtained from the people, who can, by the election of more faithful representatives, annul the acts of the usurpers."[1]

For Framers such as Madison, every citizen is unavoidably a constitutionalist, enforcing the boundaries of a limited constitution through the discerning exercise of the most potent political weapon, the popular vote. Even the most brilliant constitutional framework will fail to keep the various departments and levels of government within their respective spheres without the people serving as the ultimate constitutional safety net.

From the recognition that the people possess the authority to control the government and check the abuses of their leaders, it follows that the people are a potential source of instability. Specifically, Founding Fathers like Madison and Hamilton worried about the emergence of popular leaders who utilized demagoguery to obtain public support in service of their personal ambitions, which was ultimately destructive of the public good and individual liberty. As students of ancient history, they knew very well the turbulence that befell the governments of that era, and understood that popular governments were necessarily vulnerable to demagoguery. *The Federalist Papers* literally start and end with warning about the prospect of a demagogue. Hamilton begins the series by famously warning that "of those men who have overturned the liberties of republics, the greatest number have begun their career by paying an obsequious court to the people, commencing demagogues and ending tyrants."[2] And he ends *The Federalist* on a similar note, cautioning of the potentially dire consequences of failing to ratify the Constitution; rejecting the Constitution would, he argued, be akin to "hazarding anarchy, civil war, a perpetual alienation of the States from each other, and perhaps the military despotism of a victorious demagogue."[3]

Hamilton and Madison did not think that employing demagoguery to obtain and use political power necessarily meant that all demagogues were seeking to become tyrants; some merely used demagoguery to effectuate policies that were contrary to what they regarded as the public good. Madison worried that "men of factious tempers, of local prejudices, or of sinister designs, may, by intrigue, by corruption, or by other means, first obtain the suffrages, and then betray the interests of the people."[4] Madison cited a number of specific policies that a demagogic leader might pursue, such as a "rage for paper money, for an abolition of debts, for an equal division of property, or for any other improper or wicked project."[5]

Prior to the Constitutional Convention, the creators of the Constitution had watched nervously as these very types of measures gained traction in various state legislatures following the American Revolution, and they designed the Constitution in way that would inhibit such measures. In making his final plea for the Constitution in *The Federalist*, Alexander Hamilton specifically cited "the precautions taken against the repetition of those practices on the part of the State governments which have undermined the foundations of property and credit, have planted mutual distrust in the breasts of all classes of citizens, and have occasioned an almost universal prostration of morals."[6]

In creating the Constitution, the Founding Fathers labored hard to design a system that stymied demagogic leaders in their pursuit of political power. They sought to construct a system that, in Madison's words, made it "more difficult for unworthy candidates to practice with success the vicious arts by which elections are too often carried."[7] To this end, Madison and his colleagues bucked the traditional assumption—most conspicuously articulated by Montesquieu, who was held in high regard by virtual all of the Framers—that a republican form of government had to be confined to a small geographic area. They instead created an extended republic that could serve as a bulwark against those candidates who resorted to the "vicious arts" that they detested because, Madison argued, the "influence of factious leaders may kindle a flame within their particular States but will be unable to spread a general conflagration through the other States."[8] Armed with a deep knowledge of the history of popular governments, Madison saw the demagogue as the major threat to the stability of a republican government—it was through the use of "popular arts" that a demagogue could exploit a majority faction in a way that overwhelmed the myriad of the Constitution's deliberately designed constraints and oppressed the private rights of the minority.

What kind of behavior did Madison, Hamilton and their brethren consider to be demagogic? They worried about people being deceived by what Hamilton called "the arts of men, who flatter their prejudices to betray their interests."[9] As Hamilton saw it, the people are continually beset "by the wiles of parasites and sycophants, by the snares of the ambitious, the avaricious, the desperate, by the artifices of men who possess their confidence more than they deserve it, and of those who seek to possess rather than to deserve it."[10] At a most basic level, the Founding Fathers considered a demagogue to be a leader who capitalizes on popular prejudices by peddling false claims, by employing questionable rhetorical techniques, or by intentionally sowing divisions among different factions or interests within the body politic.

All demagoguery is not created equal. As one political scientist has explained, there is a difference in kind between "soft" demagoguery, which involves currying favor with the people through (among other things) making implausible promises, and "hard" demagoguery, which involves stirring the passions of the public through antagonism and division.[11] In either instance, the demagogue is trying to build a connection to the people, and leverage that connection for his own personal ambitions, which are at odds with the public good. Though the Founding Fathers most feared the demagogue who plays the "obsequious court to the people" and later commences a tyrant, they also worried about the political opportunist who uses "talents for low intrigue, and the little arts of popularity" to obtain office, manipulate legislators, and enact questionable public measures. The rule of law was of paramount importance: whereas the demagogue-turned-military dictator will by definition scuttle the rule of law in favor of a government based on his personal caprice, the soft demagogue will champion policies, such as the legislative redistribution of wealth and extinguishment of private debts, which tend to undermine it.[12]

****

Barack Obama ran for president as a different kind of politician. He introduced himself to the country during his 2004 convention keynote address as a figure of national unity, someone who disdained the tired "red states vs. blue states" debates of the past, and who expressed a desire for a color-blind society. A few years later, he promised that his presidential campaign would "be about reclaiming the meaning of citizenship, restoring our sense of common purpose, and realizing that few obstacles can withstand the power of millions of voices calling for change." He lamented that "our leaders in Washington seem incapable of working together in a practical, common-sense way," and pledged that, if elected, he would practice "a new kind of politics."[13]

This "new kind of politics" would transcend partisanship and the old ways of doing business in Washington. Obama chose Senator Joe Biden as his vice presidential nominee because, Obama said, Biden would help him "turn the page on the ugly partisanship in Washington so we can bring Democrats and Republicans together to pass an agenda that works for the American people."

Obama repeatedly stressed that "we've got to change the political system." And he offered, as a down-payment on this pledge, a refusal to "take money from federal registered lobbyists, because I want to answer to you when I'm in the White House." Once in office, Obama's experiment with a new kind of politics seemed to be working: a CBS poll taken during his first 100 days found that 68% of voters considered Obama to be a "different kind of politician."[14]

That this sentiment proved to be short-lived is not at all surprising. It is easy to talk about being a different kind of politician when things are going well. Before entering the presidency, Barack Obama had never really been in a tough political situation. He won his seat in the Illinois Senate by getting the other primary candidates disqualified from appearing on the ballot, and his road to the U.S. Senate was paved in part by the disclosure of the divorce records of not just his main Democratic primary opponent but also his main Republican opponent. Though he did lose his primary challenge to incumbent Rep. Bobby Rush for a seat in Congress in 2000, Obama has acknowledged that the campaign was ill fated from the start. In fact, from the time he was elected president of the *Harvard Law Review*, Obama enjoyed remarkably good political fortunes, from the national acclaim he garnered at Harvard to his surprising selection to give the keynote speech to the 2004 Democratic National Convention. He did not win a Reaganesque landslide in the electoral college, but his victory was convincing—especially in light of the two close presidential elections that preceded the 2008 election. He remained well regarded by the public throughout his first 100 days in office, sporting a public approval rating of greater than 60%.

But after ushering in a huge economic stimulus package, continuing and expanding the TARP bank bailout program and proposing economically costly restrictions on carbon emissions, Obama turned his attention to overhauling of the nation's health care system. This was by no means the most pressing issue in the minds of the American public, but had been on the wish list of progressive activists for decades. Though he did not advocate radical changes to the health care system during the campaign, Obama spoke out in favor of a Canadian-style, government-run health care system as a U.S. Senate candidate just a few years before. Taking office on the heels of a major financial crisis, Obama saw a golden opportunity to realize the most elusive (and grandest) of progressive dreams.

Soon after he started campaigning on behalf of a major federal overhaul, public opposition began to flourish. CNBC's Rick Santelli had helped launch the tea party movement when he lashed out against Obama's home mortgage bailout policies in February of 2009, and many of those tea party activists were naturally repelled by the sweeping expansion of the federal government portended by the health care overhaul. Their dissatisfaction was further aroused by the daily and devastating criticism of the various progressive health care proposals by conservative talk radio and the conservative blogosphere. Within a few months, members of Congress returning to their districts and states to attend town hall meetings were met by constituents incensed that Congress was considering a massive increase in government, especially in the midst of a terrible economic environment. In spite of this public opposition, Obama was not dissuaded from pursuing his grand health care design; but, by this time, it was clear that he would only realize his dream of a health care transformation by confounding the desires of the majority of the public.

Perhaps because of the public opposition to the health care overhaul, Obama conducted a laborious public relations campaign to help usher the bill through Congress. This debate seemed to bring out the worst in Obama, as he typically resorted to rhetoric that was at best questionable and at worst outright demagogic. One strange instance occurred at a press conference in July of 2009, when Obama was asked about how the pending health care overhaul would affect patient care, and the extent to which the government would be tasked with making medical decisions. He responded by offering a blistering critique of physician behavior:

> So if they're looking and—and you come in and you've got a bad sore throat, or your child has a bad sore throat, or has repeated sore throats, the doctor may look at the reimbursement system and say to himself, "You know what? I make a lot more money if I take this kid's tonsils out."[15]

Obama offered no evidence of physicians needlessly ripping out tonsils for profit, yet his statement stood as a blanket critique of how private doctors practice medicine. By linking the medical decisions of physicians to their ability to get reimbursements, Obama was trying to criticize the overall health care system, but the effect of his comments was to defame pediatricians.

Obama's critique of doctor behavior rested on questionable assumptions. He suggested that physicians would recklessly violate medical ethics and the Hippocratic Oath due to their own lust for profit. This reflected Obama's view of human nature and private economic behavior: he tends to see anyone engaged in a profit-generating venture as inherently suspect. The Founding Fathers, though fully cognizant of the defects in human nature, were not so quick to pass such blanket judgments. "As there is a degree of depravity in mankind which requires a certain degree of circumspection and distrust," James Madison observed in *The Federalist* No. 55, "so there are other qualities in human nature which justify a certain portion of esteem and confidence."[16]

In contrast to Madison, Obama's tonsils example presupposed that doctors were willing to elevate their own personal greed above ethics, science and patient well-being. The illustration fell flat because few believed doctors behaved in this fashion, and most understood that, even if a pediatrician was willing to needlessly rip out children's tonsils for profit, the pediatrician isn't even the one who would perform the actual procedure.

To curry favor with the public regarding his health care proposal, Obama made a number of promises that were unbelievable. Perhaps the most notorious of these promises was Obama's repeated assertion that, in spite of his desire to transmogrify the nation's health care system, the health care enjoyed by the American people would be undisturbed by his federal health care overhaul. "No matter how we reform health care," Obama declared, "we will keep this promise to the American people. If you like your doctor, you will be able to keep your doctor, period. If you like your health care plan, you'll be able to keep your health care plan, period. No one will take it away, no matter what."[17] Technically, there was a grain of truth in what Obama said, as the 2,000-plus page health care law does not contain an explicit provision forcing people to change plans. But the law affected roughly one-sixth of the entire economy, and there was no way that its implementation would not have ripple effects throughout the entire system.

Once the law was enacted, the proof was in the pudding. A number of businesses announced that, due to the changes wrought by ObamaCare, they were going to drop certain health insurance plans previously offered to their employees and/or retirees. 3M, the company that manufactures Post It notes and Scotch tape, decided to stop offering its health insurance plan to retirees because, a 3M memo explained, "health care reform has made it more difficult for employers like 3M to provide a plan that will remain competitive."[18] Principal Financial Group, an insurer that provided coverage for 840,000 people who receive employer-provided plans, chose to stop selling health insurance entirely because of the effect of the new health care law, which made it more difficult for small insurers like Principal to compete with health insurance giants like United Health Group.[19] McDonald's warned federal regulators that ObamaCare's mandates would force it to drop the modest but affordable plans that it provided for 30,000 hourly workers, and had to get a special waiver from the federal government to preserve the employee plans.[20]

Many voters were also concerned about the health care overhaul's effect on health care costs, both in terms of health insurance premiums and in terms of the stress on the federal budget. Obama made blanket promises on both fronts. Obama told the nation that, "I want to be very clear. I will not sign on to any health plan that adds to our deficits over the next decade. And by helping improve quality and efficiency, the reforms we make will help bring our deficits under control in the long term."[21] He argued that the health care overhaul would not only reduce insurance premiums, but actually *reduce* the federal budget deficit. "Our cost-cutting measures mirror most of the proposals in the current Senate bill, which," Obama claimed, "reduces most people's premiums and brings down our deficit by up to $1 trillion over the next decade because we're spending our health care dollars more wisely."[22] Obama was crystal clear in pitching his health care overhaul as a double win for the American people, who would benefit from lower premiums and enjoy the fruits of a declining budget deficit.

As the law started to take effect in 2010, it became clear that the law was not helping to restrain health insurance premiums; if anything, the law's mandates were driving additional premium increases. When confronted about the law's failure to reduce insurance premiums despite his repeated insistence that the law would reduce costs, Obama, incredibly, claimed that rising costs were something that he anticipated. "As a consequence of us getting 30 million additional people healthcare," Obama said, "at the margins that's going to increase our costs—we knew that."[23]

Within a couple of months after its enactment, the Congressional Budget Office noted that the spending associated with ObamaCare would likely be $115,000,000,000 more than was originally estimated, which further undermined the claim that ObamaCare would reduce the deficit.[24] The report from Obama's own Fiscal Commission pointed out that even these less-favorable CBO projections still "count on large phantom savings," that the long-term care program contained in ObamaCare is financially "unsustainable," and that, in spite and perhaps because of ObamaCare, Congress still must enact a "number of other reforms to reduce federal health spending and slow the growth of health care costs more broadly."[25] Within six months of its passage, Obama's promise regarding reducing costs and the budget deficit was so discredited that left-leaning interest groups such as the Herndon Alliance urged ObamaCare supporters *not* to claim that "the law will reduce costs and [the] deficit," or else run the risk of forfeiting their credibility with the public.[26]

****

With the economic malaise and the public's dissatisfaction with ObamaCare unabated, it became clear, as 2010 wore on, that Obama's Democratic Party was facing a large defeat in the midterm elections. Because independent voters had turned against Obama and his party, the best hope to stem Democratic losses rested on Obama's ability to energize the base constituencies of the party, especially racial and ethnic minorities. As the first African-American president, Obama enjoyed almost unanimous support from the black community, which gave him a 90%-plus approval rating, so these voters, once mobilized, could be expected to support his agenda at the polls.[27] Hispanics overwhelmingly supported Obama in 2008, but, if press reports are to be believed, many were less than pleased with Obama's refusal to push so-called "comprehensive immigration reform," which would legalize millions of illegal immigrants, creating, critics charged, a de facto amnesty, which is extremely unpopular. Obama thus faced the prospect not only that his party would lose Hispanic support, but also that those Hispanics who still supported him would stay home instead of voting Democratic in the midterms.

With this concern in mind, Obama decided to inject himself into the debate over the state of Arizona's immigration enforcement statute. The Arizona law made it a misdemeanor offense to be present in Arizona if in violation of federal immigration laws and required that state and local law enforcement personnel inquire about the immigration status of an individual lawfully stopped, detained or arrested—on non-immigration grounds—if "reasonable suspicion" existed that the individual is not legally present in the United States. If the individual is, in fact, present in the country illegally then the law enforcement officer has to report the individual to federal immigration authorities. The statute also provided that a "law-enforcement official or agency of this state may not consider race, color or national origin in implementing the requirements of this subsection except to the extent permitted by the United States or Arizona Constitution."[28]

The Arizona legislature passed the law because the federal government had proven itself incapable of securing the southern border, and the violent turmoil in Mexico had started to spread into Arizona. Although polls showed that the overwhelming majority of Arizonans supported the measure, left-of-center activists and left-leaning media outlets reacted strongly against the law, accusing Arizona of enacting a racial profiling scheme designed to run roughshod over the rights of ethnic minorities. U.S. Attorney General Eric Holder acknowledged that the law was not racist, but he expressed serious concerns about the measure even though he admitted that he had not yet read it.[29] He eventually filed a federal lawsuit seeking to prevent the law from taking effect.

Some accused Arizona of reincarnating Nazi Germany in the United States. Congressman Connie Mack, a Florida Republican, lashed out against Arizona for enacting SB 1070: "This law of 'frontier justice'—where law enforcement officials are required to stop anyone based on 'reasonable suspicion' that they may be in the country illegally—is reminiscent of a time during World War II when the Gestapo in Germany stopped people on the street and asked for their papers without probable cause."[30]

Politicians and activists began calling for an economic boycott of all things Arizona, and many even urged Major League Baseball to move the 2011 All Star game from Phoenix to further punish Arizona. Congressman Jose Serrano, a Democrat from New York, reasoned that "Major League Baseball, with 40 percent Latino ballplayers at all levels, should make a statement that it will not hold its All-Star Game in a state that discriminates against 40 percent of their people."[31]

Though not all criticism of the law was unreasonable—many pointed out, for example, that the law imposed a new burden on state and local law enforcement, which could hinder enforcing other state laws—the criticism levied by the likes of Mack and Serrano was not justified by the actual provisions of the statute. The use of "reasonable suspicion" as the threshold investigatory standard was identified by critics as being the foremost problem with the law because, they contended, it allowed law enforcement to target minorities based on an entirely subjective standard. But the "reasonable suspicion" standard was not invented out of whole cloth by Arizona as a way to target people based on race or ethnicity; it is a standard that has been a part of American law for decades, a standard that was devised by the Supreme Court during the high tide of pro-defendant liberal judicial activism during the 1960s, and which had been infused with objective meaning by numerous judicial decisions applying the standard to the facts of concrete cases.

As the Supreme Court stressed in the decision announcing the "reasonable suspicion" standard, when initiating law enforcement action based on "reasonable suspicion," the action must be based on "specific and articulable facts," and any inferences made by the officer must be rational in nature. In other words, if an officer acts only on the basis of an "inchoate and unparticularized suspicion or 'hunch,' then 'reasonable suspicion' does not, as a matter of law, exist." [32]

Since the Arizona law required, as a precondition to its enforcement, the existence of an otherwise lawful stop, arrest or detention and since the law specifically prohibited the use of race, color or national origin in enforcing its provisions, it did not authorize blanket detention of individuals of Mexican descent based on their appearance. With this in mind, those who argued that the Arizona law would lead to rampant racial and ethnic discrimination were essentially saying that they expected law enforcement personnel to abuse their positions and to disregard the law's clear provisions.

For his part, Obama had no interest in appraising the law in an intellectually honest fashion. Instead, sensing an opportunity to woo Hispanic voters, Obama injected himself and his administration into the controversy through patent demagoguery. At a town hall meeting in Iowa, he warned that, because of the Arizona law, "now suddenly if you don't have your papers and you took your kid out to get ice cream, you can be harassed, that's something that could potentially happen."[33]

At a joint news conference in the White House Rose Garden, Obama watched approvingly while Mexican President Felipe Calderón, whose country has draconian laws against illegal immigrants, criticized the Arizona measure as resting on "principles that are partial and discriminatory." Obama did not rebuke Calderón for assailing an American state while on U.S. soil, but instead complimented Calderón's criticism by declaring that "no law-abiding person—be they an American citizen, a legal immigrant, or a visitor or tourist from Mexico—should ever be subject to suspicion simply because of what they look like"—the implication being that the Arizona law actually sanctioned such conduct.[34]

Obama was not offended by Calderón's public criticism of American citizens while at the White House because he was more interested in fanning and exploiting racial and ethnic divisions for his political benefit. Though thoughtful and measured criticism was made about the law, none of that criticism centered upon the prospect of law enforcement targeting innocent bystanders at an ice cream shop. Obama was less concerned with a fair-minded debate about the law than he was on using the law as a wedge issue to energize Hispanic voters to vote Democratic.

Obama did not mince words in trying to mobilize Hispanic voters on behalf of his party, and he even urged Hispanic voters to approach the midterm elections by saying, "We're going to punish our enemies and we're gonna reward our friends who stand with us on issues that are important to us."[35] Obama also warned a minority radio audience that the election of a Republican majority in Congress would lead to "hand-to-hand combat" on Capitol Hill.[36] Obama was not merely trying to pitch his policies as being superior to those advanced by Republicans; he was attempting to paint Republicans as "enemies" of certain racial and ethnic minorities, thereby dividing the electorate along racial and ethnic lines.

Obama's attempts to sow racial and ethnic divisions among the electorate for his political benefit represented a palpable break from his famous invocation of an America united in the face of racial and ethnic diversity. Back then, Obama was trying to herald a new kind of politics that transcended the divisions of the past, but when his political fortunes took a turn for the worse, he tossed aside the airy platitudes of his presidential campaign in favor of deliberate attempts to sow antagonisms and division among members of the public. This demagoguery was certainly ineffective as a political tactic—Republican candidates received a far greater percentage of Hispanic votes than they had in 2008. Perhaps more significantly, Obama's resort to such rhetoric did substantial damage to his political brand, as it wiped away the remaining vestiges of the idea that Obama was a different kind of politician.

****

Obama has also habitually resorted to rhetorical techniques that, though not patently demagogic like some of his other rhetoric, represent the type of questionable popular leadership that Constitution creators like Madison and Hamilton frowned upon. Perhaps most conspicuously, Obama utilized the rhetorical technique known as the straw man to advance his political agenda. A straw man argument is a form of logically fallacious reasoning whereby a speaker takes an opponent's argument, mischaracterizes it, and then attacks the mischaracterized argument without addressing the substance of the actual argument—hence the description of the technique as "attacking a straw man." Though hailed as a gifted speaker, Obama resorted to the straw man in lieu of the soaring, inspirational rhetoric that characterized his presidential candidacy. It was the rhetorical crutch that he used to weather tough political storms.

Though Obama used the straw man in a wide variety of contexts, he habitually employed it when arguing for his expansionist view of government. He understood that the American public would not respond favorably to an explicit appeal for vast expansions of government, so he tried to elevate himself by denigrating the purported philosophy of his predecessor, as well as that of the Republican Party. Obama described that philosophy as follows: "The idea was that if we just had blind faith in the market, if we let corporations play by their own rules, if we left everyone else to fend for themselves that America would grow and America would prosper."[37] He tried to take issue with those who say that "government has no role in laying the foundation for our common prosperity."[38] And he criticized the view "that says every problem can be solved if only government would step out of the way; that if government were just dismantled…it could somehow benefit us all."[39]

Obama's criticism is simply unrecognizable for anyone with even a passing acquaintance with modern American politics. His claim that his opponents wanted to put "blind faith" in the market with no rules regarding corporations is belied by the facts. For one thing, additional corporate regulations were enacted during the tenure of the very predecessor Obama habitually lampooned, including the Sarbanes-Oxley Act of 2002, which the left-leaning editorial board of *The New York Times* has referred to as the "most significant investor-protection legislation since the Great Depression."[40] His Republican predecessor also imposed tariffs on steel imports, signed pervasive regulations of campaign money used to fund political speech, and created the bank bailout program known as TARP—none of which represents anything approaching a faith in free market economics, much less a "blind faith."

Obama's claim that his political opponents want "everyone else to fend for themselves," which implies that Republicans don't support a social safety net, is equally specious. Republicans are not known for eliminating any government programs. During the 1990s, a Republican-led Congress did replace the welfare entitlement with a temporary program designed to break the cycle of dependency and require work, but that law was signed by a Democrat, Bill Clinton, and is generally considered to have been a policy success. Other than the case of welfare entitlement, Republicans have, if anything enhanced the welfare state through programs such as the addition of a prescription drug entitlement to Medicare, which was passed in a Republican Congress in 2003 and signed into law by George W. Bush. And even those Republicans most ambitious about reigning in federal spending, such as Wisconsin Congressman Paul Ryan, have advocated changes that modernize but maintain the social safety net.

Obama's claim that Republicans regard government as having "no role" in creating conditions that can lead to economic growth is also unfounded. Even the most prominent proponents of free enterprise, from Adam Smith to Friedrich Hayek, have advocated a role for government and have spurned a truly laissez-faire system. For example, in the *Wealth of Nations*, Smith stressed the need for government to enforce the rule of law, create protections for intellectual property, and take on public works projects as a means of facilitating economic growth. Likewise, in *The Road to Serfdom*, Hayek argued that the government should address certain market inefficiencies, such as protection against poisonous substances, and should guarantee a minimum standard of living to its citizens. For their part, many Republicans have articulated a belief in a government that creates conditions that are conducive for economic growth, including stable tax policy, sound money and reasonable regulations. Certainly, no reasonable participant in the nation's political debate suggested that the government be "dismantled."

Obama employed the straw man in other contexts. In a speech discussing his goal of a world free of nuclear weapons, he claimed that those who considered his goal to be naïve were arguing "that the spread of these weapons cannot be stopped, cannot be checked—that we are destined to live in a world where more nations and more people possess the ultimate tools of destruction." Of course, those who objected to Obama's vision of a world devoid of nuclear weapons were not arguing for nuclear proliferation; many objected to rogue states like Iran acquiring nuclear weapons, but correctly surmised that America's possession of nuclear weapons helped deter potential aggressors, thereby rendering Obama's vision undesirable.

In discussing education reform, Obama described the education philosophy of his political opponents by saying that "no matter how much money you spend, nothing makes a difference, so let's just blow up the public school systems."[41] Though there exists a wide variety of conservative approaches to education reform, few approaches envision blowing up public schools; instead, these approaches seek to foster competition through parental choice, implement ways to measure student achievement, and reduce the bureaucracy and administrative overhead that prevent public funds from positively impacting students in the classroom. Obama employed this straw man because, by touting himself as an education reformer, he was picking a fight with public education unions, which inject millions of dollars into political campaigns in service of Democratic candidates. By characterizing the views of his political opponents in such extreme and inaccurate terms, Obama could distinguish himself, in the eyes of the unions, from those seemingly obnoxious views.

The straw man was also the technique of choice for Obama's pronouncements regarding the handling of unlawful enemy combatants captured during the War on Terror. Obama promised to close the detention facility at Guantanamo Bay, Cuba, arrange for the detainees to be transferred to the United States and, for the most part, prosecuted in federal civilian courts on American soil. Obama took issue with those who purportedly have "derided our federal courts as incapable of handling the trials of terrorists. They are wrong. Our courts and our juries, our citizens, are tough enough to convict terrorists."[42]

Again, Obama was battling a straw man. The issue was not whether federal courts are "tough" enough to handle trials of terrorists; there have been numerous examples in which terrorists captured in the United States have been convicted in federal courts. Instead, the question was whether it is in the national security interest of the United States to try terrorists captured outside of the United States, such as 9/11 mastermind Khalid Sheikh Mohammad, in civilian courts located in places like New York City. Critics pointed out that a trial of someone like Mohammad would create security concerns and impose financial burdens upon the host city, that unlawful enemy combatants were not entitled to the full panoply of rights of an American citizen, that soldiers do not collect evidence in the middle of a firefight in the same way that a federal agent collects evidence during a criminal investigation, and that classified information could be better protected in a military commission-style forum.

As is his practice, Obama claimed to be transcending the tired debates of the past related to the detainment and treatment of terrorist detainees. He criticized those who "make little allowance for the unique challenges posed by terrorism…who would never put national security over transparency." Though some on the far left may have made such arguments, no credible political official has claimed that the government has no interest in protecting classified information from those public disclosures which would endanger American lives. Obama also criticized those who "suggest that the ends of fighting terrorism can be used to justify any means, and that the president should have blanket authority to do whatever he wants—provided it is a president with whom they agree." While some on the right may view the president's commander-in-chief powers as being more potent than Obama and his liberal allies would like, nobody denied the importance of the congressional Authorization for the Use of Military Force following 9/11, or that the United States, including the president, is bound by the law of armed conflict. By criticizing the two philosophical extremes, Obama claimed to be transcending what he considered to be the stale debates of the past, but his use of the straw man was proof positive that he succeeded in doing no such thing.

****

That Obama has so thoroughly confounded the ideals of the Founding Fathers with respect to political leadership is surprising. After all, he came to office promising to transcend old debates, to eschew petty partisan squabbles, and to serve as a national unifying force in government. Yet, even though he could plausibly claim to be the most liberal president in 50 years, Obama was not able to maintain the same level of political support that he enjoyed during the campaign, as his performance in office left many of these previously enthusiastic supporters dejected and demoralized. Obama, it turned out, was just like any other politician.

Indeed, by the end of 2010, some progressives bemoaned the "leadership vacuum that Obama has left," and pined for a progressive movement with "the passion and single mindedness of the Tea Party movement."[43] Frank Rich, the hyper-liberal columnist for *The New York Times*, even compared Obama's failure to demonstrate progressive presidential leadership to a prisoner suffering from Stockholm Syndrome.[44] Coming on the heels of huge Republican gains in the 2010 midterm elections, these complaints were politically convenient. But the dissatisfaction was a result of the original delusion, which many progressives possessed, that Obama was a historically transcendental figure capable of monumental feats, a belief based on unrealistic, if audacious, hope.

23

THE DIPLOMACY OF DEFERENCE

After the Democratic Party's "shellacking" in the 2010 elections, left-leaning media outlets tried to draw parallels between Barack Obama's political situation and that of Ronald Reagan, who saw his party lose seats in Congress during the first midterm election of his presidency. The hope was that Obama, like Reagan, would be able to rebound to earn a convincing reelection victory. The comparison was more than a little odd. After all in *Dreams From My Father*, Obama ripped Reagan, referring to the Gipper's White House as the place "where Reagan and his minions were carrying on their dirty deeds" and mocking Reagan's "brand of verbal legerdemain."[1] As a collegian, Obama was an implacable opponent of the Reagan defense buildup that helped end the Cold War, and he penned an article in Columbia's *Sundial* student magazine in which he criticized Reagan's foreign policy for its "twisted logic," especially because Obama despised the fact that American tax dollars were going towards national defense rather than to additional social welfare programs. Obama, instead, supported a nuclear freeze, which most analysts agree would have prolonged the existence of the Soviet Union and the Cold War.

Obama's criticism of Reagan's Cold War policies is noteworthy because, before assuming the presidency, Obama spent most of his political life working towards the goal of redistributive justice. As both a community organizer and as an Illinois state senator, the issues that motivated him were generally domestic issues: supporting a Canadian-style, government-run health care system, opposing efforts to reform welfare, and envisioning a collective political salvation effectuated through government action. Thus, Obama's strong critique of Reagan's policy of "peace through strength" represents one of the most telling glimpses into how Obama viewed foreign affairs. Reagan, as well as leading advocates of the Constitution such as Alexander Hamilton and John Jay, saw the projection of strength as the most effective way to deter conflict with foreign adversaries. Obama's hostility to the Reagan defense buildup rested on the notion that the display of strength was provocative and, thus, invited further conflict. In other words, Obama thought that displaying magnanimity towards foreign enemies is the way to prompt such enemies to act in a way that is less threatening to the United States.

Other than the student article on the nuclear freeze movement, Obama's major foreign policy pronouncement occurred at an anti-war rally in Chicago during the congressional debate over authorizing the use of force against Saddam Hussein's regime in 2002. Then an obscure state senator from Hyde Park, Obama spoke out against removing Hussein from power. Calling the Iraq war a "dumb war," Obama ripped the "cynical attempt by…armchair, weekend warriors… to shove their own ideological agendas down our throats, irrespective of the costs in lives lost and hardships borne." He claimed that the war was an "attempt by political hacks like Karl Rove to distract us from a rise in the uninsured, a rise in the poverty rate, a drop in median income to distract us from corporate scandals and a stock market that has just gone through the worst month since the Great Depression." To Obama, this amounted to a "war based not on reason but on passion, not on principle but on politics."[2]

Obama used the speech, with great effect, to demonstrate his anti-war bona fides during the 2008 presidential primaries. Nevermind that the speech contained implausible factual assertions, such as Obama's claim that, during World War II, his American grandfather "heard the stories of fellow troops who first entered Auschwitz and Treblinka"—since both camps were liberated by the Soviet Union, not Patton's Army, it is unlikely that "fellow troops" said anything of the kind. To the dovish base of the Democratic Party, which was utterly disenchanted with the Iraq conflict, the speech showed Obama to be the one viable candidate who could credibly claim to have opposed the war from the start. Obama would later say that it was "the speech I am most proud of," and it was one of the most important factors that helped him best Hillary Clinton for his party's nomination.

Before the financial crisis in mid-September of 2008, foreign policy was perhaps the dominant issue in the presidential campaign. Obama aggressively ran against the "failed policies of George W. Bush," criticizing Bush for employing "tough talk and bad strategy" and disparaging John McCain for his closeness to Bush and for "grasping at the ideas of the past." Obama also bemoaned that "we've been told that tough talk and an ill-conceived war can replace diplomacy, and strategy, and foresight."[3] He envisioned an approach to foreign affairs that rested on coordination with other nations and the enhancement of America's image in the rest of the world. Obama argued that the achievement of "ultimate victory against our enemies will come only by rebuilding our alliances and exporting those ideals that bring hope and opportunity to millions of people around the globe."[4]

This soft power approach to world affairs portended, Obama claimed, a new era in international politics, one in which the United States was revered by its allies and respected by its adversaries. By striking a deferential posture in diplomatic dealings with other nations, the world's most intractable problems, from the pursuit of nuclear weapons by rogue states like Iran to the Israeli-Palestinian conflict, could be solved. During a campaign debate, he even pledged to meet, within the first year of his presidency and without preconditions, with the leaders of the world's most deplorable regimes: Iran, North Korea, Syria, Venezuela and Cuba. He ridiculed "the notion that somehow not talking to countries is punishment to them" as being "ridiculous." Obama analogized his willingness to meet with rogue leaders with the diplomatic efforts, during the Cold War, of presidents like John F. Kennedy and Ronald Reagan, who, Obama argued, "understood that we may not trust them and they may pose an extraordinary danger to this country, but we had an obligation to find areas where we can potentially move forward."[5] Kennedy, though, regarded his first meeting with Soviet premier Nikita Khrushchev as a major blunder, and Reagan was intent on defeating the Soviet Union, not trying to "move forward" with it.

Be that as it may, candidate Obama proclaimed that there was "no greater mission than keeping America safe and restoring America's image in the world," and he suggested that repairing America's image depended upon strengthening alliances with friendly nations and, perhaps more importantly, making America less disliked by its adversaries. He stressed that "the old formulas will not do," and trumpeted the need "to turn the page on the Bush-Cheney policy of not talking to leaders we don't like. That doesn't make us look tough. It makes us look arrogant. I'm not afraid that I'll lose a propaganda battle with a bunch of dictators. Strong countries and strong presidents shouldn't be afraid to talk to our adversaries to tell them where

America stands."[6] If reaching out to America's enemies meant alienating allies, then Obama appeared ready to do just that.

Obama's approach to foreign affairs as president rested on a number of questionable premises. First, true to philosophy he exhibited in his college article lauding the nuclear freeze movement, Obama believed that the road to a more peaceful world required a reduction in American strength. In a celebrated speech in Prague shortly after taking office, Obama stated "clearly and with conviction America's commitment to seek the peace and security of a world without nuclear weapons." Citing his oft-repeated campaign slogan, he told the crowd that, in response to those who criticized such a goal as undesirable, "we have to insist, 'Yes, we can.'" Obama counseled of the need to "put an end to Cold War thinking," and pledged that the United States "will reduce the role of nuclear weapons in our national security strategy," and that he would "urge others to do the same"—hoping that America's show of goodwill would incentivize other nations to act in a similar fashion.[7]

True to his word, Obama later enacted substantial changes to the nation's nuclear weapons policy. For the first time in its history, the United States explicitly committed not to use nuclear weapons against nonnuclear states in compliance with the Nuclear Nonproliferation Treaty, even if such states attack the U.S. with chemical or biological weapons or if they initiate a crippling cyber-attack.[8] The policy also renounced, over the objection of Obama's Secretary of Defense Robert Gates, the development of any new nuclear weapons. According to Obama, these changes would set an example for other nations to follow, and portended a world in which nuclear weapons were obsolete. The changes were dramatic. Obama was restricting America's ability to use nuclear weapons to deter a wide variety of threats, including chemical, biological and conventional attacks, against which previous administrations considered America's nuclear arsenal to be an efficacious deterrent.

The U.S. nuclear arsenal has served as a deterrent to a wide range of threats. When Saddam Hussein's army invaded Kuwait in August of 1990, the United States led an international diplomatic effort to negotiate the removal Iraqi forces from Kuwaiti land. On the eve of a U.S.-led military response in January of 1991, Secretary of State James Baker held a 7-hour meeting with Tariq Aziz, Iraq's foreign minister, and warned Aziz about the use of weapons of mass destruction against

U.S. and coalition forces. "If conflict ensues," Baker told Aziz, "and you use chemical or biological weapons against U.S. forces, the American people will demand vengeance. And we have the means to exact it…this is not a threat, it is a promise." According to Baker, it is likely that Iraq did not use chemical weapons against U.S. forces because he made clear that his warning "was broad enough to include the use of all types of weapons that America possessed," including nuclear weapons. "Years later," Baker told a Senate committee, "when Saddam Hussein was captured, de-briefed and asked why he had not used his chemical weapons [during the 1991 war], he re-called the substance of my statement to Aziz in Geneva."[9]

The value of such a deterrent is unassailable, yet Obama nevertheless saw fit to weaken America's nuclear posture. Just as Obama the Columbia undergraduate saw a nuclear freeze as representing a magnanimous outreach to the Soviet Union that would result in better Soviet behavior, Obama the president saw the adoption of a less aggressive nuclear posture by the United States as representing a gesture of goodwill by the United States to the rest of the world that would foster more stability and peace. Once other nations see America restricting the scenarios in which she would use nuclear weapons, so this line of thinking goes, they will be more willing to work with the United States to reduce, and eventually eliminate, the need for nuclear weapons.

This wishful thinking stems from Obama's stated belief that "the fate of each nation is inextricably linked to the fate of all nations."[10] In a speech before the United Nations, he claimed, incredibly, that "the interests of nations and peoples are shared," and that "no one nation can or should dominate another nation. No world order that elevates one nation or group of people over another will succeed. No balance of power will hold….The time has come to realize that the old habits, the old arguments, are irrelevant to the challenges faced by our people. They lead nations to act in opposition to the very goals they claim pursue."[11] Under this view, the United States should not occupy a preeminent position in world affairs; American military power, including the deterrent effect of its nuclear arsenal, is more likely to provoke hostility than to foster stability. Given that, in Obama's view, all nations share the same interests, there exists no need for one nation to possess a nuclear advantage over another nation.

To Obama, a world in which no nation, including the United States, possesses nuclear weapons will be a world in which the frequency of military conflict is reduced. Obama's approach presupposes that if the United States agrees to disarm itself, then regimes hostile to the United States would follow suit—even though American weakness would provide such regimes a golden opportunity to dramatically enhance their own power vis-à-vis the United States through the acquisition of nuclear weapons. Obama did concede that "some countries will break the rules," and that "we need a structure in place that ensures that when any nation does, they will face consequences."[12] He claimed that "rules must be binding. Violations must be punished. Words must mean something."[13]

But on the very day that he spoke those words, North Korea's communist dictatorship tested a rocket that could be used for long-range nuclear missiles. Obama acknowledged the test and proclaimed that "North Korea must know that the path to security and respect will never come through threats and illegal weapons…And that's why we stand shoulder to shoulder to pressure the North Koreans to change course."[14] Of course, North Korea well knows that it greatly *enhances* its security by possessing nuclear weapons, and, judging from its contentment at being an international pariah for more than six decades, it does not seem to view the "path to respect" as being within its national interests. Nonetheless, in spite of the failure to prevent North Korea from acquiring nuclear weapons, Obama remained convinced that the reduction and even elimination of America's nuclear arsenal was in the best interests of the United States and the world.

Obama habitually sought other ways to downplay American military and political dominance. His actions were premised on the idea that publicly minimizing the strength of the United States would grease the skids of international diplomacy. Perhaps most conspicuously, Obama adopted a practice of bowing before foreign leaders, which conveyed an image of inferiority and represented a sign of weakness. When Obama first bowed before King Abdullah of Saudi Arabia, many observers were befuddled that an American president would extend such a greeting to a foreign monarch. The bow "belittled the power and independence of the United States," the *Washington Times* remarked in an editorial. "Such an act is a traditional obeisance befitting a king's subjects, not his peer. There is no precedent for U.S. presidents bowing to Saudi or any other royals."[15]

Some of Obama's aides disputed that Obama actually bowed to the Saudi monarch, though video belied their explanation that Obama's greeting was a function of the height difference between Obama and King Abdullah. However, when Obama greeted the emperor of Japan with a full, almost ninety-degree bow, there was no room for dispute about Obama extending a bona fide bow to a foreign potentate. Though the White House claimed the bow was merely an observation of protocol, bowing is hardly customary. Officials from the United States, including then-Vice President Dick Cheney, Canada, the Philippines, Bulgaria, India, Latvia, Finland, Turkey, Loas, China, France, Peru, Israel, Vietnam, Germany, Russia, Mexico and Indonesia have all greeted Emperor Akihito with a handshake rather than a bow.[16] "There is no reason for an American president to bow to anyone," Cheney said. "Our friends and allies don't expect it, and our enemies see it as a sign of weakness."[17] According to an academic with an expertise on Japan consulted by Jake Tapper from ABC News, the "bow as [Obama] performed it did not just display weakness in Red State terms, but evoked weakness in Japanese terms….The last thing the Japanese want or need is a weak looking American president," yet Obama's bow projected such weakness.[18]

White House aides characterized the bow a deliberate attempt to project a more benevolent national image, a way for Obama "to deliver" on his campaign promise of "directly engaging friends and enemies alike."[19] Such a tactic, though, cut against the grain of traditional American behavior. As conservative William J. Bennett bluntly reminded Obama and his supporters, "We don't defer to kings or emperors."[20] Indeed, when then-President Bill Clinton performed a mini-bow in a meeting with the Japanese Emperor in 1994, even *The New York Times* asked, "If not to stand eye-to-eye with royalty, what else were 1776 and all that about?"[21] Obama, though, was unmoved. When he greeted Chinese President Hu Jintao the following spring, he supplemented the handshake he extended to the communist leader with a partial bow.

Though some naysayers dismissed Obama's penchant for bowing to foreign leaders as a non-issue, the bows were clearly premeditated by Obama. To be sure, Obama's rationale for bowing stems from his desire to show respect to other nations, which he sees as being necessary to improve the image of the United States and to create a harmonious environment for international relations. Consistent with

Obama's general foreign policy outlook, though, this rested less on paying tribute to foreign royalty than on projecting a diminished United States. Like many American critics, Obama seemed to equate American strength with "belligerence," and considered American dominance as threatening to other nations and corrosive of the international order.

Given that Obama went out of his way to portray the United States as just another country, it is not surprising that Obama failed to offer a ringing endorsement of the idea of "American exceptionalism." When asked during a foreign trip whether he believed in the idea of "American exceptionalism," Obama replied that he believed in "American exceptionalism, just as I suspect that the Brits believe in British exceptionalism, and the Greeks believe in Greek exceptionalism." In other words, America is exceptional just like other nation, which is to say it is not exceptional at all. From Obama's perspective, this awkward formulation made sense because an unabashed defense of American exceptionalism necessarily elevates the United States above other nations, undercutting Obama's larger purpose of making America merely one nation among a world of equals.

Obama also habitually called attention to (and in some instances unfairly exaggerated) America's supposed flaws, even offering unsolicited apologies. He seemed to think that characterizing his country as a deeply flawed giant would endear him to other nations and foreign audiences. Within a week after taking office, he told the Al Arabiya news network that his presidency marked the chance to improve relations between the United States and the Muslim world, suggesting that the tension in the relationship stemmed from the behavior of the United States. "We sometimes make mistakes," Obama said. "We have not been perfect." Obama also stressed that "we cannot paint with a broad brush a faith as a consequence of the violence that is done in that faith's name," which was a veiled rebuke of his predecessor, George W. Bush, even though Bush repeatedly took pains to declare that "Islam is peace," including in the week following the 9/11 attacks. He also promised Muslims that he is someone "who is listening, who is respectful," and declared, incredibly, that his job was "to promote the interests not just of the United States, but also ordinary people who right now are suffering from poverty and a lack of opportunity."[22]

When he made his first foreign presidential trip in April of 2009, Obama went out of his way to call attention to America's supposed flaws, which vindicated criticism of the United States lodged, in many instances, by those hostile to American interests. At a town hall meeting in Strasbourg, France, Obama lamented America's "failure to appreciate Europe's leading role in the world." He expressed frustration that, "instead of celebrating your dynamic union and seeking to partner with you to meet common challenges, there have been times where America has shown arrogance and been dismissive, even derisive." Obama promised a new partnership with Europe "in which America listens and learns from our friends and allies."[23] Britain's *Daily Telegraph* noted that Obama's remarks in Strasbourg "went further than any United States president in history in criticizing his own country's action while standing on foreign soil."[24]

Obama's remarks in France were just the beginning of what critics dubbed his international apology tour, during which Obama repeatedly called attention to alleged American transgressions. At the Summit of the Americas, Obama declared that, under his supposedly enlightened leadership, "we seek an equal partnership. There is no senior or junior partner in our relations."[25] When the Nicaraguan strongman Daniel Ortega gave a lengthy, rambling speech indicting the United States as the root of the world's ills and complaining of U.S. actions as far back as the Kennedy administration, Obama did not rebuke Ortega and did not offer a defense of the United States or previous presidents like JFK; instead, he remarked that he was thankful that Ortega did not blame him for things that occurred when he was a child. Obama was untroubled by withering criticism of his own country by foreign critics so long as those critics recognized the dividing line between America before and after Obama's leadership. Indeed, Obama deliberately cultivated the idea that America suffered from a series of maladies so that he could position himself as the symbol of a benevolent, deferential America eager to make peace with friend and foe alike.

Obama even invoked the purported flaws of the United States to justify his nuclear abolition agenda. Obama stressed the necessity of abolishing nuclear weapons because, "as the only nuclear power to have used a nuclear weapon, the United States has a moral responsibility to act."[26] He seemed to equate the need to prevent rogue states from acquiring nuclear weapons with the fact that the United States employed atomic bombs against Hiroshima and Nagasaki to end

World War II. No American president has ever apologized for America's use of the bomb and most agree that the use of the bomb saved, at a minimum, hundreds of thousands of American lives. What is more, immediately following World War II, the United States enjoyed a nuclear monopoly and could have conquered the entire world. That we refused to do any such thing belies Obama's suggestion that America is guilty of recklessness with nuclear weapons.

At a press conference in Japan, Obama was asked by a Japanese journalist whether he believed the United States made the "right decision" when it dropped atomic bombs on Hiroshima and Nagasaki during WWII, which devastated the two cities but which ended the war. He dodged the question and declined to rebuke Truman, probably because he knew that a direct apology would have drawn criticism from his fellow Americans. Obama did, though, tell Japanese journalists that he "would be honored to have the opportunity to visit those cities at some point during my presidency."[27] And Obama made international news when, in August of 2010, he became the first American president to send a representative from the United States to the annual Hiroshima remembrance ceremony to "to express respect for all the victims of World War II."[28] Though the American envoy did not speak at the ceremony, his presence, especially when viewed within the context of Obama's habitual apologies for the United States, represented what the son of Enola Gay pilot Paul Tibbets called "an unsaid apology." Such a de facto apology served to create a moral equivalence between the actions of imperial Japan and the United States.

Obama also drew negative attention to America for issues having nothing to do with foreign affairs. At a speech before the Turkish Parliament, Obama invoked what he called "our own darker periods of our history"—slavery, segregation and the mistreatment of Native Americans. There existed no need to invoke these issues on foreign soil, and it simply reduced America's moral authority in the eyes of the rest of the world and provided enemies of the United States with grist for their habitual criticism of America. In addition, when Mexican President Felipe Calderon publicly ripped the state of Arizona for it's immigration enforcement statute during a joint press conference with the president at the White House, Obama did not defend one of the sovereign states in his own country; instead, he buttressed Calderon's complaints by criticizing the law as discriminatory, declaring that "no law-abiding person—be they an American citizen, a legal immigrant, or a visitor or tourist from Mexico—should ever be subject to suspicion simply because of what they look like," even though the law provided for no such thing.[29]

Indeed, Obama's administration even made the Arizona immigration law an international issue by raising it in discussions on human rights with, of all countries, China. Assistant Secretary of State for Democracy Human Rights and Labor Michael Posner told reporters that the U.S. brought up the Arizona law "early and often" because it was "a troubling trend in our society, and an indication that we have to deal with issues of discrimination or potential discrimination. And these are issues very much being debated in our own society."[30]

This drew a sharp rebuke from U.S. Senators John McCain and John Kyl, both from Arizona. "You seemed to imply [the Arizona law] is morally equivalent to China's persistent pattern of abuse and repression of its people," McCain and Kyl wrote in demanding an apology. "To compare in any way the lawful and democratic act of the government of the state of Arizona with the arbitrary abuses of the unelected Chinese Communist Party is inappropriate and offensive."[31]

Though he was quick to highlight, even gratuitously, the supposed shortcomings of the United States, Obama made a deliberate effort to laud predominantly Muslim countries and to invoke their positive contributions to history. At a speech in Cairo, Obama spoke about "civilization's debt to Islam" for carrying "the light of learning through so many centuries, paving the way for Europe's Renaissance and Enlightenment....Islamic culture has given us majestic arches and soaring spires; timeless poetry and cherished music; elegant calligraphy and places of peaceful contemplation....Islam has demonstrated through words and deeds the possibilities of religious tolerance and racial equality." According to Obama, "Islam has always been a part of America's story." Perhaps because of this, Obama told the crowd that he considered it "part of my responsibility as president of the United States to fight against negative stereotypes of Islam wherever they appear."[32]

He even instructed his NASA administrator, Charles Bolden, to reorient the agency's mission away from space exploration and towards engagement with the Muslim world. According to Bolden, Obama told him that his "perhaps foremost" task was to "find a way to reach out to the Muslim world and engage much more with dominantly Muslim nations to help them feel good about their historic contribution to science, math and engineering."[33]

By taking a much more critical stance against his own country than against Muslim countries, Obama was trying to "build bridges" to the Muslim world. The hope was that by calling attention to America's alleged flaws and the Muslim world's supposed greatness, Obama could reduce tensions stemming from the War on Terrorism, the removal of Saddam Hussein, and America's historic support for the State of Israel. Part of this strategy rested on America pursuing its national interests with less vigor; under Obama, the United States would be more willing to subordinate its own interests to international institutions and to international agreements. But part of the strategy rested on cosmetics: by being exceptionally solicitous of predominantly Muslim countries, the hope was that the United States would improve its image in the eyes of Muslims in the Middle East and throughout the world.

To further advance this strategy, Obama called attention to his own Muslim roots, hoping to connect with the people of the Muslim world. During the presidential campaign of 2008, the mention of Obama's middle name of "Hussein" was considered to be outside the bounds of political decency. When a conservative radio host referred to Obama as "Barack Hussein Obama" at a rally for John McCain, McCain publicly repudiated the comments and pledged that "it will never happen again."[34] Once Obama was in office, though, he highlighted the fact that he was "an African-American with the name Barack Hussein Obama" as a way of endearing the United States with Muslims throughout the world. The notion seemed to be that, as the son of a Kenyan, as a former resident of Indonesia, as the bearer of a Muslim middle name, and as the proponent of a post-American foreign policy, Obama, as an individual, represented an effective vehicle for achieving better relations with the Muslim world. Journalists such as Andrea Mitchell, Dan Rather, and Katy Kay lauded the fact that, "with this president and his multicultural background," America was improving its image with Muslims.[35] Unfortunately, public opinion surveys taken nearly two years after Obama assumed office revealed that approval of U.S. leadership in the Middle East and North Africa was at the same level, or lower, than it was before Obama took office.[36]

Obama's Muslim outreach was part of his overall design to curry favor with those nations, such as Iran, who are avowed enemies of America. Shortly after taking office, Obama taped a New Year's message to the people and leaders of Iran. Using the title favored by the Iranian regime, "The Islamic Republic of Iran," Obama hailed Iran for its "great and celebrated culture" and for Iran's contributions to American society. He appealed to the "common humanity" between the U.S. and Iran, cited the quest for peace as stemming from the common hopes and dreams of both nations, and urged a new commitment to diplomacy. Later, in his Cairo University speech, Obama pledged to "proceed with courage, rectitude, and resolve," and to "move forward without preconditions on the basis of mutual respect."[37] Obama even lamented that the "United States played a role in the overthrow of a democratically elected Iranian government," which made him the first U.S. president to publicly acknowledge American involvement in the 1953 Iranian coup.[38] At no time did Obama question the legitimacy of the Islamic terror state.

When Iranians took to the streets to protest massive election fraud in June of 2009, Obama refused to publicly back the so-called "Green Revolution" against the regime of Mahmoud Ahmadinejad. Though the electoral chicanery was convincingly condemned by many European leaders, Obama did not forcefully rebuke the regime because, he explained, he did not want to "meddle" in Iranian affairs, meekly stating that "people's voices should be heard and not suppressed."[39] As the protests continued, Obama reemphasized that "the use of tough hard headed diplomacy, diplomacy without illusions, is critical when it comes to pursuing a core set of national security interests. We will continue to pursue a tough direct dialogue between our two countries."[40] Obama's passive response to the Iranian upheavals signaled that he was more interested in pursuing his diplomatic endeavors with Iran's despotic leaders than he was in supporting freedom for Iran's people.

Obama's attempts to engage Iran failed. On the one issue that is central to the security of the United States and allies such as Israel—preventing Iran from developing or acquiring nuclear weapons—Obama's repeated overtures to the Islamic state did not succeed in stymieing its march to a nuclear weapon. In fact, Iran engineered a deal with Brazil and Turkey, both nations that are supposed to be friendly with the United States, in which Iran agreed to send a significant portion of its enriched uranium stockpile, which can be used for weapons, to Turkey for conversion into fuel rods that can be used for power but not weapons. This still left Iran with a large amount of enriched uranium, undermined the international effort to impose sanctions on Iran through the United Nations, and embarrassed the United States. Although sanctions were adopted by a United Nations Security Council Resolution, Turkey and Brazil voted against the sanctions, and the sanctions instituted were widely viewed as ineffective at preventing the further development of nuclear weapons by the Iranian regime.

Obama's attempt to engage Iran in diplomatic discussions was fatally flawed. By displaying magnanimity towards Iran, Obama thought he was making a good faith gesture towards a regime that has been a mortal enemy of the United States for three decades, thereby creating an incentive for Iran to forego developing a nuclear weapon in favor of a more constructive relationship with the U.S. and its allies. By Iran's lights, though, Obama's gestures demonstrated weakness and reassured Iran that its continued development of nuclear weapons would not be met with a U.S. military response. Obama's push for diplomacy and his deemphasizing of U.S. strength sent the signal that the consequences of obtaining a nuclear weapon would not be fatal to the Iranian regime.

Obama pursued his strategy of seeking to curry favor with American adversaries even when it required that he disrespect, and even harm, traditional U.S. allies. In a move designed to please Russian leaders like Vladimir Putin and Dmitri Medvedev, Obama scrapped plans to deploy a missile defense shield in Poland and the Czech Republic. By reversing the pledge made to the Poles and the Czechs regarding missile defense, Obama hoped that his action would be taken by the Russians as a gesture of good faith, making them more likely to assist the U.S. with preventing the acquisition of nuclear weapons by Iran. Obama initially raised the possibility of canceling the missile defense plans in a secret letter sent to President Medvedev, though no binding commitments were ever provided by the Russians.[41] Because Obama's decision appeared to represent a unilateral concession, some U.S. allies worried that Obama's actions ran "the risk of appearing to give away too much to tough negotiating partners who may simply pocket any concessions."[42]

For steadfast American allies Poland and the Czech Republic, the reneging on commitments brokered during the Bush administration between the U.S. and the Polish and Czech governments, respectively, represented, in the words of Polish Foreign Affairs minister Radoslaw Sikorski, "the worst-case scenario" in which "Poland consents to the shield, incurs the political costs, and then the base is not built because the government changes in the United States."[43]

Obama also undermined a key American ally in service of brokering a nuclear arms control treaty with the Russians. As someone who sees nuclear disarmament as the key to global peace, Obama was desperate to reach an agreement on the so-called New START treaty. The Russians understood this and, accordingly, demanded that the U.S. provide Russia with information about Trident missiles supplied to Great Britain by the United States, even though the treaty did not concern the British. The U.S. tried to obtain U.K. approval for transferring detailed information about the British missiles to Russia, but officials in London refused. Nevertheless, Obama agreed to hand over the serial numbers for all Trident missiles supplied by the U.S. to the U.K., which allowed Russia to better gauge the size of the British nuclear arsenal—something that British officials have deliberately tried to obscure.[44]

As someone willing to engage with adversaries of all types, Obama, perhaps not surprisingly, garnered praise from some undesirable quarters. Speaking at the United Nations, Libyan strongman Moammar Gaddafi praised America's 44th president as "our Obama," and hailed the election of Obama as "the beginning of change. We are content and happy if Obama can stay forever as the president."[45] Even as Obama prepared to launch air strikes against Gaddafi's regime in March of 2011, Gaddafi wrote to Obama that "even if Libya and the United States of America enter into a war, God forbid, you will always remain my son, and I have all the love for you as a son."[46]

For his part, Venezuelan Marxist autocrat Hugo Chavez celebrated Obama's election as "the symptom that the change that has been gestating from the south of the Americas could be knocking at the doors of the United States," which Chavez saw as reflected by audaciously leftist governments such as his own.[47] Prior to Obama, Chavez explained, the "United States did not allow a government to progress if it deviated from the imperial position, but my have things changed in these past years. Now, it is worth it to wait calmly for the

United States, more so with the new administration of President Barack Obama."[48]

When Obama won the Nobel Peace Prize, Cuba's communist dictator Fidel Castro praised the award as a "positive measure" because it served as a rebuke to previous American presidents and policies, which, Castro claimed, have created the need for "an exhortation for peace and the search for solutions to assure the survival of the species."[49] The passage of the ObamaCare health law also drew praise from Castro, who considered "health reform to have been an important battle and a success of his (Obama's) government." "It is really incredible that 234 years after the Declaration of Independence," Castro remarked, "the government of that country has approved medical attention for the majority of its citizens, something that Cuba was able to do half a century ago."[50]

Given Obama's penchant for minimizing American interests, it is not surprising that he placed a high priority on international treaties and international institutions. In addition to New START, Obama also expressed support for the Convention on the Rights of Persons with Disabilities, even though the U.S. already has robust legal protections for citizens with disabilities; the Convention on the Law of the Sea, which President Ronald Reagan refused to sign because it undermined U.S. sovereignty; the Committee on the Eradication of All Forms of Discrimination Against Women, which has languished in the Senate since the Carter administration; the United Nations Arms Trade Treaty, which critics claimed undermines Americans' First and Second Amendment rights; and the Comprehensive Nuclear Test Ban Treaty, which would ban testing of nuclear weapons and could stymie American efforts to modernize its nuclear arsenal. Obama also sought to "re-engage" the United Nations by, among other things, joining the Human Rights Council (which included the likes of Libya and Cuba), embracing the Millennium Development Goals and chairing a session of the U.N. Security Council (the first president to do so).

Obama's foreign policy vision, particularly Obama's focus on international institutions and agreements, was music to the ears of the Norwegian Nobel Committee, which awarded Obama the Nobel Peace Prize. He had been in office for less than two weeks by the date of the nomination deadline, so the award was less about achievements Obama had accumulated than it was about endorsing his anti-Bush foreign policy vision. The Nobel Committee lauded Obama's "extraordinary efforts to strengthen international diplomacy and cooperation between peoples," especially "Obama's vision of and work for a world without nuclear weapons." The committee asserted that "Obama has created a new climate in international politics," which placed multilateral diplomacy in "a central position, with emphasis on the role that the United Nations and other international institutions can play." Under this new approach, rather than burnishing the possibility of force to advance important national interests, "dialogue and negotiations are preferred as instruments for resolving even the most difficult international conflicts. Only very rarely," the committee gushed, "has a person to the same extent as Obama captured the world's attention and given its people hope for a better future."

Though appreciated by the Nobel Committee, Obama's approach to foreign affairs rested on a number of premises that are, from the perspective of America's foundational principles, questionable. For one thing, Obama seems to see himself as a post-American president whose job is not limited to vindicating American interests. Under this view, Obama assumes the role of standing up for "ordinary people" throughout the world who suffer from poverty and a lack of opportunity and of policing anti-Muslim stereotypes. It is one thing for a president to assume such duties because they further the interests of the United States, but Obama the transnationalist undertakes them irrespective of whether they further U.S. goals.

Obama also emphasized identity politics in his relations with other nations. As the product of an intercontinental union between a Kenyan and a Kansan, so this line of thinking goes, Obama possesses a multicultural appeal that serves to enhance America's relationships with other nations. What is more, Obama embraced the notion that demonstrating good intentions constitutes an effective means by which to prompt nations with conflicting interests, including America's sworn enemies, to cooperate with the United States.

He adopted a more deferential nuclear posture because he thought it would lead other nations to follow America's lead. Such a move is premised on the notion that other nations will feel less threatened by American strength and, thus, will have less need for a nuclear weapon. Finally, in his zeal to reduce America's dominance in the world, Obama has adopted a practice of bowing before foreign leaders like the king of Saudi Arabia, the emperor of Japan and the president of China. And he has deliberately highlighted what he considers

America's past sins, substantiating a number of anti-U.S. criticisms and, in the process, damaging the reputation of the United States. As we will see, in each instance, the assumption on which he operated contrasted with the basic premises on which the Founding Fathers relied when they created the Constitution.

24

"The Best Possible State of Defense"

At the time of the Constitution's creation, America was little more than a fledgling republic, yet international affairs loomed large in the minds of the Founding Fathers. They saw their situation on the American continent as being Providential for the natural physical safety that it provided, but also understood that it was unrealistic to expect that international threats would simply disappear. Europe was a hotbed of hostilities, and nations like France, Great Britain and Spain still maintained a foothold on territories in the Western Hemisphere, including on land adjacent to the United States.

Supporters of the Constitution fully expected that American progress and growth would inevitably engender hostilities from abroad. As John Jay remarked in *The Federalist* No. 4, "it is easy to see that jealousies and uneasinesses may gradually slide into the minds and cabinets of other nations, and that we are not to expect that they should regard our advancement in union, in power and consequence by land and by sea, with an eye of indifference and composure." This was cause for concern because, Jay wrote, "it is too true, however disgraceful it may be to human nature, that nations in general will make war whenever they have a prospect of getting anything by it."[1]

The new nation thus needed to prepare itself for the inevitable foreign policy storm. This was not an issue tangential to the purpose or design of the Constitution but was one of its most fundamental aspects. "Among the many objects to which a wise and free people find it necessary to direct their attention," Jay observed in *The Federalist* No. 3, "that of providing for their *safety* seems to be the first. The *safety* of the people doubtless has relation to a great variety of circumstances and considerations, and consequently affords great latitude to those who wish to define it precisely and comprehensively."[2] Any credible government needed to serve this basic function.

The preeminence that the Founding Fathers placed on the safety of the people and the security of the nation meant that the new federal government had to be capable of vindicating these critical ends. For constitutionalists like Jay, Madison and Hamilton, this meant, in the first instance, to create a written constitution that provided for a strong union, one capable of ensuring the safety of the people by "forbearing to give just causes of war to other nations." Jay worried that, without a strong union, individual states would enmesh the nation into unnecessary and debilitating military conflicts with foreign nations. By instilling the federal government with the ability to protect the nation's citizens, property and territory from foreign attacks as well as with the authority to enact and enforce national policies, Jay and other constitutionalists reduced, if not eliminated, the likelihood that individual states would spark such conflicts.

At the same time, the nation needed to be constituted so as to project a clear sense of strength to the rest of the world. The safety of the people depended on "their placing and continuing themselves in such a situation as not to invite hostility or insult; for it need not be observed that there are pretended as well as just causes of war." It was the Constitution that provided the foundation that was "necessary to put and keep them in *such a situation* as, instead of *inviting* war, will tend to repress and discourage it." For Jay and other Constitution creators, "that situation consists in the best possible state of defense, and necessarily depends on the government, the arms, and the resources of the country."[3]

For the Framers, the exhibition of national and military strength represented the surest road to peace and security. They knew that foreign nations would be taking the measure of the new nation, especially because of the fact that, as Hamilton noted in *The Federalist* No. 11, "our situation invites and our interests prompt us to aim at an ascendant in the system of American affairs."[4] They fully expected other nations to pursue their own respective national interests, and knew that the projection of weakness did nothing but provide encouragement to those countries eager to further such interests at the expense of the United States. It was, they thought, foolish to expect the extension of benevolence to other nations to engender favorable treatment in return. But if other nations looked to the United States and saw a nation projecting strength militarily, financially and politically, then "they will be much more disposed to cultivate our friendship then to provoke our resentment."[5]

Hamilton, in particular, ridiculed the notion that America, due to its republican character, was immune from external dangers. Speaking about the potential for dissension among the individual states but using logic applicable to the full spectrum of foreign and military relations, he lambasted the "utopian speculations" of "visionary or designing men," who saw the republican character of America as making armed hostilities a thing of the past. Under this mistaken view, "the spirit of commerce has a tendency to soften the manners of men, and to extinguish those inflammable humors which have so often kindled into wars." Commercial republics, so the argument went, "will be governed by mutual interests, and will cultivate a spirit of mutual amity and concord." This struck Hamilton as fanciful idealism thoroughly repudiated by history. "Is it not time to awake from the deceitful dream of a golden age," Hamilton asked, "and to adopt as a practical maxim for the direction of our political conduct that we, as well as the other inhabitants of the globe, are yet remote from the happy empire of perfect wisdom and perfect virtue?"[6]

The nation needed to develop the capacity to project strength on land and sea, thereby deterring military threats. For his part, Hamilton praised the Constitution for providing the federal government with the ability to establish a strong defense, and for doing so in a way that did not create incapacitating restrictions on the use of force, which many Anti-Federalists demanded. For example, Anti-Federalists, who embraced the radical Whig fear of standing armies, wanted the Constitution to prohibit the government from maintaining an army in a time of peace.

This struck Hamilton as "the most extraordinary spectacle which the world has yet seen—that of a nation incapacitated by its Constitution to prepare for defense before it was actually invaded." Thus, "we must receive the blow, before we could even prepare to return it. All that kind of policy by which nations anticipate distant danger, and meet the gathering storm, must be abstained from," which meant that "we must expose our property and liberty to the mercy of foreign invaders, and invite them by our weakness to seize the naked and defenseless prey."[7] Such a state of affairs was flatly unacceptable to the creators of the Constitution. As President Washington noted in his first State of the Union Address, "To be prepared for war is one of the most effectual means of preserving peace."[8]

As a coastal nation, the United States also required the capacity to project power on the seas, which would not only enhance the state of American defenses but also would foster the expansion of American commerce. "If we mean to be a commercial people, or even to be secure on our Atlantic side," Hamilton wrote in *The Federalist* No. 24, "we must endeavor, as soon as possible, to have a navy."[9] This was a practical necessity but also a matter of national pride. "We have heard much of the fleets of Britain," John Jay observed, "and the time may come, if we are wise, when the fleets of America may engage attention."[10] By arming the federal government with the power to provide and maintain a navy, the Constitution provided the American people with the means to expand their commercial activity, to protect their national shorelines, and to enhance their national reputation.

Underlying the notion that building and maintaining strength by land and by sea cultivated peace and security is a hardheaded realism regarding the actions of other nations. During the Revolutionary War, Washington observed that "it is a maxim, founded on the universal experience of mankind, that no nation is to be trusted further than it is bound by its interest, and no prudent statesman or politician will venture to depart from it."[11] Washington may have appreciated the support of France in America's fight against the British, but he did not suffer under any illusions about why a prominent adversary of Great Britain supported his Continental Army in their revolutionary struggle, and he cautioned against allowing hatred of England to equate to excessive confidence in France. Indeed, Washington never wavered from this view of foreign relations. In his Farewell Address, he warned the American people "that Nations as well as individuals act for their own benefit and not for the benefit of others, unless both interests happen to be assimilated and when that is the case there requires no contract to bind them together."[12]

The presupposition that nations act in accordance with their own self-interest necessarily meant that the utility of international agreements and treaties was limited. Hamilton explained that "contracts with foreign nations…have the force of law, but derive it from the obligations of good faith. They are not rules prescribed by the sovereign to the subject, but agreements between sovereign and sovereign."[13] Because they depend on good faith, they are "subject to the usual vicissitudes of peace and war, of observance and nonobservance, as the interests or passions of the contracting parties dictate."

To underscore the limited ability of international agreements, Hamilton invoked the "epidemical rage in Europe" for compacts between nations that prevailed in the early-18th century, "from which the politicians of the times fondly hoped for benefits which were never realized." The agreements had sought to establish and maintain European peace, "but they were scarcely formed before they were broken, giving an instructive but afflicting lesson to mankind, how little dependence is to be placed on treaties which have no other sanction than the obligations of good faith, and which oppose general considerations of peace and justice to the impulse of any immediate interest or passion."[14]

Consistent with Washington's admonition regarding international agreements, many of the Founding Fathers took a measured approach to international opinion and customs. On the one hand, Framers like Madison wanted America's national councils to "possess that sensibility to the opinion of the world which is perhaps not less necessary in order to merit than it is to obtain its respect and confidence." Madison considered possessing knowledge of world opinion to be desirable because public measures "should appear to other nations as the offspring of a wise and honorable policy," and because "in doubtful cases, particularly where the national councils may be warped by some strong passion or momentary interest, the presumed or known opinion of the impartial world may be the best guide that can be followed."[15] By crafting sensible laws, American legislators could help the new nation earn the respect of other nations, contributing to the dignity and reputation of the United States.

In *The Federalist Papers*, Madison and Hamilton wrote extensively about the need for legislators to possess a broad base of knowledge about subjects such as law, political economy, and war, and they surely considered international opinions to be important sources of such knowledge. After all, when they framed the Constitution, Founders like Hamilton and Madison relied on the theories of thinkers such as Montesquieu and John Locke, and drew lessons about politics from the histories of ancient Greece and Rome. Accordingly, they were not about to dismiss, out of hand, the opinions of those in foreign nations as being irrelevant to the issues they faced in the American political theater.

At the same time, the Founding Fathers won a revolution against the most powerful nation on earth, and they pursued what they deemed to be the right and proper policies irrespective of how such policies were perceived overseas. "Is it not the glory of the people of America," James Madison asked, "that, whilst they have paid a decent regard to the opinions of former times and other nations, they have not suffered a blind veneration for antiquity, for custom, or for names, to overrule the suggestions of their own good sense, the knowledge of their own situation, and the lessons of their own experience?"[16]

This meant that, while the Founding Fathers respected the opinions of foreign nations, they were not subservient to such opinions and were quite willing to stand up to erroneous foreign views. When discussing the need for a strong union in The *Federalist* No. 11, Hamilton lambasted "the arrogant pretenses" of Europe, whose superior military and economic strength has "tempted her to plume herself as the mistress of the world, and to consider the rest of mankind as created for her benefit."

Hamilton rejected the ideas, popular among European elites, that Europeans possessed a "physical superiority" and that "all animals, and with them the human species degenerate in America—that even dogs ceased to bark after having breathed awhile in our atmosphere." He urged his fellow citizens to "disdain to be the instruments of European greatness!" It was up to the United States, Hamilton wrote, "to vindicate the honor of the human race" by "erecting one great American system superior to the control of all transatlantic force or influence and able to dictate the terms of the connection between the old and the new world!"[17]

Framers like Hamilton saw America as representing an exceptional place in the world, but they didn't see themselves, like Europeans saw themselves, as inherently superior to other people. Instead, they saw themselves as being charged with the task of vindicating certain ideas and principles regarding republican government and individual liberty in a way that would have global consequences. If they failed at their task of creating and maintaining a republic that successfully protected the God-given rights of individuals and that permitted the pursuit of happiness, the Founding Fathers believed that the idea of a government based on the consent of the governed would be discredited for all time. As James Madison observed in *The Federalist* No. 14, the Framers hoped that "posterity will be indebted for the possession, and the world for the example, of the numerous innovations displayed on the American theatre, in favor of private rights and public happiness."[18]

Perhaps because they knew that they were carrying the banner of freedom of future generations, constitutionalists like Hamilton, Jay and Washington were extremely self-conscious about the reputation of the United States. One of Hamilton's primary complaints about the Articles of Confederation was that, by failing to provide for a strong national defense, the Articles failed to produce any real degree of respectability. "We may indeed with propriety be said to have reached almost the last stage of national humiliation," Hamilton wrote in *The Federalist* No. 15. "There is scarcely anything that can wound the pride or degrade the character of an independent nation which we do not experience."

Foremost among the reasons why America suffered from such damaged pride was its inability to engender "respectability in the eyes of foreign powers," which was a crucial "safeguard against foreign encroachments." The "imbecility" of the Articles seemed to invite disrespect from other nations; according to Hamilton, "our ambassadors abroad are the mere pageants of mimic sovereignty." Rather than possess the best possible state of defense, the nation had "neither troops, nor treasury, nor government," and was beset by the injurious actions of foreign governments. These circumstances prompted an exasperated Hamilton to wonder, "are we even in a condition to remonstrate with dignity?"[19]

The Framers were protective of the new nation's reputation, and did not want to see America humiliated on the world stage, which counseled in favor of acquiring and maintaining military and economic strength. John Jay called attention to the appeasement of Louis XIV by the state of Genoa in 1685. After having offended the French monarch, Genoa was ordered to send their chief magistrate and four senators "to ask for his pardon and receive his terms. They were obliged to submit to it for the sake of peace." Jay wondered whether Louis XIV would "on any occasion either have demanded or have received the like humiliation from Spain, or Britain, or any other *powerful* nation?"[20] The question answered itself. It was the weakness of Genoa that led it to suffer the type of national embarrassment that was anathema to the Founding Fathers. As zealous guardians of their nation's reputation, they winced at the thought of a similar affront to their own nation's dignity.

****

Just like so many other issues, Barack Obama's approach to foreign affairs rests on operating assumptions that are antithetical to the principles relied upon by the Founding Fathers when they created the Constitution. Even regarding the most fundamental task of government, the need to provide for the safety of the people, there exists a difference between the outlook of Barack Obama and the American Founders. To be sure, Obama has acknowledged that the federal government has the responsibility to ensure the safety and security of the United States and its people. And though he lacked any experience with military affairs prior to taking office, Obama took his responsibility as commander-in-chief seriously enough that, under the guidance of an expert, he worked hard to learn how to perform the military salute, privately repeating it over and over until he performed it properly.[21]

At the same time, Obama's performance in office demonstrated that his primary focus was on effectuating major social welfare programs like his signature health care overhaul rather than on managing America's shooting wars abroad. He campaigned as a strong proponent of "finishing the job in Afghanistan," charging the Bush administration with neglecting the Afghan theater in favor of the Iraq campaign, yet he took almost a full year to make a decision regarding America's strategy in Afghanistan. Incredibly, he insisted on setting an 18-month deadline for withdrawal because he worried that an open-ended commitment to winning would harm his domestic agenda. "Our Afghan policy was focused as much as anything on domestic politics," one adviser told *The New York Times*. "He would not risk losing the moderate to centrist Democrats in the middle of health insurance reform and he viewed that legislation as the make-or-break legislation for his administration."[22]

Even though he campaigned tirelessly on the importance of the Afghanistan campaign to the security of the United States and even though he claimed that the failure to finish the job in Afghanistan would "create an unacceptable risk of additional attacks on our homeland and our allies,"[23] Obama was not willing to commit to a policy that would jeopardize his transformational project at home.

This says a lot about his priorities. Given that he used his 2002 anti-war speech as a way to draw an anti-war contrast with Senator Hillary Clinton, Obama may simply have cited the urgency of Afghanistan as a way of safeguarding himself against charges of weakness, which can be electorally devastating in a national election for an urban liberal like Obama. This was an inherently political tactic. Once in office, the fact that he fashioned his Afghanistan strategy around his domestic political ambitions demonstrated that his primary concern was redistributive change, not military victory.

Making redistributive change his top priority was just one way that Obama parted company with the Framers. Washington warned that policies predicated on a nation foregoing its own interests are ill advised, but Barack Obama has eschewed Washington's dictum. Rather than acknowledge that certain nations have interests that are completely at odds with the interests of the United States, Obama has trumpeted the notion that nations share the same basic interests. Under his view, since the fate of all nations is "inextricably linked," even the world's most intractable problems can be "solved" through diplomatic outreach premised on superficialities like his multicultural background, and by combining the reduction in American strength with the extension of magnanimity to America's enemies. This is precisely the type of thinking that Hamilton derided "as utopian speculations" of those foolishly advocating the "deceitful dream of a golden age."

If one accepts Washington's observation regarding the role that national interests play in determining the conduct of foreign nations, then Obama's attempt to ingratiate himself with predominantly Muslim countries by showcasing his father's Muslim roots and his middle name of Hussein was anything but a sound approach to diplomatic relations. Though he may have simply believed that calling attention to his multicultural background would change the way individual Muslims viewed the United States, the notion that Obama, as a "citizen of the world," could create a new era in U.S. relations with Muslim nations was wishful thinking. So, too, was his idea to use NASA as a vehicle of engagement with the Muslim world through lauding, in an effort to enhance the collective self-esteem of Muslim nations, the contributions of Muslims to math, science and engineering. Such an approach rests on superficialities that might be useful in a domestic political campaign but are not, as Washington warned, sufficient to govern the conduct of nations. While a U.S. president bearing the middle name of "Hussein" might be an item of interest to individual Muslims and while some Muslims might be flattered by recognition of their culture's historic achievements, such artificialities are not going to change the fact that nations like Iran and Syria conceive of their interests as antagonistic to the United States.

Obama's general outlook with respect to the role of national interests in international relations explains why his approach to international agreements diverged from the principles articulated by Washington and Hamilton. Obama pushed a flurry of agreements (bilateral, multilateral and global) regarding nuclear weapons, global warming, firearms, people with disabilities, and discrimination against women. These agreements required, in some instances, the United State to forgo its national interest in favor of international consensus and international institutions such as the United Nations. He seemed to think that if diplomats could just hammer out the right agreements, and if enough nations signed onto existing conventions and treaties, then the nations of the world could stand as one.

Though the Founding Fathers recognized the need for international agreements in certain instances (and accordingly, provided a mechanism in the Constitution for the ratification of treaties), they also knew that such agreements could not, in and of themselves, create peace between nations. It is not the written agreement but rather the confluence of interests between nations that facilitates constructive relationships. As Hamilton noted, when a signatory to an agreement faces a conflict between the provisions of the agreement and the signatory's national interest, the latter will invariably prevail. This is why Washington pointed out that, when the interests of nations are assimilated, no agreement is even necessary to bind them together.

In his quest to abolish nuclear weapons, Obama seemed to be oblivious to the way national interests influence the behavior of nations. Obama pines for comprehensive international agreements in which nuclear weapons are eradicated once and for all, believing that the creation of an international inspection regime will be able to enforce the terms of the agreement. Once the agreement is hammered out and the inspection regime is in place, nuclear weapons will supposedly be a thing of the past. For a constitutionalist like Hamilton, such a regime will inevitably collapse as nations seek to become nuclear powers in an otherwise nuclear-free world, providing an immediate and dramatic boost to their strength and influence.

Obama's nuclear policies also violated Jay's admonition regarding the need to have the "best possible state of defense." By ruling out the use of nuclear weapons to respond to chemical, biological and large-scale convention attacks, Obama unilaterally reduced the deterrent capacity of American defenses. The possibility of a nuclear response was the critical factor in convincing Saddam Hussein to forestall the use of chemical weapons against U.S. forces during Operation Desert Storm, and there can be little question that the nuclear deterrent is effective. Obama's policies rested on the notion that demonstrating the willingness of the U.S. to reduce the capacity of its defenses will lead other nations to follow suit. Under this view, the best possible state of defense is more likely to invite, rather than discourage, conflict.

From Obama's assumption that strength was threatening and thus destabilizing flowed his strategy to display magnanimity to America's enemies, to defer to foreign nations, and to criticize the United States. Obama reserved his most respectful treatment to foreign adversaries like Russia; in fact, he deliberately undercut the security of Poland, the Czech Republic and Great Britain so that he could reach an agreement with Russia regarding nuclear weapons. Obama's foreign policy was so solicitous of foreign adversaries that more than a few observers noted that, under Obama, it is better to be an enemy of the United States than a friend.

Founders like Jay recoiled at the thought of a foreign nation like Genoa being humiliated on the world stage, yet Obama adopted the practice of bowing before foreign leaders like the emperor of Japan, representing a symbolic attempt to show that the United States is just another nation in a community of equals. His habitual criticism of the United States echoed complaints about America lodged by many European elites. Hamilton was willing to rebuke the Europeans' "arrogant pretensions" when they deserved it, but Obama appeared more interested in validating prevailing critiques of the United States. Obama's apologies portrayed the United States as a flawed giant whose reckless actions were responsible for many of the world's ills, undercutting the type of national dignity that the Founders saw as a prerequisite to national respectability.

Perhaps most disturbingly, Obama's affinity for international institutions like the United Nations surpasses his fidelity to constitutional principles. When Obama authorized military intervention against the Libyan tyrant Moammar Gaddafi in March of 2011, he did not seek any approval from the United States Congress. Instead, Obama relied on a resolution from the United Nations Security Council and a statement of support from the Arab League as justification for the "kinetic" deployment of U.S. military assets in Libya. Critics complained that Obama's actions defied his previous admonition that the "president does not have power under the Constitution to unilaterally authorize a military attack in a situation that does not involve stopping an actual or imminent threat to the nation."[24] Secretary of State Hillary Clinton defended the lack of congressional authorization regarding Libya because an "internationally authorized intervention where we are one of a number of countries participating to enforce a humanitarian mission is not the kind of unilateral action that…President Obama…was speaking of several years ago."[25]

To be sure, the extent to which the Constitution requires congressional authorization before the president undertakes military action continues to be subject to much debate. At the Constitutional Convention, the delegates changed language in the Constitution regarding Congress' war powers from the power to "make" war to the power to "declare" war. The delegates worried about lodging the authority to "make" war in the legislature because they thought the legislature contained too many individuals and operated too slowly to competently manage military operations. As Alexander Hamilton wrote in *The Federalist* No. 74, the "direction of war most peculiarly demands those qualities which distinguish the exercise of power by a single hand."[26] Accordingly, James Madison and Elbridge Gerry moved to change the language so that Congress would possess the power to "declare" war, "leaving to the Executive the power to repel sudden attacks."[27]

Some interpret the history surrounding constitutional war powers to demonstrate that, other than to repel an attack, the president cannot undertake military action absent a declaration of war by Congress. Others argue that the original meaning must be viewed in light of the history of the Founding Era, which demonstrates that the use of military force absent a declaration of war was not necessarily so confined. For example, during the early years of the Republic, military force was used against France by President John Adams (the so-called "quasi-war") and against the Barbary pirates during the administration of Thomas Jefferson, yet in neither instance did Congress formally declare war (though in both instances Congress authorized support for the efforts). According to this view, the Founding Fathers saw a distinction between a formal state of war and the use of military force: while the former cannot be attained absent a congressional declaration the latter can be initiated by the executive (though many acknowledge this may require *some* type of congressional authorization, even if simply a willingness to fund the operation).

For his part, Obama simply ignored *any* constitutional requirements in favor of "authorization" from international bodies. He previously proclaimed that the president did not have the authority to initiate military force, but because he views international institutions like the United Nations as trumping the Constitution, he did not see the need to get formal congressional support. Under Obama's view, the authorization to use military force by the United Nations Security Council is sufficient legal authority to justify "kinetic" military operations. In this vein, "fundamental transformation" demands the subordination of constitutionalism to the whims of transnational progressivism—yet another instance of Obama scuttling the principles of the Founders in favor of his own ideological ambitions.

Part Eight

The National Character

25

THE CONSTITUTIONAL RENAISSANCE AND PROGRESSIVE DISCONTENTS

As the 2010 campaign entered the autumn home stretch, *The Wall Street Journal*'s Jonathan Weisman marveled at how the "tea party-fueled midterm elections of 2010 have featured a surprising group of men in a cameo role: the Founding Fathers."[1] Although tea party citizen-activists energetically engaged a variety of pressing political issues, their passionate participation was primarily rooted in a sense that the transformational project of Barack Obama and his allies in Congress represented a marked departure from the nation's foundational principles as exemplified by the political ethos of the Founders and by the Constitution they created. *The New York Times*' Adam Liptak observed that, though the movement was still in its infancy, by making "the Constitution central to the national conversation," the tea party's focus on first principles had "added something distinctive to contemporary political discourse."[2]

If anything, the fact that the tea party's focus on the country's founding principles represented a peculiar addition to modern political discourse demonstrates that the nation's ruling class has not been faithful to such principles. It should be "surprising" that seasoned reporters like Weisman and Liptak expressed incredulity at the invocation of first principles by American citizens in contemporary political debate, especially because the nation is nothing if not an application of certain fundamental truths regarding the freedom of the individual and the limited power of the state. Interestingly, a grand debate about faithfulness to the nation's original, fundamental values and principles never occurred because, Weisman noted, "for much of the debate over the United States' origins, the Democrats have ceded the field."[3] In the face of withering political attacks on their agenda of hyperkinetic government, attacks that indicted that agenda not merely for being politically undesirable but also for defaulting on the nation's core principles, the foot soldiers of transformational change remained, for the most part, awkwardly silent.

Perhaps this was for good reason. After all, on the relatively few occasions when supporters of Obama's grand designs tried to engage the debate about the nation's first principles, the result was almost invariably destructive to their own cause. From Congressman Phil Hare's declaration that he didn't worry about the Constitution when it came to ObamaCare to Congressman Pete Stark's insistence that the Constitution placed virtually no restrictions on the federal government's power, many political practitioners left the impression that, in the age of Obama, the Constitution was not even relevant.

For her part, then-House Speaker Nancy Pelosi, the famously liberal San Franciscan, attempted to link her progressive policy desires to the nation's Founding Fathers. She claimed that ObamaCare honored their dedication to the right to "life, liberty and the pursuit of happiness" asserted in the Declaration of Independence because the new law would lead to healthier lives, and she heralded the so-called DREAM Act—a controversial immigration initiative that promised a broad amnesty for children of those who came to the United States illegally—as something that was directly associated with the Founders' victory in the American Revolution. Her invocation of the Founding Fathers was so logically feeble and so obviously contrived for political purposes that it was, in both instances, counterproductive.

Seeking to capitalize on the energy of the tea party movement and on the intellectual clumsiness of progressive politicians like Pelosi, Republican members of Congress and GOP congressional candidates promised that, if given the majority in the U.S. House of Representatives following the 2010 elections, they would require that each piece of legislation cite the constitutional provision that affirmatively authorized Congress to legislate in the proposed area. After they won a sweeping victory in the midterms, Republicans did something that had not been done in all of American history: they read the entire Constitution aloud on the floor of the House of Representatives. Though members of Congress swear an oath that requires the support and defense of the Constitution (and nothing else), these two relatively modest Constitution-focused initiatives appeared to represent a sea change in how members of Congress conducted public business; Republican leaders even distributed a short memorandum informing members how to examine a bill's constitutional basis, and held training sessions for legislative aides.[4]

To activists such as Tea Party Patriots co-founder Mark Meckler, this focus on the Constitution "shows the extraordinary times now. Regular people all across the country are focused on the Constitution, and the message was sent to Congress we want them to do the same." *Washington Post* reporters Philip Rucker and Krissah Thompson characterized this newfound fidelity to the Constitution as "the tea party-ization of Congress."[5]

Tellingly, voices from the progressive chorus reacted to such changes with hostility. To Massachusetts Congressman Barney Frank, the requirement that Congress identify its constitutional authority when writing legislation represented little more that "a kiss they're blowing to the tea party," since, Frank said, laws passed that are "unconstitutional will be thrown out in court."[6] *Newsweek*'s Ben Adler argued that such a requirement was outright dangerous, labeling it an "extraconstitutional attempt to limit the powers of Congress…as it constitutes an encroachment on the judiciary," which he claimed was the sole mechanism for assessing the constitutionality of legislation.[7]

Ezra Klein, a progressive writer, dismissed the reading of the Constitution as a "gimmick" because it "has no binding power on anything." For Klein, a focus on the Constitution is a distraction—he claimed that the document "is confusing…because it was written more than 100 years ago," and because "people have different beliefs about what it says."[8] On the floor of the House, leftist Congressman Jim McDermott expressed annoyance at "silly stuff" such as "reading the Constitution."[9]

These criticisms were entirely predictable. At every step of the way—Rick Santelli's "rant heard 'round the world," the popular uprising against ObamaCare, the political shellacking delivered by voters to Obama's Democratic Party in 2010, the Constitution-focused initiatives touted by the new GOP majority in the House of Representatives—progressive pundits, politicians and Obama sycophants unleashed a torrent of criticism against anyone deigning to demand adherence to the nation's founding principles. Writing in April 2009, when the tea party movement was in its infancy, Paul Krugman of *The New York Times* snidely dismissed the impending tax day protests as "AstroTurf (fake grass roots) events, manufactured by the usual suspects."[10] By the time it was obvious that the tea party movement was a legitimate grass roots enterprise, reporter David Barstow, also writing in the *Times*, published a purported exposé that tried to delegitimize the movement by linking it to militia groups bent on perpetrating violence against the federal government.[11]

Not to be outdone, *Times* columnist Frank Rich claimed that tea party-led opposition to ObamaCare was premised not on concern for constitutional principles but on bigotry: "The conjunction of a black president and a female speaker of the House—topped off by a wise Latina on the Supreme Court and a powerful gay Congressional committee chairman—would sow fears of disenfranchisement among a dwindling and threatened minority in the country no matter what policies were in play."[12] Such criticism was little more than a thinly veiled attempt to discredit a genuine grassroots movement seen as a political threat to the progressive transformational undertaking.

Because these critics refused to take seriously the invocation of the nation's founding principles by those citizens opposed to Obama's expressed desire "to fundamentally transform the United States of America," they consistently misinterpreted the significance of the tea party movement. Barack Obama was one such critic. In June of 2009, with his popularity beginning to sag in the face of popular blowback to his proposed health care overhaul and with the tea party on his mind, Obama invited a group of left-leaning historians to the White House to discuss historical precedents for popular backlashes against the nation's ruling class. According to Peter Baker of *The New York Times*, "the historians recalled the Know-Nothings in the 1850s, the Populists in the 1890s and Father Charles Coughlin in the 1930s"—all generally regarded as negative political forces and all of which were primarily concerned with issues, be it immigration, the gold standard or "social justice," that had little relationship to the nation's founding principles as articulated at the Constitutional Convention or in *The Federalist Papers*.[13]

By analogizing the tea party movement to the discredited movements of the past, these historians reinforced Obama's own view that the tea party represented a fringe political phenomenon. As he explained to *Rolling Stone* magazine, the tea party movement was an "amalgam, a mixed bag of a lot of different strains in American politics that have been there for a long time"—strains, no doubt, that he saw as ill informed and even sinister.[14]

At a fundraiser in April 2010, Obama made clear his disdain for these citizen-activists; he declared he was "amused" by the anti-tax tea party rallies and mockingly said that, rather than protest his policies, "you would think they'd be saying thank you."[15] Though he declined to indict them for bigotry and conceded that concerns about the federal budget deficit were legitimate, Obama, like other progressives, dismissed these activists as being little more than habitual gripers incapable of governing if given the opportunity. At one point, he even demanded that tea partiers "identify, specifically, what would you do?"[16]

Like the catalogue of progressive commentators critical of the tea party, Obama failed to come to terms with what animated the movement. Indeed, many of these commentators had never even tried to understand the motivation of the movement; they had nothing but contempt for the millions of Americans who identified with the goals of the tea party, resorting to using crude vulgarisms, such as the term "teabagger," to describe their fellow citizens simply because these citizens dissented from progressive orthodoxy. They were also quick to indict anyone affiliated with the tea party movement as being intellectually deficient. Jon Stewart, a comedian who is one of the leading intellectual forces in the progressive community, even staged a "Rally to Restore Sanity" in Washington, DC, which was implicitly billed as an antidote to the tea party, one geared towards members of the so-called "reality-based community," who claim to be more informed than their fellow citizens.

Claims of superior intellect were, though, hardly justifiable. For example, when former Alaska Gov. Sarah Palin told a group of voters that a victory at the polls would enable them to "party like it's 1773," the year of the Boston Tea Party, many tea party critics, such as progressive blogger Markos Moulitsas and PBS host Gwen Ifill, ridiculed Palin for her ignorance but revealed their own historical illiteracy in the process. Nevertheless, the notion that tea party supporters are a collection of crazy imbeciles is a view widely shared by progressives, elite journalists, and Democratic politicians.

To those who saw the tea party as a political movement akin to the Know Nothings, Populists or devotees of Father Coughlin, it was natural to assume that tea partiers operated on ignorance. One critical difference, though, between these other movements and the tea party is the latter's almost singular focus on respecting the Constitution, revering the Founding Fathers, and rediscovering the nation's original principles. What is more, in the age of the internet, interested citizens did not have to make a pilgrimage to the library or take a class to better acquaint themselves with the nation's founding principles; critical sources such as the Declaration of Independence, the Constitution, *The Federalist Papers* and Washington's Farewell Address, as well as the writings of the original progressives, such as Woodrow Wilson, who criticized the Constitution and disparaged the Founders, were merely a computer click away. Now, every citizen could truly be a constitutionalist, measuring the actions of the political class against the text, history and structure of the Constitution, as well as the principles that the Constitution reflects. They were defenders of the Constitution that, in many instances (as illustrated in town hall meetings throughout the country), knew more about the Constitution that the representatives who swore an oath to uphold it.

The emphasis on the Constitution and the Founding Fathers made the tea party an inherently conservative phenomenon. Whereas the roots of the political ideology of Obama and chief lieutenants like Pelosi lie in the progressive movement—and especially in the progressive emphasis on absorbing power in a centralized bureaucracy and engaging in national planning from Washington, which the original progressives delightfully saw as conflicting with the Founders' political worldview—the tea party looked directly to the Founding Fathers for their belief in constitutionally limited government, and their desire to create a government that, above all, protected individual liberty, which is a natural, God-given right of individuals.

Of course, the components of "transformational change"—the enactment of the stimulus bill, the continuation and expansion of the bank bailout bill, the creation of more than 100 new federal bureaucracies under ObamaCare—cut sharply against this limited government tradition, and portended an era in which the federal government wielded the power to regulate virtually any conduct in the name of progressive imperatives such as "fixing" the temperature of the earth or cultivating healthier lifestyles. The addition of progressive jurists, such and Elena Kagan, to the Supreme Court, underscored the extent to which the federal government was becoming unmoored from its limited Constitution origins. During her Senate confirmation hearing, Kagan was at a loss to cite *any* congressional action, including a hypothetical federal law mandating broccoli consumption, that would exceed Congress' enumerated power to regulate interstate commerce, while, at the same time, she displayed an inclination to construe the right to keep and bear arms, protected by the Second Amendment, extremely narrowly.

Political candidates eager to court voters aligned with the tea party proudly referred to themselves as "constitutional conservatives." Though all elected officials swear an oath to uphold the Constitution, the explicit identification of oneself as seeking to conserve it was, oddly, considered by many to be a curious phenomenon. To Lincoln Caplan, a liberal editorialist from *The New York Times*, the label "constitutional conservative" is merely a "vague, highly-selective catchall," rooted in "nostalgia for an inadequate version of the country's past," that "doesn't bear close examination."[17]

Larry Kramer, a progressive professor from Stanford Law School, condescendingly saw this reverence for the Constitution as based on "some loose, ill-informed version of originalism," which is a method of interpreting the Constitution that insists that the Constitution has a stable meaning, ascertainable by reference to how each provision was originally understood by the society that ratified it.[18] Left-leaning *Newsweek* reporter Andrew Romano ridiculed the constitutional conservatives' "claim that they've distilled their entire political platform…directly from the text of the founding document," alleging that they rely on the Constitution as "an instrument of self-affirmation and cultural division."[19] The editorial board of *The New York Times* characterized constitutional conservatism as a "well-known and extreme point of view about the Constitution and about cases and issues that will be decided by the Supreme Court."[20]

These critics impugn the notion of constitutional conservatism as being "vague," "ill-informed," a tool of "cultural division," and "extreme" in part because they do not see the Constitution and the Founding Fathers as being terribly relevant to modern political discourse. As articulated by Ron Chernow, a liberal historian who has written biographies of Hamilton and Washington, the invocation of the Founding Fathers in opposition to the Obama agenda "ends up promoting an uncomfortably one-sided reading of history" because the Founders "seldom agreed about anything." "Instead of bequeathing to posterity a set of universally shared opinions," he argued, "the founders shaped a series of fiercely fought debates that reverberate down to the present day."[21] Under this view, since the Founding

Fathers disagreed about so many issues, it is futile to cite them in service of a modern political agenda because, on issue after issue, such as the role of government and the extent of federal authority, one will be able to find a leading Founding Father on either side.

This argument proves too much. If the Framers truly operated without a set of shared principles, it is unfathomable that they could have successfully crafted a durable written governing charter, much less fought a successful revolution. Even Chernow acknowledges that, "as a general rule, the founders favored limited government." Chernow stresses that they "differed sharply over those limits," but the important fact is that they all believed in *some* constitutional limits.[22] To say the least, an unshakable belief in limited government conflicts sharply with creative constructions of certain powers, such as the Commerce Clause, that transform the Constitution from one based on powers that are "few and defined" into one possessed with powers that are "numerous and indefinite."

The Framers insisted on creating a federal government that was constrained by numerous innovations—separating the government into three branches, providing each branch with a means to check the other, mandating different term lengths for House members and senators, respectively—so that it remained limited to those powers granted to it, under the Constitution, by the people. Indeed, so pervasive was the belief in limited government during the Founding Era that, had the Constitution created a government without such constitutional limitations, it almost certainly would not have even been ratified.

As a general matter, there exists a critical distinction between the fundamental first principles that united the vast majority of the Founders and which underlie the Constitution and those prevailing political issues that arouse the attention of politicians and citizens then and now. The Founders disagreed about how the Constitution was to be applied in certain circumstances, such as the ability of the federal government to charter a national bank, but their disagreements were less over first principles than over the means by which to vindicate such principles. For example, when Hamilton defended the constitutionality of the Bank of the United States to President Washington, he articulated a theory of federal power that was broader than that supported by Thomas Jefferson, yet he did not argue that the Constitution contained no limitations on the means available for use by the government to achieve its desired ends. Indeed, he specifically noted that it was constitutionally permissible to employ only those means "which are not precluded by restrictions and exceptions specified in the constitution, or not immoral, or not contrary to the essential ends of political society."

By the same token, we may never be able to know definitely what Hamilton would have thought about the effectiveness of President Obama's attempts to defeat America's enemies or whether Madison would have supported ObamaCare. But we certainly know that the Constitution provided for a potentially potent military force because, as Hamilton and John Jay discussed in *The Federalist*, strength fostered safety while weakness invited hostility. We also know that the Constitution created by Madison and his fellow delegates was designed to affect a limited number of objects but not exert a pervasive influence over American life. We can, then, judge whether the prevailing orthodoxies in the age of Obama represent a vindication of, or a departure from, these founding principles. As the eminent statesman and political theorist Edmund Burke explained, "without the guide and light of some well-understood principles, all reasonings in politics, as in everything else, would be only a confused jumble of particular facts and details."[23] Our nation's bedrock values must be the guide that animates our contemporary politics.

A desire to live up to the principles that the Constitution embodies has animated the constitutional renaissance sparked by the Obama program of transformational change, yet many of the naysayers saw this renaissance as little more than a misplaced religious devotion to the Founding Fathers and the Constitution they created. Samuel Freedman of *The New York Times* noted how, examining the tea party movement through the prism of religion, "the Constitution is the tea party's bible, and that holy book is embraced as an inerrant text."[24]

Joy Behar, a left-wing television personality, wondered whether, in light of the plan of Republicans in Congress to read the Constitution aloud in the House of Representatives, this "Constitution-loving is getting out of hand?" The tea party's invocation of first principles was certainly too much for Michael Lind, a progressive writing for Salon.com, who argued that it represented a "deeply flawed understanding of America's founding," a "superstitious veneration of particular constitutions handed down by wise demigods." He expressed disgust at the "cult of the all-wise Founders," and approvingly cited the view of "our Anglophone peers" who "regard American Constitution-worship as bizarre and quaint, like our fondness for displaying the national flag."[25]

Others reacted to what they saw as a pious reverence for the Constitution and its creators by trying to diminish the Founding Fathers and their achievements. E. J. Dionne, a liberal columnist for *The Washington Post*, lambasted the tea party movement for viewing the Constitution "as the equivalent of sacred scripture" rather than what Dionne considered it to be: merely a "collection of shrewd political compromises." Dionne cited Gordon Wood, an eminent progressive historian, for the notion that the Founding Fathers "were not outside history…they had no special divine insight into politics, and their thinking was certainly not free of passion, ignorance, and foolishness."[26] Congressman Jerrold Nadler, a Democrat from New York, called the "ritualistic reading" of the Constitution on the House floor "total nonsense," and derided those who consider the Founders to be "demigods," when, he claimed, they created a constitution that was, at best, "highly imperfect."[27]

The New York Times lambasted the Republican-led House for what it deemed to be the political stunt of reading the Constitution; according to *The Times*, it is presumptuous to claim knowledge of the meaning of the Constitution since the document doesn't establish protection for fixed, time-honored principles, but, rather, is "open to generations of reinterpretation." *The Times* then snidely remarked, "Certainly, the Republican leadership is not trying to suggest that African-Americans still be counted as three-fifths of a person"—a thinly-veiled swipe at the "unenlightened" Founding Fathers but one which revealed historical ignorance since counting slaves as less than a full person for purposes of representation benefitted anti-slavery states.[28]

This criticism of reverence for the Constitution and its creators wildly misses the mark. The Constitution, as well as the Declaration of Independence, has always served as a national unifying symbol because the United States is founded on ideas—unlike nations the world over, ours is a nation without a national ethnicity or religion but a shared political creed. Indeed, we have a civic religion, one dedicated to certain fundamental propositions about the rights of individuals and the role of government. For this reason, George Washington advised his fellow citizens that the Constitution must be "sacredly maintained," and James Madison wished for public opinion to "guarantee, with a holy zeal, these political scriptures from every attempt to add to or diminish from them."

Though both Washington and Madison believed America received the aid of Divine Providence in the struggle against the British and the creation of the Constitution, they did not consider the Constitution to be, like the Bible, the inerrant word of God. Rather, the Constitution needed to be piously followed because it contained the specific, enumerated powers delegated and limited by the people to the federal government, thereby standing as the carefully circumscribed boundaries that separated a government of laws from a government of men. Support and defense of the Constitution is a way to vindicate a government based on what Alexander Hamilton called "reflection and choice," which is a government based on the consent of the people.

Seen in this light, appreciation for the Founding Fathers lies not in a notion that they were superhuman or beyond history, which is merely a caricature typically employed by those critical of the Founders and their Constitution. Instead, the Founders stand out as monumental figures in history because they articulated and asserted the right ideas at the right time in history, demonstrating the courage of their convictions by risking their lives, their fortunes, and their sacred honor to establish a new political order for the ages. Their primary achievement—the establishment of a government based on the consent of the governed and limited by an enduring, written constitution—is sometimes taken for granted given the success of their political project, but the fact is that such success confounds the expectations of history, which has seen popular governments habitually fail.

One individual who understood the grand achievement of the Founding Fathers was a young lawyer from Illinois. In a speech to the Young Men's Lyceum in Springfield, he stressed the need to celebrate the rule of law and guard against the steady "alienation of their affections from the government" bequeathed to them by the Founding Fathers. The lawyer, Abraham Lincoln, continued:

> As the patriots of seventy-six did to the support of the Declaration of Independence, so to the support of the Constitution and Laws, let every American pledge his life, his property, and his sacred honor; let every man remember that to violate the law, is to trample on the blood of his

> father, and to tear the character of his own, and his children's liberty. Let reverence for the laws, be breathed by every American mother, to the lisping babe, that prattles on her lap – let it be taught in schools, in seminaries, and in colleges; let it be written in Primers, spelling books, and in Almanacs; let it be preached from the pulpit, proclaimed in legislative halls, and enforced in courts of justice. And, in short, let it become the political religion of the nation.[29]

Lincoln was still decades away from being elected president of the United States, yet he saw the danger that, as the memory of the Founding generation continued to fade, the nation's bedrock principles would no longer command the same level of respect, admiration and adherence. By championing the rule of law—indeed, by making it the "political religion of the nation"—Lincoln was trying to ensure continued dedication to the principles that underpinned the nation established by the "patriots of seventy-six."

Does dedication to the nation's bedrock values, as Lincoln urged, mean that no changes can be made to the Constitution? In the age of Obama, some criticized those self-described constitutionalists who, on the one hand, express a reverence for the Constitution and the Founding Fathers while, on the other hand, seek to amend the very Constitution they created. If the document is so worthy of praise, these critics maintain, then why is it in need of alteration? For one thing, the Constitution itself provides a means for amendment, so it cannot, in and of itself, be a slight against the Founding Fathers to seek to amend the Constitution they explicitly acknowledged would, from time to time, require it.

In fact, within the first fifteen years following the ratification of the Constitution, members of the Founding generation amended the document twelve times. While ten of these amendments, what later became known as the Bill of Rights, were contemplated before the Constitution was ratified, both the Eleventh Amendment (dealing with the sovereign immunity of states) and the Twelfth Amendment (clarifying the manner of election for the President and Vice President) were adopted to address problems with the operation of the new government.

The Constitution can be amended in a way that reaffirms, rather than repudiates, the nation's founding principles. This is surely what Lincoln thought he was doing when he urged support for a constitutional amendment abolishing slavery; he saw it as vindication of the principles articulated in the Declaration of Independence, even though opponents of the Thirteenth Amendment criticized the deviation from the "Constitution as is."

While it is true that many tea party supporters have supported the adoption of additional amendments to the Constitution, it is not necessarily hypocritical for them to do so provided that the proposed amendments do not represent a departure from the principles underlying the Constitution. From correcting erroneous interpretations of the Constitution by the Supreme Court (such as those failing to vindicate individual liberty, like *Plessy v. Ferguson* and *Kelo v. City of New London*) to combating the expansion of government beyond its constitutional limitations, there exist a number of ways in which amendments can serve this reaffirmative function. Though it should never be done without an appropriate amount of caution—because, in Madison's words, such "experiments are of too ticklish a nature to be unnecessarily multiplied"—amending the Constitution in this fashion represents an appropriate application of the Article V power devised by Framers.

The fact that those styling themselves as constitutional conservatives advocate, in some instances, amendments to the Constitution serves to distinguish them from their progressive critics. It cannot be said that those who espouse a progressive political philosophy *never* advocate formal amendments to the Constitution. Though they received little serious consideration, a number of amendments have, since 1990, been introduced in Congress by progressives—amendments that would, among other things, abolish the electoral college, place restrictions on political speech during campaigns, mandate taxpayer funding of welfare benefits, and require progressive income taxes. These amendments cannot be described as serving a reaffirmative function; instead, they would either replace a particular provision of the original Constitution or otherwise transform the Constitution from one that preserved liberty by limiting government's power to one that subordinated individual liberty to the collectivist appetites of the nation's governing class.

In any event, amendments to the Constitution along progressive lines have not been a major aspect of the platforms of most recent progressive politicians. This is not an accident. As *The New York Times* revealed when it criticized the reading of the Constitution on the

House floor, progressives (like the editorialists at *The Times*) do not see the Constitution as possessing a stable meaning but, instead, as remaining "open to generations of reinterpretation." This is why progressives stress the disagreements of the Founding Fathers and insist that the Constitution's original meaning is elusive; it provides them with a convenient reason to eschew fealty to the original principles underlying the Constitution in favor of their more "enlightened," avant-garde interpretations of what they want the Constitution to represent. There is no need to employ the difficult formal amendment process if the same ends can be attained through creative construction.

In the age of Obama, the progressive constitutional playbook has been on display for all to see. Under this view, there is no discernible limitation on the power of the federal government to regulate practically any aspect of everyday life. But rather than simply declare the power of the federal government to be unlimited, like was done, in an eyebrow raising fashion, by California Congressman Pete Stark, the progressive prefers to laud the courts as being the sole judge of the Constitution. As stated by Congressman Henry Waxman, when it comes to acts of Congress, the question of "whether it is constitutional or not is going to be whether the Supreme Court says it is." In other words, members of Congress do not need to confine their actions to the powers enumerated in the Constitution because the Supreme Court will decree when they have overstepped their bounds; otherwise, they are free to get away with whatever they can, such as forcing citizens to buy insurance from a private company.

Theoretically, a judiciary that faithfully enforced the limitations on the Congress' power contained in the Constitution would serve to keep progressive legislators like Waxman in check. However, because the progressive emphasizes "reinterpreting" the Constitution, jurists of a progressive bent recoil from insisting that the regulatory power of Congress is subject to constitutional limitations. These jurists subscribe to the notion, first articulated by Woodrow Wilson, that the Constitution is a "living" document, which enables them to change the meaning of the Constitution through novel interpretation. Wilson condemned the Constitution because he thought that the dispersal of power and internal checks served to frustrate the capacity of the federal government to "solve" problems through centralized planning, and the modern progressive jurist employs Wilson's "living"

Constitution theory to remove impediments to the expansion of the federal government's power. When Obama's second Supreme Court nominee, Elena Kagan, could not articulate a single example of Congress exceeding its regulatory authority under the Commerce Clause, she was singing from the progressive playbook. If jurists like Kagan are committed to giving Congress virtually unlimited regulatory discretion, then how, exactly, will legislators like Waxman be reigned in when they exceed the boundaries of the Constitution?

This awkward formulation of a judicially supreme constitutional government would be unrecognizable to the Framers, who stressed the relative weakness of the judiciary and who noted the need for legislators to scrutinize the constitutionality of legislation. This does not, of course, mean that the political branches are free to disregard judicial decisions, such as those issued by the Supreme Court, the decisions of which are final. That said, it is a mistake to think that judicial decisions invariably interpret the Constitution correctly, as there exist a number of instances in which courts failed to enforce the Constitution, such as *Plessy v. Ferguson*, which upheld the constitutionality of racial segregation by watering down the Fourteenth Amendment via the creation of a "separate but equal" doctrine. If legislators do not make an effort to abide by the Constitution, then certain rights, particularly those rights held in disrepute by progressive jurists, such as property and gun rights, will not receive the protection afforded to them in the Constitution.

The approach to the Constitution articulated by progressives in the age of Obama confounds its basic purpose. The Constitution demarcates limitations on government's power, including specific protections for certain natural rights like the freedom of speech and freedom of religion, because the Founders presupposed that certain public views, passions and mores will change over time, and they wanted a written constitution to serve as an anchor for a changing society. Free speech might not always be popular, so we need a Constitution to stand as an enduring roadblock against popular passions that might undermine it, as well as other, God-given rights upon which no government can properly infringe.

Once judges and politicians engage the progressive conceit that they have the prerogative to "reinterpret" the Constitution as they see fit, those protections are no longer the great cement of society but merely rudderless provisions that can be narrowed as a matter of course. Under this view, swearing an oath to the Constitution requires one to support and defend an elusive target, a document susceptible of transformation without any formal amendment. Having lost the full force of its restraining power, the Constitution no longer serves its intended function as an impenetrable obstacle to the infringement of liberty.

Because they embrace a form of constitutionalism that elevates the rule of men over the rule of law, the resurgence of the Constitution and the Founding Fathers necessarily puts progressives on the intellectual defensive. When Woodrow Wilson and other early 20th-century progressives complained about the Constitution and criticized the Founding Fathers, they were distressed that so many of their fellow citizens venerated the Founders and held the Constitution in high esteem. To Wilson, many governments in Europe were superior to the American government because the former facilitated the creation of a centralized administrative state, yet most Americans were not eager to erect wholesale changes to the Constitution. The "living" Constitution theory was Wilson and other progressives' answer to this conundrum; they would transcend the Constitution where they could not change it.

Such transcendence is a much taller order when the Constitution and the Founding Fathers occupy a central place in the nation's political discourse. Those citizens who invoke the nation's first principles do not consider departure from the Constitution by the ruling class to be "progress." Instead, they see the principles underlying the Constitution as representing enduring, time-tested truths about politics, government, and liberty. And they refuse to indulge those politicians who advocate interpretations of the Constitution that are insusceptible of principled application and that convert the limited Constitution into what James Madison called an "unlimited government." Given this political environment, it is no wonder that progressives reacted with such hostility to those tea party activists who demanded adherence to the Constitution and cited the Founding Fathers in support of their opposition to Obama and his allies.

26

The Future of American Constitutionalism

It is somewhat ironic that a renewed appreciation for the Constitution and the nation's first principles has unfolded in the age of Obama. After all, Obama is the product of almost monolithically leftist political influences. The animating beliefs of these influences, from his father's dreams of a centralized, redistributive political system to the radical figures he gravitated towards as a young man and budding politician, represent a political ethos far different from and, in some instances, diametrically opposed to the principles that serve as the foundation for the Constitution. He also viewed himself as a figure of supreme historical significance, someone who could usher in a fundamental transformation of the country, a transformation that reflected his own political principles and ideology but did not reaffirm the nation's original principles. He probably never anticipated that Americans from all walks of life would react to his transformational agenda by invoking first principles.

Though he paid tribute to America's founding and to the Constitution, which is virtually obligatory for any president, he did so less than many, if not all, of his predecessors. Perhaps this was because he doesn't see the nation's founding principles as particularly noteworthy. Though he confessed that did not "entirely" reject what he considered to be the "myth" of the Founding, he stressed that the Founding Era's "spirit of liberty didn't extend, in the minds of the Founders, to the slaves that worked their fields, made their beds and nursed their children."[1] With respect to the nation's birth, he refused to "brush aside the magnitude of the injustice done, or erase the ghosts of generations past, or ignore the open wound, the aching spirit that ails this country still."[2] During a press conference after the 2010 midterm elections, a noticeably agitated Obama even declared, "I couldn't go through the front door at this country's founding."[3]

Obama's indictment of the Founding Fathers is seriously flawed in two important respects. For one thing, Obama's blanket denunciation of the Founders for not extending the "spirit of liberty" to the "slaves that worked their fields" is alarmingly inaccurate with respect to a number of Founding Fathers, such as Alexander Hamilton, Benjamin Franklin and Gouverneur Morris, who opposed slavery. Morris condemned slavery at the Constitutional Convention as "curse of heaven where it prevailed," and both Hamilton and Franklin were active in anti-slavery organizations.

Second, as Charles Kessler of the Claremont Institute points out, when it comes to the Founders' dedication to natural rights, "Obama's interpretation is the opposite of Lincoln's, who devoted some of his finest pages to proving that the founders regarded slavery as a moral and political evil because it violated the rights of man."[4] Though Obama made every attempt to draw comparisons between himself and Lincoln, it is actually one of Lincoln's foremost political adversaries and one of Obama's predecessors, Stephen A. Douglas, who argued like Obama that the Founders meant to exclude non-whites from the natural rights clarion call contained in the Declaration of Independence. To Lincoln, such a view "assumes what is historically a falsehood…[because] they placed [slavery] where they understood, and all sensible men understood it was in the course of ultimate extinction."[5]

Despite his anti-Lincolnian views about the conception of the nation, Obama has other points of dispute with the Founding Fathers, which he has displayed by pressing his transformational political project. There can be little doubt that Obama and his congressional allies have little patience for the limitations on legislative power contained in the Constitution. The age of Obama has seen an expansion of government on virtually every level: citizens forced to purchase health insurance from private companies, bake sales at local schools regulated by federal authorities, massive "stimulus" spending appropriated and expended, automobile bankruptcies influenced in derogation of settled rules of law, and more than 100 new bureaucracies created. At least one of these initiatives, the individual health care mandate, represents a violation of the Constitution because it expands the Commerce Clause beyond anything the Founding Fathers would have envisioned—indeed, beyond anything that can be entertained while still plausibly considering the government to be one of limited and enumerated powers, as it was unquestionably designed. Other initiatives, when taken together and if institutionalized over the long term, portend a society in which the federal government exerts a pervasive influence over a vast range of individual behavior ranging from the consumption of energy to dietary decisions.

Perhaps the primary reason that Obama has sought to markedly expand the power of the federal government is his desire for so-called redistributive change. The notion of using the levers of political power to redistribute wealth, in a manner the political class deems appropriate, represents one of the central themes in Obama's political life and a large part of the dreams he inherited from his father. For the man whose original redistributive playground consisted of the streets of Chicago and who lamented the failure of the Warren Court to use the courts to redistribute wealth, his first two years in the White House witnessed the realization, on a grand scale, of the very type of redistributive change that he has long coveted: he dispensed generous benefits to his political supporters through the so-called stimulus bill, he injected himself into the auto company bankruptcies in a way that redistributed wealth to his union allies, he enacted a 2,000-plus page health care bill that included sweeping new taxes and heralded the redistribution of hundreds of billions, if not trillions, of dollars in taxpayer money, and he signed a voluminous financial regulatory bill that he hopes will reduce profits in the financial services industry.

Following the 2010 midterm elections, Obama struck a compromise with Republicans in Congress that postponed the tax increases due to take effect in 2011 for a period of two years. To the outrage of some of his progressive supporters, this postponement even applied to those making more than $250,000 a year in income, which is the line decreed by Obama as the demarcation point between the "rich" and those who work for a living. This was certainly something that Obama was loathe to do; after all, during the presidential campaign, he voiced support for raising capital gains tax rates even if it led to less revenue for the government because, essentially, he wanted to punish people who realized capital gains. Indeed, at the press conference announcing the compromise, Obama was visibly irritated by the very deal that he had just negotiated, demonstrating the extent to which redistributive change informs his political worldview. He made the compromise because, lagging in the polls and facing the prospect that higher taxes would impede the already anemic growth in the economy, he needed to protect his political standing with his re-election campaign on the horizon. But the press conference made clear that his heart was with the redistributive aims of his progressive supporters. Unlike Alexander Hamilton, who conceived of the tax system as a way to raise revenue for the nation's critical public needs, Obama considers tax policy to be a way to wield the power of the state in service of his vision for "redistributive justice."

Moving away from a limited government that guards against a "leveling" spirit and towards an unlimited government whose chief aim is to redistribute wealth is just one of the many ways in which the politics practiced by Obama and his allies confound the principles relied on by the Constitution's creators. Obama articulated a philosophy of jurisprudence that, in defiance of Hamilton's dictum in *The Federalist* regarding the use of will rather than judgment, championed a purposeful construction of the Constitution that relied on the (entirely subjective) personal values of the judge, thereby providing a mechanism whereby restraints on government can be eroded through constitutional interpretation. Obama and his congressional collaborators extended the government's reach into so many different areas that its operation can only be described as chronically inept—certainly a far cry from the effective administration that the Framers considered to be critical following the disastrous experience with the Articles of Confederation. And Obama eschewed notions, which Constitution creators like Hamilton and Washington embraced, regarding the need to deter adversaries through a strong defense and the futility of diplomacy premised upon foreign nations acting in defiance of their respective national interests. Instead, he sought to subordinate American interests to the concerns of the international community, and tried to engage with rogue nations that have no overlapping interests with the United States.

The 2010 midterm election represented a decisive rebuke to Obama's quest to fundamentally transform the United States. His Democratic Party lost control of the House of Representatives, and it lost a sufficient number of Senate seats to foreclose the possibility of moving gargantuan pieces of "transformative" legislation through the upper chamber. Republicans also made historic gains in state governorships and in state legislative chambers—gains that will further erode progressive power in Congress when the states redraw the congressional districts following the 2010 census. Michael Barone, the co-author of the *Almanac of American Politics*, argued that the 2010 elections might have been "the best Republican showing ever," and that the election demonstrated that "the tea party movement was a genuine popular upheaval of vast dimensions."[6]

The election was hardly an endorsement of the Republican Party. The Reagan Revolution realigned the nation's politics away from the old New Deal coalition and towards a center-right direction that eschewed some of the discredited liberal policies of the 1960s in favor of lower taxes, less government, and a strong national defense, but, by 2008, the Republican Party had lost the confidence of vast swaths of the American electorate. According to Senator Jim DeMint, a Republican from South Carolina and a leading advocate of the tea party movement, this was because "Republicans didn't do what we said we were going to do. We spent too much, we borrowed too much." After Barack Obama won the presidency, *Time*'s Michael Grunwald observed that "Republicans have the desperate aura of an endangered species," and books, such as *The Strange Death of Republican America: Chronicles of a Collapsing Party* by progressive Sidney Blumenthal, foresaw the GOP spending a generation in the political wilderness.[7]

The tea party-inspired Republican resurgence so soon after the reports of the party's demise was not due to a renewed confidence in the party of Lincoln. Instead, the GOP was the beneficiary of events largely beyond its control. First, Obama saw his election as representing a mandate for his expressed desire to "fundamentally transform the United States of America," but, in reality, he was merely the beneficiary of voter dissatisfaction with George W. Bush and voter uneasiness in the face of a jolting financial crisis. His hubris, which was fanned by fawning press coverage, led him to think, erroneously, that the public was eager for him to lead a reformulation of the nation's fundamental operating principles.

Second, Obama's attempt to transform these principles created a strong political backlash that became the tea party movement. This movement, though, was also hostile to those establishment Republicans they considered to be insufficiently faithful to America's founding principles, and it was hardly preordained that tea party activists would support Republican candidates in 2010. That the tea party tried to influence the process through the Republican Party, including by knocking off establishment-favored candidates in

Republican primaries, ensured that anti-Obama forces would be united, and represented a major political boon for the GOP.

Some simply dismissed the election results as a reflection of the economic conditions prevailing throughout the nation. With the unemployment rate high, and with economic growth sluggish, it is unlikely, so the argument goes, that any party in power would have fared much better. According to this view, there was little need for Obama to trim his sails in anticipation of his 2012 reelection campaign because his political standing would improve in line with the natural improvement in the economy. Others suggested that Obama needed a major course correction, such as was employed by Bill Clinton in 1995-96, if he wanted to win a second term. If he continued pursuing such an ideologically ambitious agenda, these critics warned, he would meet a resounding electoral defeat.

Surely, attributing the political backlash engendered by Obama's grand designs purely to the failing economy misses the entire import of the tea party movement, which is concerned with fostering more faithful constitutionalism. Nevertheless, both the state of the economy and the extent to which Obama trims his ideological sails will surely affect Obama's political standing when he faces voters in 2012. Irrespective of how Obama governs in the run up to the 2012 election, it is safe to assume that the real Obama is the self-described transformative leader that pursued a far-reaching ideological agenda during his first two years in office.

Indeed, even as he tried to position himself for reelection, Obama made a series of statements that evinced his desire for transformational change. During a speech about the nation's mounting debt, Obama proclaimed that the greatness of the United States lies not in its commitment to individual liberty but in its government spending programs, many of which did not even exist for most of American history.[8] At a town hall meeting, Obama criticized the "basic view … that no matter how successful I am, no matter how much I've taken from this country…that somehow I now have no obligation" to give back.[9]

He sees those who have achieved economic success as "taking" from the country rather than contributing to it, even though entrepreneurs from Henry Ford to Steve Jobs have dramatically enhanced the quality of life in America. Curiously, Obama equates giving back to the country with paying more taxes to the federal government, thereby enabling him to commandeer more resources to feed his transformational schemes.

To be sure, if he secures reelection, Obama will be in a position to further pursue his agenda of transformational change. This includes the institutionalization of ObamaCare in a way that pushes the nation towards a purely government-run, single-payer system, the further expansion of the regulatory state to cover individual choices regarding energy and food consumption, and additional ineffective spending programs under the guise of economic "stimulus" and "investment."

Without having to face voters again, a reelected Obama will be much more willing to press for a tax policy aimed at equalizing outcomes by penalizing success. He will also be in a position to appoint additional justices to the United States Supreme Court—including, perhaps, a replacement for Associate Justice Antonin Scalia, who is the longest serving justice. If Obama appoints a progressive jurist to replace Justice Scalia, then he will effectuate a dramatic shift in the direction of the Court, thereby immunizing his initiatives against constitutional attack and paving the way for uninhibited progressive activism.

For those inclined to be alarmed by Obama's desire to transform the country, the stakes of the 2012 presidential election are extraordinarily high. A second Obama term will see a continued drift away from those principles—regarding limitations on government, the role of the courts, the redistribution of wealth, foreign affairs, and governmental competence—that the Founding Fathers articulated in defending the Constitution.

America is at a constitutional crossroads. Obama's vision, resting heavily on progressive thought and the plethora of left-of-center political influences that have informed his worldview, is for a decidedly less exceptional America, an America more akin to governments throughout Europe, in which the state, rather than the individual, is supreme.

Such a vision is a far cry from the dreams bequeathed to us by the Founding Fathers. The voters' choice between these competing visions will define the national character for a generation and, perhaps, irrevocably. Alexander Hamilton's observation in *The Federalist* No. 1, regarding the state of affairs in his time, is equally apt to our time: "The crisis at which we are arrived may with propriety be regarded as the era in which that decision is to be made; and a wrong election of the part we shall act may, in this view, deserve to be considered as the general misfortune of mankind."[10]

NOTES

1
Fundamental Transformation

[1] This figure is based on the revised estimate of the Congressional Budget Office from August 2010 at http://www.cbo.gov/ftpdocs/117xx/doc11705/08-18-Update.pdf (accessed September 1, 2010).
[2] As quoted in Michael Barone, "The Transformative Power of Rick Santelli's Rant," *The Washington Examiner*, June 9, 2009, http://www.washingtonexaminer.com/politics/The-transformative-power-of-Rick-Santelli_s-rant-95907904.html (accessed September 1, 2010).
[3] Barack Obama, "Address to the Democratic National Convention," July 27, 2004, http://www.washingtonpost.com/wp-dyn/articles/A19751-2004Jul27.html (accessed September 1, 2010).
[4] Barack Obama, "Remarks in Grant Park," November 4, 2008, http://articles.cnn.com/2008-11-04/politics/obama.transcript_1_transcript-answer-sasha-and-malia?_s=PM:POLITICS (accessed September 1, 2010).
[5] "In Their Own Words: Obama on Reagan," *The New York Times*, http://www.nytimes.com/ref/us/politics/21seelye-text.html (accessed August 15, 2010).
[6] Barack Obama, "Announcement of Candidacy for President," February 10, 2007, http://www.barackobama.com/2007/02/10/remarks_of_senator_barack_obam_11.php (accessed August 15, 2010).
[7] Hayley Tsukyama and Liz Lucas, "Thousands Cheer Obama at a Rally for Change," *The Columbia Missourian*, October 30, 2008, http://www.columbiamissourian.com/stories/2008/10/30/obama-speaks-crowd-40000/ (accessed August 15, 2010).
[8] Allison J. Pugh, "Scholar's Passion to Help the Poor Fuels Law Career," The Associated Press, printed in *The New Orleans Times Picayune*, April 16, 1990.
[9] Michelle Obama, "Remarks in San Juan, Puerto Rico," May 14, 2008, http://www.youtube.com/watch?v=afGz0dzVSIU (accessed September 15, 2010).
[10] Abraham Lincoln, "Address at Cooper Union," February 27, 1860 in Joseph R. Fornieri, ed., *The Language of Liberty: The Political Speeches and Writing of Abraham Lincoln* (Washington, DC: Regnery Publishing 2009), 566.
[11] Dr. Martin Luther King Jr., "Speech at Civil Rights March," August 28, 1963 in Fred R. Shapiro, ed., *The Yale Book of Quotations* (New Haven: Yale University Press, 2006), 428.
[12] Dr. Martin Luther King Jr., "I've Been to the Mountain Top," April 3, 1968, http://www.americanrhetoric.com/speeches/mlkivebeentothemountaintop.htm. (accessed September 16, 2010).

[13] Editorial, "President Obama," *The New York Times*, January 20, 2009, http://www.nytimes.com/2009/01/21/opinion/21wed1.html (accessed June 8, 2010).
[14] Matthew Benjamin and Juliana Goldman, "Obama's Economic Stimulus Bill Most Ambitious Since Roosevelt," Bloomberg.com, February 17, 2009, http://www.bloomberg.com/apps/news?pid=newsarchive&sid=ajHfW4awsaho (accessed June 8, 2010).
[15] Jennifer Levitz, "Halloween Doesn't Fully Explain the Spike in Powdered Wig Sales," *The Wall Street Journal*, October 14, 2010, http://online.wsj.com/article/SB10001424052748703794104575545850961915076.html (accessed October 16, 2010).
[16] See, e.g., Ron Chernow, "The Founding Fathers Versus the Tea Party," *The New York Times*, September 23, 2010, http://www.nytimes.com/2010/09/24/opinion/24chernow.html (accessed September 24, 2010).
[17] Quoted in Editorial, "The Violence Card: Bill Clinton Plays Politics With Timothy McVeigh," *The Wall Street Journal*, April 21, 2010, http://online.wsj.com/article/SB10001424052748704448304575196310816341450.html (accessed September 2, 2010).
[18] http://www.gallup.com/poll/113968/obama-initial-approval-ratings-historical-context.aspx (accessed September 2, 2010).
[19] Carol Lee, "Obama Dissects Demonstrators," *Politico*, March 30, 2010, http://www.politico.com/politico44/perm/0310/to_a_tea_7861654c-f576-4cce-a912-ab0cd07ebcc7.html (accessed August 3, 2010).

2
"First Principles and Main Pillars of the Fabric"

[1] Alexander Hamilton, "The Federalist No. 31," in Clinton Rossiter, ed., *The Federalist Papers* (New York: NAL Penguin, 1961), 193.
[2] Quoted in Gordon S. Wood, *The Creation of the American Republic, 1176-1787* (Chapel Hill: University of North Carolina Press 1969, 1998), 393.
[3] George Washington to James Madison, November 5, 1786 in Jared Sparks, ed., *The Writings of George Washington* (Boston: Russell, Odiorne and Metcalf, 1835), 9: 206.
[4] George Washington to Alexander Hamilton, August 28, 1788 in Michael Meyerson, *Liberty's Blueprint: How Madison and Hamilton Wrote the Federalist Papers, Defined the Constitution, and Made Democracy Safe for the World* (New York: Basic Books, 2009), 141.
[5] George Washington, "Resignation Address," December 23, 1783.
[6] George Washington to Alexander Hamilton, August 28, 1788 in Sparks, ed., *The Writings of George Washington*, 9: 420.
[7] Thomas Jefferson to James Madison, November 18, 1788 in S.E. Forman, ed., *The Life and Writings of Thomas Jefferson* (Indianapolis: Bowen and Merrill Co., 1900), 214.
[8] Ron Chernow, *Alexander Hamilton* (New York: Penguin Press, 2004), 30.
[9] Ron Chernow, *Alexander Hamilton* (New York: Penguin Press, 2004), 248-251.
[10] Alexander Hamilton, "The Federalist No. 1," in Rossiter, ed., *The Federalist Papers*, 33.

[11] Benjamin Franklin, "Speech to the Federal Convention," September 17, 1787 in Max Farrand, ed., *Records of the Federal Convention of 1787* (New Haven: Yale University Press, 1911), 2: 643.
[12] Ibid., 648.
[13] Matt Welch, "Thomas L. Friedman Wants Us 'to be China for a day,' to 'authorize the right solutions,'" Reason.com, May 24, 2010, http://reason.com/blog/2010/05/24/thomas-l-friedman-wants-us-to (accessed August 10, 2010).
[14] Richard Cohen, "GOP Succumbs to Witchful Thinking," September 21, 2010, http://www.realclearpolitics.com/articles/2010/09/21/gop_succumbs_to_witchful_thinking.html (accessed September 22, 2010).
[15] http://www.newyorker.com/online/blogs/hendrikhertzberg/obama/ (accessed September 22, 2010) .
[16] American Political Science Association panel discussion, September 3, 2010, http://www.c-spanvideo.org/program/295312-1 (accessed September 4, 2010).
[17] Quoted in Gary A. Hengstler, "Marshalling His Views: Justice's Controversial Comments Break 20-year Silence," *ABA Journal*, March 1, 1988, 36.
[18] Alexander Hamilton, "Speech on the Compromises of the Constitution," June 20, 1788, New York Ratifying Convention, Poughkeepsie, NY in John C. Hamilton, ed., *The Works of Alexander Hamilton* (New York: John F. Trow, 1850), 2: 434.
[19] Farrand, *Records of the Federal Convention*, 2: 643.
[20] Gouverneur Morris, "Speech to the Federal Convention," August 8, 1787 in Farrand, ed., *Records of the Federal Convention,* 2: 222.
[21] John Adams to Hezekiah Niles, 13 February 1818 in Charles Francis Adams, ed., *The Works of John Adams* (Boston: Little, Brown and Co., 1856), 10: 283.

3
James Madison University

[1] Trevor Brown, "Obama Revs Up Area Voters," *The Daily News Leader (Staunton, VA)*, October 29, 2008; Obama explicitly spelled out his desire for a "fundamental" transformation of the country, see Hayley Tsukayama and Liz Lucas, "Thousands Cheer Obama at Rally for Change," *The Columbia Missourian*, October, 30, 2008.
[2] Interview with Tom Brokaw, "The Charlie Rose Show," October 30, 2008, http://www.charlierose.com/view/interview/9330 (accessed June 4, 2010).
[3] Jake Tapper, "Halperin Decries 'Disgusting' Pro-Obama Media Bias in Election Coverage," ABCNews.com, November 24, 2008, http://blogs.abcnews.com/politicalpunch/2008/11/halperin-decrie.html (accessed June 4, 2010).

4
The Philosophy of "Change"

[1] Benjamin Wallace-Wells, "Barack Obama's Radical Roots," *Rolling Stone*, February 22, 2007.
[2] Warner Todd Huston, "Rolling Stone Changes Headline From Obama's 'Radical Roots' to 'Destiny's Child,'" Newsbusters.org, March 15, 2008, http://newsbusters.org/blogs/warner-todd-huston/2008/03/15/rolling-stone-changes-headline-obamas-radical-roots-destinys-chi.
[3] Barack Obama, "Speech to the Democratic National Convention," July 27, 2004, http://www.americanrhetoric.com/speeches/convention2004/barackobama2004dnc.htm (accessed July 10, 2010).
[4] Tim Jones, "Barack Obama: Mother not just a girl from Kansas," Chicagotribune.com, March 27, 2007, http://www.chicagotribune.com/news/politics/obama/chi-0703270151mar27-archive,0,5853572,full.story.
[5] Barack Obama, *Dreams From My Father: A Story of Race and Inheritance* (New York: Three Rivers Press, 1995, 2004), 50.
[6] Tim Jones, "Barack Obama: Mother not just a girl from Kansas."
[7] Jonathan Martin, "Obama's Mother Known Here as 'Uncommon,'" *The Seattle Times*, April 8, 2008, http://seattletimes.nwsource.com/html/politics/2004334057_obama08m.html.
[8] Ibid.
[9] Obama, *Dreams From My Father*, 154.
[10] Ibid., 47.
[11] Ibid., 17.
[12] Ibid.
[13] As quoted in Paul Kengor, "Obama's Surrogate Anti-Colonial Father," *The American Spectator*, October 14, 2010, http://spectator.org/archives/2010/10/14/obamas-surrogate-anti-colonial (accessed October 26, 2010).
[14] Obama, *Dreams From My Father*, 97.
[15] Ibid., 98.
[16] Ibid., 145-46.
[17] Obama, *Dreams From My Father*, 50.
[18] Ibid., 50.
[19] Eye on Books interview with Barack Obama, August 9, 1995, http://www.eyeonbooks.com/obama_transcript.pdf (accessed August 16, 2010).
[20] Obama, *Dreams From My Father*, 220.
[21] Ibid.
[22] Ibid., 429.
[23] Jon Meacham, "On His Own," *Newsweek*, August 23, 2008, http://www.newsweek.com/2008/08/22/on-his-own.html (accessed August 10, 2010).
[24] Obama, *Dreams From My Father*, 429-30.
[25] Ibid., 230.
[26] Meacham, "On His Own."

[27] Barack Obama Sr., "Problems Facing Our Socialism," *East Africa Journal*, July 1965, http://www.politico.com/static/PPM41_eastafrica.html (accessed March 30, 2010).
[28] Ibid.
[29] Ibid.
[30] Ibid.
[31] Obama, *Dreams From My Father*, 100-01.
[32] Ibid.
[33] Quoted in Ronald Kessler, "Obama Espoused Radical Views in College," February 8, 2010, Newsmax.com, http://www.newsmax.com/RonaldKessler/obama-college-marxism-occidental/2010/02/08/id/349329 (accessed April 9, 2010). Video of the interview with Dr. Drew can be viewed at http://www.breitbart.tv/college-acquaintance-young-obama-was-pure-marxist-socialist (accessed April 9, 2010). See also John C. Drew, "Meeting Young Obama," *The American Thinker*, February 24, 2011, http://www.americanthinker.com/2011/02/meeting_young_obama.html (accessed March 27, 2011).
[34] Barack Obama, "Breaking the War Mentality," *Sundial*, March 10, 1983, http://graphics8.nytimes.com/packages/images/nytint/docs/obama-s-1983-college-magazine-article/original.pdf (accessed March 22, 2010).
[35] Obama, *Dreams From My Father*, 122, 135.
[36] Ibid. 133-39.
[37] Ibid. 131.
[38] Ryan Lizza, "The Agitator," *The New Republic*, March 9, 2007, http://www.discoverthenetworks.org/Articles/bobamasunlikelypoliticaledu.html (accessed March 17, 2010).
[39] Ibid.
[40] Saul Alinsky, *Rules for Radicals: A Pragmatic Primer for Realistic Radicals* (New York: Vintage Books, 1971), 10.
[41] Ibid. 11.
[42] Ibid.
[43] Ibid., 9-10.
[44] Ibid., 52.
[45] Ibid., 18-23.
[46] Ibid., 23.
[47] Barack Obama, *The Audacity of Hope: Thoughts on Reclaiming the American Dream* (New York: Vintage Books 2008), 254.
[48] Obama, *Dreams From My Father*, 274.
[49] Wright's comments can be seen at http://www.youtube.com/watch?v=617eK2XIaLk (accessed on October 2, 2010).
[50] Jodi Kantor, "A Candidate, His Minister and a Search for Faith," *The New York Times*, April 30, 2007, http://www.nytimes.com/2007/04/30/us/politics/30obama.html?pagewanted=print (accessed April 2, 2010).
[51] Obama, *Dreams From My Father*, 283.
[52] Stanley Kurtz, "Jeremiah Wright's 'Trumpet,'" *The Weekly Standard*, May 19, 2008, Volume 013, Issue 34.
[53] Obama, *Dreams From My Father*, 285.
[54] Ibid., 286.

[55] Ibid., 292-93.
[56] Sheryl Gay Stolberg, "Obama Talks About His Faith," *The New York Times: The Caucus Blog*, September 28, 2010, http://thecaucus.blogs.nytimes.com/2010/09/28/obama-talks-about-his-faith-2/ (accessed September 29, 2010).
[57] Obama, *Dreams From My Father*, 276.
[58] Jennifer A. Kingson, "Harvard Tenure Battle Puts 'Critical Legal Studies' on Trial," *The New York Times*, August 30, 1987, http://www.nytimes.com/1987/08/30/weekinreview/harvard-tenure-battle-puts-critical-legal-studies-on-trial.html (accessed April 11, 2010).
[59] David Remnick, *The Bridge: The Life and Rise of Barack Obama* (New York: Random House, 2010), 184-85.
[60] Fox Butterfield, "First Black Elected to Head Harvard's Law Review," *The New York Times*, February 6, 1990, http://www.nytimes.com/1990/02/06/us/first-black-elected-to-head-harvard-s-law-review.html (accessed April 11, 2010).
[61] Alison J. Pugh, "No Cushy Post for this Pioneer: Harvard Law Review Chief Plans to Work in Inner City," *The Akron-Beacon Journal*, April 19, 1990.
[62] Deanna Bellandi, "Obama's Neighborhood Rich in Diversity," *USA Today*, July 23, 2007, http://www.usatoday.com/news/topstories/2007-07-23-2766958871_x.htm (accessed June 3, 2010).
[63] See http://www.chicagoelections.com/pctlevel3.asp?Ward=4&elec_code=90&race_number=3 (accessed October 1, 2010) as reported in Jay Cost, "What We Learned From Obama's *Rolling Stone Interview*," *The Weekly Standard*, September 30, 2010, http://www.weeklystandard.com/blogs/obama-democrat?page=3 (accessed October 1, 2010).
[64] Dinitia Smith, "No Regrets for Love of Explosives: In a Memoir of Sorts, a War Protester Talks of Life With the Weatherman," *The New York Times*, September 11, 2001, http://www.nytimes.com/2001/09/11/books/no-regrets-for-love-explosives-memoir-sorts-war-protester-talks-life-with.html. (accessed September 9, 2010).
[65] Andrew Ferguson, "Mr. Obama's Neighborhood," *The Weekly Standard*, June 16, 2008, Vol. 13, No. 38.
[66] Democratic Presidential Debate, April 17, 2008, http://latimesblogs.latimes.com/showtracker/2008/04/stephanopoulos.html (accessed September 9, 2010).
[67] Ben Smith, "Obama Once Visited 60s Radicals," *Politico*, February 22, 2008, http://www.politico.com/news/stories/0208/8630.html (accessed September 10, 2010); Stanley Kurtz, "Obama and Ayers Pushed Radicalism on Schools," *The Wall Street Journal*, September 23, 2008, http://online.wsj.com/article/SB122212856075765367.html (accessed September 10, 2010); Michael Dobbs, "Obama's Weathermen Connection," February 19, 2008, http://blog.washingtonpost.com/fact-checker/2008/02/obamas_weatherman_connection.html (accessed September 10, 2010); Scott Shane, "Obama and 60s Bomber: A Look Into Crossed Paths," *The New York Times*, October 3, 2008, A1.
[68]Michael Powell, "Obama Addresses Critics on Centrist Moves," *The New York Times: The Caucus Blog*, July 8, 2008,

http://thecaucus.blogs.nytimes.com/2008/07/08/obama-addresses-critics-on-centrist-moves/ (accessed August 1, 2010).
[69] Woodrow Wilson, *Congressional Government* (Cambridge, MA: The Riverside Press, 1885), 4-5.
[70] Richard Hofstadter, *Age of Reform: From Bryan to F.D.R.* (New York: Vintage Books, 1955), 200.
[71] Herbert Croly, *The Promise of American Life* (Norwood, MA: Norwood Press, 1909), 209.
[72] Ibid., 153.
[73] Ibid., 274.
[74] Woodrow Wilson, *Constitutional Government in the United States* (New York: Columbia University Press, 1908), 69-70.
[75] Ibid.
[76] Ibid.; James Ceaser, *Presidential Selection: Theory and Development* (Princeton: Princeton University Press, 1979), 172.
[77] Ibid., 65.
[78] Geoffrey Hodgson, *Woodrow Wilson's Right Hand: the Life of Colonel Edward M. House* (New Haven: Yale University Press, 2006), 6.
[79] Edward M. House, *Philip Dru: Administrator* (New York: B.W. Heubsch, 1912), 2.
[80] George F. Will, "Obama in the Wilsonian Tradition," March 11, 2010, http://www.realclearpolitics.com/articles/2010/03/11/in_the_wilsonian_tradition_104733.html (accessed April 1, 2010).
[81] Mark Landler and Helene Cooper, "Obama Seeks a Course of Pragmatism in the Middle East," *The New York Times*, March 10, 2011, http://www.nytimes.com/2011/03/11/world/africa/11policy.html?_r=1 (accessed March 11, 2011).

5
The Philosophy of Liberty

[1] Thomas Jefferson to John Adams, August 30, 1787 in Thomas Jefferson Randolph, ed., *Memoirs and Correspondence of Thomas Jefferson* (London: Colburn and Bentley, 1829), 1: 228
[2] Ralph Ketcham, *James Madison: A Biography* (Charlottesville: The University Press of Virginia), 25-51.
[3] Ron Chernow, *Alexander Hamilton* (New York: Penguin Press, 2004), 52-53.
[4] Garret Ward Sheldon, *The Political Philosophy of James Madison* (Baltimore: Johns Hopkins University Press, 2001), 16.
[5] Alexander Hamilton, "The Farmer Refuted," February 23, 1775 in Harold C. Syrett, ed., *The Papers of Alexander Hamilton* (New York: Columbia University Press, 1961), 122.
[6] Garret Ward Sheldon, "Religion and Politics in the Thought of James Madison," in David Dreisbach, Mark Hall and Jeffry Morrison, ed., *The Founders on God and Government* (Lanham, MD: Rowman & Littlefield, 2004), 89-90; Garret Ward Sheldon, *The Political Philosophy of James Madison* (Baltimore: Johns Hopkins University Press, 2001), 1-26.

[7] James Madison, "The Federalist No. 37," in Clinton Rossiter, ed., *The Federalist Papers* (New York: NAL Penguin, 1961), 230-31.
[8] Benjamin Franklin, "Remarks at the Federal Convention," Thursday, June 28, 1787 in Max Farrand, ed., *Records of the Federal Convention* (New Haven: Yale University Press, 1911), 1: 450-52.
[9] George Washington, "Letter to the Roman Catholics," March 15, 1790 in John Frederick Schroeder, ed., *Maxims of Washington: Political, Social, Moral and Religious* (New York: D. Appleton and Co., 1855), 86.
[10] The Enlarged Salem Covenant of 1636 found in Williston Walker, *The Creeds and Platforms of Congregationalism* (Boston: The Pilgrim Press, 1960), 116-18.
[11] This phenomenon is detailed in Donald S. Lutz, *The Origins of American Constitutionalism* (Baton Rouge: Louisiana State University Press, 1988).
[12] James Madison, "The Federalist No. 53" in Rossiter, ed., *The Federalist Papers*, 331.
[13] Alexander Hamilton, "The Federalist No. 9," in Rossiter, ed., *The Federalist Papers*, 72.
[14] John Locke, *Second Treatise of Government*, Ch. V, Sec. 45.
[15] Ketcham, *James Madison*, 330.
[16] Adam Smith, *An Inquiry into the Nature and Causes of the Wealth of Nations* (New York: Collier, 1937).
[17] Roy C. Smith, *Adam Smith and the Origins of American Enterprise: How the Founding Fathers Turned to a Great Economist's Writings and Created the American Economy* (New York: St. Martin's Press, 2002), 188.
[18] Edward G. Bourne, "Alexander Hamilton and Adam Smith," *The Quarterly Journal of Economics* 8: 328-344.
[19] James Madison, "The Federalist No. 20," in Rossiter, ed., *The Federalist Papers*, 138.
[20] Carl J. Richard, *Greeks and Romans Bearing Gifts: How the Ancients Inspired the Founding Fathers* (Lanham, MD: Rowan And Littlefield, 2008).
[21] John Adams, "A Defence of the Constitutions of Government of the United States of America," March 22, 1778 in George Wescott Carey, ed., *The Political Writings of John Adams* (Washington, DC: Regnery Publishing, 2000), 121.
[22] James Madison, "Address to the Federal Convention," Notes of Yates, Tuesday, June 19, 1787 in Farrand, ed., *Records of the Federal Convention*, I: 326.
[23] James Madison, "Vices of the Political System of the United States," April 1787 in Ralph Ketcham ed., *Selected Writings of James Madison* (Indianapolis: Hackett Publishing Co., 2006), 38-40.

6
Ancient and Modern

[1] Barack Obama, "Remarks at White House Ramadan Dinner," August 14, 2010, http://www.whitehouse.gov/blog/2010/08/14/president-obama-celebrates-ramadan-white-house-iftar-dinner (accessed August 16, 2010).
[2] Hank De Zutter, "What Makes Obama Run?" *Chicago Reader*, December 7, 1995, http://www.chicagoreader.com/chicago/what-makes-obama-run/Content?oid=889221 (accessed May 17, 2010).

[3] Barack Obama, "Speech to the NAACP Annual Convention," July 14, 2008, http://www.msnbc.msn.com/id/25678384/ (accessed May 17, 2010).
[4] Barack Obama, "Remarks at the Hispanic Congressional Caucus Institute Awards Gala," September 15, 2010, http://www.whitehouse.gov/the-press-office/2010/09/15/remarks-president-congressional-hispanic-caucus-institutes-33rd-annual-a (accessed September 30, 2010); Barack Obama, "Remarks to the DCCC/DSCC," September 23, 2010, http://www.whitehouse.gov/the-press-office/2010/09/23/remarks-president-a-dcccdscc-dinner (accessed September 30, 2010). For an overview of numerous other instances in which Obama has omitted reference to the "Creator" when speaking of inalienable rights, see Terence P. Jeffrey, "Obama Again Omits 'Creator' when Speaking of 'Inalienable Rights' Cited in the Declaration of Independence," September 27, 2010, http://cnsnews.com/news/article/75843 (accessed September 30, 2010). On October 18, 2010, Obama again delivered a speech in which he quoted directly from the Declaration of Independence; the text of his prepared remarks omits any mention of the Creator. See http://www.whitehouse.gov/the-press-office/2010/10/19/remarks-president-a-dscc-dinner-rockville-maryland (accessed October 21, 2010).
[5] Barack Obama, Eye on Books Interview, August 8, 1995, http://www.eyeonbooks.com/obama_transcript.pdf (accessed September 21, 2010).

7
"Spread the Wealth Around"

[1] http://blogs.abcnews.com/politicalpunch/2008/10/spread-the-weal.html (accessed March 27, 2010).
[2] Barack Obama, "Interview on Chicago Public Radio," January 18, 2001, http://blogs.vocalo.org/jandrews/2008/10/barack-obamas-radio-days/639 (accessed March 27, 2010).
[3] Dennis Jacobs, "Americans Oppose Income Redistribution to Fix the Economy, Gallup.com, June 27, 2008, http://www.gallup.com/poll/108445/americans-oppose-income-redistribution-fix-economy.aspx (accessed March 30, 2010).
[4] Debate Transcript, Democratic Presidential Primary Debate, April 16, 2008, http://abcnews.go.com/Politics/DemocraticDebate/Story?id=4670271&page=3 (accessed March 30, 2010).
[5] Debate Transcript, Presidential Debate, September 26, 2008, http://edition.cnn.com/2008/POLITICS/09/26/debate.mississippi.transcript/ (accessed April 2, 2010).
[6] Barack Obama, "Address to Congress," February 24, 2009, http://www.nytimes.com/2009/02/24/us/politics/24obama-text.html (accessed April 2, 2010).
[7] Barack Obama, "Speech to the AFL-CIO of Illinois," June 30, 2003 at http://www.pnhp.org/news/2008/june/barack_obama_on_sing.php (accessed April 5, 2010).
[8] Gerald F. Seib, "In Crisis, Opportunity for Obama," *The Wall Street Journal*, November 21, 2008, A2.

[9] Robert Samuelson, "Obama's Illusions of Cost Control," *The Washington Post*, March 15, 2010.
[10] Quoted in Laura Litvan, James Rowley and Catherine Dodge, "Senate Approves Final Changes to Health Care Overhaul," *Business Week*, March 25, 2010, http://www.businessweek.com/news/2010-03-25/senate-approves-final-changes-to-landmark-health-care-overhaul.html (accessed March 27, 2010).
[11] Howard Dean, "Remarks on CNBC," March 25, 2010, http://www.breitbart.tv/howard-dean-of-course-health-care-law-is-redistribution-of-wealth/ (accessed April 2, 2010).
[12] David Leonhardt, "In Health Bill, Obama Attacks Wealth Inequality," *The New York Times*, March 23, 2010, http://www.nytimes.com/2010/03/24/business/24leonhardt/html (accessed April 2, 2010).
[13] Dr. Donald Berwick, "Speech to the National Health Service," July 8, 2010, http://www.kaiserhealthnews.org/Stories/2010/July/07/berwick-british-NHS-speech-transcript.aspx (accessed August 17, 2010).
[14] Quoted in Eamon Javers, "Obama Picks Fight with 'Speculators,'" Politico.com, April 30, 2009, http://www.politico.com/news/stories/0409/21935.html (accessed May 15, 2010).
[15] Neil King, Jr. and Jeffrey McCracken, "U.S. Forced Chrysler's Creditors to Blink," *The Wall Street Journal*, May 11, 2009.
[16] Katherine Burton, Sree Bhaktavatsalam, and Pierre Paulden, "Yale, Haliburton and Gates Foundation Listed as Chrysler Lenders," Bloomberg.com, May 2, 2009, http://www.bloomberg.com/apps/news?pid=newsarchive&sid=a109vAXclorI (accessed May 15, 2010).
[17] Michael Barone, "White House Puts UAW Ahead of Property Rights," *The Washington Examiner*, May 6, 2009.
[18] Quoted in Margaret Chadbourn, "Senate Defeats Mortgage 'Cram-Down' as Democrats Balk," Bloomberg.com, April 30, 2009, http://www.bloomberg.com/apps/news?pid=newsarchive&sid=aJ_sqd73P0Wk (accessed March 22, 2010).
[19] Barack Obama, "Remarks to the Editorial Board of the *San Francisco Chronicle*," January 2008, http://hotair.com/archives/2008/11/02/obama-well-bankrupt-any-new-coal-plants/ (accessed June 23, 2010).
[20] Declan McCullagh, "Obama Admin: Cap and Trade Could Cost Families $1,761 A Year," CBSNews.com, September 15, 2009, http://www.cbsnews.com/8301-504383_162-5314040-504383.html (accessed March 17, 2010).
[21] Calvin Woodward, "Promises, Promises: Obama Tax Pledge up in Smoke," The Associated Press, April 1, 2009, http://www.breitbart.com/article.php?id=D979POSG0 (emphasis added) (accessed March 27, 2010).
[22] Charles Hurt, "Obama 'VAT' of Tax Trouble," *The New York Post*, April 22, 2010, http://www.nypost.com/p/news/national/obama_stirring_up_vat_of_tax_trouble_fGATEXgBC548BMlG4HpgHP (accessed April 3, 2010).
[23] Third Point LLC, "Second Quarter 2010 Investor Letter," August 27, 2010, http://cache.dealbreaker.com/uploads/2010/08/Third-Point-Q2-2010-Investor-

Letter.pdf (accessed September 2, 2010); Andrew Ross Sorkin, "Why Wall St. is Deserting Obama," *The New York Times*, August 30, 2010, B1.
[24] Video clip at http://www.youtube.com/watch?v=BnMMo8lVG5M (accessed October 1, 2010).
[25] Associated Press Report, October 5, 2010, http://www.boston.com/news/politics/articles/2010/10/05/obama_panel_veer_into_debate_on_tax_cuts/ (accessed October 15, 2010).
[26] Evan Glass, "Pelosi Fires Back at Gingrich Over Food Stamps," CNN.com, October 6, 2010, http://politicalticker.blogs.cnn.com/2010/10/06/pelosi-fires-back-at-gingrich-over-food-stamps/ (accessed October 15, 2010).
[27] Quoted in David Leonhardt, "After the Great Recession," *The New York Times*, April 28, 2009, http://www.nytimes.com/2009/05/03/magazine/03Obama-t.html?_r=1&hp (accessed May 5, 2010).

8
"The First Object of Government"

[1] James Madison, "Vices of the Political System of the United States," April 1787 in Ralph Ketcham, ed., *Selected Writings of James Madison* (Indianapolis: Hackett Publishing Co., 2006), 39.
[2] James Madison, "Federal Convention Speech," June 26, 1787 in Ralph Ketcham, ed., *Selected Writings of James Madison* (Indianapolis: Hackett Publishing Co., 2006), 60.
[3] Ibid.
[4] Alexander Hamilton, "Federal Convention Speech," June 26, 1787 in Harold C. Syrett, ed., *The Papers of Alexander Hamilton* (New York: Columbia University Press, 1962), 4: 218.
[5] James Madison, "The Federalist No. 10," in Clinton Rossiter, ed., *The Federalist Papers* (New York: NAL Penguin, 1961), 78-79.
[6] Ibid.
[7] Ibid.
[8] Ibid., 80-81.
[9] Ibid.
[10] Ibid., 84.
[11] Alexander Hamilton, "The Federalist No. 85," in ibid., 521-22.
[12] James Madison, "Speech to the Virginia Constitutional Convention," December 2, 1829 in Ralph Ketcham, ed., *Selected Writings of James Madison* (Indianapolis: Hackett Publishing Co., 2006), 354-55.
[13] Montezuma, "Anti-Federalist No. 9," October 17, 1787, http://www.utulsa.edu/law/classes/rice/Constitutional/AntiFederalist/09.htm (accessed March 17, 2010).
[14] Alexander Hamilton, "The Federalist No. 60," in Rossiter, ed., *The Federalist Papers*, 370-71
[15] Alexander Hamilton, "The Federalist No. 85," in ibid., 522.
[16] Alexander Hamilton, "The Federalist No. 36," in ibid., 217-18.
[17] Alexander Hamilton, "The Federalist No. 8," in ibid., 69.
[18] Alexander Hamilton, "The Federalist No. 11," in ibid., 85.

[19] Gordon S. Wood, *Revolutionary Characters: What Made the Founders Different* (New York: Penguin Press 2006), 128-29.
[20] Alexander Hamilton, "The Federalist No. 36," in ibid., 222.
[21] Alexander Hamilton, "The Federalist No. 35," in ibid., 216-17.
[22] Alexander Hamilton, "Report on Public Credit," January 9, 1790 in Harold C. Syrett, ed., *The Papers of Alexander Hamilton* (New York: Columbia University Press, 1962), 6: 73-79.
[23] Ibid.
[24] Debate in the House of Representatives, February 15, 1790 in Thomas Hart Benton, ed., *Abridgment of the Debates of Congress from 1789 to 1856* (New York: D. Appleton and Co., 1857), 211-23.

9
Obamanomics and American Constitutionalism

[1] Barack Obama, "Remarks in Quincy," April 28, 2010, http://www.realclearpolitics.com/video/2010/04/28/obama_to_wall_street_i_do_think_at_a_certain_point_youve_made_enough_money.html (accessed on October 2, 2010).
[2] Alexander Hamilton, "Defence of the Funding System," July 1795, in Harold C. Syrett, ed., *The Papers of Alexander Hamilton* (New York: Columbia University Press, 1961), 19: 32.
[3] Barack Obama, "Remarks on the Economy in Parma, Ohio," September 8, 2010, http://www.whitehouse.gov/the-press-office/2010/09/08/remarks-president-economy-parma-ohio (accessed September 12, 2010).
[4] Nancy Pelosi, " Remarks on Fairness," October 18, 2010, http://www.realclearpolitics.com/video/2010/10/18/pelosi_need_to_address_fairness_of_ownership_and_equity_in_america.html (accessed on October 22, 2010).
[5] Barack Obama, "Speech to the National Press Club," April 26, 2005, http://obamaspeeches.com/014-National-Press-Club-Obama-Speech.htm (accessed September 22, 2010).
[6] Barack Obama, "Speech at Parma, OH,: September 8, 2010, http://www.whitehouse.gov/the-press-office/2010/09/08/remarks-president-economy-parma-ohio (accessed September 22, 2010).
[7] Barack Obama, *Dreams From My Father: a Story of Race and Inheritance* (New York: Three Rivers Press, 2004), 135-38.
[8] Barack Obama, "Commencement Address at Arizona State University," May 13, 2009, http://www.nytimes.com/2009/05/13/us/politics/13obama.text.html?pagewanted=1 (accessed September 21, 2010).

10
Legislative Incompetence

[1] Alexander Hamilton, "The Federalist No. 68," in Clinton Rossiter, ed., *The Federalist Papers* (New York: NAL Penguin, 1961), 414.
[2] Alexander Hamilton, "The Federalist No. 70," in ibid., 423.
[3] Alexander Hamilton, "The Federalist No. 15," in ibid., 105-112.
[4] Alexander Hamilton, "The Federalist No. 9," in ibid., 71-72.
[5] James Madison, "The Federalist No. 45," in ibid., 289.
[6] James Madison, "The Federalist No. 46," in ibid., 295.
[7] James Madison, "The Federalist No. 63," in ibid., 386.
[8] James Madison, "The Federalist No. 53," in ibid., 332.
[9] Alexander Hamilton, "The Federalist No. 35," in ibid., 216.
[10] Alexander Hamilton, "The Federalist No. 33," in ibid., 203-04.
[11] "Congressman: 'I Don't worry About the Constitution' on Health Care Overhaul," FoxNews.com, April 2, 2010, http://www.foxnews.com/politics/2010/04/02/democratic-lawmaker-dont-worry-constitution-health-care-overhaul/ (accessed May 22, 2010).
[12] Ibid.
[13] Kay Hagan, "Interview on Rush Radio 94.5," April 22, 2010, http://www.youtube.com/watch?v=tZ7LjBetLE4 (accessed April 30, 2010).
[14] *Wickard v. Filburn*, 317 U.S. 111, 125 (1942).
[15] Centers for Medicare and Medicaid Services, "NHE Fact Sheet," https://www.cms.gov/NationalHealthExpendData/25_NHE_Fact_Sheet.asp (accessed March 22, 2011).
[16] Robert J. Myers, "How Bad Were the Original Actuarial Estimates for Medicare's Hospital Insurance Program?" *The Actuary*, February 1994, 6-7.
[17] Seymour E. Harris, "The British Health Experiment: The First Two Years of the National Health Service," *The American Economic Review*, Vol. 41, No. 2, May 1951, 655.
[18] http://www.cbo.gov/ftpdocs/115xx/doc11553/ForecastingAccuracy.pdf (accessed September 30, 2010).
[19] Ceci Connolly, "How Obama Revived His Health Care Bill," *The Washington Post*, March 23, 2010, http://www.washingtonpost.com/wp-dyn/content/article/2010/03/22/AR2010032203729.html (accessed June 12, 2010).
[20] Quoted in Joseph Ryan, "Melissa Bean Will Vote in Favor of Health Care Reform Proposal," *The Daily Herald*, March 20, 2010.
[21] Richard S. Foster, Memorandum: Estimated Financial Effects of the "Patient Protection and Affordable Care Act," Centers for Medicare and Medicaid Services, April 22, 2010.
[22] Editorial, "Details of McKinsey Study Reveal ObamaCare Flimflam," *The Washington Examiner*, June 22, 2011, http://washingtonexaminer.com/opinion/2011/06/details-mckinsey-study-expose-obamacare-flimflam (accessed June 25, 2011).
[23] Richard Brake, "Elected Officials Flunk Constitution Quiz," AOL News, January 14, 2011, http://www.aolnews.com/2011/01/14/opinion-who-are-the-constitutional-illiterates/.

11
"Voluminous and Incomprehensible"

[1] James Madison, "The Federalist No. 62," in Clinton Rossiter, ed., *The Federalist Papers* (New York: NAL Penguin, 1961), 376-82.
[2] Dan Testa, "Residents Question Health Care Bill, Call for Additional Doctor at Clinic," *The Flathead Beacon*, August 24, 2010.
[3] Robert Pear, "Baffled by Health Plan? So are Some Lawmakers," *The New York Times*, April 12, 2010, A14.
[4] Ryan Byrnes and Edwin Mora, "Democratic Senator Predicts None of His Colleagues 'Will Have the Chance' to Read Final Stimulus Bill Before Vote,' *CNS News*, February 12, 2009, http://www.cnsnews.com/news/article/43478 (accessed April 3, 2010).
[5] Congressional Budget Office, Budget and Economic Outlook: an Update, August 2010, http://cbo.gov/ftpdocs/117xx/doc11705/08-18-Update.pdf (accessed August 30, 2010)
[6] Michael Grabell and Christopher Weaver, "In Stimulus Bill: An Earmark by Any Other Name," *Pro Publica*, February 5, 2009, http://www.propublica.org/article/welcome-in-the-stimulus-bill-an-earmark-by-any-other-name (accessed April 28, 2010).
[7] http://www.readthestimulus.org/hr1_final.pdf (accessed July 9, 2010).
[8] James Madison, "The Federalist No. 62," in Rossiter, ed., *The Federalist Papers*, 381.
[9] Editorial, "Cash for Clubbers: Congress's fabulous golf cart stimulus," *The Wall St. Journal*, October 17, 2009, A12.
[10] James Madison, "The Federalist No. 62," in Rossiter, ed., *The Federalist Papers*, 381.
[11] Gary Fields, "Political Uncertainty Puts Freeze on Small Business," *The Wall Street Journal*, October 28, 2009, A18.
[12] Hannah Hager, "Business Owners Confused and Uncertain About Health Care," *The Loudon Times*, April 15, 2010.
[13] Sarah E. Needleman, "Companies Confused by Health Care Legislation," *The Wall Street Journal*, March 25, 2010.
[14] Editorial, "ObamaCare is Just the Beginning," *The Washington Examiner*, August 4, 2010, http://washingtonexaminer.com/opinion/obamacare-just-beginning (accessed August 5, 2010).
[15] James Madison, "The Federalist No. 57," in Rossiter, ed., *The Federalist Papers*, 352-53.
[16] Ben Domenech, "Some Interesting Provisions for Senior Democrat Staffers Who Helped Write the Bill," *The New Ledger*, March 23, 2010, http://www.cbsnews.com/stories/2010/03/23/opinion/main6324480.shtml (accessed April 12, 2010).
[17] A USA Today/Gallup Poll conducted on March 26-28, 2010—just after the passage of Obama's health care bill—found that 40% of Americans believed that the overhaul would make their own health care situation worse, whereas only 22% held the view that the overhaul would improve their own health care.
[18] Laura Meckler and Naftali Bendavid, "Unions Cut Special Deal on Health Taxes," *The Wall Street Journal*, January 15, 2010,

http://online.wsj.com/article/SB10001424052748704281204575003040695279432.html (accessed April 13, 2010).
[19] Editorial, 'Cadillac' Tax Plan Shrinks in Obama-Union Deal," *The Washington Post*, January 16, 2010.
[20] Manu Raju, "Nebraska Governor to Ben Nelson: Keep the Money," *Politico*, December 24, 2009, http://www.politico.com/news/stories/1209/30947.html (accessed March 22, 2010).
[21] http://www.dol.gov/federalregister/PdfDisplay.aspx?DocId=23967 (accessed September 12, 2010).
[22] James Madison, "The Federalist No. 62," in Rossiter, ed., *The Federalist Papers*, 381.

12
The People's Representatives

[1] James Madison, "The Federalist No. 62," in Clinton Rossiter, ed., *The Federalist Papers* (New York: NAL Penguin, 1961), 378.
[2] John Boehner, "Remarks on the House Floor Regarding Health Care," March 22, 2010, http://johnboehner.house.gov/News/DocumentSingle.aspx?DocumentID=177587 (accessed April 2, 2010).
[3] Ed Rendell, "Interview for 'On the Record,'" April 8, 2010, http://www.foxnews.com/story/0,2933,590563,00.html (accessed April 21, 2010).
[4] James Madison, "The Federalist No. 10," in Rossiter, ed., *The Federalist Papers*, 77-84.
[5] Edmund Burke, "Speech to the Electors at Bristol," November 3, 1774 in *The Writings and Speeches of Edmund Burke* (Boston: Little Brown and Co., 1901), 2: 89-98.
[6] James Madison, "The Federalist No. 63," in Rossiter, ed., *The Federalist Papers*, 386.
[7] Alexander Hamilton, "The Federalist No. 70," in ibid., 428-29.
[8] Alexander Hamilton, "The Federalist No. 71," in ibid., 432.
[9] Ibid.
[10] James Madison, "The Federalist No. 63," in ibid., 384.

13
"Manifest and Irresistible Proofs"

[1] Imus in the Morning, November 10, 2008.
[2] Editorial, *The San Francisco Chronicle*, November 5, 2008, B16.
[3] Obama for President, Campaign Press Release, February 7, 2008, http://www.barackobama.com/2008/02/07/barack_obama_to_lay_out_progra.php (accessed May 12, 2010).
[4] David Von Drehle, "Why History Can't Wait," *Time*, December 17, 2008, http://www.time.com/time/specials/packages/article/0,28804,1861543_1865068_1867013-2,00.html#ixzz0xrCbLYYV (accessed May 5, 2010).

[5] Terry Moran, Interview with Mediabistro.com, http://www.realclearpolitics.com/video/2009/02/moran_obama.html (accessed May 21, 2010).
[6] Evan Thomas, Interview on MSNBC's Hardball, June 5, 2009, http://www.realclearpolitics.com/video/2009/06/05/newsweek_editor_evan_thomas_obama_is_sort_of_god.html (accessed July 11, 2010).
[7] David Remnick, *The Bridge: The Life and Rise of Barack Obama* (New York: Alfred A. Knopf, 2010), 274.
[8]Jennifer Loven, "He Won But For What?" October 9, 2009, http://www.realclearpolitics.com/news/ap/politics/2009/Oct/09/analysis__he_won__but_for_what_.html (accessed March 13, 2010).
[9] Brett Baier, "Media Reacts to Obama's Nobel Prize Win," *Special Report*, http://www.foxnews.com/story/0,2933,564303,00.html (accessed March 17, 2010).
[10] Statement of the Norwegian Nobel Committee, October 9, 2009, http://nobelprize.org/nobel_prizes/peace/laureates/2009/press.html (accessed April 30, 2010).
[11] Alexander Hamilton, "The Federalist No. 27," in Clinton Rossiter, ed., *The Federalist Papers* (New York: NAL Penguin, 1961), 176.
[12] Laura Meckler, "Housing Bailout at $275 Billion: Obama Plan Would Fund Loan Modifications, Cover More Losses at Mortgage Titans." *The Wall St. Journal*, February 19, 2010, http://online.wsj.com/article/SB123496582087411241.html (accessed April 24, 2010).
[13] Peter S. Goodman, "U.S. Loan Effort Is Seen as Adding to Housing Woes," *The New York Times*, January 2, 2010, A1.
[14] Report: Obama Mortgage Aid Plan Won't Help Many, April 14, 2010, http://www.cbsnews.com/stories/2010/04/14/business/main6394446.shtml (accessed June 2, 2010).
[15] Patrice Hill, "'Green' Jobs No Longer Golden in Stimulus," *The Washington Times*, September 9, 2010, http://www.washingtontimes.com/news/2010/sep/9/green-jobs-no-longer-golden-in-stimulus/ (accessed September 12, 2010).
[16] Ed Tibbetts, "Grassley Questions "Green Jobs" Spending," *The Quad-City Times*, June 8, 2010, http://qctimes.com/news/local/government-and-politics/article_7eafa33c-7370-11df-8243-001cc4c002e0.html (accessed September 12, 2010).
[17] http://watchdog.org/1556/your-guide-to-the-stimulus-district-by-phantom-district/ (accessed August 7, 2010).
[18] Barbara Hollingsworth, "Stimulus Watch: Now its Fake Zip Codes," *The Washington Examiner*, January 4, 2010, http://www.washingtonexaminer.com/opinion/blogs/beltway-confidential/Now-its-fake-zip-codes-80627972.html (accessed August 7, 2010).
[19] Michael Cooper and Ron Nixon, "Reports Show Conflicting Number of Jobs Attributed to Stimulus Money," *The New York Times*, November 4, 2009, A16.
[20] Louise Radnofsky, "Stimulus Checks Sent to Dead, Incarcerated," *The Wall Street Journal*, October 7, 2010, http://online.wsj.com/article/SB10001424052748704696304575538483156036168.html?mod=googlenews_wsj (accessed October 10, 2010).

[21] Wendy Gruel, "Audit of Federal Stimulus Funds in Los Angeles Shows $111 million in ARRA Grants Has Only Created 55 Jobs," *Huffington Post*, September 16, 2010, http://www.huffingtonpost.com/wendy-greuel/audit-of-federal-stimulus_b_719817.html (accessed October 10, 2010).
[22] Barack Obama, "Interview on Meet the Press," December 7, 2008, http://www.msnbc.msn.com/id/28097635/ (accessed June 3, 2010).
[23] Louise Randofsky, "A Stimulus Project Gets All Caulked Up," *The Wall Street Journal*, September 21, 2010, A1.
[24] Louise Randofsky, "White House Under Fire for Unspent Infrastructure Cash," *The Wall Street Journal*, August 16, 2010, http://online.wsj.com/article/SB10001424052748704532204575397061414483040.html (accessed September 17, 2010).
[25] Peter Baker, "The Education of President Obama," *The New York Times Magazine*, October 12, 2010, http://www.nytimes.com/2010/10/17/magazine/17obama-t.html?_r=1&pagewanted=all (accessed October 14, 2010).
[26] Charles Krauthammer, "The Union-Owned Democrats," *The Washington Post*, June 16, 2011, http://www.washingtonpost.com/opinions/the-union-owned-dems/2011/06/16/AGRYNqXH_story.html (accessed June 16, 2011).
[27] Campbell Robertson, "Efforts to Repel Oil Spill Described as Chaotic," *The New York Times*, June 14, 2010, A1.
[28] Jake Tapper and Huma Khan, "'Political Stupidity': Democrat James Carville Slams Obama's Response to BP Oil Spill," May 26, 2010, http://abcnews.go.com/GMA/Politics/bp-oil-spill-political-headache-obama-democrats-slam/story?id=10746519 (accessed July 2, 2010).
[29] Chris Kirkham, "Red Tape Keeps Prized Oil-Fighting Skimmers from Gulf, Coastline," *The New Orleans Times-Picayune*, June 29, 2010, http://www.nola.com/news/gulf-oil-spill/index.ssf/2010/06/red_tape_keeps_prized_oil-figh.html (accessed July 7, 2010).
[30] Patrik Jonsson, "Top Five Bottlenecks in the Gulf Oil Spill Response," *The Christian Science Monitor*, July 1, 2010, http://www.csmonitor.com/USA/2010/0701/Top-five-bottlenecks-in-the-Gulf-oil-spill-response (accessed July 7, 2010); Mark Guarino, "BP Oil Spill: Will the 'Sweeping Arm System' from the Dutch Help?" *The Christian Science Monitor*, June 1, 2010, http://www.csmonitor.com/USA/2010/0601/BP-oil-spill-Will-the-sweeping-arm-system-from-the-Dutch-help (accessed July 7, 2010).
[31] Jeffrey M. Jones, "Americans' Image of the 'Federal Government' Mostly Negative," Gallup.com, October 11, 2010, http://www.gallup.com/poll/143492/Americans-Image-Federal-Government-Mostly-Negative.aspx (accessed October 15, 2010).
[32] Lydia Saad, "Majorities in the U.S. View Government as Too Intrusive and Powerful," Gallup.com, October 13, 2010, http://www.gallup.com/poll/143624/Majorities-View-Gov-Intrusive-Powerful.aspx (accessed October 15, 2010).
[33] Rasmussen Reports, "Daily Presidential Tracking Poll," October 16, 2010, http://www.rasmussenreports.com/public_content/politics/obama_administration/obama_approval_index_history (accessed on October 16, 2010).

[34] Lydia Saad, "Congress Only Growing Less Popular With Americans," Gallup.com, September 20, 2010, http://www.gallup.com/poll/143054/congress-growing-less-popular-americans.aspx (accessed October 17, 2010).
[35] Todd Purdum, "Washington, We Have a Problem," *Vanity Fair*, September 2010, http://www.vanityfair.com/politics/features/2010/09/broken-washington-201009?currentPage=all (accessed October 4, 2010).
[36] Baker, "The Education of President Obama."

14
Limited and Enumerated

[1] David Leonhardt, "Obama's Budget Plan Sweeps Away Reagan Ideas," *The New York Times*, February 27, 2009, http://www.nytimes.com/2009/02/27/business/economy/27policy.html (accessed August 27, 2010).
[2] Barack Obama, "Inaugural Address," January 20, 2009, http://abcnews.go.com/Politics/Inauguration/president-obama-inauguration-speech-transcript/story?id=6689022&page=2 (accessed August 12, 2010).
[3] Barack Obama, "Address to a Joint Session of Congress," February 24, 2009, http://www.whitehouse.gov/the_press_office/Remarks-of-President-Barack-Obama-Address-to-Joint-Session-of-Congress/ (accessed August 12, 2010).
[4] Barack Obama, "Presidential Press Conference," April 29, 2009, http://www.cbsnews.com/8301-503544_162-4979228-503544.html (accessed August 12, 2010).
[5] Peter Baker, "For Obama, A Steep Learning Curve as Chief in War," *The New York Times*, August 29, 2010, A1.
[6] Ed Morrissey, "Schakowsky: Those Radical Republicans Talk About Self-Government," *Hot Air*, October 2, 2010, http://hotair.com/archives/2010/10/02/schakowsky-those-radical-republicans-talk-about-self-government/ (accessed October 5, 2010).
[7] James Madison, "The Federalist No. 45," in Clinton Rossiter, ed., *The Federalist Papers* (New York: NAL Penguin, 1961), 292-93.
[8] Ibid., 293.
[9] Alexander Hamilton, "The Federalist No. 84," in ibid., 512-13.
[10] Ibid., 513-14.
[11] Ibid., 515.

15
Obama and the Demise of Limited Government

[1] Stephen Dinan, "Judge Rules Against Health Law, Cites Obama's Words," *The Washington Times*, January 31, 2011, http://www.washingtontimes.com/news/2011/jan/31/judge-uses-obamas-words-against-him/ (accessed February 1, 2011).

[2] Barack Obama, "Remarks by the President to a Joint Session of Congress," September 9, 2009, http://www.whitehouse.gov/the_press_office/remarks-by-the-president-to-a-joint-session-of-congress-on-health-care/ (accessed November 22, 2010).
[3] Jennifer Haberkorn, "CBO Ups Health Care Cost Projections," *Politico*, May 12, 2010, http://www.politico.com/news/stories/0510/37081.html (accessed August 14, 2010).
[4] Editorial, "No, Congressman, Government Does Have Limits," *The Washington Examiner*, August 3, 2010, http://washingtonexaminer.com/opinion/examiner-editorial-no-congressman-government-does-have-limits (accessed August 7, 2010).
[5] Nicholas Ballasy and Edwin Mora, "Sen. Mark Warner: 'No Place in Constitution that says Health Care," *CNS News*, September 4, 2009, http://www.cnsnews.com/news/article/53580 (accessed August 7, 2010).
[6] Ben Cardin, "Town Hall Meeting," August 10, 2009, http://www.youtube.com/watch?v=ygInRIabq_g&feature=player_embedded (accessed August 7, 2010).
[7] James Madison, "The Federalist No. 41," in Clinton Rossiter, ed., *The Federalist Papers* (New York: NAL Penguin, 1961), 263.
[8] James Madison to John Robertson, April 20, 1831 in John Curtis Sample, *James Madison and the Future of Limited Government* (Washington, DC: Cato Institute, 2002), 194.
[9] James Madison to Edmund Pendleton, January 21, 1792 in Ibid., 34.
[10] Ceci Connolly, "Like Car Insurance, Health Coverage May be Mandated," *The Washington Post*, July 22, 2009, http://www.washingtonpost.com/wp-dyn/content/article/2009/07/21/AR2009072103410.html?sid=ST2009072103763 (accessed June 12, 2010).
[11] Ibid.
[12] Edwin Mora, "Sen. Reed: Forcing People to Buy Health Insurance is Constitutionally Justified Because It's Like Making People 'Sign Up for the Draft,'" *CNS News*, November 10, 2009, http://www.cnsnews.com/node/56971 (accessed June 29, 2010).

16
First, Do No Harm

[1] James Madison, "The Federalist No. 48," in Clinton Rossiter, ed., *The Federalist Papers* (New York: NAL Penguin 1961), 311.
[2] James Madison, "The Federalist No. 55,"in ibid., 345.
[3] Editorial, "Send Biden Back to History Class," *The Washington Examiner*, October 27, 2010, http://washingtonexaminer.com/editorials/2010/10/examiner-editorial-send-biden-back-history-class (accessed November 1, 2010).
[4] Barney Frank, Interview on MSNBC, October 26, 2009, http://www.realclearpolitics.com/video/2009/10/26/frank_we_are_trying_on_every_front_to_increase_the_role_of_government.html (accessed October 30, 2010).

[5] Barack Obama, "Democratic Convention Acceptance Speech," August 28, 2008, http://www.nytimes.com/2008/08/28/us/politics/28text-obama.html?pagewanted=3 (accessed May 5, 2010).
[6] Jennifer Haberkorn, "Four Companies Mulled Dropping Health Insurance Plans," *Politico*, May 7, 2010, http://www.politico.com/news/stories/0510/36926.html (accessed September 12, 2010).
[7] Robert Pear, "Coverage Now for Sick Children? Check the Fine Print," *The New York Times*, March 28, 2010, http://www.nytimes.com/2010/03/29/health/policy/29health.html (accessed July 8, 2010).
[8] N. C. Aizenman, "Major Health Insurers to Stop Offering Child-Only Policies," *The Washington Post*, September 20, 2010, http://www.washingtonpost.com/wp-dyn/content/article/2010/09/20/AR2010092006665.html (accessed September 12, 2010).
[9] Laurie McGinley and Mary Agnes Carey, "Kids With Preexisting Illness Get New Protection For Coverage But Hurdles Remain," *Kaiser Health News*, September 23, 2010, http:www.kaiserhealthnews.org/Stories/2010/September/23/kids-preexisting-conditions.aspx (accessed September 30, 2010); Christoper Conover, "Health reform and Preexisting Conditions for Children," *Health Reform Report*, September 23, 2010, http://healthreformreport.com/2010/09/health-reform-and-pre-existing-conditions-for-children.php (accessed September 30, 2010).
[10] John Dingell, Interview with WJR's Paul W. Smith, March 23, 2010, http://www.wjr.com/Article.asp?id=1742921&spid=34612 (accessed November 2, 2010).
[11] Jason Millman, "Number of Healthcare Reform Law Waivers Climbs Above 1000," TheHill.com Health Watch Blog, March 6, 2011, http://thehill.com/blogs/healthwatch/health-reform-implementation/147715-number-of-healthcare-reform-law-waivers-climbs-above-1000 (accessed March 8, 2011).
[12] Kate Nocera, "Anthony Weiner: Waiver Might Work for New York," *Politico*, March 23, 2011, http://www.politico.com/news/stories/0311/51840.html (accessed March 24, 2011).
[13] Jason Roberson, "Sebelius Warns Insurers Against Blaming Health Law for Rate Hikes," *The Dallas Morning News*, September 10, 2010, http://www.dallasnews.com/business/headlines/20100910-Sebelius-warns-insurers-against-blaming-health-2187.ece (accessed September 29, 2010).
[14] Mike Allen and Josh Gerstein, "GM CEO Resigns at Obama's Behest," *Politico*, March 30, 2009, http://www.politico.com/news/stories/0309/20625.html (accessed June 5, 2010).
[15] Editorial, "Government Motors," *The Washington Post*, May 26, 2009, http://www.washingtonpost.com/wp-dyn/content/article/2009/05/25/AR2009052502135.html (accessed June 5, 2010).
[16] Editorial, "Busy Not Running GM," *The Wall Street Journal*, June 3, 2009, A13.
[17] Ibid.
[18] James Madison, "The Federalist No. 14," in Rossiter, ed., *The Federalist Papers*, 102.
[19] Alexander Hamilton, "The Federalist No. 17," in Rossiter, ed., *The Federalist Papers*, 118-19.

[20] Katherine Skiba, "Stimulus Signage Has GOP Outraged," The Chicago Tribune, July 15, 2010, http://articles.chicagotribune.com/2010-07-15/news/ct-stimulus-sign-controversy0716-20100715_1_billion-stimulus-signs-transparency-board (accessed August 2, 2010).
[21] Tom Fitton, "The Rest of the Story on Those Andy Griffith ObamaCare Ads," *The Washington Examiner*, December 3, 2010, http://washingtonexaminer.com/opinion/op-eds/2010/12/tom-fitton-rest-story-those-andy-griffith-obamacare-ads#ixzz17lIEldsJ (accessed December 5, 2010).
[22] Sheryl Gay Stolberg, "Childhood Obesity Battle Is Taken Up by the First Lady," *The New York Times*, February 9, 2010, A16.
[23] Jim Geraghty, "The Campaign Spot," *National Review Online*, February 20, 2008, www.nationalreview.com/campaign-spot/10312/barack-will-never-allow-you-go-back-your-lives-usual (accessed December 3, 2010).
[24] Penny Starr, "Michelle Obama on What Kids Eat: 'We Can't Just Leave it Up to the Parents,'" *CNS News*, December 13, 2010, http://www.cnsnews.com/news/article/michelle-obama-45-billion-child-nutritio (accessed December 15, 2010).
[25] Mary Clare Jalonick, "Hold the Brownies! Bill Could Limit Bake Sales," *The Washington Post*, December 3, 2010, http://www.washingtonpost.com/wp-dyn/content/article/2010/12/03/AR2010120305042.html.

17
Government as Schoolmaster

[1] Alexis de Tocqueville, *Democracy in America* (New York: HarperPerennial, 1988), 690-95.
[2] As discussed in James Buckley, *Reflections on Politics, Liberty and the State* (New York: Encounter Books, 2010).
[3] Philip Klein, "The Empress of ObamaCare," *The American Spectator*, June 4, 2010, http://spectator.org/archives/2010/06/04/the-empress-of-obamacare (accessed August 21, 2010).
[4] Jeffrey H. Anderson, "ObamaCare 'Rule,' 347 Pages, 118,072 Words," *The Weekly Standard*, November 17, 2010, http://www.weeklystandard.com/blogs/obamacare-rule-347-pages-118072-words_518084.html.
[5] Rich Lowry, "The Rule of Sebelius," *National Review Online*, December 28, 2010, http://www.nationalreview.com/articles/255980/rule-sebelius-rich-lowry.
[6] Robert Pear, "Obama Returns to End-of-Life Plan That Caused Stir," *The New York Times*, December 26, 2010, A1.
[7] Robert Pear, "U.S. Alters Rule on Paying for End-of-Life Counseling," *The New York Times*, January 5, 2011, A15.
[8] Prescriptions Blog, "Lawmakers Detail Obama's Pitch," *The New York Times*, November 7, 2009, http://prescriptions.blogs.nytimes.com/2009/11/07/lawmakers-detail-obamas-pitch/.
[9] Peter Slevin, "Obama Defends Priorities, Makes Plea for Civility," *The Washington Post*, May 2, 2010, http://www.washingtonpost.com/wp-dyn/content/article/2010/05/01/AR2010050102039.html.

[10] James Madison, "The Federalist No. 57," in Clinton Rossiter, ed., *The Federalist Papers* (New York: NAL Penguin 1961), 353.

18
Laws and Men

[1] James Madison, "The Federalist No. 47," in Clinton Rossiter, ed., *The Federalist Papers* (New York: NAL Penguin, 1961), 301.
[2] Max Farrand, ed, *Records of the Federal Convention* (New Haven: Yale University Press, 1911), 1: 35.
[3] Farrand, ed., *Records of the Federal Convention,* 2: 77.
[4] James Madison, "The Federalist No. 51," in Rossiter, ed., *The Federalist Papers*, 320-25.
[5] White House, "President Signs Campaign Finance Reform Act," news release, March 27, 2002, www.whitehouse.gov/news/releases/2002/03/20020327.html (accessed March 14, 2010).
[6] Brutus, "Anti-Federalist No. 15," March 20, 1788 in Stephen L. Schechter, ed., *Roots of the Republic: American Founding Documents Interpreted* (Lantham, MD: Rowan and Littlefield, 1990), 411-15.
[7] Alexander Hamilton, "The Federalist No. 78," in Rossiter, ed., *The Federalist Papers*, 465.
[8] Ibid., 465-66.
[9] Ibid., 466-67.
[10] Ibid.
[11] Ibid., 468-69.
[12] Alexander Hamilton, "The Federalist No. 81," in ibid., 482.
[13] *Marbury v, Madison*, 5 U.S. (1 Cranch) 137 (1803).
[14] Ibid., 485.
[15] George Washington, "Farewell Address," September 19, 1796 in Matthew Spalding and Patrick Garrity, eds., *A Sacred Union of Citizens: George Washington's Farewell Address and the American Character* (Lanham, MD: Rowan and Littlefield, 1996), 175-88.

19
Activism and Abdication

[1] Thomas Jefferson to Judge Johnson, June 12, 1823 in Henry Augustine Washington, ed., *The Writings of Thomas Jefferson* (New York: Derby and Jackson, 1859), 7: 296.
[2] Quoted in Drew R. McCoy, *The Last of the Fathers: James Madison and the Republican Legacy* (Cambridge: Cambridge University Press, 1989), 76.
[3] *Dred Scott v. Sanford*, 60 U.S. (19 How.) 393 (1857).
[4] Ibid.
[5] Abraham Lincoln, "A House Divided," June 16, 1858 in Joseph R. Fornieri, *The Language of Liberty: Political Speeches and Writings of Abraham Lincoln* (Washington: Regnery Publishing, 2009), 229.

[6] Marianne M. Jennings, *Real Estate Law* (Thomson South-Western: 2008), 544.
[7] *Kelo v. City of New London*, 545 U.S. 469 (2005).

20
Not of Laws but of Men

[1] Abdon M. Pallasch, "Professor Obama Was a Listener, Students Say," *The Chicago Sun-Times*, February 12, 2007, http://www.suntimes.com/news/politics/obama/253391,CST-NWS-prof12.stng (accessed May 27, 2010).
[2] Shira Schoenberg, "Law Expert: Obama Will Preserve Constitution," *The Concord Monitor*, November 14, 2007, http://www.concordmonitor.com/article/law-expert-obama-will-preserve-constitution (accessed May 27, 2010).
[3] Barack Obama, *The Audacity of Hope: Thoughts on Reclaiming the American Dream* (New York: Vintage Books, 2008), 107.
[4] Barack Obama, "Interview on Chicago Public Radio," January 18, 2001, http://blogs.vocalo.org/jandrews/2008/10/barack-obamas-radio-days/639 (accessed June 2, 2010).
[5] As cited in Ben Smith's Blog, *Politico*, October 27, 2008, http://www.politico.com/blogs/bensmith/1008/Obama_advisor_pushes_back_on_redistribution.html (accessed May 28, 2010).
[6] Jake Tapper, ABC News Political Punch, October 27, 2008, http://blogs.abcnews.com/politicalpunch/2008/10/mccain-to-attac.html (accessed May 27, 2010).
[7] Barack Obama, Memorandum to Students in Con Law III, 1996, http://thecaucus.blogs.nytimes.com/2008/07/30/inside-professor-obamas-classroom/ (accessed April 25, 2010).
[8] Senator Barack Obama, Speech on the Senate Floor, September 22, 2005, http://www.barackobama.com/2005/09/22/remarks_of_senator_barack_obam_10.php (accessed May 2, 2010).
[9] Neil A. Lewis, "Sharp Contrast Between McCain and Obama in Judicial Wars," *The New York Times*, May 28, 2008, http://www.nytimes.com/2008/05/28/us/politics/28judges.html (accessed December 1, 2010).
[10] Jess Bravin, "Barack Obama: The Present is Prologue," *The Wall Street Journal*, October 7, 2008, http://online.wsj.com/article/SB122333844642409819.html?mod=article-outset-box (accessed November 7, 2010).
[11] Roberts had only been a judge for a couple of years at the time of his appointment as Chief Justice, so it is unclear if Obama was also indicting Roberts for representing "powerful" clients while in private practice.
[12] Sonia Sotomayor, "Judge Mario G. Olmos Memorial Lecture," October 26, 2001, http://berkeley.edu/news/media/releases/2009/05/26_sotomayor.shtml (accessed April 7, 2010).
[13] Alexander Hamilton, "The Federalist No. 78," in Rossiter, ed., *The Federalist Papers*, 469.

[14] Senate Judiciary Committee, Confirmation Hearings, July 14, 2009, http://epic.org/privacy/sotomayor/sotomoyor_transcript.pdf (accessed November 11, 2010).
[15] Ari Shapiro, "Sotomayor Differs With Obama on 'Empathy' Issue," NPR, July 14, 2009, http:///www.npr.org/template/story/story.php?storyId=106569335&refresh=true (accessed June 9, 2010).
[16] Christopher Neefus, "Senate to Vote Thursday on Appeals Court Nominee Who Said Judges Can Amend the Constitution with Judicial 'Footnotes,'" CNSNews.com, November 18, 2009, http://www.cnsnews.com/news/article/57375 (accessed May 3, 2010).
[17] Goodwin Liu, "Rethinking Constitutional Welfare Rights," *Stanford Law Review*, Vol. 61 (2008), 203-04.
[18] Nathaniel Ghorum, "Remarks at the Federal Convention," July 21, 1787 in Max Farrand, ed., *Records of the Federal Convention* (New Haven: Yale University Press, 1911), 2: 73.
[19] Adam Liptak, "Sotomayor Guides Court's Liberal Wing," *The New York Times*, December 28, 2010, A10.
[20] Ibid.
[21] Oral Argument, *Citizens United v. Federal Election Comm'n*, No. 08-205, March 24, 2009, http://www.supremecourt.gov/oral_arguments/argument_transcripts/08-205.pdf (accessed May 22, 2010).
[22] *Citizens United v. Federal Election Commission,*130 S.Ct. 876 (2010) (Roberts, C.J., concurring).
[23] Barack Obama, "Speech to the Graduates of Hampton University," May 9, 2010, http://www.politicsdaily.com/2010/05/09/president-obamas-remarks-at-hampton-university-commencent-cerem/ (accessed May 11, 2010).
[24] Barack Obama, "Speech to the Graduates of the University of Michigan," May 1, 2010, http://www.cbsnews.com/stories/2010/05/01/national/main6450952.shtml (accessed May 11, 2010).
[25] Cass Sunstein, *Republic.com 2.0* (Princeton University Press, 2007), 137.
[26] *Abrams v. United States*, 250 U.S. 616, 630 (1919) (Holmes, J., dissenting).
[27] Elena Kagan, "Private Speech, Public Purpose: The Role of Governmental Motive in First Amendment Doctrine," *The University of Chicago Law Review*, Vol. 63, No. 2 (Spring, 1996), 413-517.
[28] *United States v. Stevens*, No. 08-769, http://www.supremecourt.gov/opinions/09pdf/08-769.pdf (accessed November 17, 2010).
[29] Barack Obama, "Remarks Regarding the Nomination of Elena Kagan to the United States Supreme Court," May 10, 2010, http://www.whitehouse.gov/the-press-office/remarks-president-and-solicitor-general-elena-kagan-nomination-solicitor-general-el (accessed May 15, 2010).
[30] Oral Argument, *Citizens United v. Federal Election Comm'n*, No. 08-205, September 9, 2009, 66, http://www.supremecourt.gov/oral_arguments/argument_transcripts/08-205%5BReargued%5D.pdf (accessed April 15, 2010).
[31] April Fulton, "Kagan, Coburn Spar Over Fake Veggie Law Instead of Health Law," NPR.com, June 30, 2010,

http://www.npr.org/blogs/health/2010/06/30/128211446/kagan-coburn-spar-over-fake_veggie_law_instead_of_health_law (accessed August 3, 2010).

21
Hubris and Humility

[1] Michael Saul, "Oprah Rallies Iowa for Obama," *The New York Daily News*, December 10, 2007, http://www.nydailynews.com/news/politics/2007/12/08/2007-12-08_oprah_rallies_iowa_for_barack_obama.html#ixzz15Dn0rmoL
[2] Ben Smith and David Paul Kuhn, "Messianic Rhetoric Infuses Obama Rallies," *Politico*, December 11, 2007, http://www.politico.com/news/stories/1207/7281.html
[3] Gerard Baker, "So Which Spouse Wins the House?" *The Times*, February 8, 2008, http://women.timesonline.co.uk/tol/life_and_style/women/article3327479.ece
[4] Joel Achenbach, "Swept Up in the Obama Moment," *The Washington Post*, January 6, 2008, http://blog.washingtonpost.com/44/2008/01/swept-up-in-the-obama-moment-1.html.
[5] William Lowther, "Barack Obama Criticized Over 'Cult-Like' Rallies," *The Telegraph,* February 23, 2008, http://www.telegraph.co.uk/news/worldnews/1579618/Barack-Obama-criticised-over-cult-like-rallies.html.
[6] Paul Krugman, "Hate Springs Eternal," *The New York Times*, February 11, 2008, http://www.nytimes.com/2008/02/11/opinion/11krugman.html
[7] Joe Klein, "Inspiration vs. Substance," *Time*, February 7, 2008, http://www.time.com/time/politics/article/0,8599,1710721,00.html.
[8] Barack Obama, "Remarks in St. Paul," *The New York Times*, June 3, 2008, http://www.nytimes.com/2008/06/03/us/politics/03text-obama.html?pagewanted=4.
[9] Carrie Budoff Brown, "Obama Tries to Dial Down Politics," *Politico*, July 22, 2008, http://dyn.politico.com/printstory.cfm?uuid=4A670F03-3048-5C12-002034DF88C14E66.
[10] Barack Obama, "Speech in Berlin," *The New York Times*, July 24, 2008, http://www.nytimes.com/2008/07/24/us/politics/24text-obama.html.
[11] Charles Krauthammer, "The Audacity of Vanity," *The Washington Post*, July 18, 2008, http://www.realclearpolitics.com/articles/2008/07/obamas_egoaccomplishment_gap.html.
[12] Ibid.
[13] Dana Milbank, "President Obama Continues Hectic Victory Tour," *The Washington Post*, July 30, 2008, http://www.washingtonpost.com/wp-dyn/content/article/2008/07/29/AR2008072902068.html.
[14] David McCullough, *Truman* (New York: Simon and Schuster, 1992), 436.
[15] Quoted in David Mendell, *Obama: From Promise to Power* (New York: HarperCollins, 2007), 2.
[16] John M. Broder, "The Great Seal of Obamaland?" *The New York Times: The Caucus Blog*, June 20, 2008, http://thecaucus.blogs.nytimes.com/2008/06/20/the-great-seal-of-obamaland/.

[17] Jake Tapper, "The Audacity of Hype," ABC News Political Punch Blog, June 20, 2008, http://blogs.abcnews.com/politicalpunch/2008/06/the-audacity-of.html.
[18] Bill Sammon, "Obama Campaign Drops Seal on Podium," *The Washington Examiner*, June 23, 2008, http://www.washingtonexaminer.com/local/obama_campaign_drops_seal_on_podium2008-06-23T21_11_00.html.
[19] Sara Burnett, "Obama's Nomination Speech Moves to Invesco," *The Rocky Mountain News*, July 7, 2008, http://www.rockymountainnews.com/news/2008/jul/07/obamas-nomination-speech-moves-invesco/
[20] Ibid.
[21] John Heilemann, "The West Wing, Season II," *New York*, January 23, 2011, http://nymag.com/news/politics/70829/index2.html.
[22] Mark Silva, "Obama: I Have a Gift," *The Chicago Tribune*, April 27, 2009, http://www.swamppolitics.com/news/politics/blog/2009/04/obama_i_have_a_gift.html.
[23] Dan Balz and Anne E. Kornblut, "Obama Joins Race With Goals Set High," *The Washington Post*, February 11, 2007, http://www.washingtonpost.com/wp-dyn/content/article/2007/02/10/AR2007021001544_2.html
[24] "Obama Gives Loaded iPod to the Queen," *Chicago Sun-Times*, April 2, 2009, http://www.suntimes.com/entertainment/1508272,obama-queen-elizabeth-ipod-040209.article.
[25] John F. Harris and Glenn Thrush, "The Ego Factor: Can Barack Obama Change?" *Politico*, November 5, 2010, http://www.politico.com/news/stories/1110/44732.html.
[26] Barack Obama, "Remarks on the 20th Anniversary of the Berlin Wall," November 9, 2009, http://www.youtube.com/watch?v=MQqdBfaZh4Q.
[27] Jonathan Stein, "Barack Obama's Messiah Complex," *Mother Jones*, February 13, 2008, http://motherjones.com/mojo/2008/02/barack-obamas-messiah-complex.
[28] Barack Obama, "Remarks to the International Olympic Committee," October 2, 2009, http://www.whitehouse.gov/the-press-office/remarks-president-and-first-lady-international-olympic-committee.
[29] Editorial, "We Like Chicago, Too," *The New York Times*, October 3, 2009, A22.
[30] Barack Obama, "Remarks to a Fundraiser in Sand Francisco," April 6, 2008, in Mayhill Fowler, "Obama: No Surprise that Hard-Pressed Pennsylvanians Turn Bitter," *The Huffington Post*, April 11, 2008, http:www.huffingtonpost.com/mayhill-fowler/Obama-no-surprise-that-ha_b_96188.html.
[31] Peter Baker, "The Education of a President," *The New York Times*, October 12, 2010, http://www.nytimes.com/2010/10/17/magazine/17obama-t.html?pagewanted=all.
[32] Carol E. Lee, "President Obama: 'Fear and Frustration' Drive Voters," *Politico*, October 16, 2010, http://www.politico.com/news/stories/1010/43706.html.
[33] Charles Krauthammer, "Obama Underappreciation Syndrome," *The Washington Post*, October 22, 2010, http://www.washingtonpost.com/wp-dyn/content/article/2010/10/21/AR2010102104856.html.
[34] John M. Broder, "White House Editing Caused Drilling Ban Dispute," *The New York Times: Green Blog*, November 10, 2010,

http://green.blogs.nytimes.com/2010/11/10/white-house-editing-caused-drilling-ban-dispute/.
[35] Robert Samuelson, "High-Speed Pork," *Newsweek*, October 29, 2010, http://www.newsweek.com/2010/10/29/why-high-speed-trains-don-t-make-sense.html.
[36] James Madison, "Convention Notes," May 25, 1787 in Erastus Howard Scott, ed., *Journal of the Federal Convention* (Clark, NJ: The Lawbook Exchange, 2008), 54.
[37] Quoted in Joseph J. Ellis, *His Excellency: George Washington* (New York: Random House, 2004), 189.
[38] Quoted in William Roscoe Thayer, *George Washington* (Boston: The Riverside Press, 1922), 65.
[39] Jeffry H. Morrison, *The Political Philosophy of George Washington* (Baltimore: Johns Hopkins University Press, 2009), 41-43.
[40] Stanley Weintraub, *General Washington's Christmas Farewell* (New York: Free Press, 2003), 162.
[41] Quoted in Ellis, *His Excellency*, 139.
[42] Quoted in Richard Brookhiser, *Founding Father* (New York: Free Press, 1996), 103.
[43] Max Farrand, ed., *Records of the Federal Convention* (New Haven: Yale University Press, 1911), 1:66.
[44] Ibid., 103.
[45] For an overview of the Farewell Address, see Matthew Spalding and Patrick J. Garrity, *A Sacred Union of Citizens: George Washington's Farewell Address and the American Character* (Lanham, MD: Rowan and Littlefield Publishers, Inc., 1996).

22
The Vicious Arts

[1] James Madison, "The Federalist No. 44," in Clinton Rossiter, ed., *The Federalist Papers* (New York: NAL Penguin, 1961), 286.
[2] Alexander Hamilton, "The Federalist No. 1," in ibid., 35.
[3] Alexander Hamilton, "The Federalist No. 85," in ibid., 527.
[4] James Madison, 'The Federalist No. 10," in ibid., 82.
[5] Ibid., 84.
[6] Alexander Hamilton, "The Federalist No. 85," in ibid., 522.
[7] Ibid.
[8] James Madison, "The Federalist No. 10," in ibid., 84.
[9] Alexander Hamilton, "The Federalist No. 71," in ibid., 432.
[10] Ibid.
[11] Jeffrey K. Tulis, *The Rhetorical Presidency* (Princeton: Princeton University Press, 1987), 28-30 (citing James Ceaser, *Presidential Selection: Theory and Development* (Princeton: Princeton University Press, 1979)).
[12] Michael Signer, *Demagogue: The Fight to Save Democracy From Its Worst Enemies* (New York: Palgrave MacMillan, 2009).
[13] Barack Obama, "Announcement of Presidential Candidacy," February 10, 2007, http://www.cbsnews.com/stories/2007/02/10/politics/main2458099_page3.shtml?tag=contentMain;contentBody (accessed October 11, 2010).

[14] Poll results can be found at http://www.cbsnews.com/htdocs/pdf/poll_042709_Obama_3pm.pdf (accessed October 11, 2010).
[15] Barack Obama, "Presidential Press Conference," July 22, 2009, http://blogs.suntimes.com/sweet/2009/07/obama_july_22_2009_press_confe.html (accessed March 15, 2010).
[16] James Madison, "The Federalist No. 55," in Rossiter, ed., *The Federalist Papers*, 346.
[17] Mary Lu Carnevale, "Obama: 'If you Like Your Doctor, You Can keep Your Doctor,'" *The Wall Street Journal: Washington Wire Blog*, June 15, 2009, http://blogs.wsj.com/washwire/2009/06/15/obama-if-you-like-your-doctor-you-can-keep-your-doctor/ (accessed August 17, 2010).
[18] Janet Adamy, "3M to Change Health-Plan Options for Workers," *The Wall Street Journal*, October 4, 2010, http://online.wsj.com/article/SB10001424052748703859204575526953379583836.html?mod=googlenews_wsj (accessed October 10, 2010).
[19] Reed Abelson, "Insurer Cuts Health Plans as New Law Takes Hold," *The New York Times*, September 30, 2010, B1.
[20] Janet Adamy and Avery Johnson, "Rules Eased for Some Health Plans," *The Wall Street Journal*, November 23, 2010, B1.
[21] Quoted in Sheryl Gay Stolberg, "Obama Says Health Plan Won't Add to the Deficit," *The New York Times*, July 19, 2009, A18.
[22] Barack Obama, "Remarks by the President on Health Insurance Reform," March 8, 2010, http://www.whitehouse.gov/the-press-office/remarks-president-health-insurance-reform-arcadia-university (accessed June 11, 2010).
[23] Barack Obama, "Presidential Press Conference," September 10, 2010, http://www.realclearpolitics.com/video/2010/09/10/obama_we_knew_that_health_care_costs_would_go_up.html (accessed September 15, 2010).
[24] Letter from Douglas Elmendorf to Rep. Jerry Lewis, May 11, 2010, http://www.cbo.gov/ftpdocs/114xx/doc11490/LewisLtr_HR3590.pdf (accessed June 3, 2010).
[25] The National Commission on Fiscal Responsibility and Reform, "The Moment of Truth," December 2010, http://www.fiscalcommission.gov/sites/fiscalcommission.gov/files/documents/TheMomentofTruth12_1_2010.pdf (accessed December 22, 2010).
[26] Ben Smith, "Dems Retreat on Health Care Cost Pitch," *Politico*, August 20, 2010, http://www.politico.com/news/stories/0810/41271.html (accessed September 7, 2010).
[27] Jeffrey M. Jones, "Obama Approval Averages 45% in September," Gallup, October 4, 2010, http://www.gallup.com/poll/143354/Obama-Approval-Averages-September.aspx (accessed October 15, 2010).
[28] http://www.azleg.gov/FormatDocument.asp?inDoc=/legtext/49leg/2r/bills/hb2162c.htm (accessed October 11, 2010).
[29] Jerry Markon, "Holder is Criticized for Comments on Ariz. Immigration Law, Which He Hasn't Read," *The Washington Post*, May 14, 2010, http://www.washingtonpost.com/wp-

dyn/content/article/2010/05/14/AR2010051404231.html (accessed September 17, 2010).
[30] Elysa Batista, "Mack: Arizona Immigration Law a Blow to Freedom," NaplesNews.com, April 29, 2010, http://www.naplesnews.com/news/2010/apr/29/connie-mack-arizona-immigration/ (accessed September 17, 2010).
[31] Scott Mayerowitz, "Will Immigration Law Cost Arizona All Star Game?" ABCNews.com, April 29, 2010, http://abcnews.go.com/Travel/immigration-law-cost-arizona-star-game-push-boycott/story?id=10511724 (accessed October 11, 2010).
[32] *Terry v. Ohio*, 392 U.S. 1 (1968).
[33] Brian Montopoli, "Obama Again Hits Arizona Immigration Bill," CBSNews.com, April 27, 2010, http://www.cbsnews.com/8301-503544_162-20003600-503544.html (accessed September 17, 2010).
[34] Barack Obama and Felipe Calderon, "Join Press Availability," May 19, 2010, http://www.whitehouse.gov/the-press-office/remarks-president-obama-and-president-calder-n-mexico-joint-press-availability (accessed September 17, 2010).
[35] Brian Stetler, "New Political Muscle, In Whatever Language," *The New York Times*, November 2, 2010, A19.
[36] Michael A. Memoli, "GOP Takeover of Congress Would Mean 'Hand-to-Hand Combat,' Obama Warns," October 7, 2010, http://www.latimes.com/news/custom/topofthetimes/national/la-pn-obama-base-20101008,0,6063786.story (accessed October 10, 2010).
[37] Barack Obama, "Remarks in Parma, OH," September 8, 2010, http://www.whitehouse.gov/the-press-office/2010/09/08/remarks-president-economy-parma-ohio (accessed September 10, 2010).
[38] Barack Obama, "Address to Congress," February 24, 2009, http://www.whitehouse.gov/the_press_office/Remarks-of-President-Barack-Obama-Address-to-Joint-Session-of-Congress/ (accessed September 10, 2010).
[39] Barack Obama, "Remarks at the 102nd Abraham Lincoln Association Annual Banquet," February 12, 2009, http://www.whitehouse.gov/the-press-office/remarks-president-102nd-abraham-lincoln-association-annual-banquet (accessed September 10, 2010).
[40] Editorial, "Dangerous Work," *The New York Times*, December 4, 2009, A34.
[41] Barack Obama, "Presidential Press Conference," February 9, 2009, http://www.cbsnews.com/stories/2009/02/10/politics/100days/main4789627.shtml (accessed May 15, 2010).
[42] Barack Obama, "Speech at the National Archives," May 21, 2009, http://www.whitehouse.gov/the-press-office/remarks-president-national-security-5-21-09 (accessed June 1, 2010).
[43] Robert Kuttner, "Saving Progressivism From Obama," *The Huffington Post*, November 21, 2010, http://www.huffingtonpost.com/robert-kuttner/post_1307_b_786612.html (accessed November 23, 2010).
[44] Frank Rich, "All the President's Captors," *The New York Times*, December 5, 2010, WK8.

NOTES

23
The Diplomacy of Deference

[1] Barack Obama, *Dreams From My Father: A Story of Race and Inheritance* (New York: Three Rivers Press, 2004), 133, 203.
[2] Barack Obama, "Remarks Regarding Iraq," October 2, 2002, http://www.barackobama.com/2002/10/02/remarks_of_illinois_state_sen.php (accessed September 2, 2010).
[3] Barack Obama, "Acceptance Speech," August 28, 2008, http://www.npr.org/templates/story/story.php?storyId=94087570 (accessed September 2, 2010).
[4] Barack Obama, "Announcement for President," February 10, 2007, http://blogs.suntimes.com/sweet/2007/02/obamas_presidential_announceme.html (accessed September 1, 2010).
[5] Byron York, "Obama's Bad Night," *National Review*, July 24, 2007, http://www.nationalreview.com/articles/221670/obamas-bad-night/byron-york (accessed September 2, 2010).
[6] Barack Obama, "Remarks at a Labor Day Rally," September 3, 2007, http://www.barackobama.com/2007/09/03/remarks_of_senator_barack_obam_22.php (accessed September 10, 2010).
[7] Barack Obama, "Remarks in Prague," April 5, 2009, http://www.whitehouse.gov/the_press_office/Remarks-By-President-Barack-Obama-In-Prague-As-Delivered/ (accessed September 10, 2010).
[8] David E. Sanger and Peter Baker, "Obama Limits When U.S. Would Use Nuclear Arms," *The New York Times*, April 5, 2010, http://www.nytimes.com/2010/04/06/world/06arms.html?pagewanted=print (accessed September 10, 2010).
[9] James A. Baker, III, "Opening Statement," Senate Foreign Relations Committee, May 19, 2010, http://foreign.senate.gov/imo/media/doc/BakerTestimony100519p.pdf (accessed November 5, 2010).
[10] Barack Obama, "Remarks by the President to the International Olympic Committee," October 2, 2009, http://www.whitehouse.gov/the_press_office/Remarks-By-the-President-And-the-First-Lady-to-the-International-Olympic-Committee/ (accessed September 12, 2010).
[11] Barack Obama, "Remarks by the President to the United Nations General Assembly," September 23, 2009, http://www.whitehouse.gov/the-press-office/2010/09/23/remarks-president-united-nations-general-assembly (accessed September 12, 2010).
[12] Barack Obama, "Remarks in Prague," April 5, 2009, http://www.whitehouse.gov/the_press_office/Remarks-By-President-Barack-Obama-In-Prague-As-Delivered/.
[13] Ibid.
[14] Ibid.
[15] Editorial, "Barack Takes a Bow," *The Washington Times*, April 7, 2009, http://www.washingtontimes.com/news/2009/apr/7/barack-takes-a-bow/ (accessed May 10, 2010).

[16] A group of college Republicans put together a video montage containing photographs of other leaders greeting the Japanese emperor. None of them appeared to bow. See http://www.dailymotion.com/video/xb62fc_obama-bows-to-japanese-emperor-akihito_news (accessed May 10, 2010).
[17] Mike Allen, "The Diplomacy of Deference," *Politico*, November 17, 2009, http://www.politico.com/news/stories/1109/29614.html (accessed May 11, 2010).
[18] Jake Tapper, "On President Obama's Bow to the Japanese Emperor, An Academic Friend Writes That Both the Left and the Right Are Wrong," ABCNews.com, November 15, 2009, http://blogs.abcnews.com/politicalpunch/2009/11/on-president-obamas-bow-to-the-japanese-emperor-an-academic -friend-writes-that-both-the-left-and-the-right-are-wrong.html (accessed May 10, 2010).
[19] Allen, "The Diplomacy of Deference."
[20] AFP, "Outrage in Washington Over Obama's Japan Bow," Breitbart.com, November 16, 2009, http://www.breitbart.com/article.php?id=CNG.50fd6792b83ac59fea414195ebeb58b3.2d1 (accessed December 1, 2010).
[21] Douglas Jehr, "The President's Inclination: No, it Wasn't a Bow-Bow," *The New York Times*, June 19, 1994, http://www.nytimes.com/1994/06/19/weekinreview/the-world-the-president-s-inclination-no-it-wasn-t-a-bow-bow.html.
[22] Barack Obama, "Interview with Al-Arabiya," January 27, 2009, http://www.msnbc.msn.com/id/28870724/ns/politics-white_house/ (accessed November 1, 2010).
[23] Barack Obama, "Remarks at Strasbourg Town Hall," April 3, 2009, http://www.whitehouse.gov/the_press_office/Remarks-by-President-Obama-at-Strasbourg-Town-Hall/ (accessed November 1, 2010).
[24] Toby Harnden, "Barack Obama: 'Arrogant U.S. Has Been Dismissive' to Allies," *The Daily Telegraph*, April 3, 2009, http:///www.telegraph.co.uk/news/worldnews/northamerica/usa/barackobama/5100338/Barack-Obama-arrogant-US-has-been-dismissive-to-allies.html (accessed November 1, 2010).
[25] Barack Obama, "Remarks at the Summit of the Americas," April 17, 2009, http://www.whitehouse.gov/the_press_office/Remarks-by-the-President-at-the-Summit-of-the-Americas-Opening-Ceremony/ (accessed November 1, 2010).
[26] Barack Obama, "Remarks in Prague," April 5, 2009, http://www.whitehouse.gov/the_press_office/Remarks-By-President-Barack-Obama-In-Prague-As-Delivered/ (accessed November 1, 2010).
[27] Blaine Harden, "Hiroshima: the Dreaded Invitation," *The Washington Post*, November, 13, 2009, http://www.washingtonpost.com/wp-dyn/content/article/2009/11/12/AR2009111210925.html (accessed November 30, 2010).
[28] Warren Kozak, "A Hiroshima Apology?" *The Wall Street Journal*, August 6, 2010, http://online.wsj.com/article/SB10001424052748703748904575411123599873634.html (accessed November 30, 2010).
[29] Brian Montopoli, "Obama, Calderon Slam Arizona Immigration Law," *CBS News*, May 19, 2010, http://www.cbsnews.com/8301-503544_162-20005395-503544.html (accessed November 30, 2010).

[30] Ben Smith, "Apologizing for Arizona," *Politico*, May 17, 2010, http://www.politico.com/blogs/bensmith/0510/Apologizing_for_Arizona.html (accessed November 30, 2010).
[31] Kasie Hunt, "John McCain, John Kyl Demand Apology," *Politico*, May 18, 2010, http://www.politico.com/news/stories/0510/37416.html (accessed November 30, 2010).
[32] Barack Obama, "Speech at Cairo University," June 4, 2009, http://www.huffingtonpost.com/2009/06/04/obama-speech-in-cairo-vid_n_211215.html (accessed November 30, 2010).
[33] Michelle Spitzer, "NASA Chief Bolden's Muslim Remark to Al-Jazeera Causes Stir," *Florida Today*, July 7, 2010, http://www.space.com/8725-nasa-chief-bolden-muslim-remark-al-jazeera-stir.html (accessed November 30, 2010).
[34] "McCain Repudiates 'Hussein Obama' Remarks," *The New York Times: The Caucus Blog*, February 26, 2008, http://thecaucus.blogs.nytimes.com/2008/02/26/mccain-repudiates-hussein-obama-remarks/ (accessed December 2, 2010).
[35] "The Chris Matthews Show," September 12, 2010, http://www.realclearpolitics.com/video/2010/09/12/chris_matthews_show_obamas_middle_name_hussein_means_good_relations_with_muslim_countries.html (accessed December 2, 2010).
[36] Jenney Marlar, "U.S. Approval Gains Nearly Erased in Middle East/North Africa," Gallup.com, September 30, 2010, http://www.gallup.com/poll/143294/Approval-Gains-Nearly-Erased-Middle-East-North-Africa.aspx (accessed December 2, 2010).
[37] Barack Obama, "A New Year, A New Beginning," March 19, 2009, http://www.whitehouse.gov/Nowruz/ (accessed August 17, 2010).
[38] Barack Obama, "Remarks in Prague," April 5, 2009, http://www.whitehouse.gov/the_press_office/Remarks-By-President-Barack-Obama-In-Prague-As-Delivered/ (accessed August 17, 2010).
[39] Report, "Obama Says Iran Should Not Suppress People's Voices," *Reuters*, June 16, 2009, http://in.reuters.com/article/2009/06/16/iran-election-obama-idINN1626113920090616 (accessed August 18, 2010).
[40] Jim Sciutto and Stephen Splaine, "Pro and Anti-Government Rallies Blanket Iranian Capitol," ABCNews.com, June 16, 2009, http://abcnews.go.com/International/story?id=7849084&page=3 (accessed August 17, 2010).
[41] Peter Baker, "Obama Offered Deal to Russia in Secret Letter," *The New York Times*, March 2, 2009, http://www.nytimes.com/2009/03/03/washington/03prexy.html (accessed November 15, 2010).
[42] Marc Champion and Peter Spiegel, "Allies React to U.S. Missile U-Turn," *The Wall Street Journal*, September 18, 2009, http://online.wsj.com/article/SB125317801774419047.html (accessed November 15, 2010).
[43] Kejda Gjermani, "The Missile-Defense Betrayal," *Commentary*, December 2009, http://www.commentarymagazine.com/article/the-missile-defense-betrayal/ (accessed November 15, 2010).
[44] Matthew Moore, Gordon Rayner, and Christopher Hope, "WikiLeaks Cables: U.S. Agrees to Tell Russia Britain's Nuclear Secrets," *The Daily Telegraph*, February 4, 2011,

http://www.telegraph.co.uk/news/worldnews/wikileaks/8304654/WikiLeaks-cables-US-agrees-to-tell-Russia-Britains-nuclear-secrets.html# (accessed February 10, 2011).
[45] Keith B. Ricgburg, "Gaddafi Praises Obama at U.N.," *The Washington Post*, September 23, 2009, http://www.washingtonpost.com/wp-dyn/content/article/2009/09/23/AR2009092303488.html (accessed November 20, 2010).
[46] "Qadhafi Writes Obama," *Politico*, March 19, 2011, http://www.politico.com/politico44/perm/0311/my_son_7ffb5ed0-e8dd-4f6a-a33a-fbeb3a337336.html (accessed March 20, 2011).
[47] Javier Doberti, "Latin American Leaders Laud Obama's 'Historic' Victory," CNN.com, November 5, 2008, http://articles.cnn.com/2008-11-05/politics/obama.latin.america_1_latin-american-leaders-barack-obama-government?_s=PM:POLITICS (accessed November 10, 2010).
[48] *Agencia Bolivariana de Noticias (ABN), Embassy of the Bolivarian Republic of Venezuela Press Office, "Venenzuela's Chavez Praises Obama," January 23, 2009,* http://venezuelanalysis.com/news/4139 (accessed November 10, 2010).
[49] Jeff Franks, "Fidel Castro Lauds Nobel Prize for Obama," *Reuters*, October 10, 2009, http://www.reuters.com/article/2009/10/10/us-nobel-peace-obama-castro-idUSTRE5991C120091010 (accessed November 10, 2010).
[50] Paul Haven, "Cuban leader Applauds U.S. Health Care Reform Bill," The Associated Press, March 25, 2010, http://finance.yahoo.com/news/Cuban-leader-applauds-US-apf-124808403.html?x=0&.v=1 (accessed November 10, 2010).

24
"The Best Possible State of Defense"

[1] John Jay, "The Federalist No. 4," in Clinton Rossiter, ed., *The Federalist Papers* (New York: NAL Penguin, 1961), 46.
[2] John Jay, "The Federalist No. 3," in ibid., 42.
[3] John Jay, "The Federalist No. 4," in ibid., 47.
[4] Alexander Hamilton, "The Federalist No. 11," in ibid., 85.
[5] John Jay, "The Federalist No. 4," in ibid., 49.
[6] Alexander Hamilton, "The Federalist No. 6," in ibid., 54, 56.
[7] Alexander Hamilton, "The Federalist No. 25," in ibid., 165-66.
[8] Quoted in Steven F. Hayward, *The Age of Reagan: The Fall of the Liberal Order 1964-1980* (New York: Three Rivers Press, 2001), 467.
[9] Alexander Hamilton, "The Federalist No. 24," in Rossiter, ed., *The Federalist Papers*, 162.
[10] Jay, "The Federalist No. 4," in ibid., 48
[11] Quoted in Joseph J. Ellis, *His Excellency: George Washington* (New York: Vintage Books, 2005), 123.
[12] George Washington, "Farewell Address," September 26, 1796 in Jared Sparks, ed., *The Writings of George Washington* (Boston: American Stationers' Company, 1837), 7: 392-93.

[13] Alexander Hamilton, "The Federalist No. 75," in Rossiter, ed., *The Federalist Papers*, 450-51.
[14] Alexander Hamilton, "The Federalist No. 15," in ibid., 109.
[15] James Madison, "The Federalist No. 63," in ibid., 382.
[16] James Madison, "The Federalist No. 14," in ibid., 104.
[17] Alexander Hamilton, "The Federalist No. 11," in ibid., 90-91.
[18] James Madison, "The Federalist No. 14," in ibid., 104.
[19] Alexander Hamilton, "The Federalist No. 15," in ibid., 106-07.
[20] John Jay, "The Federalist No. 3," in ibid., 45.
[21] Carol Lee, "President Obama's Evolution as Commander-in-Chief," *Politico*, January 23, 2010, http://www.politico.com/news/stories/0110/31896.html (accessed December 5, 2010).
[22] Peter Baker, "For Obama, Steep Learning Curve as Chief in War," *The New York Times*, August 29, 2010, A1.
[23] Barack Obama, "Address to the Cadets at West Point," December 1, 2009, http://www.whitehouse.gov/the-press-office/remarks-president-address-nation-way-forward-afghanistan-and-pakistan (accessed December 5, 2010).
[24] Charlie Savage, "Barack Obama's Q and A," *The Boston Globe*, December 20, 2007, http://www.boston.com/news/politics/2008/specials/CandidateQA/ObamaQA/ (accessed March 20, 2011).
[25] Hillary Clinton, "Interview on This Week," March 27, 2011, http://abcnews.go.com/ThisWeek/week-transcript-hillary-clinton-robert-gates-donald-rumsfeld/story?id=13232096 (accessed March 28, 2011).
[26] Alexander Hamilton, "The Federalist No. 74, in Rossiter, ed., *The Federalist Papers*, 447.
[27] Debate of August 17, 1787 in Max Farrand, ed., *Records of the Federal Convention* (New Haven: Yale University Press, 1911), 2: 318.

25
The Constitutional Renaissance and Progressive Discontents

[1] Jonathan Weisman, "Tea Party Gives Founding Fathers a Role in the Midterms," *The Wall Street Journal*, October 20, 2010, http://blogs.wsj.com/washwire/2010/10/20/tea-party-gives-founding-fathers-a-role-in-midterms/ (accessed November 1, 2010).
[2] Adam Liptak, "Tea-ing Up the Constitution," *The New York Times*, March 13, 2010, WK1.
[3] Jonathan Weisman, "Tea Party Gives Founding Fathers a Role in the Midterms," *The Wall Street Journal*, October 20, 2010, http://blogs.wsj.com/washwire/2010/10/20/tea-party-gives-founding-fathers-a-role-in-midterms/.
[4] Philip Rucker and Krissah Thompson, "Two New Rules will Give Constitution a starring Role in GOP-controlled House," *The Washington Post*, December 30, 2010, http://www.washingtonpost.com/wp-dyn/content/article/2010/12/29/AR2010122901402.html?sid=ST2010122901409 (accessed January 12, 2011).

[5] Ibid.
[6] Jonathan Strong, "New GOP Constitution Rule Irks House Democrats," *The Daily Caller*, December 22, 2010, http://dailycaller.com/2010/12/22/new-gop-constitution-rule-irks-house-democrats/#ixzz19oaQxWli (accessed January 12, 2011).
[7] Ben Adler, "GOP's 'Pledge to America' Looks Unlikely to Inspire," *Newsweek*, September 22, 2010, http://www.newsweek.com/blogs/the-gaggle/2010/09/22/gop-pledge-to-america-looks-unlikely-to-inspire.html (accessed January 12, 2011).
[8] http://www.realclearpolitics.com/video/2010/12/30/wapos_ezra_klein_constitution_confusing_because_it_is_old.Html (accessed January 12, 2011).
[9] Jim Geraghty, "WA Democrat: 'I'm Tired of Reading the Constitution and All the Silly Things,'" *National Review Online*, March 31, 2011, http://www.nationalreview.com/campaign-spot/263532/wa-democrat-im-tired-reading-constitution-and-all-silly-things (accessed April 1, 2011).
[10] Paul Krugman, "Tea Parties Forever," *The New York Times*, April 13, 2009, A21.
[11] David Barstow, "Tea Party Lights Fuse for Rebellion on Right," *The New York Times*, February 15, 2010, A1.
[12] Frank Rich, "The Rage is Not about Health Care," *The New York Times*, March 27, 2010, WK10.
[13] Peter Baker, "The Education of a President," *The New York Times*, October 12, 2010, MM40.
[14] Jann Wenner, "Obama in Command: The Rolling Stone Interview," *Rolling Stone*, September 28, 2010, http://www.rollingstone.com/politics/news/obama-in-command-br-the-rolling-stone-interview-20100928 (accessed October 1, 2010).
[15] Barack Obama, "Remarks at Political Fundraiser," April 16, 2010, http://www.realclearpolitics.com/video/2010/04/16/obama_on_tea_partiers_you_would_think_theyd_be_saying_thank_you.html (accessed October 1, 2010).
[16] Sam Stein, "Obama to Tea Party: 'Identify, Specifically, What Would You Do?'" *The Huffington Post*, September 20, 2010, http://www.huffingtonpost.com/2010/09/20/obama-to-tea-party-identi_n_731770.html (accessed October 1, 2010).
[17] Lincoln Caplan, "Exploring the Meaning of 'Constitutional Conservatism,'" *The New York Times*, December 1, 2010, http://www.nytimes.com/2010/12/02/opinion/02thu4.html (accessed December 3, 2010).
[18] Adam Liptak, "Tea-ing Up the Constitution," *The New York Times*, March 13, 2010, WK1.
[19] Andrew Romano, "America's Holy Writ," *Newsweek*, October 17, 2010, http://www.newsweek.com/2010/10/17/how-tea-partiers-get-the-constitution-wrong.html (accessed October 29, 2010).
[20] Editorial, "Justice Scalia and the Tea Party," *The New York Times*, December 19, 2010, WK7.
[21] Ron Chernow, "The Founding Fathers Versus the Tea Party," *The New York Times*, September 24, 2010, A29.
[22] Ibid.

[23] Edmund Burke, "Speech on the Petition of the Unitarian Society," 1792 in Peter J. Stanlis, ed., *Edmund Burke: selected Writings and Speeches* (Washington: Regnery Publishing, 1997), 377.
[24] Samuel Freedman, "Tea Party Rooted in Religious Fervor for the Constitution," *The New York Times*, November 6, 2010, A17.
[25] Michael Lind, "Let's Stop Pretending the Constitution is Sacred," *Salon.com*, January 4, 2011, http://www.salon.com/news/politics/war_room/2011/01/04/lind_tea_party_constitution (accessed January 12, 2011).
[26] E. J. Dionne, "What a G.O.P. Congress Might Bring," *The Washington Post*, January 3, 2011, http://www.washingtonpost.com/wp-dyn/content/article/2011/01/02/AR2011010202380.html (accessed January 12, 2011).
[27] Jason Horowitz, "Reading Between Constitution's Lines," *The Washington Post*, January 5, 2011, http://www.washingtonpost.com/wp-dyn/content/article/2011/01/04/AR2011010405252.html (accessed January 12, 2011).
[28] Editorial, "Pomp, and Little Circumstance," *The New York Times*, January 5, 2011, A22.
[29] Abraham Lincoln, "The Perpetuation of Our Political Institutions: Address to the Young Men's Lyceum of Springfield," January 27, 1838 in Roy P. Basler, ed., *Lincoln: Speeches and Writings, 1832-1858* (New York: Penguin Putnam, 1989), 32.

26
The Future of American Constitutionalism

[1] Barack Obama, *The Audacity of Hope: Thoughts on Reclaiming the American Dream* (New York: Vintage Books, 2006), 114.
[2] Ibid., 115.
[3] Barack Obama, "Presidential Press Conference," December 7, 2010, http://www.realclearpolitics.com/video/2010/12/07/obama_i_couldnt_go_through_the_front_door_in_this_countrys_founding.html (accessed December 10, 2010).
[4] Charles Kessler, "The Audacity of Barack Obama," *Claremont Review of Books*, October 17, 2008, http://www.realclearpolitics.com/articles/2008/10/the_audacity_of_barack_obama.html (accessed December 15, 2010).
[5] Abraham Lincoln, "Rejoinder to Judge Douglas," October 13, 1858 in Joseph Fornieri, ed., *The Language of Liberty: The Political Speeches and Writings of Abraham Lincoln* (Washington, DC: Regnery Publishing, 2009), 500.
[6] Michael Barone, "The Depth and Breadth of GOP Victories," November 8, 2010, http://www.realclearpolitics.com/articles/2010/11/08/gop_poised_to_reap_redistricting_rewards_107871.html (accessed November 10, 2010).
[7] Michael Grunwald, "The Republicans in Distress," Time, May 7, 2009, http://www.time.com/time/politics/article/0,8599,1896588,00.html#ixzz1AY8wyJRY (accessed December 22, 2010).

[8] Barack Obama, "Remarks by the President on Fiscal Policy," April 13, 2011, http://www.whitehouse.gov/the-press-office/2011/04/13/remarks-president-fiscal-policy (accessed April 15, 2011).
[9] Barack Obama, "Remarks by the President at a Facebook Town Hall," April 20, 2011, http://www.whitehouse.gov/the-press-office/2011/04/20/remarks-president-facebook-town-hall (accessed April 23, 2011).
[10] Alexander Hamilton, "The Federalist No. 1," in Clinton Rossiter, ed., *The Federalist Papers* (New York: NAL Penguin, 1961), 33.

INDEX